THE AGE OF ALIGNMENT

The Age of Alignment

Electoral Politics in Britain
1922–1929

CHRIS COOK

University of Toronto Press
Toronto and Buffalo

Published in the United Kingdom 1975 by
The Macmillan Press Ltd

First published in Canada and the United States 1975 by
University of Toronto Press
Toronto and Buffalo

ISBN 0-8020-2204-9

Printed in Great Britain

To my parents

Contents

Acknowledgements

This book originated in research undertaken at Nuffield College, Oxford, into constituency politics and electoral change in the period surrounding the first Labour Government.

I owe a special debt to the Warden and Fellows of Nuffield College for my election to a Research Studentship at the college. I also owe a particular debt to my college supervisor at Nuffield, Dr David Butler, for his constant help and encouragement in my research.

A variety of people have given generously of their time and expert knowledge at various stages in the production of this book. I must particularly thank Professor Michael Kinnear who, at an early stage of my research, loaned me a considerable amount of statistical material. David Marquand, MP, was kind enough to allow me to consult the draft chapters of his life of Ramsay MacDonald, covering the period of the first Labour Government. For help on particular points I should like to thank John Barnes, Maurice Cowling, Roy Douglas, Ross McKibbin, Kenneth Morgan, John Rowett and Trevor Wilson. I am very indebted to John Ramsden for help with proof-reading.

I must also thank my colleagues at the London School of Economics, in particular Philip Jones, Josephine Sinclair and Jeffrey Weeks, who have worked with me over the past years on the Political Archives Investigation. For help with typing I am very much indebted to Mrs Jean Ali, Miss Eileen Pattison and Mrs E. M. Smith.

Finally, I owe my greatest debt, for his advice and encouragement over many years, to my former supervisor, Mr A. J. P. Taylor. No research student could have asked for better guidance or kindlier criticism.

For permission to consult papers in their possession, I am extremely indebted to the Librarians of the following institutions:

Beaverbrook Library (Beaverbrook MSS., Davidson MSS, Bonar Law MSS, Lloyd George MSS, St Loe/Strachey MSS);

Bodleian Library (Altrincham MSS, Asquith MSS, H. A. L. Fisher MSS, Donald Maclean MSS);

British Library (Herbert Gladstone MSS, C. P. Scott MSS, J. A. Spender MSS);

Cambridge University Library (Baldwin MSS);

Leeds City Library (Sheepscar Branch) (archives of the Society of Certified and Associated Liberal Agents; the Leeds Liberal Federation; the Yorkshire Liberal Federation).

This study has also relied heavily on the surviving archives of the political parties at local and regional level. I would like to express my grateful thanks to the many secretaries and agents who gave me permission to quote from documents in their possession. These sources are more fully listed in the bibliography (pp. 344–53). The Librarian of the National Liberal Club kindly made available to me the unique collection of election addresses held by that library: Miss Enid Lakeman, of the Electoral Reform Society, generously gave me access to the useful volumes of press cuttings held by the Society.

To any other copyright-holder who may inadvertently have been omitted from this list, I would like to offer my apologies.

CHRIS COOK

Part One

The State of the Parties

1 Elections and Politics 1918–1922

Between the fall of the Lloyd George Coalition in 1922 and the general election of October 1924, the face of British politics was transformed. In the space of two years, Bonar Law succeeded Lloyd George as Prime Minister, Baldwin launched his party into an unwanted and disastrous tariff election, whilst Ramsay MacDonald presided over the short-lived first Labour Government. In this period of British politics in transition the fate of the Liberal Party was decided. From reunion and revival in December 1923, the party went on to ruin in October 1924.

This book is a study of constituency politics and electoral change from the fall of the Coalition to the general election of 1929. Throughout this period, emphasis has been directed towards the changing fortunes of the Liberal Party – for the fate of the party (and with it the shape of British politics) was finally decided in these years. Within the electoral politics of this period, four themes dominate this study: the state of the Liberal Party and its rivals at constituency level in the immediate post-1918 period; the general election of 1923; the electoral politics of the first Labour Government; and finally, the crucial general election of October 1924 and its aftermath.

The general election of 1922 provides the most convenient opening for a detailed study of electoral politics in this period. But the election of 1922 itself needs to be seen against the perspective of the 'coupon' election of December 1918.

The 'coupon' election of 1918 was fought both on different constituencies and with a much enlarged electorate from the previous general election in December 1910. In that election the electorate had numbered 7,709,981. Under the Representation of the People Act, which became law in February

1918, the electorate had risen to 21,392,322. The 'coupon' election of 1918 was thus the first election in this country fought on the basis of universal adult male suffrage for those over 21.[1] Women, however, were less fortunate, only those over the age of 30 being as yet enfranchised.

This very important extension of the franchise in 1918 was accompanied by an equally far-reaching redistribution of constituencies. Such a redistribution – the first since 1885 – was long overdue. By 1915 the largest constituency, Romford, numbered 60,878 electors, while the smallest, Kilkenny, had only 1,702.[2]

This redistribution, however, was mainly to the advantage of the Conservatives. The areas of greatest population growth after 1885 were the urban centres of London, Birmingham, Liverpool and Glasgow – areas in which the Conservatives were relatively strong compared with the Liberals. Meanwhile the areas of greatest population decline had been rural Scotland and Wales (where the Liberals were entrenched) and Southern Ireland (by now solid Nationalist territory).

Any redistribution was therefore of direct benefit to the Conservatives. It has been calculated that if the election of December 1910 had been fought on the redistributed constituencies of 1918, the Conservatives would have gained between 25 and 30 seats.[3] This bonus enjoyed by the Conservatives at the 'coupon' election was one factor – albeit slight – in the Coalition landslide.

It was a bonus, however, that neither Lloyd George nor Bonar Law needed. The election results of December 1918 were nothing short of a complete triumph. It was a Coalition landslide greater than the Liberal victory of 1906 and as

---

[1] In addition, those who had served in the war were enfranchised at 19. The 1918 election was also the first occasion when each constituency polled on the same day.

[2] M. Kinnear, *The British Voter* (1969) p. 70.

[3] Ibid., p. 70. Kinnear's calculations for 1910 if redistribution had applied, compared with the number of seats actually won (in parentheses), were: Conservatives 306 (272), Liberals and Labour 322 (314), Nationalists 79 (84).

sweeping as the success of Ramsay MacDonald and the National Government in 1931.

The full results of the 'coupon' election are given in Table 1.1.[4] The Lloyd George Coalition returned 332 couponed

TABLE 1.1
General Election, 1918

		Total votes	% share	Candi-dates	MP's elected
Coalition	Co. Con.	3,472,738	32·5	362	332
	Co. Lib.	1,396,590	12·6	145	127
	Co. Lab.	53,962	0·4	5	4
	Co. Ind.	9,274	0·1	1	1
	Co. NDP	156,834	1·5	18	9
	(Total Co.)	(5,089,398)	(47·1)	(531)	(473)
Non-Coalition	Conservative	671,454	6·1	83	50
	Liberal	1,388,784	13·0	276	36
	Labour & Co-operative	2,303,562	21·4	361	58
	Sinn Fein	497,107	4·6	102	73
	Others	836,513	7·8	260	17
		10,786,818	100·0	1,623	707

Conservatives, 127 Coalition Liberals, and 14 other couponed Independents or National Democratic Party members. In addition to these 473 supporters, a further 47 uncouponed Conservatives and 3 Ulster Unionists gave the Coalition general support.

The opposition benches presented a sorry state of disarray. The largest group, the 73 Sinn Fein Members, never took

[4] Classification of candidates in 1918 is extremely difficult. I have in general followed the figures in F. W. S. Craig, *British Parliamentary Election Statistics, 1918–1968* (1969) pp. 1–2. For convenience, the Labour and Co-operative totals have been amalgamated. The 'Others' category includes the National Party, the uncouponed National Democratic Party candidates and five nominees of the NFDSS (National Federation of Discharged and Demobilized Sailors and Soldiers).

their seats.[5] Labour could muster only 60.[6] The remnant of 'Wee Free' Liberals numbered a mere 36, while a further 17 assorted 'Independents' also generally voted against the government.

The landslide of 1918 was quickly attributed by the Independent Liberals to the allocation of the 'coupon'.[7] This judgement was mistaken. The overwhelming success of the 'couponed' candidates (473 out of 541 were returned) has disguised the exact nature of the Coalition victory. The idea that success was due to the coupon does not stand up long to investigation. The 1918 victory was essentially a victory of the Right, and couponed Liberals were successful, not so much because they possessed the coupon, but because they were guaranteed no Conservative opposition. Thus, in such areas as Liverpool and Manchester, even uncouponed Conservatives gained easy and substantial victories.

Even this explanation is only half correct. The subtlety of 1918 was that, at a time when the electors were in an unusually radical mood, Lloyd George and his Conservative allies, by exploiting the wave of patriotic sentiment that followed the end of the war, persuaded them to return a massive majority of Conservatives and Coalition Liberals to Parliament.

For the Independent Liberals led by Asquith, the results were both a rout and a humiliation on a scale almost

[5] Strictly, their actual number was 69, since four Sinn Fein candidates were returned for two constituencies.

[6] The number of Labour and Co-operative candidates elected was 58, but two others (J. J. Jones in West Ham Silvertown and Brig.-Gen. Sir O. Thomas in Anglesey) joined the Labour Party immediately after being elected.

[7] The 'coupon' itself was a letter of support signed by Bonar Law and Lloyd George and sent to each favoured candidate. In all, the coupon was distributed to 541 candidates (362 Conservatives, 145 Liberals, 18 to the ephemeral National Democratic Party and 6 to other right-wing Independents). The actual allocation of the coupon was complex. Thus, George Lambert, the loyal Lloyd George supporter from South Molton, was denied the coupon, whereas Josiah Wedgwood, who did not want the coupon, was allocated it. The details of the coupon are well discussed in T. Wilson, *The Downfall of the Liberal Party (1966)* pp. 157–9.

unparalleled in British politics. A mere 36 uncouponed Liberals had survived the massacre.[8]

Virtually all the leaders of the pre-1914 party were defeated. Asquith, Sir John Simon, Walter Runciman, Reginald McKenna, Herbert Samuel and the Chief Whip, J. W. Gulland, all failed to return to Westminster.[9] Two ex-Ministers, Sir Charles Hobhouse in Bristol East and T. McKinnon Wood in the St Rollox division of Glasgow, both suffered the added humility of a lost deposit at the foot of the poll in a three-cornered contest. McKenna, Runciman, Samuel and H. J. Tennant were all similarly placed in three-cornered contests.

Even the most traditional of Liberal strongholds fell before the onslaught. In Frome, the sitting Member, who had represented the division since 1892, obtained less than 9 per cent of the total votes. Nor were the 36 survivors of the election based on any firm regional or geographical basis. Indeed, as Roy Douglas has written, even among the tattered band who did scramble home, good luck played a large part. Fewer than twenty had defeated a Coalition opponent. Fewer

[8] This is in fact an overestimate of the number of non-Coalition Liberals, as nine who had not received the official Coalition 'coupon' (the endorsement given only to officially approved Coalition candidates) accepted the Coalition whip upon election. They were: Sir F. D. Blake, Bt. (Berwick-upon-Tweed), G. P. Collins (Greenock), Hon. W. H. Cozens-Hardy (South Norfolk), J. Gardiner (Kinross and West Perthshire), Major S. G. Howard (Sudbury), Rt Hon. G. Lambert (South Molton), Capt. J. T. T. Rees (Barnstaple), Sir W. H. Seager (Cardiff East) and Lt-Cmdr E. H. Young (Norwich).

A few other Liberals were, with reservations, general supporters of the Coalition, and the number of anti-Coalition Liberals (commonly called 'Free' or 'Asquithian' Liberals) who were prepared to follow Asquith's leadership was estimated by *The Times* in January 1919 to be about 14 Members who could be relied upon consistently to oppose the Coalition Government.

[9] The fate which befell the Chief Whip was shared by all his Assistant Whips – Geoffrey Howard, Walter Rea and Sir Arthur Marshall. Only three non-Coalition Liberals who had ever sat on a Front Bench survived the catastrophe – George Lambert, F. D. Acland and William Wedgwood Benn.

still had withstood a three-cornered contest. The Liberal pacifists were totally obliterated.[10]

For this forlorn group, led by Sir Donald Maclean until Asquith returned to Parliament in the Paisley by-election of February 1920, the political future seemed doubtful and uncertain.

For the Labour Party, the results of the election produced a mixture of disappointment and solid advance. With 371 candidates in the field, compared with 56 in December 1910, the number of Labour Members returned rose from 42 to 60.[11] If this total was relatively disappointing, there was much more comfort in the total votes polled for Labour – 2,245,777 compared with 371,772, in 1910. In a wide variety of industrial seats Labour finished second, forcing the Liberals into third place – itself a distinct advance on the pre-1914 position. Yet the 60 seats won by Labour were not particularly good evidence for the supposed new-found strength of the party. Eleven of these were unopposed, whilst a variety of other Labour MPs had faced only left-wing 'Socialist' opponents. Similarly, Labour failed to make more than partial inroads even into such mining areas as South Wales, West Lancashire and Yorkshire. Such overwhelmingly industrial seats as Aberdare, Pontypridd, and the Gorbals and Bridgeton divisions of Glasgow, all returned Coalition Liberals. In the whole of the Greater London area, Labour secured only four seats. In the confused politics of 1918, Labour also won a few unexpected seats which it failed to secure regularly again – such as Holland-with-Boston and Clitheroe (this latter was not won again until 1945).

The uneven Labour performance was reflected in the almost total defeat of the 'pacifist' wing of the party. MacDonald was defeated in Leicester West by 14,223 votes. Snowden was equally heavily defeated in Blackburn. Arthur

[10] R. Douglas, *History of the Liberal Party, 1895–1970* (1971) pp. 130–1. Of the Liberal pacifists, C. P. Trevelyan in Elland, R. L. Outhwaite in Hanley and D. M. Mason in Coventry were not even supported by their Liberal Associations, and stood as Independents with Asquithian Liberals among their opponents.

[11] If the Co-operative MP for Kettering is included. Of these 60 seats, 44 were in England, 9 in Wales and 7 in Scotland.

Henderson, whose inability to retain seats became something of a disease, came third in East Ham South.

A consequence of the defeat of MacDonald and Snowden was that the party was left largely leaderless in the Commons (the nominal party leader was William Adamson) and composed very much of a solid phalanx of trade union-sponsored MPs.

These difficulties for Labour, however, were relatively unimportant compared with the débâcle that had overtaken the Liberals under Asquith. And yet some Liberals were able to put a brave face on events. There were exceptional factors about the election – the electoral pact, the low turnout, the inadequate register, the emotional tone of the campaign – which helped explain the disaster. One defeated Liberal candidate wrote to his constituency secretary that there was no need for undue Liberal depression, since in 1918 'conditions were so peculiar that it cannot be regarded as representing the normal views of the electorate'. [12]

These views were possible consolations for the disaster of the 'coupon' election. No such comforting explanations were possible, however, for the Liberal by-election record up to the 1922 general election.

After such a landslide victory in the 1918 election, it was not surprising that the by-elections rapidly showed a pronounced swing away from the Coalition. Indeed, the first by-elections of 1919 seemed to suggest that the Asquithian Liberals might be on the way to a sustained revival. The Independent Liberals won Leyton West (1 March), Hull Central (29 March) and Central Aberdeenshire and Kincardine (16 April). Of these results, J. M. Kenworthy's victory in Hull Central on a swing of 32·9 per cent was the most sensational.

These results, however, proved to be a false dawn. After Central Aberdeenshire the by-elections suddenly, but consistently, showed that the initiative in the constituencies had passed from the Liberals to Labour. During the remainder of 1919, in the three contests fought by Conservative, Liberal

[12] Harborough Division Liberal and Radical Association Papers, Percy Harris to Alderman Black, 28 Jan 1919.

and Labour, the Liberals came bottom in all three. Up to the
1922 general election the Independent Liberals won only two
other by-elections. These were Louth, a traditional rural
Nonconformist seat that had returned a Liberal at every
election since 1885 (except for January 1910), and Bodmin, a
similarly traditional Liberal West Country stronghold.

The greatest disappointment for the Independent Liberals
came in three-cornered contests. In such seats as Manchester
Rusholme, Plymouth Sutton and Ilford, Labour forced Liberals into third place. In the 24 three-cornered by-election
contests between 1918 and 1922, the votes were cast as
follows:

Coalition Conservative and		
Coalition Liberal	233,037	(40·1%)
Labour	203,887	(35·1%)
Independent Liberal	144,138	(24·8%)

Indeed, much the most significant feature of the by-elections
during the lifetime of the Coalition was the advance of
Labour. During 1919 the party won Bothwell (16 July) and
Widnes (30 August) from Coalition Conservatives and, in a
closely fought contest, gained Spen Valley on 20 December.
Labour also polled some extraordinarily high votes in several
suburban and middle-class areas. In December 1919, in
straight fights against Conservatives, Labour took 42·4 per
cent of the vote in St Albans and 47·5 per cent in Bromley.
Both were constituencies which Labour had not fought in the
'coupon' election.

Coalition losses to Labour continued during 1920. Labour
won Dartford on 27 March and South Norfolk on 27 July.
This latter was another remarkable victory; indeed, Labour
had decided only at the last minute to contest this Coalition
Liberal-held seat at all. The loss of South Norfolk produced
considerable despair among Conservative supporters of the
Coalition at the fate of their Liberal allies. Sir George
Younger, the party chairman, wrote to Bonar Law:

This constant loss of C[oalition] L[iberal] seats becomes serious and I see no chance of any improvement. With poor candidates and no organisation of their own, the attrition is bound to go on and the indecision of the Downing Street staff does no good. They arrive, spend money lavishly, but cut little ice.[13]

Meanwhile, in March 1921, Labour scored a further series of gains, capturing Dudley, Kirkcaldy and Penistone within the space of three days. Curiously, these Labour victories were preceded by the only genuine by-election victory won by the Coalition during this Parliament – Woolwich East, where the defeated Labour candidate was Ramsay MacDonald.[14]

After March 1921 the tide of Labour's advance slackened, although the party gained Heywood and Radcliffe on 8 June. During the winter of 1921–2 Labour's advance picked up again, with the party capturing Southwark South-East (14 December 1921), Manchester Clayton (18 February 1922), Camberwell North (20 February) and Leicester East (30 March). Before the fall of the Coalition, Labour made a final gain at Pontypridd on 25 July 1922.

During the last two years of the Coalition, although Labour had continued to win seats, the party had not contested by-elections on anything like the scale of 1919 and 1920.[15] It is, in fact, easy to exaggerate the extent of Labour's by-election advance. Although the party gained 14 by-election victories between 1918 and 1922, all except two of these were in working-class constituencies that remained generally

---

[13] Bonar Law Papers, 99/4/16, Younger to Bonar Law, 12 Aug 1920.

[14] He was defeated by Capt. R. Gee, VC, an ex-miner and war-hero. The campaign was centred almost entirely on MacDonald's pacifist record.

[15] This point is demonstrated by the following statistics:

	1919 and 1920	1921 and 1922
Number of by-elections	38	51
Number in Coalition-held seats	31	44
Number in Coalition-held seats contested by Labour	23 (74%)	18 (41%)

C. Cook and J. Ramsden (eds.), *By-Elections in British Politics* (1973) p. 20, n. 6.

faithful to Labour throughout the inter-war period.[16] Indeed, the Coalition polled remarkably well in such seats as Penistone, which it came close to winning in the face of Labour and Independent Liberal opposition. In this sense, the Coalition was probably more embarrassed by the success of the Anti-Waste League and right-wing Independents winning safe Conservative seats than by Labour victories in such areas as Pontypridd or Kirkcaldy.[17]

Labour was itself well aware that the votes it had polled in such seats as Dudley (the only really 'safe' Conservative seat won by Labour) were as much a protest at the Coalition as a positive swing to Labour. In the longer term, however, the significance of the by-elections was the extent to which (outside the old Nonconformist rural areas) protest votes were finding their home with Labour rather than with the Asquithian Liberals.

In part this was due to the large number of seats left uncontested by Independent Liberals at by-elections. No Independent Liberals were brought forward at by-elections in such seats as Bromley, Woodbridge, Dover or Taunton. This lack of a wide by-election challenge was itself evidence of the disastrous collapse of constituency organisation which occurred after 1918 (see pp. 27–48).

This disintegration of Liberal morale at constituency level reflected the wider dilemmas facing Liberals – the continued and growing split of the Independent and Coalition Liberals at national level.

In fact, the Asquithian Liberals were slow to realise that Lloyd George intended a permanent separation. During 1919, however, as Lloyd George continued to employ the 'coupon' in by-elections, the nature of his intentions became clearer.[18] The defeat of Sir John Simon in Spen Valley marked

[16] The two exceptions (Spen Valley, and Heywood and Radcliffe) were both won on a fortunate split of the anti-Socialist vote.

[17] The Anti-Waste League won Westminster St George's (7 June 1921) and Hertford (16 June 1921), and narrowly missed winning Westminster Abbey (25 Aug 1921). Right-wing Independents won the Wrekin (7 Feb 1920) and Dover (12 Jan 1921).

[18] Internal Liberal politics in these months are well discussed in Douglas, *History of the Liberal Party*, pp. 132–65.

an important step in this process of separation. The final break – and the establishment of a separate Coalition Liberal organisation – came with the failure of Lloyd George's attempts to create a 'Centre Party' by fusing the two wings of the Coalition. Throughout 1919 and 1920, Lloyd George's political objective had been to create a 'Centre Party' which would, by uniting the Coalition Liberals and Conservatives at all levels, provide a permanent base to fight off Socialism. The idea had been mooted with H. A. L. Fisher and Christopher Addison as early as September 1919.[19] At that time, Lloyd George believed it would be the Unionists who would provide the main obstacle. However, after some persuasion, both Bonar Law and Younger agreed. Lloyd George took the acceptance of his own party for granted.

In this, however, Lloyd George was to be rudely awakened. Whilst such Liberal Ministers as Churchill and Addison were enthusiastic for fusion – although for different reasons – they were isolated voices. When, on 16 March 1920, Lloyd George faced his Liberal colleagues at a crucial meeting intended to be the preliminary to public fusion with the Conservatives, he met firm opposition. The net result was that when Lloyd George met the Coalition back-bench MPs two days later, he made only vague appeals for 'closer co-operation' in the constituencies, rather than demanding fusion. Even this mild appeal met with a burst of criticism.

The net result was that, unable to deliver his party's own support, Lloyd George could clearly not approach the Unionists. As Morgan has written, the Coalition Liberals remained Liberals still and, whether he liked it or not, so did Lloyd George.[20]

This attempt at fusion, though it ended in failure, had important consequences. In March 1920 the Asquithian Liberal Party declared war on the Coalition Liberals. This declaration was echoed from constituency to constituency as Liberal Associations passed resolutions condemning both the

[19] Fisher's diary, 23 Sep 1919, quoted in Wilson, *The Downfall of the Liberal Party*, p. 193.

[20] See Kenneth O. Morgan, 'Lloyd George's Stage Army', in A. J. P. Taylor (ed.), *Lloyd George: Twelve Essays* (1971) p. 247.

Coalition and the policy of close co-operation with the Conservatives.

This growing animosity came to a head at the general meeting of the National Liberal Federation at Leamington in May 1920. Several Coalition Liberal MPs attended the gathering. However, when the Coalition case was argued from the platform, interruptions steadily mounted. T. J. Macnamara, who had spoken against Simon in the Spen Valley by-election, received a rowdy reception. This was nothing, however, compared with the general pandemonium which occurred when F. G. Kellaway declared that during the Boer War Asquith had been unfaithful to Liberalism. As tempers mounted Sir Gordon Hewart, the Attorney-General, stated that, in protest at these unruly proceedings, the Coalition Liberals would withdraw. Amid loud cheers, the Coalition Liberals left. The divisions in the party had become finalised.

After the Leamington conference, the Coalition Liberals began the creation of a separate party organisation in the constituencies and federations. Despite lavish expenditure from the Lloyd George Fund, the party organisation never really provided the Coalition Liberals with real roots (see pp. 43–6). When by-elections fell vacant, dreary reports came in of the lack of any Coalition Liberal organisation.[21] In a general review of the dismal Coalition Liberal performance at by-elections, F. E. Guest wrote to Lloyd George: 'New methods will have to be adopted, and many of our old methods will have to be scrapped, if the new and vast electorate is to be got at.'[22]

Guest was right. But it was Labour, not the Coalition Liberals, who were to set themselves the task. By 1921 it was increasingly apparent that the Coalition Liberals were a party of chiefs without Indians. In fact, the Lloyd George Liberals contained an impressive array of talent. In addition to Winston Churchill, H. A. L. Fisher and Sir Alfred Mond, the

[21] For Penistone, see report of James Parker (Coalition Liberal MP for Cannock) in Lloyd George Papers, F/22/3/7. Parker was even more depressing in his report on Kirkcaldy, where he found the industrial villages to be 'practically unorganised'.

[22] Lloyd George Papers, Guest to Lloyd George, 9 Mar 1921.

party possessed Edwin Montagu, Christopher Addison and Hilton Young. However, the further away one came from Downing Street, the more peripheral was the influence of the Coalition Liberal Party.[23] Certainly, in the Commons, the Liberals were never an effective parliamentary force. Although the party possessed its own Whips, it occupied no distinct place in the House separate from the Conservatives. Moreover, few of the back-bench Coalition Liberals were figures of any consequence.[24] In the constituencies, their political organisation was minimal. It is hardly surprising that the Coalition Liberals who supported Lloyd George have been the most unloved of political parties.

By 1922, however, Lloyd George himself was becoming the most unloved of politicians. His own position was becoming increasingly difficult. Coalition Liberal discontent was rife, yet Lloyd George did little about it. The Liberal back-benchers were treated with complete indifference. With the exception of Churchill, Lloyd George's main colleagues and confidants were all Conservatives – in particular, Austen Chamberlain, Sir Robert Horne, Lord Birkenhead and Sir Laming Worthington-Evans. Those Liberals left in the government were becoming increasingly isolated.

Meanwhile, in the Conservative constituency associations, the movement to sever the Coalition links was rapidly rising. On 2 June 1922, 11 Conservative peers and 30 MPs published a manifesto in the press declaring that 'to drift further with ever changing policies must quickly produce chaos, disaster and ruin'. The signs of revolt were becoming more evident.

With all these portents, it was remarkable that it was not until August 1922, when an imminent general election seemed likely, that Lloyd George set up a committee, consisting of Mond, Kellaway and Macnamara, to investigate the Coalition Liberal Party machine.

---

[23] See Morgan, in *Lloyd George: Twelve Essays*, p. 225.

[24] Wealthy industrialists – such as Sir Charles Sykes of Huddersfield and Sir Beddoe Rees of Cardiff – were much in evidence in the party. The Coalition Liberals were, perhaps, strongest in terms of bank balances rather than political expertise.

By the autumn of 1922, against a long background of by-election reverses, Coalition Liberal morale had all but disappeared. Lloyd George's bellicose handling of the Chanak crisis did nothing to calm the party. It was this crisis in October 1922 which, by threatening the Coalition with a new rebellion anyway, decided the Cabinet to take the plunge and hold an immediate election.

On 19 October the Conservative MPs were summoned to the Carlton Club by Austen Chamberlain, in an effort to secure their consent to fight the election as a Coalition. The meeting at the Carlton Club resolved that the Conservatives would not be the allies of the Coalition Liberals at the next election; it thereby destroyed the Coalition.

Lloyd George resigned as Prime Minister the same afternoon. On Monday 23 October, Bonar Law was unanimously elected leader of the Conservative Party to succeed Austen Chamberlain – who had himself replaced Bonar Law only nineteen months previously. Three days later, Parliament was dissolved. The date of the general election was fixed for 15 November.

The fall of the Coalition left both Lloyd George and his Liberal supporters without a power base. Despite a plea by Mond that the Coalition Liberals should fight during the subsequent election as Liberals desiring a reunited party, the bulk of the Coalition Liberals decided to act with the pro-Coalition Conservatives during the campaign.

With the fall of the Coalition, Lloyd George was left without any clear direction in which to try to lead his followers. In a speech at Leeds on 21 October, he was palpably engaged in an exercise to buy himself time. He offered no positive programme, and he carefully avoided defining his relations with the other parties. A similar lack of positive policy was again apparent when he spoke at the Hotel Victoria on 26 October. For once, Lloyd George was in the unhappy position of a leader with nothing to say.

Indeed, to some extent he was also a leader with nothing to lead. For, with the fall of the Coalition, the Lloyd George Liberals now discovered what had long been a political fact: they were a party without roots. The coming of the election meant that they must fend for themselves. Such electoral arrangements as they could make with other parties would have to be at constituency level.

Apart from North Wales, where Coalition Liberalism was strong in its own right, the most fortunate were the Lloyd George Liberals in Scotland. Feeling in the Scottish Unionist ranks was strongly in favour of a continued Coalition.[25] As it was, the Eastern Division of the Scottish Unionist Association formally decided not to oppose sitting National Liberal Members. In return, the Scottish National Liberals agreed not to oppose sitting Conservatives. Apart from such isolated constituencies as Perth and Glasgow Cathcart, the National Liberals in Scotland enjoyed a Coalition in 1922.

South of the Border, however, Coalition Liberals were forced to make such arrangements as they could to secure local Conservative support. So, in London, Macnamara in Camberwell North-West, as well as Arthur Lever in Hackney Central and Lt.-Col. M. Alexander in Southwark South-East, received official Conservative support only after they had given specific pledges of support to a Bonar Law Ministry. Others were less fortunate. Despite repeated attempts to secure Conservative support in Sunderland, Sir Hamar Greenwood was faced with two Conservative opponents in this double-Member constituency.

The rapid increase in the number of Conservatives coming forward to attack Coalition Liberal seats was likely to produce electoral disaster for Lloyd George's supporters. Yet Lloyd George was powerless to prevent it. His threat to bring forward candidates against sitting Conservatives was hardly practical politics. Though urged to adopt this course by Mond and Rothermere, nothing came of the 'phantom host' of candidates promised by C. A. McCurdy, the Chief Whip. As Churchill rightly observed, nothing was to be gained, and much would be lost, by spreading the war.

In the event, moderation prevailed. Only 144 Coalition Liberals were eventually adopted. Only 24 of these were in constituencies that had not been allocated to Coalition Liberal or National Democratic candidates in the 'coupon'

[25] Only 5 Scottish Unionists had voted to end the Coalition at the Carlton Club.

election. Only seven of these 24 fought against sitting Conservatives. The bulk of the attack was directed at Labour. In addition to Scotland and the East End of London, the Coalition continued virtually undisturbed in such towns as Bristol and Newcastle. Some 121 Coalition Liberals (Churchill among them) escaped any Conservative opposition.

Apart from the variety of dilemmas surrounding Lloyd George and the Coalition Liberals, the rest of the events of the 1922 election were much as expected. The Conservatives brought forward 482 candidates. Labour fielded 414, its largest contingent so far. The Asquithian Liberals made a widespread and determined challenge with 333 candidates. In all, 1,441 candidates came forward for the election. The outcome is given in Table 1.2.

TABLE 1.2
General Election, 1922

	Total votes	% share	Can- didates	MPs elected	Unopposed returns
Conservative	5,502,298	38·5	482	344	42
Liberal	2,668,143	18·9	333	62	6
National Liberal	1,412,772	9·4	144	53	4
Labour	4,237,349	29·7	414	142	4
Communist	33,349	0·2	5	1	–
Nationalist	112,528	0·5	5	3	1
NDP	52,233	0·4	7	–	–
Others	373,370	2·4	51	10	–
	14,392,330	100·0	1,441	615	57

The result disguised a variety of cross-currents. The Conservatives under Bonar Law gained 45 seats, but lost 63, while Labour gained 86 seats for the loss of only 19. Together, the two Liberal factions gained 36 seats but lost 75.

A closer analysis of the Liberal performance reveals just how disturbing the results were for both Asquith and Lloyd George.

With 333 candidates, the Independent Liberals fielded a large challenge with little reward. Admittedly, their numbers elected rose to 62, but this was only a meagre success.[26] Yet even this advance could hardly disguise several disturbing features. Fourteen of the seats won in 1918 had been lost, nine of them to Labour. The Liberals fared particularly badly in the mining areas. In Durham the three remaining Liberal constituencies, Consett, Seaham and Spennymoor, were all lost. Other traditional Liberal mining strongholds lost included Peebles and South Midlothian (Sir Donald Maclean's constituency), Leigh, and North-East Derbyshire.

On the other hand, the Independent Liberals managed to gain 43 seats. Of these, 10 were won from Coalition Liberals, 32 from Conservatives and Independents, but only one from Labour. It was significant that the best results for the Asquithian Liberals were in the traditionally Liberal rural seats lost in the 1918 débâcle. Thus, in Scotland, the Liberals recaptured such constituencies as Dumfries, Forfar and East Fife.[27]

However, the most disturbing feature of this partial revival, outside the occasional area such as rural Scotland or the West Country, was its lack of a secure regional base. Very many traditional Liberal seats, especially in the cities, had not been recovered, while several of the Liberal victories were in areas which had not returned Liberals for a generation. In Oxford, Frank Gray's success was the first Liberal victory since 1885. Likewise, the Liberal gain in Bootle was the first victory after forty years in the wilderness. Similar remarkable results occurred in Worcester, Blackpool and Great Yarmouth.

In fact, one Liberal Federation Secretary noticed that party organisation bore little relation to success. In many cases, the worse the organisation, the better the party fared.[28] The explanation lies in the fact that in 1922, the Liberals gathered the protest votes at the shortcomings of the Coalition.

[26] This figure does not include two National Liberals, T. M. Guthrie (Moray and Nairn) and J. Hinds (Carmarthen), who accepted the Independent Liberal whip after election.

[27] In the North of Scotland the Independent Liberals recaptured Caithness and Sutherland and Orkney and Shetland from the Coalition, but forfeited the Western Isles to a Lloyd George Liberal.

[28] Midland Liberal Federation, Minutes, Report of Federation Secretary on 1922 Election.

This was particularly true of the series of Liberal victories in rural seats which had rarely, if ever, returned Liberals before 1922. These victories owed little to the Liberal Party's own agricultural policy. Rather, they were a direct reaction to the failure of the Coalition to tackle the depression in farm prices.[29] Typical of Liberal gains in these areas were the victories in Grantham, Horncastle, Holderness and Taunton. The net result was that the Conservatives held only 48 of the 86 most rural constituencies in 1922.

A further disturbing feature for the Liberal Party was that its best results were, almost without exception, in straight fights against the Conservatives. In the 31 constituencies in which Independent Liberals enjoyed straight fights with Conservatives in 1918 and 1922, the Liberal share of the vote increased by over 10 per cent. These seats, however, were almost exclusively rural or residential. In the 54 constituencies which the three major parties contested in 1918 and 1922, the Liberals increased their share of the vote by only 4·5 per cent from 22·7 per cent to 27·2 per cent. The Liberal recovery in industrial working-class seats was, in general, conspicuously absent. The occasional exception, such as Walsall, which Pat Collins won for the Liberals, only made the general pattern more obvious.[30]

In the rural seats, however, the presence of Labour candidates had less effect, and in such seats as Westbury and Chippenham the Liberals were still able to regain lost territory.[31] In the small mixed-industry towns, such as York, Gloucester and Ayr, and in mixed county constituencies such

[29] For the decline of agricultural prices, see Kinnear, *The British Voter*, p. 43.

[30] A partial exception to this rule was to be found in the occasional Lancashire or Yorkshire seat, e.g. Darwen, Bradford South and Manchester Blackley.

[31] The figures in Chippenham were:

	1918			1922	
Con.	8,786	(53·0%)	Lib.	10,494	(48·6%)
Lib.	4,839	(29·2%)	Con.	10,006	(46·3%)
Lab.	2,939	(17·8%)	Lab.	1,098	(5·1%)

as Harborough, the Liberal recovery went hand in hand with a rise in the Labour vote. Conservatives were returned on a minority vote with the radical vote divided.[32]

However, if the 1922 election was one of disappointment for the Asquithians, for the Lloyd George Liberals the results constituted an unmitigated disaster. Among the many casualties were Churchill in Dundee, Sir Hamar Greenwood in Sunderland, Kellaway in Bedford and Guest in East Dorset. Guest suffered the added indignity of losing his seat to an Independent Conservative.

In 1918, 138 Coalition Liberals had been returned. Only 60 survived the 1922 election. No fewer than 81 seats were lost, 21 of which had even lacked defenders. Whilst 57 seats were retained, only three new seats were won. Only one of these, Wellingborough, was taken from Labour.

In the industrial areas the rout assumed the proportions of a massacre. In Sheffield, only the Park division survived as the lone outpost of Coalition Liberalism. Attercliffe was lost to Labour on a swing of 33·5 per cent; Hillsborough fell on a similar huge swing of 29·6 per cent.

South Wales was the scene of a similar débâcle. Neath was lost on a swing of 24·3 per cent, while Labour also captured Aberdare, Llanelli, Merthyr, Aberavon and Swansea East, which the Coalition Liberals had narrowly retained in the by-election of July 1919.[33]

In Scotland, despite the continuation of local Conservative–National Liberal agreements, it was the same story of industrial Liberal seats swamped by a Labour tide. Eight of the twelve seats in industrial Scotland were lost.[34]

[32] The result in Harborough prompted Percy Harris, the Liberal candidate, to write to the secretary of the association that a Liberal would never win the seat against Labour. See Harborough Division Liberal and Radical Association, correspondence, 19 Dec 1922.

[33] For the by-elections of the 1918–22 period in Wales, see Kenneth O. Morgan, 'The Twilight of Welsh Liberalism: Lloyd George and the Wee Frees, 1918–35', *Bulletin of the Board of Celtic Studies*, XXII, 4 (May 1968).

[34] The size of the swing to Labour in these eight constituencies was: Dunbarton, 17·1 per cent; Edinburgh Central, 6·6 per cent; Glasgow Bridgeton, 18·9 per cent; Montrose, 21·6 per cent; Stirling and Falkirk, 17·6 per cent; Kilmarnock, 12·4 per cent; Rutherglen, 14·2 per cent; West Renfrewshire, 15·8 per cent.

Only in its stronghold of rural North Wales was Coalition Liberalism able to survive unaided against Conservative and Labour attacks.[35] The net result of 1922, as far as the Coalition Liberals were concerned, was a disaster.

For the Labour Party, however, the results were little short of a triumph. The party returned with 142 seats, having fielded 414 candidates compared with 371 in 1918. This total of 142 was made up of four unopposed returns, 52 other seats successfully defended and 86 new seats won.[36] Labour failed to hold 19 of the seats it was defending.[37] Although the party possessed only 26 more seats than the combined Liberal forces, its position was infinitely more secure. No fewer than 89 of Labour's 142 seats were held with a majority of the votes cast, compared with the many Liberal seats won on minority votes.[38]

The Labour seats were concentrated in certain well-defined areas. Mining districts provided 39 of the 86 Labour gains, while 28 more came from Glasgow, Greater London, Tyneside and Sheffield. The Glasgow returns provided the most striking result, with Labour taking ten of the seats it contested, usually on large swings. Yet Labour's position was not as strong as it appeared at first sight. Admittedly the party won slightly more votes than the Liberals (29·4 per cent compared with 29·1 per cent), but if conflicting Liberal candidatures had been avoided, the Liberals would have won four Conservative seats and ten Labour. It has been calculated, on this basis, that the overall result of this would have been to give the combined Liberal ranks 134 to Labour's 133.[39]

---

[35] In such constituencies as Denbigh, the Coalition Liberals easily warded off the Labour and Conservative challenge. By contrast, the industrial Wrexham constituency was lost to Labour.

[36] The four unopposed returns were Abertillery, West Fife, Wentworth and Rother Valley.

[37] 11 of these 19 were in seats won in by-elections, while the loss in Birmingham Duddeston was in a constituency in which the MP elected in 1918 had subsequently joined Labour.

[38] Kinnear, *The British Voter*, p. 42.

[39] M. Kinnear, *The Fall of Lloyd George: The Political Crisis of 1922*, (1973) pp. 198–9.

Again, Labour's advance in 1922 was far from even. Whilst, overall, the Labour vote rose from 22·2 per cent in the 1918 'coupon' election to 29·4 per cent, the main areas of increase were heavily concentrated in mining areas, Glasgow and the Clyde, Sheffield and parts of London. These areas produced 64 of the 86 Labour gains. In 85 seats Labour actually lost ground compared with 1918. In 64 seats Labour did not contest seats fought in the 'coupon' election. In the 83 seats fought by Labour in 1922 but not in 1918, support for the party rarely exceeded 15 per cent. Since Labour did not contest 135 seats either in 1918 or 1922, and with withdrawals in 64 and declining support in a further 85, there were no fewer than 284 seats in which, even where a Labour candidate was seen, support was minimal. The party, although on the road to becoming a truly national party, still had far to go. The fact that, within fifteen months, Labour was to form its first government has tended to disguise this fact.

The seats where Labour lost heavily in 1922 came in two main categories: agricultural seats, especially in the South Midlands, together with the textile districts of East Lancashire and West Yorkshire.

Throughout the inter-war period Labour failed to make any real inroads into the agricultural constituencies. In the 86 most rural seats in Britain – those in which over 30 per cent of the employed male workforce were engaged in agriculture – Labour never won more than five of these in any inter-war election, a total the party achieved in 1923 and 1929.[40] The only constituency to return a Labour representative consistently was North Norfolk.[41]

It is essential, when examining the rise of the Labour Party in Britain, to realise just how little success the party met with in the countryside. In 1922, however, this weakness was far overshadowed by the dramatic gains in the industrial regions, symbolised in the sweeping victories along the Clyde.

[40] In 1918 Labour won only one (Holland-with-Boston), in 1924 only one (North Norfolk) and none in 1931.

[41] North Norfolk returned Noel Buxton from 1922 until July 1930. Buxton, however, had fought the seat as a Liberal in 1918, and with his defection the local Liberal Association had collapsed (*Norwich Mercury*, 17 Nov 1923).

The net outcome of 1922 for the Labour Party was its growth from a relatively ineffective and insecurely based force to the position of a vigorous and determined opposition, securely based in several major industrial regions.

If Labour had many occasions for rejoicing, the Conservatives had perhaps most to celebrate. Freed from the Coalition, the party had been returned with a clear majority of seats, although they were far short of a majority of votes cast. The exact figure of the Conservative majority is impossible to state accurately because a variety of candidates stood successfully as Independent Conservatives, Anti-Wasters or Constitutionalists.[42] Excluding the Members in this category, the Conservative majority was 39. However, Bonar Law's government could also count on the regular support of many Lloyd George Liberals. The government could thus be sure of a perfectly sufficient majority which could rise as high as 150. Certainly, Bonar Law's majority was quite adequate to maintain him for a five-year period in office.

This Conservative victory had been achieved with few major casualties. The only important Minister to suffer the indignity of defeat was Sir Arthur Griffith-Boscawen in Taunton.[43]

In fact, the results of the 1922 election distorted public opinion by giving the Conservatives a larger number of seats than they deserved. With 38·5 per cent of the votes they won a clear majority of seats – the lowest percentage of votes obtained by any majority government this century (and 5·2 per cent less votes than the Conservatives had captured in the 1906 Liberal landslide).

Table 1.3 indicates the comparative over-representation of the Conservatives in 1922. Partly these percentages are explained by the narrowness of many majorities in 1922. As Kinnear has written:

[42] 13 Independent Conservatives, 4 Constitutionalists, 2 'Unionist and Anti-Waste' candidates and one 'Unionist and Agriculturalist' were elected.

[43] Griffith-Boscawen had only been elected for Taunton in April 1921 after unsuccessfully seeking re-election in Dudley on his appointment as Minister of Agriculture. In addition to Taunton, Major J. W. Hills, the Financial Secretary to the Treasury, lost the Durham City seat.

... each of the three main parties got approximately a third of the vote, and no fewer than 103 MPs, a sixth of the total, had majorities of under 1,000 votes. Conservatives won 38 of these contests. In each of these constituencies a turnover of 500 votes would have changed the result. In addition, a further 38 MPs had majorities between 1,001 and 1,500.[44]

TABLE 1.3

Election	Con. % of vote	Con. seats	Con. % of seats
1922	38·5	343	55·8
1923	38·1	258	41·9
1929	38·2	260	42·3

These figures can be seen in perspective in Table 1.4, for the inter-war period.

TABLE 1.4
Number of MPs with Majorities under 1,000

1918	54	1929	68
1922	103	1931	21
1923	123	1935	48
1924	65		

Several other features of the Conservative victory need emphasising. The Conservatives nominated fewer candidates in 1922 than in 1923 or 1929, but they contested nearly all the seats where they had much chance. The Conservatives took 95 seats in 1922 on minority votes, and a further 19 in straight fights where their candidates had majorities of under 1,000 votes, for a total of 114 seats which were insecure by any usual reckoning.

If the Conservatives enjoyed several circumstances (especially during the campaign) which favoured their position, and if they were to some extent lucky in their total number of seats (compared with their percentage of the total poll), the areas which actually returned this large complement of Conservatives were the traditional inter-war strongholds of

---

[44] Kinnear, The Fall of Lloyd George, p. 152.

the party: London, the South-East, Birmingham, West Lancashire, and the agricultural seats of North Yorkshire and the West and South Midlands.

The Conservatives won no fewer than 158 of the seats with a middle-class proportion of the electorate above 20 per cent. The Conservatives also won 48 of the 86 seats in which the proportion of the employed male work-force engaged in farming was over 30 per cent. With the exception of 1923, this total was the lowest of any interwar election.

Faced with the dramatic increase in Labour support, and with the Conservatives under Bonar Law secure with a comfortable overall majority, it is hardly surprising that the Liberal Party found little comfort in the verdict of November 1922. Over breakfast with C. P. Scott, editor of the *Manchester Guardian*, Lloyd George asked him for his views on the result. Scott replied that the election constituted a disaster for the Liberal Party worse than 1918 because there was less excuse for it.[45]

Though Lloyd George realised the seriousness of the Liberal position, even he did not awake to the reality of the new position. To have restored Liberal fortunes, it would have needed an invigorated and active leadership in a united Liberal Party. The Liberals would need organisation, finance and policy. Above all, the party would need active, eager constituency associations, willing with missionary zeal to recoup the years in which the only propaganda that had been seen had come from Labour.

1922 was a severe Liberal defeat. It was also a challenge. The following chapters examine the response the Liberal party made in the months after 1922.

---

[45] Scott Papers, BM Add. MSS 50,906 f. 206, entry in diary for 6 Dec. 1922.

2 Constituency Organisation and Morale: The Counties

Although the results of 1922 demonstrated how far, in electoral terms, the divided party had fallen, they concealed the extent to which organisation, propaganda and political activity had collapsed at local level.

It is a remarkable comment on the existing historiography of the Liberal Party that virtually no work has been done at regional or constituency level on the inter-war decline of the party. There is no study, for example, of the decline of Scottish Liberalism, or of the continuing strength of Liberalism in the West Riding or Lancashire.[1]

A comprehensive survey of constituency Liberal Associations would require enormous space. By selecting area case studies, however, a representative picture can be assembled which enables firm conclusions to be drawn on the state of the party in mid-1923.[2]

The gravity of the position to which Liberalism at constituency level had deteriorated after 1918 was not lost on certain Liberals. One person to have no illusions was Viscount Gladstone, the director of Liberal Headquarters. Gladstone was later to write of the position after 1918:

> The result of 1918 broke the party, not only in the House of Commons but in the country. Local associations perished or

[1] A partial exception is the excellent study of Wales, in Kenneth O. Morgan, 'The Twilight of Welsh Liberalism: Lloyd George and the Wee Frees, 1918–35', *Bulletin of the Board of Celtic Studies*, XXII, 4 (May 1968).

[2] The areas in which detailed surveys have been undertaken are East Anglia, the West Midlands, Scotland, South Wales and the southern Home Counties.

maintained a nominal existence. Masses of our best men passed away to Labour. Others gravitated to Conservatism or independence.

He continued:

Over and over again, our remnants in the constituencies declined even to hold meetings. In the election of 1922, many constituencies actually refused to fight, even though candidates and funds were available.[3]

Was this picture exaggerated? Or was Gladstone's observation essentially correct? The first case study, of the area within the Eastern Counties Liberal Federation, provides a test of the accuracy of Gladstone's report. This was a region with three marked characteristics, all of which might have suggested an area of thriving constituency Liberalism. To begin with, the region had a strong Liberal tradition. In 1906 the 36 constituencies then within the Federation had returned 31 Liberals to Westminster. In the election of December 1910 the ratio had still been 21 Liberals to 15 Conservatives.

Linked with this Liberal tradition, the region contained many constituencies with a strong Nonconformist vote. In nine constituencies the proportion of Nonconformists, as calculated by Kinnear, exceeded 10 per cent, while in Horncastle, Gainsborough, Ipswich and Lincoln this figure exceeded 12 per cent. The regional average for the 28 constituencies, of 8·5 per cent, was one of the highest in the country.[4]

The third characteristic of the region was the high proportion of the adult working population engaged in agriculture. In eight constituencies this amounted to over half the employed male labour force. In every constituency except Brigg, Peterborough and Lowestoft over one-third were employed in agriculture.

Despite these factors, the Eastern Counties in mid-1923 presented a picture of dormant associations and a demoralised party. To the Liberal Federation Secretary, three major problems faced the party: the need to retain agents, the

[3] Gladstone Papers, BM Add. MSS 46,480, f. 133, Memorandum on the General Organisation of the Liberal Party, 18 Nov 1924.
[4] Derived from Kinnear, *The British Voter*, pp. 126–9.

problem of derelict constituencies and the urgent question of finance.[5]

In October 1923, only 15 of the 28 constituencies still possessed an agent, and several of these were only retained in spite of financial difficulties. In Gainsborough, for example, the Federation had to assist with a £50 grant to help maintain the agent. In Huntingdonshire the agent had been dismissed but was continuing in a voluntary capacity. Lincoln was less fortunate. The association still existed, but was in debt and the agent had gone. Similarly, Peterborough no longer possessed an agent, which may account for Liberal reluctance even to defend their council seats.

The position was made worse by the fact that the Federation was rapidly becoming unable to support weak associations financially. In April 1923 Liberal Headquarters terminated the £375 annual grant to the Federation, although still continuing to pay the salary of the Federation Secretary. Henceforth the Federation had to raise constituency subsidies from its own resources.[6]

These two factors – financial difficulties and lack of agents – were symptoms of a deeper malaise. This was the total lack of any form of Liberal activity in many constituencies. This was true of the two North Lincolnshire constituencies of Brigg and Grimsby. In Brigg, old-fashioned Liberalism had died a lingering death since 1918 in this former Liberal stronghold, whilst in Grimsby, though possessing sufficient funds to field a candidate, the association did not put one forward until 1924.[7] The party was simply dormant.

The most derelict area within the Federation, however, was Norfolk. In the South-West division, where the sitting Liberal, Sir Richard Winfrey, was a Lloyd George supporter, the old Liberal Association was defunct and the agent had gone. Meanwhile, Labour was carefully nursing the division.[8]

---

[5] The following material is derived from the Report of the Secretary of the Eastern Counties Liberal Federation, in Eastern Counties Liberal Federation, Minutes, Executive Committee, 5 Oct 1923 hereafter abbreviated to ECLF.

[6] ECLF, Minutes, Executive Committee, 20 Apr 1923.

[7] *Yorkshire Post*, 14, 24 Nov 1923.

[8] *Norwich Mercury*, 17 Nov 1923.

The split between Asquith and Lloyd George had played an important part in the South Norfolk division. Two rival Liberal candidates at a by-election in July 1920 gave Labour victory on a minority vote, despite the fact that, at first, Labour had not even intended to fight the seat.[9] Since the by-election defeat, Liberal organisation had further disintegrated.

In the North Norfolk division, Liberal organisation had completely collapsed when Noel Buxton, who had unsuccessfully fought the division in 1918, defected to Labour. In late 1923, with the agent gone, the association was still defunct.

Defection in another direction had further demoralised the Liberal ranks in the double-Member constituency of Norwich. Hilton Young, the sitting National Liberal, defected to the Conservatives early in 1923. Earlier, in June 1922, the Federation had received a letter from Young's agent stating that, in view of his position, he could no longer maintain his connection with the Federation.[10] Against this background of events, the Federation Secretary could only report that the position was 'clarifying itself'.

The adjacent county of Suffolk presented, with the exception of the Eye division, an equally derelict scene. At Ipswich the association was moribund, the agent had left, and no Liberal contested the seat until 1929. At Lowestoft the party was seriously divided, and once again the agent had left. Perhaps the most desolate of all constituencies was the safe Conservative seat of Bury St Edmunds. The Federation Secretary had the name of only one Liberal contact, a journalist on the *Bury Free Press*. The Liberal Association had completely disintegrated.

The Rutland and Stamford division, another very safe Conservative seat, presented a further example of constituency decay. The constituency was in debt and without an agent. A by-election vacancy occurred in September 1923, and the Federation Secretary warned his Executive: '. . . if we leave this seat to Labour our position for the future will be

---

[9] ECLF Annual Report, 1920. The figures at the by-election were: Labour 8,594, Coalition Liberal 6,476, Independent Liberal 3,718.
[10] ECLF, Minutes, Executive Committee, 9 June 1922.

sadly prejudiced.'[11] The warning went unheeded. No Liberal contested the by-election, and no attempt was made to improve constituency organisation before the general election.

This picture of dormant associations, however, was not universal. Elsewhere within the Federation, constituencies were active or undertaking reorganisation.

This was true of the agricultural divisions of North Lincolnshire. In Louth, for example, where the Liberals had gained a by-election victory in June 1920, and retained the seat at a second by-election in September 1921 despite Labour intervention, the local organisation was 'developed to perfection' and active propaganda work was being undertaken. The adjacent Horncastle division provided a parallel example. Once again, unexpected victory in 1922, in a constituency which had previously returned a Conservative at every election since 1885, had served to stimulate party organisation and morale. These examples were paralleled in the active divisions of King's Lynn, Yarmouth and Grantham.[12]

Similarly, the Secretary's report provided evidence of Liberals reorganising dormant constituencies. In Cambridgeshire a new agent had been appointed, reform of the Ely association was under way, and similar revival was planned for East Norfolk.

The net result of all this was that, of 28 divisions within the Federation, 7 were active and healthy, 13 totally dormant and defunct, and 8 either reorganising or facing financial stringency.

The second case study, of the Home Counties of Sussex and Surrey, finds close parallels with the Eastern Counties except that, as an area with little Liberal tradition, the decay in organisation had gone even further.[13]

[11] ECLF, Minutes, Executive Committee, 1 Oct 1923.

[12] In Yarmouth the Secretary reported that the sitting Liberal was 'ably maintaining his position', while in Lynn a woman organiser had been at work for two months and an active constituency campaign was under way.

[13] It is perhaps symbolic that the records of the Home Counties Liberal Federation (hereafter abbreviated to HCLF) do not survive before 1924. However, the Annual Reports after 1924 make frequent reference to the failure of attempts to organise constituencies between 1918 and 1923.

This was certainly true of the six county divisions in Sussex. In Lewes, which the Liberals had last fought in January 1910, the Liberal machine was totally defunct. In the adjacent Horsham and Worthing constituency the Liberal Party had similarly lain dormant for seven years. The Annual Report of the Federation could only remark that these were constituencies 'in which we failed to fan any semblance of Liberalism into life in the years after the war'.[14] The Chichester division was a similarly desolate scene. On the eve of the 1923 election no candidate was in sight and the association was dormant. According to one observer, there were only 12 known Liberals in the whole constituency.[15] Only in the Rye and Eastbourne divisions were the local associations sufficiently active to field candidates in 1922.

The position was the same in the Sussex boroughs of Brighton and Hastings. Of Brighton, a double-Member constituency, one newspaper commented: Liberalism in Brighton is in a more or less moribund state. There is in existence the nucleus of an organisation, but the party's activities for some years have been confined to the election contest.'[16] Another paper supported this view, commenting that Brighton found a source of considerable amusement in the lethargy with which the Liberals took up the electoral challenge in 1923.[17]

The seven Surrey divisions provided an equally desolate scene. Liberal organisation had totally collapsed in Reigate; the Conservative MP, Brigadier-General G. K. Cockerill, was not opposed until a Labour candidate was brought forward in 1924. The Epsom constituency defied all attempts to resuscitate organisation until the fortunate occurrence of a by-election in 1928 galvanised a little life into the local Liberals.[18] East Surrey displayed an equal lack of activity. In the Guildford division the Liberal campaign in 1923 provided the town with the first public meeting held by the Liberals

[14] HCLF, Annual Report, Executive Committee, May 1925.
[15] H. A. L. Fisher's diary, 9 Dec 1923, quoted in Wilson, *The Downfall of the Liberal Party*, p. 260.
[16] *Daily Telegraph*, 14 Oct 1924.
[17] *The Times*, 27 Nov 1923.
[18] HCLF, Annual Report, 1929.

since pre-war days. The position in Croydon was even less hopeful. In the South division, Liberal organisation was 'little better than hasty improvisation' during the 1923 campaign, and unity between the two wings of Liberalism was only achieved 'at the 11th minute of the 11th hour'.[19] The North Croydon Liberals were completely derelict.

Perhaps the best summary of the state of Surrey Liberalism was the deliberate understatement of one correspondent, that Liberal machinery would need considerable oiling before the Wey was set on fire.[20]

The net result of the collapse of these local Liberal Associations, and the subsequent lack of Liberal activity, can be seen in the numbers of Liberal candidates fielded: from 1918 to 1924 inclusive, of 39 possible contests in Sussex, Liberals fought only 17. In Surrey, for 51 possible contests, only 22 Liberals came forward.

The third case study, in the West Midlands, reveals the same dreary condition of the Liberal Party at the grass roots, except that there were signs of reorganisation setting in. The Secretary of the Midland Liberal Federation, in his report on the 1922 general election, commented dispiritedly: 'The most dreadful feature of our work during the past four years has been the difficulty of arousing any interest whatsoever'[21] After 1922, however, a renewal of interest had taken place.

The Secretary's report continued:

Since the elections were completed, there are many signs of a thoroughly awakened and revived party. . . . After the defeat of 1918, everything fell dead . . . but on this occasion . . . Liberals are already preparing to take action and preparing themselves for the next trial of strength.

There was some evidence to support this optimism. Reorganisation was under way in the derelict Evesham constituency. Large-scale meetings were planned in Worcester, and also in Walsall, both constituencies unexpectedly electing Liberals in

[19] *Croydon Advertiser*, 10, 17 Nov 1923.
[20] *Surrey Weekly Press*, 16 Nov 1923.
[21] Midland Liberal Federation, Minutes, Report of Federation Secretary on the 1922 General Election (hereafter abbreviated to MLF).

1922.[22] A Women's Advisory Council for the Federation was established in May.

Elsewhere, however, parts of the Federation paralleled the position found in Sussex and Surrey. The Burton division was completely dormant. In Tamworth no Liberal candidate had appeared since 1910, and the association was virtually defunct.

The defunct condition of Ludlow Liberalism became only too evident in the by-election of April 1923. The mixed industrial and agricultural Staffordshire constituencies were all derelict or dormant. In Kingswinford there had been a total cessation of all Liberal activities.[23] In Newcastle-under-Lyme, Josiah Wedgwood's defection to Labour had brought about the virtual collapse of the Liberal Association. In future, lacking any vitality, the Liberals hovered between independence and throwing in their lot with the Conservatives.[24] Continued inactivity in the Wrekin division as late as mid-1925 brought a protest from neighbouring, more active associations.[25]

The worst scene of Liberal decay was in the industrial constituencies of Birmingham and the Black Country. The Smethwick and Wednesbury divisions remained totally unorganised until 1925.[26] In Dudley the Liberal candidate in 1923 admitted that there was no organisation at the outset of the campaign. One result of the moribund Liberal condition was that 80 per cent of the local Labour Party were 'good old Liberals'.[27] In the Bilston division of Wolverhampton, despite a strong Liberal tradition in the industrial villages, the local association was defunct.

The final case study, of constituency Liberalism in Scotland, is perhaps the most revealing of all. All the symptoms of a serious malaise were present. Organisation was defunct,

[22] MLF, Minutes, Executive Committee, 2 Feb, 5 Oct 1925.

[23] *Birmingham Post*, 16 Nov 1923; *Dudley Chronicle*, 13 Dec 1923.

[24] F. Bealey, J. Blondel and W. P. McCann, *Constituency politics: A Study of Newcastle-under-Lyme* (1965) p. 405.

[25] MLF, Minutes, Executive Committee, 12 June 1925, letter of Shrewsbury Liberal Association to Federation Secretary.

[26] MLF, Minutes, Executive Committee, 20 Nov 1925.

[27] *Dudley Chronicle*, 13 Dec 1923; *Birmingham Post*, 21 Nov 1923.

finance was not forthcoming, speakers and candidates were obtained only with difficulty.

After the 1922 election the Executive of the Scottish Liberal Federation carried a resolution urging on all local associations 'the immediate necessity of taking advantage of the interest and work aroused by the General Election to improve organisation in the constituencies'.[28] There is little evidence that this advice was acted on. The Secretary of the Eastern Organising Committee of the Scottish Liberal Federation reported in July that 'the replies on Organisation had not been very satisfactory'.[29] It was, in many cases, a serious understatement.

Liberal constituency organisation had totally collapsed in several of its former citadels. Thus, one correspondent wrote of the West Stirlingshire division: 'The Liberal Association in the constituency seems to have died a natural death. At the last election, owing to the division of the party, there was no organisation capable of representing Liberal opinion in West Stirlingshire'.[30] Similarly, in the Bute and North Ayrshire division, Liberal organisation was moribund, while in South Ayrshire even the issue of Free Trade could raise only 'a stirring of life in the isolated tents of South Ayrshire Liberalism.'[31]

Most of Lanarkshire provided an equally derelict scene. It was agreed that special assistance by the Scottish Liberal Federation would have to be given to resuscitate Coatbridge and Airdrie, and Lanark.[32] The association in North Lanarkshire was moribund, while the Liberal votes in South Lanarkshire were compared by one correspondent with 'the lost tribe'.[33]

The most derelict of all areas was Glasgow itself. As *The Times* correspondent aptly remarked, Liberalism in Glasgow

[28] Scottish Liberal Federation, Minutes, Executive Committee, 8 Dec 1922 (hereafter abbreviated to SLF).

[29] Eastern Organising Committee of the SLF, Minutes, Executive Committee, 13 July 1923.

[30] *Glasgow Herald*, 21 Nov 1923; *Dundee Advertiser*, 15 Nov 1923.

[31] *Scotsman*, 21 Nov 1923. For a criticism of organisation in South Ayrshire from a pro-Liberal paper, see *Ayrshire Post*, 14 Dec 1923.

[32] SLF, Minutes, Executive Committee, 19 Dec 1923.

[33] *Lanarkshire Press*, 29 Nov 1923.

was in a waterlogged position. Even where a Liberal candidate was brought forward in 1923, few Liberals had any illusions on the likely result – a place at the foot of the poll.[34] Together with moribund organisation, finance was also a major problem. At the end of 1922 the Secretary of the Eastern Finance Committee reported that:

> He had been informed . . . that the grants that had been given in the past would probably be halved, and this in itself was serious enough, but several very good friends who had rendered valuable financial assistance were unwilling to subscribe.[35]

The only response by the Eastern Finance Committee to this position was that expenses 'should be met by the usual Bank Overdraft'.

At the heart of both the decay in organisation and the financial difficulties was the party split. The bitterness between the two rival Liberal camps was probably as deep in Scotland as anywhere. At the 1922 elections, of the 12 National Liberals elected, 11 had 'represented organisations that were not connected with the old Asquithian Scottish Liberal Federation'.[36] The exception was Kirkcaldy Burghs, where the association was still affiliated but was not very active. In a report on the by-election of March 1921, one National Liberal found a total lack of organisation in the mining areas of Methil and Dysart and in the industrial villages.[37]

Outside Kirkcaldy, in the 11 constituencies with a rival National Liberal organisation, the picture facing the Liberal Party was not encouraging. Typical of the position was the Moray and Nairn division. With the old association supporting the Coalition Liberals, a new Asquithian organisation had been set up. However, this had made no formal application to

---

[34] As Asquith wrote of the prospects of the Liberal candidate in Glasgow Central, there was not the 'shadowiest chance' of being anywhere except at the bottom of the poll. H. H. A., *Letters of the Earl of Oxford and Asquith to a Friend,* 2nd series (1933–4), p. 85.

[35] Eastern Finance Committee of the SLF, Minutes, 28 Dec 1922.

[36] SLF, Minutes, Executive Committee, 28 Mar 1923.

[37] Lloyd George Papers, F/22/3/7, report of James Parker, MP, on Kirkcaldy Burghs by-election.

join the Federation, as it intended first to open up negotiations with the old association with a view to arriving at an understanding.[38]

By the autumn of 1923 no 'understanding' had arrived. Not until the election were the two wings reconciled in Moray, or in such divisions as Montrose, Dundee, the Western Isles and Aberdeen.[39] Not even the election healed the breach in Ross-shire, Argyll and Inverness-shire. The net result of decaying organisation, the party split and financial difficulties could be seen in the number of prospective candidates, a mere four when the Dissolution was announced, outside seats already held by Liberals.[40]

The preceding evidence in these four case studies can be verified by examining the records which still survive for two aspects of Liberal organisation: the number and membership of the women's branches, and the numbers of affiliated party agents.

An examination of these two aspects from the national level suggests that the picture drawn up in the area studies was not exaggerated. The membership and morale of the Women's National Liberal Federation presented a far from satisfactory position after 1918.[41] The Annual Report of the Federation for 1922 could only comment that some of the associations had 'still not regained the strength and membership of pre-war days'. This was a disastrous understatement. In mid-1920 the Federation claimed 732 branches with 95,217 members. By mid-1922 membership had fallen by 30 per cent to 67,145.

Although the Annual Report for 1921–2 claimed that almost the whole country was covered with a network of women's associations, in reality there were scores of associations which had decayed since 1918.

---

[38] SLF, Minutes, Executive Committee, 28 Mar 1923.

[39] SLF, Minutes, Executive Committee, Report of Secretary on 1923 Election, 19 Dec 1923.

[40] SLF, Minutes, Executive Committee, 19 Dec 1923.

[41] The following material, except where stated, has been compiled from the Annual Reports of the Women's National Liberal Federation from 1918 to 1925.

Numerous once flourishing branches had totally collapsed. Grimsby and Kendal, each with 1,500 members in 1919, had vanished. This position was paralleled in such constituencies as Bournemouth, Brighton, Wimbledon, Frome and Leek. Even in such rural seats as Westmorland, where in 1918 the membership of the local branches had totalled 950, by 1923 there were only 210 members. In the Cirencester division, only one out of five branches still remained. Examples of the disastrous slump in membership in ten once active branches are set out in Table 2.1. From over 10,000 members in 1919, membership had slumped by 65 per cent in 1923 to only 3,600. Occasionally, as in such West Country seats as Tavistock and Tiverton, reorganisation had taken place, but in general the position was desolate. After 1923, membership fell slightly to 66,200 in 1924, despite an increase of 16 in the number of branches to 746. By 1925 membership had risen to 75,000 and to 88,000 in 1926. The number of branches was 820 in 1925 and 919 in 1926.

TABLE 2.1

Branch	1919	1923
Darwen	1,500	1,051
Lincoln	1,071	636
Colchester	750	263
Hartlepools	710	300
Rochdale	540	360
Exeter	1,000	240
Hastings	730	180
Barnstaple	1,000	120
Boston	550	210
Blackburn	2,400	252
	10,251	3,612

This slump in membership was doubly serious since it has to be seen against a rapid expansion in the rival Conservative women's organisation. In 1921 the number of women's branches was 1,340. By 1922 this total had risen to 2,102, and by 1923 to 3,600.[42] Overall membership figures do not exist, but at regional level there were, in 1923, 62,000 members in the South-east counties, 60,000 in Lancashire and Cheshire and 45,600 in the East Midlands.[43] Some individual constituencies boasted very large membership totals.[44] In such divisions as Plaistow and Luton, constituency organisation was virtually a monopoly of the women.[45] Overall, the position was one of complete contrast to the declining membership and diminishing activity of the Liberal women's organisation.

The number and morale of full-time Liberal Party agents provides a barometer which confirms the comments made earlier on party organisation. The Annual Reports of the Society of Certificated and Associated Liberal Agents record an uninterrupted decline in the numbers of agents affiliated to the society.[46]

From 357 subscribing members in January 1920, this total had fallen to 337 a year later, and to 289 by January 1922. Twelve months later, at the beginning of 1923, although this figure had held steady at 286, the position was critical. A voluntary levy was held after the 1922 election 'to assist out of work agents who were in distress'. The Annual Report concluded that 1922 ended 'in a most depressing manner for agents generally'. The position had not improved by the 1923 election.

These figures, however, greatly exaggerate the number of agents actually at work in the constituencies. Thus, of 292 affiliated members in 1924, no fewer than 90 had retired, or

[42] Women's Unionist Organisation, 4th Annual Conference Report, May 1923. An indication of the growing importance of the women's organisation was the increasing number of delegates to annual conference. From 400 in 1920 and 600 in 1921, the figure had risen to 1,600 in 1923.

[43] Ibid. For the East Midlands, see report in *Derby Mercury*, 26 Nov 1923, of the East Midlands Area Conference of the Women's Unionist Organisation.

[44] Chippenham, for example, had 3,000 subscribing members. Derby possessed 1,550. *The Times*, 19 Nov 1923; *Derby Mercury*, 26 Nov 1923.

[45] *The Times*, 29 Nov 1923; *Bedfordshire and Hertfordshire Telegraph*, 8 Dec 1923.

[46] The following material has been compiled from the Annual Reports, account books and other records of the Society of Certificated and Associated Liberal Agents.

were employed at Abingdon Street or at Federation offices. A further 13 were unemployed, leaving only 189 full-time agents at work in England and Wales. The line of agents at work in mid-1923 was thinly spread. Whilst the North-West boasted 59 subscribing members, and the Yorkshire Federation 33, there were only 21 paid-up agents in the whole of the Midland Liberal Federation and only 10 in the Northern Counties.

Although all this supports a pessimistic view of constituency Liberal health in mid-1923, a further more fundamental weakness can be seen in the inability of local Liberal Associations to raise finance themselves. Almost without exception, even where an active association existed, the constituency Liberals relied on a wealthy candidate and on subsidies from Headquarters. Radical candidates were popular. Wealthy radicals who could also pay the bills were even more popular.

An example of the extent to which a constituency Liberal Association was dependent on the wealth of an individual can be found in the Harborough division.[47] At the beginning of 1919, correspondence on the subject of finance took place between Percy Harris, the Liberal candidate in the 1918 election, and the local association. Explaining how much he was willing to contribute, Harris wrote to the constituency chairman:

> In the past, I paid £150 per annum to the Association, and £10–10–0 per month to Mr Coppock personally. I prefer to pay the whole sum to the Association, in other words I am prepared to contribute £276 per annum[48]

This offer was later extended to cover 'heavy expenses', including hotel bills and car hire. However, even this offer proved unacceptable, as the association wanted £400 per annum. Harris then wrote back to the association agent:

> I cannot see my way to contribute £400 . . . if Liberal Associations have to ask such large annual subscriptions from candidates,

[47] The following material has been taken from the constituency records of the Harborough Division Liberal and Radical Association (hereafter abbreviated to HDLRA).

[48] HDLRA, Minutes, Percy Harris to J. W. Black, 28 Jan 1919. Mr. Coppock was the association agent.

their choice is likely to be circumscribed and limited to very rich men.[49]

As a result, the Executive Committee withdrew the invitation to Harris to stand as candidate, 'due to his inability to contribute £400 per annum', and a new selection committee was appointed.[50] This committee settled on J. W. Black, who proceeded to finance the association for the next few years. Thus, the Annual Report of the Executive Committee for 1920 commented:

> Mr Black is contributing very handsomely, but from every point of view it is undesirable that any one man should be either unduly taxed or in a position to dominate the Association.

This, however, continued to be the case. Each time an annual deficit occurred, the candidate and the same few subscribers went to the rescue. Once J. W. Black departed, the association was faced with a major financial crisis.[51]

A parallel example to the Harborough division was to be found in Nottingham East. The enormous expense of a sitting Liberal MP can be seen in a letter Norman Birkett wrote to his cousin after the 1924 election:

> . . . it has also been a terribly expensive year, with an extra election thrown in following on so quickly the other . . . my brief tenure of Parliament cost me little less than £2,000, what with getting in, staying in and getting out.[52]

Just as constituencies were financed by a wealthy candidate, where one could be found, so Liberal Headquarters was itself financed by the donations of a very limited number of subscribers. Total donations to the Independent Liberal Headquarters for the 1922 election amounted to £45.523.[53]

[49] HDLRA, Percy Harris to Coppock, 13 Feb 1919.
[50] HDLRA, Minutes, Executive Committee, 26 Feb, 15 Mar 1919.
[51] J. W. Black stopped paying the salary of the association's full-time secretary in January 1925; the Executive Committee dismissed him in December 1925. The association was forced to cease its annual payment to the Midland Liberal Federation in March 1927.
[52] H. M. Hyde, *The Life of Lord Birkett of Ulverston* (1964) p. 128. Birkett was Liberal MP for the division from December 1923 to October 1924. He regained the seat in 1929.
[53] Excluding the separate Scottish list of £3,360. See Asquith Papers, Box 10, p. 45.

This was raised from only 34 people. Of this total, 12
subscribers between them contributed over £38,000. Lord
Cowdray contributed £12,000, Runciman £10,000 and Lord
Forteviot £3,000.

In the 1922 election, 112 constituencies received financial
assistance from Headquarters. This was particularly prevalent in London and the Home Counties. No fewer than 46
constituencies in the London area and 21 in the Home
Counties received substantial assistance.[54] However, the extent to which constituencies relied on grants from Headquarters is best illustrated in 1923, when £116,955 was distributed
between 220 constituencies. No fewer than 74 constituencies
in London and the Home Counties, 29 in the Midlands, 26 in
the North-West and 23 in Scotland were substantially assisted. Table 2.2 sets out the sums in detail.

TABLE 2.2
Headquarters Grants to Liberal Federations, December 1923 Election

Federation	Total HQ contribution	No. assisted	Average grant
Devon and Cornwall	£6,342	10	£634
Eastern Counties	£8,493	16	£530
Home Counties	£21,740	38	£572
Lancashire, Cheshire and North-West	£13,239	26	£509
London	£18,103	36	£503
Midland	£15,008	29	£517
Northern	£8,856	14	£632
Western	£6,002	13	£461
Yorkshire	£7,117	15	£474
Scotland	£12,055	23	£524
	£116,955	220	£532

Once again, the number of subscribers to the Independent
Liberal funds was a small circle. Of the £74,186 raised from
donations in 1923, no less than £67,000 was raised from 14

[54] Gladstone Papers, BM Add. MSS 46,480/49.

people. Lord Cowdray and Lord Inchcape each contributed £20,000.[55]

The net result of these Headquarters subsidies, which had been particularly heavy in the 1910–14 period, was not lost on such people as Gladstone.[56] The effect had been to discourage local initiatives towards financial self-sufficiency. When the subsidies were not forthcoming, as in 1924, the result was the inability of Liberal Associations to field candidates. In this sense, an added reason for the decline of the Liberal Party must be found in this field of constituency finance.

However, the bulk of the preceding evidence has related only to the Independent Liberal Party. What was the state of the Coalition Lloyd George wing of constituency Liberalism? Did the National Liberals present an active local force? Or were they in as similar sorry plight as their Asquithian rivals?

After the National Liberal Federation meeting at Leamington in May 1920, the Lloyd George Liberals had begun the creation of separate constituency and regional organisations. Money was generously provided and in a few areas (such as London) National Liberal Associations mushroomed. But these were few and far between.

Nothing like a comprehensive constituency organisation ever materialised. A close adviser of Lloyd George, Sir William Sutherland, warned that unless the Coalition Liberals were fully organised in every constituency, the party would never possess effective local influence.[57] The warning went unheeded. Outside the constituencies in which there were Lloyd George candidates, only 21 new local associations were established.

Nominally, some 224 constituencies possessed a Coalition Liberal Association. Many, as Lloyd George later admitted, had only a propaganda value and lacked real local activity.

[55] Asquith Papers, Box 10, Cash Book No. 3 (1923 Election). Inchcape's contribution was largely Cowdray's work: Gladstone Papers, BM Add. MSS 46,477/112, Cowdray to Gladstone, 19 Nov 1923.

[56] For Gladstone's criticism of Headquarters policy, see Gladstone Papers, BM Add. MSS 46,480/196.

[57] Lloyd George Papers, F/35/1/39, Sir William Sutherland to Lloyd George, 18 Mar 1922.

From August 1922 until October 1923 no mention at all of 123 of these associations was made in the *Lloyd George Liberal Magazine*. A further 69 associations would seem to have held only three meetings or fewer, while only 10 had met on more than six occasions.[58]

Among the few active associations after the 1922 election were Bolton, with 26 social functions between August 1922 and October 1923, and Sunderland, where in March 1923 20 meetings were held, with one social attracting over 1,000 people. Similarly, Coalition Liberalism was reported active at Westhoughton, where there was a programme of weekly meetings and whist drives, and at Crewe, where daily open-air meetings in the railway works were attracting up to 400 people.[59]

In the Midlands, the Wellingborough division provided a rare example of an active local association. After a national Liberal gain from Labour in the 1922 election, there had been a 'striking recrudescence' of local activity, with new branches in such centres as Finedon, and the whole organisation had undergone a 'vigorous spring-cleaning'.[60]

In Scotland the Coalition Liberals claimed that such associations as Rutherglen were active. These claims hardly stand up to close investigation.[61] It would seem that, during the early summer of 1923, the Coalition Liberals made an attempt to expand their constituency organisation. The Secretary of the Eastern Organising Committee of the Scottish Liberal Federation reported that:

> ... the National Liberals were evidently making an attempt to improve their organisation in various constituencies and had been, through their officials, offering their services to certain of the associations that still remained affiliated to us, and in other

[58] Kinnear, *The British Voter*, p. 92.

[59] *Lloyd George Liberal Magazine*, Apr 1923, p. 561.

[60] *Lloyd George Liberal Magazine*, July 1923, p. 727. Active associations in the London area included Camberwell North-West and Hackney Central. A membership drive in Hackney in June 1923 added 200 new members.

[61] Rutherglen was claimed to be the most active constituency in the West of Scotland, yet no Liberal candidate was brought forward in 1923. *Lloyd George Liberal Magazine*, May 1923, p. 639.

cases trying to set up National Liberal organisations where they had none.[62]

However, the Secretary's report continued, 'In none of the cases that were known had the movements to get their services accepted, or to get organisation going, been successful'. The claim of the Coalition Liberals, that 'arrangements are now completed all over the country for the resumption of the vigorous work of the National Liberal organisation during the winter', clearly needs treating cautiously.

However, perhaps the best example of the almost complete lack of constituency National Liberal activity can be found in the area which ought to have been most active – in Wales itself.

One Liberal to have no illusions about the gravity of the position was W. C. Jenkins of Swansea. Sir Alfred Mond, National Liberal MP for the West division, conveyed his views in a letter to Lloyd George.[63] Jenkins found that the Liberals, in their 'Rip van Winkle' sleep, had made 'only sporadic efforts' to counter the spread of Socialism. In several South Wales constituencies the party was 'without agents, to say nothing of political activity'. The deterioration had gone so far that Jenkins believed the Liberals should not have fought the mid-1922 by-elections in Gower or Pontypridd. The only hope was 'reorganisation on new lines with an industrial policy'.[64]

Reorganisation never came. The constituency associations had further deteriorated by November 1923. Liberal organisation had totally collapsed at Merthyr and at Newport.[65] Nothing had been heard of Liberal activity in Bedwellty or Abertillery.[66] In Cardiff the Liberals had no agent, no offices and not even an executive committee.

[62] Eastern Organising Committee of the SLF, Minutes, 13 July 1923.

[63] Lloyd George Papers, F/37/2/17, Mond to Lloyd George, 10 Aug 1922.

[64] For an equally pessimistic picture of Liberal organisation and morale in the Ebbw Vale by-election, see Lloyd George Papers, F/22/1/1, Revd Towyn Jones to J. T. Davies, 14 Jan 1920; for Abertillery, see Lloyd George Papers, F/22/3/2, F. E. Guest to Lloyd George, 6 Jan 1921.

[65] Western Mail, 17, 19 Nov 1923.

[66] South Wales News, 14 Nov 1923; Western Mail, 19 Nov 1923.

This moribund picture was punctuated by occasional bright spots. Social activities were reported from such constituencies as Caerphilly, Llanelli and Aberavon, whilst at Neath and Ebbw Vale attempts were under way to resuscitate the old association.[67]

These indications of activity and reorganisation have to be treated cautiously. Thus, in Ebbw Vale the Liberals claimed to have formed an association at Tredegar, and new branches were in the process of formation at Rhymney and Ebbw Vale itself, whereas the Political Organiser of the South Wales Miners' Federation denied that anything had come of these attempts.[68] Possibly some of the Liberals in Aberavon were active, but in October 1922 Mond had written of the candidate in the constituency to Lloyd George: 'Jack Edwards has so neglected Aberavon that the Liberals have been talking of withdrawing him in favour of a Tory in order to beat Ramsay MacDonald'.[69] Of Wales generally, Mond added, 'everything has been allowed to drift until the last moment'.

That observation was still true in 1923. Comparing general elections to market days, one pro-Liberal paper commented: '... in between the markets, the market place is a scene of desolation and silence as far as the Liberal vendor is concerned'.[70] The essential conclusion from a study of the Coalition Liberals is that, on reunion in November 1923, Lloyd George brought with him not an active, vital, radical party, but a party without constituency roots which was daily becoming more of an anachronism.

This evidence of Independent and Coalition Liberal organisation suggests that in virtually every part of the country, in a whole variety of traditional Liberal areas, party organisation had collapsed or was surviving only with difficulty. The position was particularly serious in three main groups.

One group was made up of the safe Conservative seats in which, even before 1914, Liberalism had never been strong.

[67] *Lloyd George Liberal Magazine*, Apr 1923, p. 560; Sep 1923, p. 884.
[68] *South Wales News*, 14 Nov 1923.
[69] Lloyd George Papers, G/14/5/1, Mond to Lloyd George, 29 Oct 1922. Similarly, if the Llanelli division was active, there was still no prospective candidate ready (*South Wales Evening Express*, 14 Nov 1923.)
[70] *Glamorgan Free Press*, 14 Dec 1923.

Examples of this in the case study of East Anglia were Bury St Edmunds and Rutland and Stamford. Similar examples can be found in such areas as the North Riding of Yorkshire or the Kent seats.

Much more surprising than this group were those county constituencies, largely agricultural, with a strong mining element. Prior to 1914 these had proved reliable Liberal territory. After the war, organised Liberalism totally collapsed in such seats as Frome, the Forest of Dean, Leek and the Wrekin.[71] The third group was made up of the predominantly mining seats. Here party organisation and morale had almost completely collapsed. After 1922 virtually the only mining seats which Liberals fought consistently were in Nottinghamshire and Derbyshire.[72].

TABLE 2.3
Liberal Candidates in Mining Seats, 1922–9[73]

Area	Total possible contests	Liberal candidates	%
Notts/Derby	32	26	81·3
South Wales	60	38	63·3
Durham	56	34	60·7
Scotland	52	27	51·9
Yorkshire	32	14	43·8
Lancashire	28	8	28·6
	260	147	56·5

In none of the remaining coalfields did the Liberals fight more than two-thirds of the possible contests during the

[71] For lack of organisation in the Forest of Dean, see *Western Mail*, 15, 17 Nov 1923. In Frome, Liberal organisation collapsed completely after the defeat of Sir John Barlow, the sitting Member, in the 'coupon' election (*Bristol Times and Mirror*, 15 Nov 1923.)

[72] For the miners' loyalty to Liberalism in this area, see J. Williams, *The Derbyshire Miners* (1962) pp. 821–9. Barnet Kenyon represented Chesterfield as a Liberal until 1929; Ilkeston, North-East Derbyshire and South Derbyshire all polled high Liberal votes in 1923.

[73] I have followed Dr Kinnear's definition of a mining seat as one in which more than 20 per cent of the employed male work-force was engaged in mining. For a list of these, see Kinnear, *The British Voter*, pp. 116–18.

period 1922–9 (see Table 2.3). In these mining seats the
Liberals were already a party that had lost the will to fight. In
Lancashire, for example, no Liberal contested the Ormskirk,
Ince or Newton divisions in any inter-war election. Even in
the 1923 election, Liberal Associations made local agree-
ments with the Conservatives to form anti-Socialist fronts.

It is true that, outside these areas, in some agricultural
seats, Liberal organisation and morale had revived, frequently as the luck of a by-election brought in outside help and
finance. This was particularly true of such rural areas as
Lincolnshire or the West Country, where the Liberals clearly
benefited from the farmers' revolt against the Coalition.
There were, indeed, some areas relatively unaffected by the
split. Cheshire provides one such example. Liberal Associations in such seats as Altrincham, Knutsford and the Wirral
were all thriving.[74] At the county council level, Cheshire
Liberalism was an established and potent force throughout
the inter-war period.[75] But such bright spots were few in the
counties. They were even fewer, as the following chapters
attempt to demonstrate, in urban and industrial England.

[74] *Warrington Examiner*, 27 Oct, 24 Nov 1923; *Chester Guardian*, 6 Nov
1923; *Liverpool Post*, 15 Nov 1923.
[75] The survival of Cheshire Liberalism at county council level is well
detailed in J. M. Lee, *Social Leaders and Public Persons: A Study of County
Government in Cheshire since 1888*, (Oxford, 1963).

3 Municipal Politics: The Provincial Boroughs

Several difficulties, in particular the lack of surviving constituency archives, face any attempt to trace the decline of the Liberal Party in the major cities. However, in municipal electoral activity there is one vital source of evidence which provides rich and hitherto untouched material for an analysis of the decline of the party.

An analysis of the numbers of wards contested annually by each party, the type of seat won and the candidates brought forward, together with the existence of local party alliances, provides a wealth of information on constituency political activity. This evidence is particularly valuable because after the expansion of the local government franchise in 1918, municipal elections took on an added importance.[1] This was reflected in relatively few uncontested elections. Between 1919 and 1926, 72 per cent of the wards falling vacant each November in Nottingham, 61 per cent in Leicester, 82 per cent in Northampton, 93 per cent in Leeds and no less than 98 per cent in Bradford were contested.

Municipal electoral evidence is particularly valuable for a study of the Liberal Party. If, at this level, it can be shown that the party was already a declining force in the major cities,

[1] Figures for the proportion of the population who possessed the local government franchise before 1914 varied from town to town. The figures in 1911 were: Leicester, 19·6 per cent; Sheffield, 18·5 per cent; Manchester, 17·1 per cent; Leeds, 19·7 per cent; Bristol, 18·3 per cent ; Cardiff, 14·8 per cent; Swansea, 16·2 per cent. After 1918 these proportions approximately doubled. Compiled from *London County Council: Comparative Municipal Statistics* (1912–13) vol. I, pp. 124–5. See also B. Keith-Lucas, *The English Local Government Franchise* (Oxford, 1952).

being forced to make electoral pacts for its survival and unable to attract young candidates or formulate a relevant policy, then this material will clearly add a new perspective to the debate on the fall of the party. Although the value of municipal political evidence for the period after 1945 is being recognised, for the inter-war period virtually no attention has been devoted to municipal politics.[2]

One useful barometer of Liberal activity in the provincial boroughs was the number of candidates fielded each November. Table 3.1 indicates the massive Labour challenge together with the marked weakness of the Liberals. The decline in the Liberal percentage continued after 1925. It fell to 15·6 per cent in 1926, 13·6 per cent in 1927, 12·6 per cent in 1928 and 12·4 per cent (less than one in eight of all candidates) in 1929.

TABLE 3.1
Percentage of Candidates Fielded for Provincial Borough Elections, 1921–5[3]

	Con.	Lab.	Lib.	Ind.	Sample
1921	31·0	35 1	18·6	15·2	1,772
1922	31·8	37·7	17·7	12·8	1,701
1923	30·3	34·6	17·3	17·8	1,833
1924	31·3	38·5	17·0	13·2	1,676
1925	29·6	38·9	15·0	16·5	1,856

These figures demonstrate very clearly the contrast between the Labour and Liberal performance. In 1921 the Liberals had fielded 18·6 per cent of the above sample of candidates. By 1929, after an almost uninterrupted decline, this figure had fallen to only 12·4 per cent. In direct contrast, the Labour attack gradually expanded, so that by 1929 44 of every 100 candidates for municipal office were put forward by Labour.

The same pattern of Liberal decline and rising Labour strength can be seen in the gains and losses of the parties each

[2] A partial exception is the important study of Wolverhampton in G. W. Jones, *Borough Politics: A Study of Wolverhampton Borough Council* (1969).

[3] *The Times*, 2, 3 Nov 1921 and annually to 1929. The sample was based on candidates brought forward for the 70 largest provincial boroughs.

November. The most dramatic result occurred in the municipal elections of November 1919, the first to be held since 1913. Although the results were distorted by a low turnout, they showed a massive breakthrough for Labour.

Labour gained ten seats in Liverpool, Bradford and Swindon. Nine gains were registered at Gateshead and Plymouth, eight at Derby. Nottingham and Coventry each provided seven gains, while at Crewe Labour swept every seat. In several cases, such as Dudley, Labour secured its first representatives in the history of the borough.[4] Only in the smaller, more residential towns was this landslide halted. Many of the individual Labour gains were nothing short of sensational. In the Wolverhampton Dunstall ward, Labour took 60 per cent of the poll in a ward consistently Liberal for the previous twenty-five years. In the Victoria ward of Newport, Labour unseated a Liberal ex-mayor who had represented the ward since 1902. Indeed, a persistent feature of the returns was Labour's success in wards with a tradition of Liberal representation.[5] The results in 1919 not only vastly increased Labour strength, but also precipitated the formation of Liberal–Conservative pacts against the Socialists.

In reaction to these victories, the municipal elections in 1920 showed an equally massive swing to the Right. The size of the reaction to Labour's victories in 1919 can be judged from the swing to the Conservatives of 16 per cent in the comparable wards of ten of the largest provincial boroughs.[6] Labour failed to secure a single ward in such towns as Bradford, Nottingham, Liverpool, Huddersfield or Portsmouth. In the 34 largest towns, only 103 of Labour's 441 candidates were successful. In contrast, Labour's most successful towns were Stoke (11 of 19 candidates elected) and Wigan (9 of 12).

After the landslide in 1919 and the reaction in 1920, Labour secured persistent gains in the following years. In

---

[4] *The Times*, 3 Nov 1919; *Manchester Guardian*, 3 Nov 1919.
[5] For example, such wards as Neepsend (Sheffield), Wyggeston (Leicester) and Sutton (Plymouth).
[6] The ten boroughs analysed were Bradford, Manchester, Liverpool, Birmingham, Plymouth, Northampton, Salford, Nottingham, Wigan and Leicester.

1921 the party gained 78 seats, losing 42. In 1923 the party
won 66 seats for the loss of 38, while in 1924 Labour made a
net gain of 20. After 1924 Labour's advance gathered
increasing momentum, culminating in 146 net gains in 1926
and 95 in 1927. The only exception to this steady Labour
progress was 1922, when the party lost 163 seats which it had
won in the 1919 landslide.

The Liberal fortunes were exactly the reverse. The party
suffered shattering and unprecendented losses in 1919 and
continued to lose seats in every year except 1922, when it
secured a small net gain of 22. Otherwise the party lost 44
seats in 1921, 24 in 1923, 24 again in 1924 and 53 in 1926.

Whilst these statistics need to be treated with some caution,
since they omit aldermanic by-elections, nonetheless they are
useful evidence of Liberal inability to withstand the Labour
advance after 1919.

Perhaps the most valuable evidence from municipal politics
can be found, not in these national figures, but in case studies
of individual boroughs, ranging from towns in which the
Liberal Party had all but disappeared, through such towns as
Bristol where at local level the party had amalgamated with
the Conservatives, and on to those cities in which an independent, radical Liberal Party still flourished.

Parts of industrial Lancashire provide several local examples of a party that had almost totally disappeared by 1923.
One such town was St. Helens, where in the 1919 elections
five wards were contested. Not a single Liberal candidate
came forward. Of the eight contests in 1920, and a further
seven in 1921, there was again no Liberal candidate.[7] The net
result was that, by the election of November 1927, no
Liberals remained on the local council.

The working-class areas of Manchester, unlike the residential wards of the town, were similarly desolate Liberal
territory.

The four industrial constituencies of Gorton, Clayton,
Ardwick and Platting closely paralleled the position in St
Helens. In the Gorton constituency, only one Liberal ever
contested a council seat in the ten years after 1919. This was

[7] *St Helens Examiner*, 3 Nov 1919, 2 Nov 1920, 2 Nov 1921.

in a straight fight in the South Gorton ward in 1927. Otherwise, in Openshaw and North Gorton wards, only the Conservatives intermittently challenged Labour in these industrial strongholds.

In the Clayton constituency no Liberal contested the Beswick or Bradford wards in the decade after 1919, whilst in Newton Heath ward the Liberals fought only in 1921, 1924 and 1927, enjoying straight fights on each occasion.

In the Platting division none of the four wards making up the constituency was contested on more than one occasion. In the Collyhurst ward a solitary Liberal enjoyed a straight fight with a Conservative in 1921, but did not come forward again to contest the seat. There was a three-cornered contest in Harpurhey ward in 1920, and in Miles Platting in 1922, but in each case the Liberal was at the foot of the poll. Not a single Liberal fought the St Michael ward.

The Ardwick constituency was equally devoid of Liberal activity. All ten contests in Ardwick itself from 1918 to 1928 were straight fights between Conservative and Labour. In New Cross ward, only one Liberal ever fought for a council seat, exactly as in St Mark ward.

Clearly, in these working-class areas of Manchester the party at municipal level had totally lost any claim to vitality. Elsewhere in the city, it is true, the Manchester Liberals still fought on an active scale for more residential wards, but the industrial territory had been handed over to Labour.

In the industrial wards of neighbouring Salford, almost exactly the same decline was at work. Liberals rarely contested wards, even allowing territory they had recently held (such as the Docks ward in 1924) to fall by default. Only five Liberals came forward in the 12 contested wards in 1919, while only three ventured to fight in the 15 contested wards in 1924. The net result was that, by 1928, Liberal representation on the council had steadily declined until it stood at only 9, compared with 23 Conservatives and an equal number of Labour councillors.

In many wards the position in Liverpool, the second largest provincial borough in England, was equally devoid of Liberal activity. This was true of such wards as Breckfield, in the West Derby division, the Walton and Fazakerley wards in Walton division and much of West Toxteth.[8] The net result was a persistent decline in Liberal strength on the council. By 1923, only 12 Liberal representatives remained in a council of 152.

A final example in Lancashire, in Wigan, both confirms the picture of St Helens and Manchester and yet provides the unusual phenomenon of a lingering Liberal–Labour 'understanding'.

In the 1919 municipal election, only three Liberal candidates were fielded for Wigan's 14 wards. However, one of these was unopposed, and the other two enjoyed straight fights against Conservatives.[9] This was clearly a legacy of the pre-war understanding between Liberal and Labour.[10]

In 1920 the only two Liberal candidates were returned unopposed. With the exception of one three-cornered contest in 1921, this lingering Liberal–Labour entente continued until 1924, when three of the remaining six Liberals in Wigan went over *en bloc* to Labour.

In all, of 70 possible municipal contests in Wigan in the five years after 1919, the Liberals brought forward only 11 candidates. That nine of these were elected was due, not to any independent Liberal strength, but to Labour's willingness to allow them unopposed returns.

In addition to this desolate municipal Liberal territory in industrial Lancashire, a second equally derelict area can be found in the West Midlands, most particularly in Birmingham. As one local editor commented on the state of Birmingham Liberalism in 1921: 'The old Liberal Party is in the melancholy condition of a gradual and persistent decline in its fortunes . . . it looks as if it will disappear, as indeed a "Middle Party" with no constructive policy is bound to'[11]

The steady Liberal decline in the council is set out in Table 3.2. From 17 representatives in November 1919, the Liberal

[8] *Liverpool Post*, 3 Nov 1919, 2 Nov 1920, 2 Nov 1921.

[9] *Wigan Observer*, 7 Nov 1919.

[10] In 1913, 5 Liberals and 8 Labour candidates enjoyed straight fights against Conservatives. The result was that, for the first time since 1864, the Conservatives lost control of Wigan. *Wigan Observer*, 1, 8 Nov 1913.

[11] *Birmingham Mail*, 2 Nov 1921. This statement might well have been made before 1914, for neither in 1906 nor in 1910 could the Liberals win a single seat in Birmingham.

TABLE 3.2
Party Representation, Birmingham City Council, 1921–6[12]

	Total	Con.	Lab.	Lib.	Others	Lib %
1919	120	67	27	17	9	14·2
1920	120	71	22	16	11	13·3
1921	120	67	28	13	12	10·8
1924	120	77	20	10	13	8·3
1926	120	73	29	8	10	6·7

total had fallen to 8 in 1926. The 1921 election was particularly disastrous, for the Liberals lost the three working-class wards they were defending.[13] In fact, not a single ward was ever consistently fought each year by a Liberal. Only five wards ever returned a Liberal between 1919 and 1929; of these, King's Norton, won on four occasions, was the best Liberal territory.[14]

In general, Liberal candidates were conspicuous only by their absence. Only two Liberals fought the 30 Birmingham wards in 1922, and again in 1924 and 1925. Only a solitary ward, Sparkbrook, was contested in 1927. In all, in the six years from 1922 to 1927 inclusive, only 13 Liberals contested the 180 vacant council seats.

Birmingham, of course, since the defection of Joseph Chamberlain, had long been barren Liberal territory. Liberal weakness in the West Midlands, however, was not confined to Birmingham. Such towns as Wednesbury and Smethwick were equally unpromising areas.

Although the examples of towns where municipal Liberalism had virtually died can be extended, the numbers were relatively limited. Much more numerous were the towns

[12] Figures taken from *Birmingham Post*, November of each year.

[13] These were Rotton Park, St Martin's and Ladywood. Ladywood was not even contested by a Liberal. *Birmingham Mail*, 2 Nov 1921.

[14] King's Norton was won in 1920, 1922, 1926 and 1929. The four other wards to return Liberals were: Small Heath, won in 1920 with Conservative support, won unopposed in 1923, lost to Labour in 1926 and never contested again: Lozells, won in 1919, 1922 and 1928; St Bartholomew, won in 1919, 1921 and 1924; and finally Washwood Heath, won in 1920 and 1923 with Conservative support; not contested when, in 1926, the sitting Liberal fought as a 'Constitutionalist'.

where Conservatives and Liberals combined to defeat Labour, either by a formal amalgamation or by means of an electoral pact. The effect and significance of these municipal pacts is a vital but neglected theme in constituency history, for these agreements both prepared the way for parliamentary co-operation against Labour, and also forced the radical working-class Liberal vote into the Labour camp.

A perfect example of a formal amalgamation at local level against Labour can be seen in Sheffield. Prior to 1914, some local arrangements against Labour had been agreed. The real coming together of the anti-Socialist parties at municipal level, however, took place in 1919.

Early in 1919 the Sheffield Trades and Labour Council announced its determination to contest every ward in the city at the forthcoming municipal election. Faced with this challenge, the Conservatives and Liberals arranged an electoral pact, to last initially for three years, under which they agreed not to oppose each other's candidates.[15] Despite this arrangement, the older parties failed to stem the Socialist tide. Labour polled 25,812 votes out of a total 57,705, taking eight seats, including four gains from the Liberals.[16]

This Labour success had its repercussions on the anti-Socialist parties. It resulted in the formation of the Sheffield Citizens' Association, led by Sir William Clegg, a prominent local Liberal. The deputy leader was the Conservative Alderman Cattell.

The object of the Citizens' Association was 'to fight municipal elections on non-party lines with the aim of finding the best men for the city'.[17] The Citizens' Association was reformed in 1929 under the label of the 'Progressive Party', and for the rest of the inter-war period an anti-Socialist alliance continued.

---

[15] For the negotiations preceding this agreement, see Sheffield Municipal Elections Committee of the Sheffield Federation of Conservative and Unionist Associations, Minutes, 23 Sep, 13 Oct 1919.

[16] *Sheffield Daily Telegraph*, 3 Nov 1919. Not a single Liberal was successful.

[17] See *Sheffield Annual Year Book and Record, 1920*; for a survey of Sheffield politics, see H. K. Hawson, *Sheffield: The Growth of a City* (Sheffield, 1968) pp. 291–3.

Despite an article in the *Sheffield Independent* by 'A Free Liberal' expressing grave warnings on the consequences of an anti-Socialist pact, no Independent Liberal challenge ever really emerged in Sheffield.[18] As the condition of Liberalism in Sheffield continued to deteriorate, much of the blame was laid at the door of this municipal coalition.[19]

An almost identical, and equally enduring, municipal alliance was organised at Bristol, which succeeded in uniting the anti-Socialist vote at almost every election. In Parliamentary politics also, Bristol remained a town where local coalition continued throughout the 1920s.[20]

A less well-known but equally 'model' pact was organised in Crewe. Following a sweeping Labour victory in November 1919, the Conservative and Liberal parties made approaches for an anti-Socialist alliance.[21] The result was the formation of the Crewe Progressive Union in October 1920. Its objective was 'the good government of the town on sound business lines of progress and development, with due regard for economy'. To achieve this end, the Progressive Union was to 'sink party politics in municipal affairs, and to support men of moderate views and proved business capacity'.[22] As in Sheffield and Bristol, the pact in Crewe was to be a feature of municipal politics throughout the inter-war period. Anti-Socialist alliances were particularly to be found in such railway towns as Derby and Swindon.[23]

---

[18] Only three Independent Liberals came forward in 1920; only one was returned. *Sheffield Daily Telegraph*, 2 Nov 1920.

[19] *Manchester Guardian*, 25 Oct 1924.

[20] It was noticeable that, under the arrangement, the party to suffer most from the amalgamation was the Liberals. *The Times*, 1 Nov 1923.

[21] This was not the first example of co-operation. For the municipal 'general election' of November 1908 an anti-Labour pact succeeded in eliminating Socialist representation. This subsequently lapsed: see W. S. Chaloner, *Social and Economic Development of Crewe* (Manchester, 1950) p. 168.

[22] Ibid., p. 169.

[23] At Derby, for example, the Conservatives and Liberals combined to form the Derby Municipal Alliance, 'a combination of the old parties for the common good' (*Derby Mercury*, 2 Nov 1922). For the Citizens' League in the railway town of Swindon, see *Swindon Advertiser*, 2 Nov 1923.

In addition to this type of anti-Socialist agreement, there were several towns in which, although no formal amalgamation of Conservatives and Liberals for municipal purposes took place, the two parties had a written pact to maintain a united anti-Labour front.

A perfect illustration of an anti-Socialist 'pact' of this type can be seen in Wolverhampton. As in Sheffield, 1919 proved to be the crucial year. In October 1919, after negotiations with the Liberals, the secretary of the West Wolverhampton Conservative Association was able to report to his Executive Committee 'that Alderman Bantock on behalf of the Liberals and himself on behalf of the Association, had agreed not to oppose one another's candidates but to work as a Coalition to assist each other's candidates'.[24] The result of this agreement was that the Liberals were given a straight fight against Labour in the East division where Conservative organisation was virtually non-existent, while the Conservatives enjoyed a similar privilege in the West division.[25] Conflicting Conservative and Liberal candidatures were avoided and relations between the anti-Socialist parties grew increasingly intimate. Thus, for the municipal 'general election' of March 1927, the Conservatives and Liberals pooled resources, planned the election campaign together and issued a joint election address. Despite protests from within the Liberal ranks, this municipal pact continued until, in 1945, the last elected Liberal disappeared from the council.[26]

Another Midland town to produce a very similar anti-Socialist pact was Coventry. Once again, the decisive year was 1919. A sub-committee of the Coventry Liberal Municipal Committee was established to arrange an electoral agreement with the Conservatives.[27] The sub-committee was able to

[24] West Wolverhampton Conservative Association, Minutes, Management Committee, 22 Oct 1919.

[25] Jones, *Borough Politics*, p. 53.

[26] See, for example, the Young Liberal resolution of protest at the pact passed in January 1928, ibid., p. 55.

[27] This approach was particularly significant since, from 1907 to 1914, the Coventry Liberals made repeated overtures for an agreement with Labour. All were unsuccessful.

report a completely successful outcome from these negotiations.[28]

Despite the pact, Labour won seven of the twelve wards in 1919. A year later, on 9 October 1920, a meeting of Conservative and Liberal councillors was arranged to 'consider the question of arriving at a mutual understanding with regard to the nomination of candidates for municipal elections'. The result was an arrangement almost identical to that of the previous year.[29]

After 1920 the pact was renewed annually, gradually being extended in scope.[30] For the 1923 elections the arrangements were settled as early as the preceding April. A joint conference agreed that no candidates standing as 'Independents' should receive official support, while a detailed agreement was made over future aldermanic elections.[31]

This 1923 agreement, drawn up for a three-year period, precipitated considerable acrimony in the local Liberal Association. The constituency association passed a resolution asking that the pact should not be extended beyond a twelve-month period without being submitted to the association Executive for approval. After a meeting between the Liberal council members and the association Advisory Committee, the councillors and aldermen finally won the day.[32]

[28] Coventry Liberal Municipal Committee, Minutes, 9 Oct 1919 (hereafter abbreviated to CLMC). The agreement took the form that no Liberal would oppose the seven retiring Conservatives, and no Conservative oppose the five retiring Liberals. Each party with no candidate of its own was actively to assist the other.

[29] CLMC, Minutes, 5 Nov 1920. The Liberals agreed not to oppose the retiring Conservatives in Bablake, Cheylesmore, Swanswell and Stoke wards. The Conservatives agreed not to oppose the seven Liberals seeking re-election, while it was agreed that the Greyfriars ward should revert to the Liberal Party on the retirement of the sitting Conservative.

[30] Thus, it was agreed that when seats held by Labour fell vacant, the Conservatives and Liberals would hold a joint conference to decide the course of action to be taken.

[31] CLMC, minutes, 4 Apr 1923.

[32] This joint meeting passed the following resolution: 'whether the pact is to be renewed should be left in the hands of a committee consisting of the Liberal Aldermen and Councillors, and six members of the Executive of the Association'. For details of this argument, see CLMC, Minutes, May 1925.

This incident at Coventry throws a significant light on the division between the Liberal council members, eager for a pact with the Conservatives, and many of the rank-and-file members angered at not having the right to field Liberals as and when they wanted. One ward to protest against the pact was Bablake, which officially asked the Advisory Committee to be allowed to nominate municipal candidates. The reply was a firm negative.[33]

In the short term, no doubt, the Liberal party benefited from this pact in Coventry. Over the longer period, however, the alliance served only to force the working-class Liberal vote into the Socialist camp. Despite the protests of such wards as Bablake, the pact was only rarely broken. On only two occasions between 1919 and 1926 did Liberal candidates oppose Conservatives.

Both Wolverhampton and Coventry provide examples of a 'model' anti-Socialist pact observed throughout the city. A more complex example can be seen in Bradford. Here, municipal relations between Conservative and Liberal varied from constituency to constituency and from ward to ward. The correlation that stands out is of anti-Socialist pacts in working-class wards, and continued Liberal–Conservative contests in the residential areas.

Of the Bradford constituencies, the North division was the most residential.[34] In this division, of the 30 possible contests in this period, 10 three-cornered fights took place. Although a relatively small figure, the total was considerably higher than in any other division. In the Allerton and Bolton wards, however, a local anti-Socialist pact operated.

Outside the Bradford North division, three-cornered contests were virtually non-existent. The contests in the South and East divisions illustrate the almost mathematical

---

[33] The Advisory Committee's reply, whilst recognising the 'awkward position' of Bablake, could only point out that the Conservatives were in a similar position in other wards.

[34] In Bradford North the ratio of rooms per person, a useful index of social composition, was 1·17, compared with 0·96 in the East division, 0·92 in the Central division and 0·99 in the South. Registrar-General, Census of England and Wales (1921) 8 vols.

precision with which local anti-Socialist arrangements were organised. In 23 of the 25 contests in Bradford South, and 17 of the 20 in Bradford East, no Liberal ever fought a Conservative.

In September 1923, following increasingly vocal demands within Bradford for Protection, the two wings of Liberalism were reunited.[35] This reunion had no significance for municipal politics. Of the 21 contested wards in November 1923, in only two cases were Conservatives opposed by Liberals.

After 1923 the degree of anti-Socialist co-operation was in fact tightened. Not a single example of a Liberal opposing a Conservative can be seen in any November election in Bradford East and Bradford South from 1924 to 1929. Only one example occurred in Bradford Central over this period, in Manningham ward in 1925.

The exception after 1924, as before, was in Bradford North. Of the 36 contests here, 14 involved all three parties, although Allerton and Bolton wards still maintained their local pacts. With this exception, Bradford was a city in which independent municipal Liberalism had ceased to give battle.

The two Midland cities of Nottingham and Leicester, each with a tradition of radical politics, might have been expected to be towns of active independent Liberalism. Both, in fact, closely paralleled the position in Bradford, with the Liberal party persistently seeking accommodation with the Conservatives.

In the 16 wards of Nottingham, no Liberal opposed a Conservative in 1919, 1920 or 1921. Only two clashes in twelve contested wards occurred in 1922.[36] As in Bradford, local Protectionist demands were prominent in 1923, but the revival of this old controversy did not disturb the anti-Socialist pact. None of the ten contested wards saw Liberals opposing Conservatives.[37] Of the 80 possible ward contests from 1919 to 1923, in only two cases had Liberals and Conservatives come into conflict. As one successful Liberal councillor explained, the older parties were 'banding together

[35] For these demands, see *Liberal Magazine,* Oct 1923.
[36] These were in Wollaton and St Mary wards. *Nottingham Guardian,* 2 Nov 1922.
[37] *Nottingham Guardian,* 2 Nov 1923.

to fight a common danger in the Socialists and their revolutionary doctrines'.[38]

To a certain extent, this anti-Socialist co-operation was
interrupted after 1923. In 1924, six Conservatives were
opposed by Liberals; in 1928, eight were similarly opposed.
Prior to 1928, however, several wards had still maintained an
obvious pact. No Conservative ever opposed a Liberal, or
vice versa, in Broxtowe, Trent, Byron, Robin Hood, Bridge
or Meadow wards. Most of the Conservative–Liberal rivalry
was confined to such residential wards as Mapperly and
Sherwood where there was little danger of a Labour victory.

A very important local exception to this rule was the St
Ann's ward. As early as 1923, the Conservative councillor
complained that the St Ann's Liberals were 'passive resisters'
to the agreement, and that they had provided no active
assistance.[39] Two years later the pact was broken completely
when a three-cornered contest occurred. The explanation
seems to be that St Ann's ward was a Nonconformist centre,
where the old rivalries had not subsided.[40]

With this occasional exception, Nottingham Liberals continued a policy of co-operation with their former opponents.
As in Bradford, no desire was forthcoming to fight on
anything like a sustained broad front as an independent party.

The neighbouring Midland town of Leicester provided a
very similar example to Nottingham. The position was again
one of tacit or open co-operation with the Conservatives to
thwart Labour.

This was already to be seen in the elections of 1919, when
Labour captured six seats. In every ward contested by
Labour, the party faced a straight fight.[41] The same phenome-
non occurred in 1920. The 'Grand Holy Alliance', as the
Leicester Pioneer termed the Conservative–Liberal pact, en-
sured that Labour faced six straight fights with Liberals and

[38] *Nottingham Guardian*, 2 Nov 1921. The same paper described the
1921 municipal election as a 'straight fight between the local Coalition on
the one hand and the more recent aspirants for power on the other'.

[39] *Nottingham Guardian*, 2 Nov 1923.

[40] *Nottingham Guardian*, 2 Nov 1925.

[41] Labour faced 7 Liberals, 4 Conservatives and one National Democratic Party candidate. *Leicester Journal*, 2 Nov 1919.

five with Conservatives.[42] Again in 1921, the Conservatives and Liberals avoided conflicting candidatures.

The position in Latimer ward, a working-class area of the city, reflected Liberal fortunes. In 1921 the party failed even to defend a seat which had frequently returned Liberals. Labour won the seat unopposed.[43] No doubt part of this collapse of morale and organisation was due to the chronic split in the Leicester Liberal ranks between the Coalition and Independent Liberals.[44] However, the fact that this continued throughout the succeeding years was an indication of more permanent weakness.

Thus, in 1925, when four Liberals and four Conservatives enjoyed straight fights against Labour, co-operation reached very close levels. The Conservatives handed in nomination papers for the Liberals in such wards as West Humberstone and Spinney Hill, while the Conservative MP for Leicester South was able to write to the local press expressing his satisfaction that 'party differences had been sunk in Leicester and that Liberals and Conservatives were fighting shoulder to shoulder against Socialism'. After the election, the successful Liberals in Abbey and Charnwood wards returned to the Constitutional Club to thank their Conservative friends. As one Liberal councillor explained, as constitutionalists, Liberals and Conservatives must always be hand in hand and glove in glove.[45]

This sentiment certainly prevailed in 1928. Of the twelve Labour candidates, six faced only Liberal opposition, five faced Conservative and one was opposed by an 'Independent'. Once again, all five elected Liberals marched off to the Constitutional Club, where the Liberal returned in Westcotes

---

[42] *Leicester Pioneer*, 3 Nov 1920; *Leicester Daily Post*, 2 Nov 1920.

[43] *Leicester Pioneer*, 4 Nov 1921.

[44] This division reached its climax at the annual meeting of Leicester Liberal Federation in March 1921. A motion expressing a desire for the Lloyd George Coalition to continue was rejected by 93 votes to 85. This caused the resignation of the president, chairman, treasurer and vice-chairman of the Leicester Liberal Federation. See Leicester Liberal Federation Papers, Minutes, Annual General Meeting, 18 Mar 1921.

[45] *Leicester Mail*, 3 Nov 1925.

ward explained that the pact was wise, since half a loaf was better than no bread.[46]

It is true that, from time to time, occasional breaks in this co-operation occurred. Three triangular contests took place in 1922, six in 1924 and three in 1926. It was significant that, in the three seats Liberals were defending in three-cornered contests in 1926, all were lost to Labour. As one local reporter graphically commented, the bust of Gladstone at the foot of the staircase in the Leicester Liberal Club positively shivered at the results.[47]

These occasional forays into three-party contests were never sustained or continuous, gradually fading completely until, in the six years after 1928, 61 of the 64 contested elections were straight fights against Labour.

In many respects, municipal politics in Northampton paralleled the position in Leicester or Nottingham, except that the Northampton Liberals retained a vitality and independence considerably stronger than in the other Midland towns. Although, in the four years from 1919 to 1922, only one three-cornered contest occurred, afterwards the position changed. Three clashes between Conservatives and Liberals took place in 1923, four in 1924 and five in 1925. In the St Lawrence ward, in which a Conservative had straight fights with Labour up to 1922, after 1923 the Liberals then contested the ward on every occasion.

Northampton, however, very well demonstrates how municipal politics varied not only between cities but between wards. In the St Crispin ward, for example, a local pact continued throughout this period. Again, whilst Liberals resumed fighting such wards as St Lawrence after 1923, no Liberal ventured forth in the North or Castle wards.

It is significant that even in Northampton, where Liberal–Conservative hostility persisted, the Liberal municipal challenge was still weaker than both Conservative and Labour. During the eleven years from 1919 to 1929, including unopposed returns, the Conservatives fielded 90 candidates,

[46] *Leicester Mercury*, 2 Nov 1928.
[47] *Leicester Mail*, 2 Nov 1926.

Labour brought forward 111, but the Liberals only 64. The Liberal challenge, if independent, was decidedly anaemic.

To find provincial towns in which the Liberal Party persistently fought virtually all wards as an independent radical party is far from easy. The two following examples, of Plymouth and Leeds, both demonstrate that even where the party retained a strong degree of local vitality, its position was still insecure.

In Plymouth the persistence of an independent Liberal challenge, reflected in the large percentage of three-cornered contests, was very marked. The 206 contests in Plymouth in this period were made up of 72 three-cornered contests (34·9 per cent of the total), 90 Conservative–Labour straight fights (43·6 per cent), 31 Liberal–Labour straight fights (15·0 per cent) and 13 others.

The total number of candidates fielded by the main parties was 477. Of these, the Conservatives fielded 171 (35·8 per cent), Labour 197 (41·3 per cent) and Liberals 109 (22·9 per cent). Even in Plymouth the Liberal total trailed the Conservatives and was only half the Labour figure. Despite a persistent Liberal challenge in certain areas, in such wards as Vallefort, Stoke and Vintry the local Liberals were conspicuously absent.

As in Plymouth, even during the 1919–22 period the Leeds Liberals had maintained their independence from party embroilments. Leeds elections in this period again showed a similar pattern to Plymouth, with a large percentage of three-cornered contests. In the 85 elections from 1919 to 1923 inclusive, there were 24 triangular contests, 20 Liberal–Labour straight fights, 16 Conservative–Labour straight fights and 12 Conservative–Liberal contests. It is significant, however, that even in Leeds there were signs of Liberal municipal weakness. Of the 188 candidates fielded from 1919 to 1923, the Liberal challenge was still marginally weaker than either Conservatives or Labour: Labour fielded 65 candidates, the Conservatives 58 and Liberals 57.

After 1924, in the period up to 1928, the figures for candidates fielded were: Labour 81, Conservative 65, Liberal 56, Independents 6. The contests were made up of 40 triangular fights, 20 Conservative–Labour straight fights, only 12 Liberal–Labour straight fights and a mere 3 Conservative–Liberal contests. In the whole period, no Liberal enjoyed the luxury of an unopposed return.

Thus, even in Leeds, where the party fought on a radical municipal programme in a city with a long tradition of Liberal council strength, the party had fallen into third place at this local level.[48].

It is a remarkable comment on the decline of municipal Liberalism that in none of the boroughs examined so far was the Liberal Party the most important local force. To find towns where this was still true in 1923 is a difficult task. These towns were virtually confined to the textile areas of Yorkshire and Lancashire and to the occasional isolated borough.

Perhaps the best example of Liberal municipal survival in Yorkshire was to be seen in Huddersfield. Here the party remained entrenched, so that throughout the 1920s control of the council was an uninterrupted Liberal monopoly. In 1923 the party's strength was 30, compared with 3 Labour and 21 Conservatives. In 1927 the Liberals still dominated the scene, with 32 representatives to 4 Labour and 21 Conservatives.[49] However, by 1927 Huddersfield was the only town with a population above 75,000 in which the Liberals enjoyed an overall majority over their opponents.

Again, the relatively large numbers of unopposed returns was a rare feature of municipal politics.[50] Excluding these unopposed returns, the type of contest in Huddersfield local elections was quite different from elsewhere. In the 1919–28 period, of the 122 contested elections, only 17 (14·7 per cent) were straight fights between Conservative and Labour, whereas 36 (31·0 per cent) were Liberal–Labour straight fights, whilst there were 41 (35·3 per cent) three-cornered fights and 22 (19·0 per cent) were between Conservative and Liberal only. The totals for all candidates fielded, opposed and unopposed, in this period were: Liberals 116 (36·7 per

[48] For the radical municipal policy advocated in Leeds, see the document 'Liberal Municipal Policy' issued for the 1927 local elections in Leeds Liberal Federation, Minutes, Executive Committee, Nov 1927.

[49] *Yorkshire Observer*, 2 Nov 1927.

[50] 28 of 150 elections in the period 1919–28 were unopposed. Two-thirds of these were Liberals.

cent), Labour 98 (31·0 per cent), Conservative 93 (29·4 per cent) and Independents 9 (2·9 per cent).

Fielding the strongest municipal challenge, returned unopposed in several wards and able to deny Labour any very considerable municipal advance, the Huddersfield Liberals were in a happy position enjoyed by almost no other Liberal Association.

The persistence of an entrenched local Liberalism in Huddersfield, a town with a tradition of Nonconformist strength, was less remarkable than the continuing strength of municipal Liberalism in Oxford, a very different community.

In municipal politics at Oxford the decade after 1919 saw an entrenched and active local Liberal Party, together with a very weak Labour Party which failed to secure continuous representation in any ward.

TABLE 3.3
Party Representation, Oxford City Council, 1919–27
○ = Con.   ◉ = Lab.   ● = Lib.

	1919	1920	1921	1922	1923	1924	1925	1926	1927
South	●●●	●●●	●●●	●●●	●●●	●●●	●●●	●●●	●●●
East	○●●	○●●	○●●	●●●	●●●	○●●	○●●	●●●	○●●
West	○○◉	○○○	○○○	○○○	○○◉	○○●	○○○	○○●	○○○
North	○○●	○●●	○●●	○●●	○●●	○○○	○○○	○○●	○○●

The political allegiance of Oxford's four wards after 1919 is shown in Table 3.3.[51] The South ward returned Liberals without interruption in this period; the East ward returned 21 Liberals and only 6 Conservatives. The Conservatives fared best in the West ward, yet this was the only ward to return a Labour councillor, whilst the North ward was also preponderantly Conservative.

[51] Each ward elected three councillors annually. After 1928 three new wards were created – Cowley and Iffley, Headington, and Summertown and Wolvercote – and each ward returned two councillors annually.

The 108 councillors returned from these four wards were made up as follows: Liberals 60 (55·6 per cent), Conservatives 46 (42·6 per cent) and Labour 2 (1·8 per cent). The Liberals in Oxford thus won more council seats than both other parties combined. In their best year, 1923, nine of the twelve councillors elected were Liberals.

Perhaps a better barometer of party activity can be seen, not in the number of seats won, but in the number of seats fought in the period 1919–27. Of 209 major-party candidates, the Liberals fielded the largest single total of 83 (39·7 per cent), the Conservatives fielded 81 (38·8 per cent) and Labour 45 (21·5 per cent). In no year did Labour field a candidate for every vacant seat.[52] In the year of Labour's most determined challenge, in 1921, the party polled only 16·7 per cent of the votes cast; the Liberals polled 42·6 per cent and the Conservatives 40·7 per cent. Labour made virtually no attempt to fight the North ward, fighting only the West ward at all consistently.

Oxford thus provides a rare example of a borough in which the rise of local Labour strength was conspicuously absent until the 1930s. Even after the redrawing of ward boundaries in 1928, the strength of the council was: Liberal 21, Conservative 20, Independents 12, University representatives 9 and Labour nil. Unlike the Liberal strength in Huddersfield, however, which extended to other small mill towns in the West Riding, the Liberal strength in Oxford was not repeated in neighbouring towns. Neither Swindon nor Reading, for example, saw an active local Liberal party.

Perhaps the best illustration of just how rare such towns as Huddersfield or Oxford were in local politics can be seen from Table 3.4, which sets out the composition of the council in 1927 for every provincial borough in England and Wales with a population of over 75,000. From these figures it can be seen that in only one town (Huddersfield) did the Liberals possess a majority over all other parties, whilst in only an additional four boroughs (Sunderland, Middlesbrough, Burnley and Halifax) was the party still the largest, or equal largest, single

[52] The nearest occasion was 1921, when Labour made a determined attempt to increase its representation. *Oxford Times*, 28 Oct 1921.

TABLE 3.4

Party Representation in the Major Provincial Boroughs, November 1927

	Con.	Lib.	Coalition	Lab.	Ind.
Birmingham	71	6	–	33	10
Liverpool	92	12	–	25	23*
Manchester	66	25	–	45	3
Sheffield	–	–	24	39	5
Leeds	27	8	–	33	–
Bristol	41	25	–	26	–
West Ham	–	–	13	51	–
Hull	25	11	–	23	5
Bradford	21	25	–	38	–
Newcastle	21	22	–	24	9
Nottingham	28	13	–	23	–
Portsmouth	35	19	–	3	3
Stoke	–	–	73	39	–
Leicester	20	16	–	27	–
Salford	22	12	–	21	9
Plymouth	46	11	–	23	–
Cardiff	19	17	–	13	3
Croydon	–	–	51	5	–
Bolton	54	11	–	31	–
Southampton	–	–	56	12	–
Sunderland	25	29	–	9	1
Swansea	8	22	–	27	–
Birkenhead	22	5	–	29	–
Oldham	20	19	–	9	–
East Ham	–	–	25	15	–
Middlesbrough	15	18	–	12	1
Derby	26	12	–	23	3
Coventry	No municipal elections in November 1927				
Blackburn	36	5	–	11	4
Gateshead	7	6	–	16	11
Stockport	39	18	–	17	8
Norwich	27	11	–	25	1
Preston	20	–	–	18	10
South Shields	20	18	–	22	–
Huddersfield	21	32	–	4	–
Southend	26	11	–	3	–
Burnley	20	20	–	8	–
St Helens	10	–	–	25	1
Wolverhampton	21	11	–	13	7
Halifax	17	25	–	17	1
Walsall	14	10	–	7	1
Newport	9	6	–	13	2

TABLE 3.4 *(continued)*

	Con.	Lib.	Coalition	Lab.	Ind.
Reading	–	–	42	10	–
Northampton	27	14	–	6	–
Wallasey	29	13	–	6	8
Wigan	15	3	–	38	–
York	25	10	–	9	4
Grimsby	33	6	–	9	–
Merthyr Tydfil	5	4	–	21	2
Ipswich	20	12	–	8	–
Warrington	17	5	–	13	–
Bootle	25	4	–	13	2
Smethwick	9	–	–	15	–

* This figure included 21 Catholic representatives.

group. In a further thirteen boroughs the Liberals were still the second largest party.

Moreover, it has to be remembered that these Liberal figures are distorted by the relatively large numbers of aldermen who were Liberal, and also that many of these seats were retained only because of an alliance with the Conservatives. In all, despite the occasional centre such as Oxford, the evidence of provincial Liberal politics assembled in this chapter provides a fairly damning indictment of the vitality of the party at constituency level.

This position was in fact even more serious, since the condition of the party in the most important city of all – London – was even weaker than elsewhere.

4 Municipal Politics: The Metropolitan Boroughs

A study of metropolitan politics after 1919 confirms very strongly the main features of local politics seen in the last chapter: a Liberal Party clearly in decline, a massive and mounting Labour challenge and a coming together of the anti-Socialist parties.[1]

Even before 1914, the decline of the Progressives was unmistakably evident on the London County Council.[2] From 83 representatives out of a total of 118 in 1904, the Progressives had been reduced to 50 by 1913. Herbert Morrison later wrote of the Progressive Party at the end of the war: 'It was doubtful whether the Progressives had any future: their period of achievement and advance seemed more or less ended. Electorally, their prospects were poor'.[3] The election of March 1919 proved Morrison correct. Labour entered this election faced with a continuation of the war-time coalition of Progressives and Municipal Reformers. In Southwark North, for example, Labour was faced with two Progressive candidates, each enjoying Municipal Reform support. In Hackney Central a Municipal Reformer and a Progressive candidate in harness were returned unopposed.[4]

A second feature of the election was the weakness of the Progressive challenge. No Progressive candidate was fielded

[1] No published work on metropolitan politics exists for the inter-war period to continue the valuable study of the pre-1914 period in P. Thompson, *Socialists, Liberals and Labour: The Struggle for London, 1885–1914* (1967).

[2] Liberals fought London elections under the label 'Progressives'; the Conservatives fought as 'Municipal Reform'.

[3] H. Morrison, *An Autobiography* (1960) p. 74.

[4] *London Labour Chronicle*, Oct 1919.

in such seats as Woolwich, Fulham, Hammersmith, Hampstead or Deptford.

The Progressives also presented the spectacle of a party facing both ways simultaneously. In such seats as Camberwell North and Lambeth Kennington the party was running in alliance with Labour, while in seven seats the Progressives enjoyed straight fights against Labour.

The result in 1919 was a further decline in Progressive strength. The new council was composed of 67 Municipal Reformers, 40 Progressives, 15 Labour and one Independent.

In a sense, excuses could be made for the poor Progressive performance in 1919. Turnout, for example, was exceptionally low, whilst party organisation had still to recover after the war. In 1922, however, these excuses could not be brought forward.

Whereas Labour fielded 94 candidates, exactly double its numbers in 1919, the Progressive Party virtually sold itself to an alliance with the Municipal Reformers. Only ten three-cornered fights took place, whereas Labour faced only Progressives in ten divisions, and Municipal Reform candidates in 25. Some 13 Municipal Reform candidates were returned unopposed, together with one Progressive.

On the surface, the results of 1922 give the appearance of Municipal Reform gains at the expense of Progressive losses. The Municipal Reformers increased their representation from 68 to 82, whilst the Progressives fell from 38 to 26 and Labour from 17 to 16. In fact, the true picture disguised by these figures is that Labour had lost seats to Municipal Reformers, but gained them from Progressives. The Progressives lost in both directions.

Whilst Labour lost seats in such areas as Deptford, Finsbury and Lambeth Kennington, the party was compensated with gains from the Progressives in Bermondsey Rotherhithe, Bermondsey West, Whitechapel and Camberwell North.[5]

The Progressive losses constituted not so much a defeat as a humiliation. In the ten three-cornered contests the party

[5] The loss of Lambeth Kennington involved the defeat of the Labour leader, Harry Gosling, by a Progressive–Municipal Reform pact. Labour's only loss to a Progressive was in Shoreditch.

obtained over 25 per cent of the poll in only three seats.[6] All except four of the Progressive seats were dependent on the goodwill of the Municipal Reform Party.

After the 1922 election the *London Labour Chronicle* wrote: 'The electoral power of the Progressive Party – we say it as a fact not as a gibe – is negligible: the electorate declines to take the party seriously'. Essentially, this judgement was correct. Although, nominally, the Progressives constituted the largest opposition party, in fact they provided the spectacle of an opposition that did not oppose.

The election of 1925 virtually eliminated Progressive representation. The party lost 19 seats, not registering a single gain, to return only six members.[7] Of these six Progressives, two were returned for Bethnal Green South-West and two for Southwark Central, in each case without Municipal Reform opposition.[8] No Progressive was elected in a three-cornered contest. In only one three-cornered contest could the Progressives poll more votes than Labour.[9]

The majority of the Labour victories in 1925 were at the expense of the Progressives.[10] After 1925 the eclipse of the party had gone so far that, despite attempts at revival, the Progressives were never again to be a major force in London. In 1928 the Liberals attempted to stage a major recovery, fielding 82 candidates, compared with 108 Labour and 124 Municipal Reformers. This challenge proved in vain, as

---

[6] These were Stepney Whitechapel (35·5 per cent), Lambeth North (33·4 per cent) and Wandsworth Balham and Tooting (26·2 per cent).

[7] *The Times*, 8 Mar 1925. Party representation before and after the 1925 election was: Municipal Reform 83 (82), Labour 35 (17), Progressive 6 (25).

[8] In addition, a single Progressive was elected in Islington West, in harness with a Municipal Reform candidate, while one was also returned in Southwark North as 'Progressive Ratepayer', again running with a Municipal Reform candidate.

[9] In Hackney North. Overall, in the three-cornered contests, the Progressives polled 18·8 per cent, Labour 38·8 per cent and Municipal Reform 42·4 per cent.

[10] The Labour gains in 1925 were Shoreditch, Hackney South, Southwark South-East and Bethnal Green North-East. Labour also took one seat in Peckham and Southwark North.

Progressive representation was further reduced to five.[11] The result in 1928 proved the accuracy of Herbert Morrison's prophesy in 1925: the election had witnessed the complete destruction of the party. In future it would never rise again.[12]

In a decisive way, the evidence of Progressive decline in London confirms all the features of municipal Liberalism in the provincial boroughs. A final confirmation of this thesis can be seen in the 28 metropolitan boroughs.

In these metropolitan boroughs the Progressives entered the elections of November 1919 against a background of rapidly declining strength. In 1912, for example, only 252 Progressives had been returned, compared with 1,002 Municipal Reformers, 48 Labour and 60 Independents, whilst only three boroughs, Bethnal Green, Southwark and Battersea, were under Progressive control.

The election of November 1919, with an electorate more than doubled since 1914, changed the face of metropolitan politics.[13] Whereas prior to this date Labour held only 48 seats, 15 of them concentrated in Woolwich, after 1919 their representation soared to 573. The Municipal Reform ranks were decimated, from 1,002 to 598. The already depleted Progressive strength fell from 252 to 131, while at a single blow Labour captured 13 boroughs. The Progressives now controlled none, although they were still the largest single party in Bermondsey (where they had 27 members compared with 24 Labour).

As in the LCC election, a variety of local coalitions was organised against Labour in such areas as Hackney and Poplar. In general, however, 1919 proved to be a highly confused election. In the occasional area such as Deptford a lingering Progressive–Labour entente still survived.[14] In

[11] The Progressives lost four of the seats won in 1925, but gained Bethnal Green North-East together with one seat in Hackney Central.

[12] *London News*, May 1925, p. 4.

[13] The electorate had risen from 777,861 in 1912 to 1,684,397 in 1919.

[14] An example of Labour–Progressive alliance was the Deptford South ward, where three Labour and three Progressive candidates faced six Municipal Reform nominees.

other boroughs Labour was still too unorganised to field a full quota of candidates.[15]

Apart from these fairly isolated examples, the most apparent feature of the election was the weakness of the Progressive challenge. Not a single Progressive was among the 77 candidates fighting for 42 seats in Hampstead, nor was there any Progressive candidate in Holborn or St Marylebone.

A perfect example of Liberal collapse at the grass roots can be seen in Greenwich. In September 1918 the Greenwich Labour Party was formed. The effect of this new Labour organisation on the old Liberal Association was immediate and catastrophic. Three senior Liberal officials defected, whilst the association, too demoralised to field a candidate for the 'coupon' election, resolved to support the Labour candidate. Several prominent Liberals then signed the nomination papers of the Conservative candidate.[16]

The Liberal Association had not reorganised itself for the elections of November 1919. Of 61 candidates fighting for 30 seats, the Progressives numbered only six, all of these confined to Marsh ward.[17] Labour fielded a full complement of candidates.

In view of the weakness of the Progressive challenge, the humiliating defeat in 1919 was perhaps to be expected. This fact, and the sweeping Labour victories, increased the moves towards anti-Socialist pacts for the 1922 elections. These moves attracted forthright opposition from sections of the Liberal press. The *Daily News* declared:

> The Moderate Party has been the steady enemy of London. . . . There is no 'temporary' alliance, for any Progressive, with such a Party as that. There is no touching such pitch without most enduring defilement.[18]

---

[15] In Finsbury, a borough in which the Labour ranks had been constantly divided before 1914, only 10 of the 108 candidates fighting for 54 seats were put forward by Labour. Only five were elected, all in St James ward.

[16] M. Benney, A. P. Gray and R. H. Pear, *How People Vote: A Study of Electoral Behaviour in Greenwich* (1956) pp. 41–2.

[17] *Greenwich Mercury*, 3 Nov 1919.

[18] *Daily News*, 25 Aug 1922.

The language of the *Star* was equally strong:

> The Moderate Party is an organisation of all the interests which
> have plundered London. . . . If the Progressive leaders carry out
> an agreement to ally themselves with this party of reaction and
> robbery . . . they will learn the truth of an old question 'What will
> it profit a man if he gain the whole world and lose his own soul'.[19]

These warnings went unheeded. The coalition which Mor-
rison had prophesied was to materialise. An independent
Progressive challenge was virtually limited to Shoreditch,
Bermondsey, Camberwell North and parts of St Pancras.[20]

Elsewhere, local coalitions were arranged. Thus, in Ham-
mersmith, Labour faced the combined forces of Progressives,
Municipal Reformers, the Ratepayers' Association and the
British Legion.[21]

The position in Hammersmith was similar to Hackney, and
also to Stepney, where the anti-Socialists came forward as
'Ratepayers' candidates', fighting for economy, efficiency and
lower rates.[22] In Bethnal Green the anti-Socialists stood as
'People's candidates', again nominated by the local
Ratepayers' Association. Outside these areas of coalition,
several boroughs did not see a single Progressive candidate.
In the nine wards of the largest borough, Wandsworth, no
Progressive was fielded.[23]

The result of the election was a triumph for Municipal
Reform, whose representation increased from 596 to 806. In
addition, there were 187 Ratepayers' Alliance candidates
elected. The Labour ranks were reduced from 573 to 253,
whilst the Progressives fell again from 129 to a mere 84.[24]

The Labour reverse was particularly heavy in working-
class areas. The party lost 31 seats in Hackney, removing its

[19] *Star*, 24 Aug 1922. For a similar warning in the *Westminster Gazette*,
see issue dated 24 Aug 1922.

[20] Even in St Pancras, in seven wards Progressives and Municipal Reform
either ran on a single ticket or came to an agreement not to oppose each
other. *London Labour Chronicle*, Jan 1923.

[21] *London Labour Chronicle*, Dec 1922.

[22] *Eastern Post and City Chronicle*, 28 Oct 1922. The candidates were
nominated by the Union of Stepney Ratepayers.

[23] *South Western Star*, 3 Nov 1922.

[24] *Westminster Gazette*, 3 Nov 1922.

representation completely from the council. There were 21 losses in both Paddington and Lambeth. Twelve boroughs were entirely without Labour representation. However, this Labour disaster was only temporary, and could partly be ascribed to defective organisation and the 'Bolshevist' scare used against the party, as well as to the effects of local coalition.[25]

The outcome for the Progressives was disastrous. After the 1922 election Progressive councillors had disappeared from 18 of the 28 metropolitan boroughs. In only the two councils of Stepney and Shoreditch did Progressives constitute more than one-quarter of the council membership.

In 1922 Labour suffered along with the Progressives. Three years later this was no longer true. Labour increased its representation from 253 to 362. Although the Municipal Reform total held fairly steady, slipping from 993 in 1922 to 933 in 1925, the Progressives were further reduced to a mere 54 members, less than 4 per cent of the total councillors elected.

The results had confirmed the sorry plight of the Progressives, with the party suffering further heavy losses to Labour, as in Finsbury where 11 Labour gains removed the last Progressives from the council. This time, unlike 1922, pacts were no longer sufficient safeguards.[26] Labour reclaimed its working-class seats; the whole of the East End was now solidly Labour.

The elections of November 1928 confirmed the downfall of the Progressives. Labour increased its representation from 362 to 458. The Municipal Reform total fell from 932 to 888, whilst the Progressives were further reduced from 54 to 37. This total is rendered misleading by the one success the Progressives achieved – in Bethnal Green, where the party gained 18 seats, returning a completely Liberal council. It was

[25] For criticism of Labour organisation in Paddington, Lewisham and Camberwell North-West, see *London Labour Chronicle*, Dec 1922 and Jan 1923.

[26] There was some opposition, especially in Whitechapel, to these anti-Socialist pacts. See *Daily Herald*, 22 Oct 1925.

a spectacular but isolated success.[27] Outside Bethnal Green the Progressives lost 35 seats, with heavy losses to Labour in Hackney and Lambeth. Only seven Progressive councillors were elected outside Bethnal Green. The election had removed the Liberals from most of the few remaining councils on which they were represented. It was the end of the road for London Liberalism.

This evidence from the metropolitan boroughs and the London County Council, together with the earlier surveys of local politics in the provincial boroughs and county constituencies, provides a fairly damning verdict on the vitality and independence of the Liberal Party at constituency level in this period. Whilst there are dangers in attempting to quantify constituencies by degrees of activity or inactivity (since this is not a stable, unchanging condition), nonetheless it is useful to construct the following picture of constituency activity:

		No.	%
Group A:	Safe Liberal seats (i.e. contested and won on every occasion, 1918–29)	22	(3·6)
Group B:	Seats won by Liberals in three or more general elections, 1918–29, where organisation and morale were essentially sound	53	(8·6)
Group C:	Seats requiring considerable stimulus of finance, propaganda and organisation	382	(62·1)
Group D:	Seats derelict or semi-derelict (i.e. not contested in 1923)	158	(25·7)
		615	(100·0)

Whilst these figures can only remain approximate, the most significant single statistic is that only 75 seats, a mere 12 per cent, fell into the top two groups. These figures do not attempt

[27] The Progressives gained 9 Labour, 8 Communist and one Municipal Reform seat. The explanation of this Liberal success is difficult. Probably the division in the Labour ranks, with rival Communist candidates, was one factor. In addition, the Liberals controlled the largest drinking club in the area. See Kinnear, *The British Voter*, p. 110.

to argue that it would not have been possible to revive organisation and morale, but rather that the task – even in mid-1923 – was already a massive one.

In those seats already in Group D by 1923, it would seem that there were clearly more long-term, fundamental weaknesses in the party than can be explained by the divisions caused by the war and the Asquith – Lloyd George split. Many of these were industrial, urban constituencies. It is useful to look more closely at possible explanations why constituency Liberal Associations were showing obvious signs of weakness reflected in wards left uncontested, candidates not fielded and anti-Socialists pacts.

One explanation behind the inability of the Liberals to contest municipal elections is fundamental to an understanding of the decline of the party; it is simply that the Liberal party had no distinctive policy to offer. The issues which had brought Liberals into local politics prior to 1914 were denominational issues, such as education, together with the need for public economy.[28]

After 1914 the Nonconformist issues declined. The old controversies faded as the era of chapel politics passed. With the decline of Nonconformity the Liberals had no compelling urge to enter municipal politics.

In those areas where Nonconformity remained a powerful social as well as religious force, most particularly where trade unionism was weak, local Liberal support thrived. This was true of Wolverhampton East, and parts of Oxford and Nottingham, as well as more obvious areas such as Huddersfield and the mill towns.

In general, however, with much of the old religious cleavage gone, there was little at municipal level to distinguish Liberals and Conservatives. The party labels had, in many cases, become empty of real content – bottles with bits of the old labels but with no inspiring liquor left.

A major factor in the decline of the Liberal Party was this failure to develop a distinctive municipal policy that went beyond a mere call for economy. The party put forward no

<hr/>

[28] For a discussion of this point, see J. P. Bulpitt, *Party Politics in English Local Government* (1967) pp. 6–9.

constructive radical policy at council level. As Jones commented of Wolverhampton municipal politics, the Liberal
groups had no policy beyond the need to resist Socialist
dictation and opposition to 'wild and extravagant schemes'.[29]

A similar observation was made of Bradford municipal
politics in 1930 by Alderman Gadie, the leader of the
Conservative group, who found that upon the broad policy of
municipal administration there had been no difference between Conservative and Liberal members on the city
council.[30] Likewise, the *Bradford Pioneer* suggested that one
of the seven wonders of the modern world was to be
discovered in finding any difference between Conservative
and Liberal policy.

In Nottingham the ease with which local Liberals co-
operated with the Conservatives can be explained only by the
fact that no vital issues separated them. The municipal
Liberal campaign at Nottingham was repeatedly directed at a
call for economy, reductions in the rates and an end to
wild-cat Socialist schemes.[31] Similarly, in Leicester, Liberals
joined the Conservative attack on these same targets of
Poplarism, extravagance and extremism.[32]

With only the occasional exception, such as Leeds, where
the Liberals fought locally on a radical programme, the
municipal Liberal challenge was one of negation and defence.
The party locally offered little to attempt to retain working-
class support.

Partly a consequence, partly perhaps a cause of this lack of
policy, was the inability of the Liberals to attract young
recruits willing to stand municipally after 1919. Some years
earlier, at one municipal election in pre-war Leicester, a
Labour candidate ungraciously accused the Liberals of
being able to field only 'worn-out old veterans'.[33] After
1919 this accusation became increasingly justified. At

[29] Jones, *Borough Politics*, p. 57.

[30] *Bradford Pioneer*, 31 Oct 1930.

[31] For examples of this, see *Nottingham Guardian*, 2 Nov 1921, 2 Nov
1926.

[32] See *Leicester Mercury*, 20, 21, 29 Oct 1925.

[33] *Leicester Daily Post*, 24 Oct 1911.

Wolverhampton, for example, the average age of new Liberal councillors entering the council between 1919 and 1929 was 49 years. The average Labour age was ten years younger.[34]

There is similar evidence for Leeds. Of the 342 councillors elected in Leeds whose age on entry to the council chamber can be determined, the difference between the comparative youth of Labour entrants and the age of Liberals was considerable (see Table 4.1). Only one Liberal in five was under 40 years old when first elected to the council, but over one-third of Labour men were under this age.

TABLE 4.1
Age of New Council Entrants, Leeds City Council[35]

	Liberals (81)		Labour (97)	
	No.	%	*No.*	%
Under 30	3	(3·7)	5	(5·1)
30–39	14	(17·3)	31	(32·0)
40–49	29	(35·8)	39	(40·2)
Over 50	35	(43·2)	22	(22·3)
	81	(100·0)	97	(100·0)

The Liberals persistently showed the largest proportion of older councillors, frequently businessmen and shopkeepers entering the council as the crowning glory of their careers. In addition, the Liberals not only fielded older candidates, but very rarely fielded working-class men. The party relied almost exclusively on the higher and middle classes.

Two examples of the Liberal inability, or unwillingness, to field working-class candidates can be seen in Leeds and

[34] Jones, *Borough Politics*, Table XXIV, p. 380
[35] See B. Powell, 'A Study in the Change of Social Origins, Political Affiliation and Length of Service of Members of the Leeds City Council, 1888–1953, unpublished M.A. thesis (Leeds, 1958) p. 167.

Wolverhampton. Of 27 elected Liberals in Leeds during the period 1906–18 whose occupations can be traced, not one was from the working class. Of 13 newcomers to the council in the 1919–28 period, not a single working-class representative was to be found. In each group, manufacturers, professional men and small shopkeepers were the most numerous. Over the whole period 1888–1935, no fewer than 153 of 158 new Liberal councillors were from the upper or higher middle classes.[36]

The occupation and social class of the Liberal councillors in Wolverhampton closely follows the pattern of Leeds. Not a single working-class representative was elected as a Liberal in the period 1888–1919, nor in the period 1919–45. Once again, the bulk of Liberal councillors were shopkeepers, manufacturers and professional men.[37]

Perhaps the most important single consequence of these municipal anti-Socialist alliances was to prepare the ground for accommodation at parliamentary level. A quite definite correlation can be seen in the 1924 election, and even in 1923, of these two phenomena. The intimacy of Liberal–Conservative parliamentary relations in December 1923 in such towns as Bristol, Bolton, Derby and Accrington must be seen against the background of this continuing municipal co-operation. In 1924 these examples were multiplied many times.

For whatever reasons, one conclusion is of paramount importance from an analysis of municipal elections. By 1923 the Liberal Party was rapidly losing the allegiance of the great majority of working-class wards. Municipal politics, like parliamentary politics, was clearly dividing on lines of class. The urban, working-class wards were becoming, with only rare exceptions, loyal to the Labour Party, whilst the Liberals were increasingly being forced into residential middle-class areas.

[36] Ibid., p. 151.
[37] Jones, *Borough Politics*, p. 370. Of the 32 new Liberals elected after 1919, 13 were shopkeepers, 9 were manufacturers and 5 were professional men. By contrast, 11 of the 13 Labour men were of working-class status.

Perhaps the best illustration of this municipal division along class lines was to be found in Glasgow. Using the data of the 1921 Census, which gives detailed figures for housing and overcrowding on a ward basis, the 37 Glasgow wards can be conveniently divided into three main social types. These were as follows:

Group A: Areas of severely overcrowded working-class housing. The 8 wards in this group consisted of Dalmarnock, Mile End, Hutchesontown, Provan, Parkhead, Shettleston, Cowcadden and Cowlairs.

Group B: Areas of overcrowding, still working-class dominated, but with less poverty and deprivation than Group A. The 14 wards in this group consisted of Calton, Springburn, Govan, Fairfield, Maryhill, Ruchill, Anderston, Whitevale, Gorbals, Kingston, Kinning Park, Woodside, Exchange and Townhead.

Group C: Wards with relatively good housing and with residential development. The 15 wards in this group consisted of Govanhill, Partick West, Sandyford, Partick East, Blythswood, Whiteinch, Pollokshaws, North Kelvin, Denniston, Camphill, Cathcart, Langside, Park, Pollokshields and Kelvinside.

In the municipal elections from 1920 to 1926 inclusive, Labour won 139 (41·7 per cent) of the 333 seats in this period, the Moderates taking 194 (58·3 per cent). When these results are broken down into the three social groups described above, some very different results emerge, as shown in Table 4.2. No less than 84·7 per cent of the wards in Group A were secured by Labour, compared with 61·1 per cent in Group B and a negligible percentage in the residential wards in the final group. In marked contrast, 69·1 per cent of all wards ever won by the Moderates were concentrated in Group C. The Moderates won every single ward on every possible occasion in Group C, with the solitary exception of Sandyford ward in 1926, where Labour snatched victory solely as the result of a split in the Moderate ranks.

TABLE 4.2
Wards won by Moderates and Labour in Glasgow, 1920–6

No.	Type of ward	Won by Lab.	%	Won by Mod.	%	Total
8	Group A	61	(84·7)	11	(15·3)	72
14	Group B	77	(61·1)	49	(38·9)	126
15	Group C	1	(0·7)	134	(99·3)	135
		139	(41·7)	194	(58·3)	333

The correlation of class and municipal voting behaviour in Glasgow can be paralleled in virtually every major city in England, with the exception in local politics as in national of Birmingham and Liverpool.

Thus, if the 35 wards in Manchester are rearranged into groups based on housing conditions, some revealing figures can be assembled. From 1919 to 1923, of the 175 wards at stake in Manchester, the Conservatives won 83 (47·4 per cent), Labour won 47 (26·9 per cent), the Liberals 40 (22·9 per cent) and Independents 5 (2·8 per cent). In the five years from 1924 to 1928, for the same total to wards, the figures were: Conservative 71 (40·6 per cent), Labour 65 (37·1 per cent), Liberal 35 (20·0 per cent) and Independents 4 (2·3 per cent).

Although the Liberal percentage held fairly well, on each occasion the party was easily the weakest. The extent to which Labour had secured the working-class areas, and forced the Liberals to the residential wards, is set out in Table 4.3.[38] It is an interesting comment on Manchester Liberalism that, from 1919 to 1923, 62 per cent of the wards won by Liberals occurred in Group A, the most residential areas. Between 1924 and 1928 this total had risen to 69 per cent. Even here,

---

[38] The wards in Group A were Withington, Didsbury, Chorlton, Crumpsall, Rusholme, Moss Side West, Longsight, Moss Side East, Levenshulme, Exchange, Cheetham, St Ann and Oxford. Those in Group B were St Luke, Blackley, Moston, All Saints, Gorton South, Harpurhey, Newton Heath, Gorton North, Ardwick, Medlock and St George. Those in Group C were Bradford, Openshaw, St Mark, Beswick, Collegiate, Collyhurst, St John, Miles Platting, St Clements, St Michael and New Cross.

only one ward (Rusholme) returned a Liberal at every
election. Labour, meanwhile, was steadily increasing its grip
on the working-class wards. Some 62 per cent of their
victories came in Group C in the period 1919–23, whilst in the
1924–8 period this proportion rose to 66 per cent. In the ten
elections after 1919 the Liberals won on only four occasions
in any ward in Group C.

TABLE 4.3
Wards Won by Party in Manchester
(a) 1919–23

Category	No.	Seats	Con.	Lib.	Lab.	Ind.
Group A	13	65	36	25	–	4
Group B	11	55	25	12	18	–
Group C	11	55	22	3	29	1
	35	175	83	40	47	5

(b) 1924–8

Category	No.	Seats	Con.	Lib.	Lab.	Ind.
Group A	13	65	37	24	–	4
Group B	11	55	23	10	22	–
Group C	11	55	11	1	43	–
	35	175	71	35	65	4

These main features of municipal politics in Manchester
were repeated in Leicester. Arranging the 16 wards according to overcrowding, Table 4.4 illustrates the position.[39]
No less than 78·3 per cent of the wards won by Labour
in the 1919–23 period, and 67·6 per cent in the 1924–8
period, were concentrated in the working-class wards. On the
other hand, 85·7 per cent of the Liberal victories in the early
period, and 94·7 per cent in the 1924–8 period, were in the

[39] The wards in Group A were Knighton, De Montfort, Wycliffe, Spinney
Hill, Westcotes and Belgrave. Those in Group B were Charnwood, West
Humberstone, Abbey, Aylestone and Castle. Those in Group C were
Latimer, St. Margarets', Newton and Wyggeston

TABLE 4.4
Wards Won by Party in Leicester
(a) 1919–23

Type	No.	Seats	Con.	Lab.	Lib.	Ind.
Group A	6	30	19	–	10	1
Group B	5	25	4	5	14	2
Group C	5	25	2	18	4	1
	16	80	25	23	28	4

(b) 1924–8

Type	No.	Seats	Con.	Lab.	Lib.	Ind.
Group A	6	30	20	2	8	–
Group B	5	25	4	9	10	2
Group C	5	25	1	23	1	–
	16	80	25	34	19	2

better-housed areas of the city, in such wards as Belgrave and West Humberstone.

This evidence from Manchester and Leicester was representative of all the major provincial boroughs. From Bristol to Leeds, or from Norwich to Bradford, the main fact was that the former working-class Liberal wards had been forfeited to Labour.

The occasional exception was in each case explicable by peculiar localised circumstances. Thus, in Wolverhampton East the working-class wards remained Liberal because of the lack of union organisation in this old heart of the Black Country. The peculiar Liberal revival in Bethnal Green in 1928 was equally localised. There was no substantial area of the country in which the Liberal Party in the 1920s was able to withstand simultaneously both the Labour and Conservative challenge.

It is quite clear that this municipal Liberal decline cannot be explained simply by the Asquith–Lloyd George split. It was the work of long-term factors. Indeed, although outside the scope of this work, it is quite certain that the beginnings of this Liberal decline were in evidence in several cities well before 1914. Certainly, in such towns as Sheffield, West Ham or Bristol, frequent examples of co-operation to thwart Labour existed in the pre-war period. In such towns as Leicester or Coventry, Liberal fears over their future relations with Labour were already in evidence.

Whatever date is given to the beginnings of this municipal decline – and many individual studies will need to be undertaken before sufficient definitive evidence is accumulated – the position of the Liberal Party by mid-1923 in the major cities of England can be clearly stated: it was the position of a party lacking vitality, youth, policy or purpose; it was a party that had lost the will to live and whose inheritance had already been considerably eroded by the rising and expanding power of Labour.

5   The Elusive Goal:
Attempts at Liberal
Reunion

The extent to which, if Liberal reunion had been achieved in the months after the 1922 general election, the organisation and morale of the party both in the constituencies and at higher levels would have been transformed, can never finally be decided. Reunion in fact did not occur until, with Baldwin's call for an election on Protection, it came too late to affect Liberal chances in 1923.

Throughout 1923 the Liberals spent considerable time grappling with the problem of reunion. Unlike the other difficulties facing the party, it was a problem about which they might do something. However, the circumstances and conduct of the 1922 election had hardly given reunion a good start. With the notable exceptions of such areas as Manchester and Leeds, the two Liberal factions had spent the 1922 election fighting each other.

And, as Trevor Wilson has written, for most Independent Liberals, including Asquith, the only satisfaction to be derived from the election results was in 'gloat(ing) over the corpses which have been left on the battlefield'.[1] There was indeed no lack of Coalition Liberal corpses. They included Churchill, Guest, Kellaway, Edwin Montagu and Hamar Greenwood. After the election, memories of these bitter scenes presented a major obstacle to reunion. Yet, to members in both wings, it seemed a vital and pressing question. Many Coalition Liberals saw reunion as giving them a more definite place in politics. Independent Liberals hoped that it would reclaim a leader possessing the vision and vigour their

---

[1] Wilson, *The Downfall of the Liberal Party*, p. 243.

party lacked. On this point, the Independent Liberals were divided. To C. P. Scott and F. D. Acland, Lloyd George's return would bring back a lost leader of dynamism and brilliance. Yet others, such as A. G. Gardiner (the former editor of the *Daily News*) and C. F. G. Masterman, vowed to join Labour if Lloyd George returned to the Liberal Party.

Overall, however, in both wings of the party, there was a general and genuine desire for reunion. It was reflected when, shortly after the general election, George Lambert (MP for South Molton) called a meeting of Liberal MPs to discuss the position.[2] At the same time, Lambert asked Asquith and Lloyd George to put their position on reunion to him.

In his reply (dated 24 November 1922) Lloyd George offered to meet the leaders forthwith to discuss the subject. Only in connection with the holding of a meeting of the rank and file did he propose any delay, and that only for a formal preliminary declaration. Four days later, on 28 November, Asquith replied in rather different vein:

> I have received and given careful attention to your letter. I regard a united Liberal Party, pursuing Liberal policy on Liberal lines, as a vital necessity to the State. I have never placed, and never shall place, obstacles in the way of its achievement. So far as the House of Commons is concerned, the most promising road would appear to me to be by co-operation in debate and in the division-lobby.

As the *Manchester Guardian* commented, it was not exactly cordial, even if it did not convey an actual repulse.

On 27 November 1922 a reunion discussion meeting was convened by Maxwell Thornton, the MP for Tavistock. The meeting elected Lambert chairman and, according to the official account, about 16 of the 'nearly one hundred' Liberal MPs present spoke in favour of reunion, while none spoke against. Two days later C. A. McCurdy, Lloyd George's Chief Whip, stated that he favoured reunion and that Lloyd George would be 'perfectly prepared to serve under Mr Asquith's leadership'.[3] These were indeed encouraging signs from the Coalition Liberals. They met with no response from Asquith. Indeed, one result of the 27 November meeting was Asquith's

---

[2] Lambert had chaired a meeting with similar aims (and similar lack of success) in February 1919.

[3] Kinnear, *The Fall of Lloyd George*, p. 211.

subsequent dismissal on 10 February 1923 of J. M. Hogge (the joint Liberal Whip) for supporting reunion. He was replaced by Vivian Phillipps, a strong opponent of reunion.

During the first weeks of December the supporters of reunion were active, but not much advance was made. The Hon. Alexander Shaw, in an article in *Reynolds' Newspaper*, strongly advocated 'the sponging of the slate'. That some Independent Liberals expected a show of penitence from the other section was illustrated by the *Westminster Gazette's* remark that the mutineers could always come back to duty if they pleased, but need not expect any fatted calf for the occasion.

At this juncture the bitterest opponent of unity was undoubtedly the *Nation*, which described the proposal for reunion as either silly or shameless, or both. 'Wayfarer', in that journal on 9 December, declared that 'The most melancholy feature of this revolting business is the part which the *Manchester Guardian* has played'.

The New Year hardly opened on a promising note. During January, Lloyd George was abroad. On his return, the National Liberals wanted to offer him dinner at the National Liberal Club, but the committee of that club, when asked for the use of their large dining-room, ungraciously refused the request. During February rather more friendly initiatives got under way with Hilton Young's invitation on behalf of the National Liberals to the Independent Liberals to co-operate in moving a joint amendment to the Address in reply to the King's Speech. This offer was accepted. In the division, 92 Liberals voted together.

The next step was to bring again a pro-reunion resolution which had been handed round in the previous session by the Hon. Alexander Shaw. Almost immediately Liberals of both groups, to the extent of much more than a clear majority of the combined total, appended their signatures. These encouraging signs received a sharp rebuff when, on 24 February, the *Westminster Gazette* published a letter from C. F. G. Masterman, in which he stated that many Liberals, as a protest against union with former Coalition Members, would withdraw from politics or join some other party.

The most important event during February came with a major speech by Lloyd George at Edinburgh on reunion. Having stressed the necessity to face 'the common enemy' (i.e. Labour), Lloyd George went on to ask for the ending of recriminations. He suggested that those responsible for the leadership in both sections should come together frankly to consult. He denied that he sought leadership. He was willing to follow any leader who possessed the necessary vision, resolution, wisdom, courage and inspiration to lead the nation to the acceptance of a faith that would save it from 'the despair of reaction and from the devastation that follows in the wake of revolution'. Nevertheless, to use the words of the *Sunday Express*, Sir John Simon at Spen Valley immediately opened fire upon the dove that Lloyd George had sent on its peaceful mission. He appeared to commit his party to a noncommittal attitude and described the consultation proposal as a proposal for a 'secret conclave'.

The initiative in fact failed to move the party any nearer reunion. Asquith continued to insist that a first prerequisite of reunion should be regular and continuous co-operation between both wings of the party in the division lobby. At a party meeting on 22 March, with Asquith in the chair, Sir Godfrey Collins proposed a resolution on exactly these lines.[4] At this meeting, Asquith delivered an uncompromising negative on the suggestions that had been mooted for the establishment of a 'Consultative Parliamentary Committee' (consisting of Asquith, Simon, Lloyd George and Mond) to discuss policy in the House and plan common action. According to the *Lloyd George Liberal Magazine* (which was broadly repeating press reports of the meeting), Asquith poured scorn on such a Consultative Committee. The magazine went on:

> ... he [Asquith] adopted an attitude entirely hostile to the proposal, treating the whole idea of a Consultative Committee

---

[4] The text ran: 'That while fully desirous of every effort being made to secure joint action in the House of Commons this meeting is of opinion that regular and continuous co-operation in the division lobby and the constituencies shall be a condition precedent to setting up any formal machinery for Liberal reunion.'

with scorn. If he and Mr Lloyd George met, what were they to talk about – the weather or the winner of the Grand National? The reunion movement, he said, was being run by the National Liberals as the Parliamentary expedient of persons in peril of their political souls. He added: 'Grateful as I am for all you have done, and much as I love all of you, if you put this proposal upon me, I will put my hat on my head and go out of the door'.

The idea of setting up formal machinery for a unity that so far did not exist on important questions of policy was ridiculed, and the meeting accepted Asquith's lead in rejecting the proposal with loud applause. The same evening, Lloyd George defended his position, declaring:

> I have been agreed to all the suggestions for united action which have been put forward by bodies of Liberal members of both groups, and I certainly accept this proposal. It is obvious that effective co-operation in the lobbies and in the country is impossible without consultation. If we do not reunite, Liberalism is done as a national driving force. For that reason I have welcomed every proposal for reunion put forward by Liberals of both sections, and I do not see what more I can do.[5]

There can be little doubt that – for whatever underlying reasons – Lloyd George wanted reunion (and reunion quickly) whilst Asquith was adopting a largely negative approach.

A further instance of Asquith's unhelpful approach came in April, when the Leeds Liberal Federation invited both Asquith and Lloyd George to luncheon – in the hope that the meeting would provide a suitable occasion for a step towards reconciliation. Lloyd George promptly accepted. Asquith's reply was not prompt and was not an acceptance; he preferred to wait until he could see a further advance in the process of Liberal co-operation in the House and in the constituencies. On the receipt of that refusal, the Leeds Liberals decided to postpone the luncheon to some future occasion.

Although regret was expressed in many parts of the country at the failure of this effort, some Independent Liberals seemed glad that it had broken down. The *Sheffield Independent* maintained that reunion would be reflected in the division lobby and not in the dining-room.

[5] *Lloyd George Liberal Magazine*, Apr 1923, p. 528.

Asquith's insistence that co-operation in the lobbies was an essential prerequisite was in fact a hyprocritical stance. Asquith continued to make reference to two divisions as examples of lack of co-operation. In one of these, Lloyd George's supporters had in fact gone almost equally into the government lobby and the opposition's, but, as Kinnear points out, he did not mention that in the second division which he used as an example of cooperation, the Asquithians had been divided. Even Asquith's own supporters refuted his argument.[6] The *Liberal Magazine* provided statistics showing that the Lloyd Georgians voted with the Asquithians three-quarters of the time. Taking 40 important divisions on such issues as tariffs, trade union legislation, land values, old-age pensions and similar subjects, it calculated that the Lloyd Georgians voted with the Asquithians on 30, against them on 8 and were split on 2. Moreover, on all but one of the divisions where they opposed the Lloyd Georgians, the Asquithians were divided. Lord Gladstone, however, calculated his figures on votes on all issues in Parliament. He calculated that, from the 1922 general election until the Easter recess of March 1923, in 53 divisions, the National Liberals voted 649 times with the Conservative Government and only 299 times against.[7] On these figures, only six National Liberals voted more often against the government than for the Conservatives.[8] Otherwise, Table 5.1 illustrates the extent to which some National Liberals were Conservatives in all but name.

To some extent, these figures lend credence to Asquith's complaints. But they tell only half the story. These figures were the right-wing rump of the old Coalition. Many were to finish their careers in the Conservative Party. Some were already deserting the National Liberal ship even in 1923. Two MPs to transfer allegiance were Arthur Evans in Leicester

[6] *Kinnear, The Fall of Lloyd George,* p. 214.
[7] Figures derived from Lord Gladstone's calculations, in Gladstone Papers, BM Add. MSS 46,480/51.
[8] These were: Fiddes (Stockport), Hutchinson (Kirkcaldy), Lewis (University of Wales), Parry (Flintshire), Stephenson (Sheffield Park) and E. A. Strauss (Southwark North).

TABLE 5.1

Member	Constituency	Voted	For govt	Against govt
A. H. Moreing	Camborne	48	43	5
Lt-Col. M. Alexander	Southwark South-East	31	29	2
A. England	Heywood and Radcliffe	33	25	8
H. A. Evans	Leicester East	34	25	9
G. W. S. Jarrett	Dartford	45	38	7
H. Philipson	Berwick-upon-Tweed	30	24	6
T. Robinson	Stretford	25	24	1
Brig.-Gen. E. L. Spears	Loughborough	25	22	3
Major W. Waring	Berwick and Haddington	25	24	1
Sir T. C. Warner	Lichfield	17	17	0

East and G. H. Roberts in Norwich.[9] To these should be added A. E. Martin in Romford, who had openly stated his intention to fight the next election as a Conservative, but withdrew from politics owing to ill-health.[10] They were the forerunners of many.

The most conspicuous feature of the National Liberals in Parliament in 1923 was that they did precisely nothing. They were at times almost a rare sight in the lobbies. Thus, when the Asquithian Liberals put forward a motion empowering local authorities to levy rates on land values, only twelve National Liberals voted at all. Six voted for, and six against. Lloyd George himself voted only twice between the 1922 general election and the Easter recess, on both occasions against the government.

Lacking in leadership, uncertain on policy, and unwelcomed and unloved by the Independent Liberals, the cohesion and morale of the Coalition Liberals was fading. Hence, no doubt, Lloyd George's conciliatory gestures to Asquith. The way back to the Conservatives was blocked; the

[9] With Evans the change was not very marked. He had given unequivocal pledges of support to a Conservative Government in 1922, and his campaign was fought on an anti-Socialist platform.
[10] *Essex County Standard*, 24 Nov 1923.

Independent Liberals remained the only sure mooring in an uncharted sea. The irony was perfect. Owing to the exigencies of politics, Lloyd George, the heretic who had split the party, was keen on reunion. Asquith, not for the first time, had everything to gain by waiting and seeing. But Lloyd George's willingness for reunion went only so far. At no time did he attack the Bonar Law government outright. As Trevor Wilson succinctly commented, it did not obviate for the future a new alliance with the Conservatives.[11]

C. P. Scott's diary provides important evidence of what was going on in Lloyd George's mind in the spring of 1923. After lunch with Lloyd George (where Hogge and C. F. Entwistle were also present), Scott recorded in his diary:

> Lloyd George evidently keen for reunion, though he put the need for immediate action on the ground that otherwise the Labour party would make all the running and the Liberal party would sink into impotence. He was prepared to go a long way in the way of conciliation but 'I will not crawl. I will not crawl on my belly.'[12]

Here, indeed, was the crunch. Lloyd George, more than Asquith, could see the realities of the political situation after Labour's advance in 1922. And yet a lingering pride prevented submission, whilst Asquith seemed to want nothing less than just that.

This position in the spring of 1923 continued unchanged as summer approached. At the same time, growing evidence of the desire for reconciliation in the constituencies became apparent. In two by-elections in Anglesey and Ludlow, local reunion was achieved. In Anglesey, Sir Robert Thomas, who had been a Coalition Liberal in the last Parliament, now stood as a Liberal without prefix, and there was a powerful lining-up of the two wings. Sir John Simon spoke for him; Ian Macpherson and several Welsh National Liberal MPs addressed meetings.

The happy relations of the campaign, however, did not carry from the hills of Wales to Westminster. Thomas's victory was followed by a general demand that the two sections should be represented by the sponsors who

[11] Wilson, *The Downfall of the Liberal Party*, p. 245.
[12] Scott's diary, entry dated 8 Mar 1923.

introduced him to the House when he took his seat. He himself wrote to Lloyd George and Asquith, asking if he might be introduced by them. Lloyd George acquiesced; Asquith refused. It was then suggested that the two Chief Whips should officiate. Hilton Young agreed to do so; Vivian Phillipps declined to act in that way with the National Liberal Whip. The *Manchester Guardian* recommended that Sir John Simon and Ian Macpherson would be appropriate sponsors, but this proposal was similarly shelved.

The evidence throughout the spring and early summer of 1923 revealed National Liberal reconciliation initiatives being summarily brought to a halt. Thus, the Welsh National Liberals held a meeting in March to consider the reunion position and appointed nine delegates with full power to meet Independent Liberals in any conference. This was communicated to a meeting at Shrewsbury of the Welsh Liberal Federation. The response to this friendly gesture was not encouraging. The Federation passed the following resolution: 'That the consideration of the letter from the National Liberal Council be deferred for six months.' A further major speech by Lloyd George – on 28 April at Manchester – again produced only a frosty reception from Asquith. Supplied with an opportunity of accepting the hand of friendship, Asquith chose as an alternative, in a speech at Bournemouth, to catalogue some of the difficulties. National Liberals had been voting with Conservatives. They had supported the government on a dockyard question. They were inclined to declare war against Labour. May produced no further real moves towards Liberal reunion, except in the constituencies, where the *Lloyd George Liberal Magazine* reported: 'The month has seen a considerable increase in the number of resolutions from rank-and-file organisations throughout the country advocating co-operation and consultation between the Party leaders as the first step towards complete reunion.'[13]

In determining the course of Liberal reunion, the annual conference of the National Liberal Federation at Buxton was of crucial importance. The concrete results of Buxton in terms of Liberal reunion were virtually nil. It was true that the

---

[13] *Lloyd George Liberal Magazine*, June 1923, p. 697.

delegates put on record their satisfaction with the growing desire for party union. It was also the case that the friendly reception given to such National Liberals as Mond and McCurdy contrasted very favourably with the hostility shown at Leamington in 1920 to Hewart and Addison. Nevertheless, the conference rejected an amendment which had the object of translating the opinion of the conference into immediate practical action. This amendment proposed to include in the pro-reunion resolution a recommendation to the Independent Liberal leaders to discuss with the National Liberal leaders the best means of promoting party unity. It is unclear what would have happened to that amendment if the chairman, Sir Donald Maclean, had asked each delegate to vote upon it in accordance with his or her own desire. Probably it would have been carried. Sir Donald adopted a very different course; he proclaimed that the Federation's Executive would regard the recommendation as indicating a lack of confidence in Asquith as their leader. After that pronouncement, the amendment's rejection was natural in an assembly so largely composed of Asquithian Liberals.

Maclean went on to embitter relations towards the National Liberals still further. As the *Star* commented in a leading article:

> The National Liberal Federation has decided, by an emphatic majority, to continue to indulge its grouch at the expense of expediency. Sir Donald Maclean said that he was asked if the time has not come to let bygones be bygones. He replied: 'Yes, if there is repentance.' We must conclude from the character of the vote that there is not repentance, or not sufficient repentance, and that Mr Lloyd George and his friends must continue to wear a white sheet.[14]

The *Manchester Guardian*, in its comments on the Buxton proceedings, declared that the blunt truth revealed by the gathering was that the party was so dangerously preoccupied with its internal problems that it had little time for the external problems of policy, especially domestic policy. How, it asked, could Liberal leaders hope to rouse enthusiasm until

[14] This, and subsequent quotations, are cited in the *Lloyd George Liberal Magazine*, July 1923, pp. 779 ff.

they had themselves enough enthusiasm to endure one another for the good of the cause?

There is little doubt that Buxton was the moment of lost opportunity for Liberal reunion. As Hogge rightly stated, by the summer of 1923 'the insistent call today is for reunion'.[15] Yet conference had turned an almost deaf ear. This was reflected in a growing number of associations making their own local arrangements for reunion. In the Heywood and Radcliffe division the Liberal Executive took steps to promote reunion at a meeting at which the sitting National Liberal Member, Colonel A. England, was present, while the chair was occupied by C. Pickstone, who had stood as Independent Liberal against England at a by-election in 1921. The Liberal Association at Ashton-under-Lyne registered by resolution an expression of its regret at 'the deplorable result of the vote on the amendment at Buxton'. At Macclesfield the Liberal Executive passed a resolution declaring conferences between the Liberal leaders to be essential. National Liberals and Independent Liberals of the Thornbury division met at Bristol and decided to join forces locally.

At the same time that the moves towards reunion at local level were increasing, Scott's diary provides interesting evidence that Asquith's intransigence in ever readmitting Lloyd George to real power within a reunited party was increasing. Thus, after a long talk with Lord Gladstone, Scott wrote:

> ... he [Gladstone] opened up at once on the subject of Lloyd George and the Liberal party. To begin with, he said, one point might be regarded as fixed and irrevocable: for whatever reason, whether arising from his own feelings or the pressure of his [domestic] entourage, he [i.e. Asquith] was resolved never again to accept Lloyd George as a colleague. I said I had already understood this, but what exactly did that imply? I gathered that Asquith was not unwilling to confer with Lloyd George and had often done so on the day to day procedure and tactics in the House. He said that was so and that they met on quite friendly terms. What Asquith refused to do was to admit Lloyd George into the 'inner council' of the party.[16]

[15] *Daily Chronicle*, 15 June 1923.
[16] Scott's diary, 1 July 1923.

The more Gladstone talked, the more it seemed that this desire to exclude Lloyd George was linked with the question of who should succeed Asquith. Scott's diary continued:

> There was the question of the succession. What of Sir John Simon? It was generally recognised that Asquith was no longer effective as an active Leader. Was Lloyd George then to succeed him, as he inevitably must, by force of personality and past position, if once accepted and recognised as a full member of the party? That would disintegrate the party. It was not merely the other leaders who would not accept him (and he himself should decline with the rest), but in most of the constituencies there were important men who could never be brought to accept Lloyd George and who would go out of active politics if he were once more brought in in an important position.

If this version is correct, the sad paradox of Liberal history stands out: Asquith succeeded in keeping out Lloyd George until October 1926, but at the cost of seeing the party destroyed. Lloyd George became leader when only a rump was left for him to lead. And Simon – whom Asquith perhaps saw as heir apparent – repaid his former chief by leading a breakaway Liberal National Party a decade later.

Meanwhile, to add to the multitude of political cross-currents at work in July 1923, Lloyd George was once again – having despaired of Liberal reunion – refusing to abandon his contacts with the Conservatives. It was all Made worse by such people as Sir Edward Grigg, Lloyd George's former private secretary and MP for Oldham, openly seeking to renew a crusade with the Conservatives against Labour. Lloyd George was still refusing to declare outright against the government or to exclude completely the possibility of a new Coalition.[17] Not surprisingly, when Scott relayed the gist of his long talk with Gladstone to Lloyd George, the latter merely became angry, indignant and unrepentant of his continuing Conservative contacts. Scott's diary recorded:

> He [Lloyd George] said nothing could be done till he was accepted on terms of full equality in the councils of the party. I told him what Lord Gladstone had said to me as to the permanent impossibility of that, and he said if that were so it ought to be

[17] Kinnear, *The Fall of Lloyd George*, p. 246.

publicly stated. While he was to be shut out W. M. R. Pringle was actually now being put forward as the possible future Liberal leader, even in preference to Simon. At that rate the Tory party would be in power for 20 years or more and then there would be a big reaction and Labour would come in. He was blamed for keeping up relations with Austen Chamberlain, but Chamberlain was in fact a Liberal . . . . The Tory party from time to time absorbed Liberals (McKenna to wit); why should not the Liberal party absorb Tories?[18]

And so matters rested.

With the months of August and September relatively empty of political activity, the position regarding reunion remained unchanged. With the exception of local reunion in Bradford (largely caused by the raising of Tariff Reform by Baldwin), this was the position when in September 1923 Lloyd George set off for what was to become a triumphant lecture tour of America. By the time he returned, Baldwin's unexpected announcement of his conversion to Protection had transformed the political climate.

[18] Scott's diary, 26 July 1923, quoted in Wilson, *The Downfall of the Liberal Party*, p. 443.

Part Two

The Liberal Revival:
The General Election of
December 1923

6 The Political Background

While the Liberals had thus wasted a valuable year in inconclusive negotiations leading only to increasing suspicion, the national political scene had greatly changed. A paradox of the 1922 election was that such a confused campaign should have had such clear and lasting significance for each party.

The election gave the Conservatives only two-fifths of the votes cast but a working majority of 77. Labour consolidated its position as the official opposition, while the anti-Coalition Conservatives headed by Bonar Law enjoyed the fruits of office. Indirectly, as Kinnear has pointed out, the election pushed Stanley Baldwin and Neville Chamberlain to prominence, since both owed their rapid promotion in 1923 to the fact that numerous Conservatives, better known than they were, were out of office when Bonar Law retired in May.[1]

It was in the Conservative Party that the most immediate consequences of the 1922 result were felt. Just after the election, the Conservative party shifted to the right, and two die-hards, Colonel John Gretton and A. B. Boyd-Carpenter, displaced two supporters of the old coalition on the Executive of the National Unionist Association. In March 1923 Bonar Law appointed two other strong opponents of the Coalition, Sir Reginald Hall and Stanley Jackson, to important posts in the Conservative organisation.

During the 1922 campaign, Churchill had caustically labelled Bonar Law's Cabinet as 'the second eleven' whilst Birkenhead had described the new Ministers as second-class intellects. The months of 1923 not only partially upheld the

[1] Kinnear, *The Fall of Lloyd George*, p. 197.

truth of the gibes of Birkenhead and Churchill, but showed how many problems faced the Bonar Law administration. Foreign affairs – in particular the German problem – remained a vexing question. The problem of the decontrol of rents, on which the government for once acted decisively, caused considerable electoral unpopularity and the government suffered a succession of by-election reverses in March.

More than any individual issue, however, it was the inexperience and limited ability of Bonar Law's Ministers that was the chief problem. Bonar Law had told Sir Archibald Salvidge that he expected to have to make quick replacements. His judgement proved correct. In addition, some 25–30 Conservative MPs persisted in supporting Austen Chamberlain, so that the government's nominally large majority was frequently reduced. Indeed, in April the government was actually defeated in the House on a motion relating to the employment of ex-servicemen. As Kinnear wrote of the government's position after this relatively minor defeat:

> . . . taken in conjunction with the Government's fumbling over war debts, the occupation of the Rhineland, rents, housing, the Irish deportations and similar matters during the first three months of the year, it showed that the Government was losing its grip. The Government retained little support from the Independent sectors of the Press which had backed it in the 1922 election, and even the clerk of the privy council, Sir Almeric Fitzroy, reflected the general disenchantment.[2]

It was against this background that Bonar Law's health gave way. In May 1923 Baldwin succeeded Bonar Law. With Austen Chamberlain (the obvious choice) not a practical candidate, Curzon was Baldwin's only real rival.

The arrival of Baldwin was to mark a watershed in British political history. Yet, at the time, there was little noticeable change. Whereas Bonar Law's government had drifted

---

[2] Ibid., p. 207. In his diary, Sir Almeric Fitzroy described Bonar Law's Cabinet as 'well-intentioned and amiable gentlemen whose virtues are more impressive than their intellects'. Fitzroy added that the government was unable to cope with the 'problems of such menacing urgency' that faced it.

almost aimlessly from crisis to crisis between November 1922 and May 1923, Baldwin was more fortunate. Without having any more definite policy or programme than Bonar Law, there were less immediately pressing or urgent problems for Baldwin to face.

Furthermore, although Austen Chamberlain and Birkenhead were not in the new government, the old wounds of the Coalition were showing the first signs of healing. Worthington-Evans (and some other Chamberlainites) joined Baldwin's government. It needed only, in Baldwin's eyes, a positive policy and a bold platform to act as the spur to reunite the party and maybe separate the old Coalitionists for all time from the Liberals. Faced with the mounting problem of unemployment, one issue seemed to offer salvation on all fronts – Protection.

Other changes were also taking place in the months of 1923 before Baldwin decided on his great gamble of a tariff election. Whilst the organisation of the Liberals at constituency level was only too frequently moribund, the Conservatives were busily reviving their organisation and morale in the constituencies after the period of Coalition.

By mid-1923 the number of constituencies without any form of Conservative organisation was limited to a few mining or heavy industrial seats.[3] Elsewhere, with the exception of such traditionally stony ground as Highland Scotland, the Conservatives had at least a rudimentary organisation.[4] During 1923 the Conservatives steadily rebuilt party organisation after the Coalition. Speaking to the annual dinner of Conservative agents, Jackson, the Chairman of the Party Organisation, eulogised the position of constituency organisation.[5] Whilst, compared with the Coalition years, the difference was very great, the position was not as optimistic as Jackson stated. Several months after the 1922 election, rebuilding from the confusion of the Coalition was still far

[3] For example, the Wentworth and Don Valley divisions. *Sheffield Daily Telegraph*, 16 Nov, 8 Dec 1923.

[4] Conservative organisation was totally absent in Caithness and Sutherland, the Western Isles, Banffshire, and Orkney and Shetland. *Glasgow Herald*, 16 Nov 1923; *Scotsman*, 23 Nov 1923.

[5] For this speech, see *Conservative Agents' Journal*, Nov 1923.

from complete. In such London seats as Hackney Central, East Ham South and Walthamstow West the Coalition tangle was still being unsorted. Rural examples of this kind can be found in Berwick and Haddingtonshire and the Eye division.[6]

As a case study of a Conservative constituency association rebuilding from the Coalition period, standing in marked contrast to the dormant Liberal Associations, the Harborough division provides a typical example. Despite winning this traditionally Liberal seat in the 'coupon' election, the Conservative position was far less healthy than might be supposed. In 1919 subscriptions had reached their lowest recorded level, whilst the Annual Report two years later complained of the great amount of apathy still prevalent.[7] The position in mid-1923 had improved only slightly, with 32 of the 52 polling districts still requiring organisation, and with several village associations still defunct.[8] Nonetheless, the position was steadily being righted thereafter. In this respect the Harborough association very much resembled the position in the Peterborough division.[9]

Divisions such as Harborough were, however, relatively unusual compared with the generally well-organised Conservative constituency associations. Compared with the Liberals, the Conservatives could view a general election with much more comfort in the autumn of 1923 than would have been the case even a few months earlier. Nor had Labour failed to use the months of 1923 to consolidate its major advances in the 1922 general election. The general election of 1922 had a marked impact on the Labour Party. The Parliamentary Labour Party moved from being a relatively weak trade union group to an effective force with a more positive leadership and a wider base in Parliament than hitherto. Whereas between 1918 and 1922 the Labour MPs had

---

[6] *Scotsman*, 8 Dec 1923; for the position in Eye, see Eastern Provincial Division, National Union of Conservative and Unionist Associations, Minutes, Executive Committee, 12 Dec 1922.

[7] Harborough Division Conservative Association, Annual Report, 1921.

[8] Ibid., Annual Report, 1923.

[9] For similar complaints of apathy and difficulty in maintaining subscriptions, see Peterborough and North Northamptonshire Conservative Association, Minutes, Executive Committee, 12 July 1922.

outnumbered the Asquithians, they had not emerged clearly as an alternative government, partly because of ineffective leadership and partly because their position as the official opposition had seemed to be the artificial result of temporary Liberal divisions. After the 1922 election, Labour had 23 more MPs than the Liberals, and Liberal factional differences left Labour effectively unchallenged as the official opposition. The most marked change was in the character of the parliamentary party, which became less obviously trade unionist than before the election.[10] The selection of Ramsay MacDonald as leader also added to this impression of a broader-based Labour Party. He was a marked improvement on J. R. Clynes. In all, the new middle-class Labour MPs and the new leader helped create the impression that the Labour Party was becoming a truly national party.

The most obvious result of the 1922 election for Labour was its great increase in seats. However, at the same time that the Parliamentary Labour Party was changing in composition and strength, the constituency organisation of the party was being rapidly extended.

By the time of the annual conference of June 1923, the Labour Party claimed that all but six of the 603 constituencies (excluding Ulster) possessed some form of Labour organisation. In all, the party boasted 2,653 divisional and local Labour Parties or Trades Councils, an increase of 253 on the preceding year. There were in addition 1,031 women's sections, with a total membership of 120,000. The women's organiser could report that the year had been one of great growth in numbers and in enthusiasm.[11]

However, several of these claims of organisation in the rural constituencies were exaggerated. Over 30 constituency associations, for example, existed in name only, failing to pay an affiliation fee to the national Labour Party.[12] In many others, organisation was embryonic. Labour efforts in the South-West were still of a purely propaganda nature.[13] The

[10] A Liberal journal, the *Nation*, put the number of middle-class Labour MPs at 54, out of a total Labour contingent of 142.

[11] Labour Party, *Annual Conference Report, 1923*, p. 5.

[12] Ibid.

[13] *Daily Herald*, 27 Oct 1924.

rural areas of such countries as Yorkshire, and the whole of the Welsh Border country, were equally barren.

It is a common fallacy to believe that the Labour Party swept across Britain like some irresistible tide after 1914 or 1918. This may have been true of urban England, but in rural England this was never so. Labour always remained weak in any country area lacking an organised trade union base. In most rural seats, such Labour organisation as existed was often little more than a local trade union branch. The important fact is not the complete weakness of Labour organisation but that, from even such rudimentary organisation, and lacking finance, the party was able to field parliamentary candidates with increasing regularity. Admittedly, outside Norfolk these candidates were usually at the foot of the poll, but the vital significance was that these Labour candidates were often able to poll sufficiently to deny the Liberals victory.

A further result of the extension of Labour constituency organisation into rural and residential areas was to reinforce the dilemma of relations between the Liberal and Labour parties. The consequences of the 1922 election hit the Liberal Party hardest. As the last chapter demonstrated, the Liberals, in contrast to the other two parties, received the greatest setback for they remained divided over leadership. A further consequence was that Labour and Conservative leaders tended to be less accommodating to Liberals seeking alliances than they had been during the 1922 election campaign, when they had anticipated a Parliament without a majority.

The by-elections in the period from November 1922 to October 1923 both reflected the national changes brought about by the 1922 general election and also provided an indicator of the relative electoral fortunes of the rival parties.

At Portsmouth South (13 December 1922), in a by-election caused by the resignation of H. R. Cayzer, the sitting member, the Conservative candidate was opposed only by an Independent. The Liberals, who had fought in 1922, failed to raise sufficient energy to field a candidate. The Conservatives easily retained the seat, with turnout falling from 73·7 per cent to 57·7 per cent. In the Newcastle East by-election, interest was added to the contest when Arthur Henderson was brought forward as Labour candidate (he had been defeated at Widnes in the 1922 general election). Henderson's goodwill was vital to electoral co-operation between Liberals and Labour if it was to be carried beyond scattered local pacts. The Liberal, Harry Barnes, had voted for a capital levy in 1919 and was on the radical wing of the party. Barnes had been opposed by a Lloyd Georgian candidate and also by Labour in 1922; the two Liberals had taken 56·8 per cent to Labour's 43·2 per cent. Since the total Liberal poll had exceeded Labour's, and since Barnes had been the MP up to 1922, it was too much to expect him to withdraw in favour of Henderson, especially with no rival Liberal.

The significance of the result in Newcastle East was the inability of the Liberal candidate to make headway against Labour in a traditionally Liberal industrial seat. Labour was in fact able to increase both its vote and its percentage of the poll.

The succeeding by-election in Whitechapel produced a similar result. Despite the withdrawal of a Conservative candidate, Labour very substantially increased its hold on this East End seat, raising its share of the total poll from 40·2 per cent to 57·0 per cent. In the Darlington by-election on 28 February 1923 a straight fight took place, although the Liberals had contested the seat at the previous election. The by-election result again demonstrated the ability of Labour to capture a further portion of the former Liberal vote.

In none of these by-elections had seats actually changed hands. This position was rapidly altered by a batch of by-elections held early in March. Partly as a result of government plans to decontrol rents, and partly as a result of an internal Conservative quarrel, the first of these by-elections, at Mitcham, produced a dramatic result. In a constituency in which in 1922 the Conservatives had taken 65 per cent of the poll in a straight fight with the Liberals, in the by-election the seat was sensationally won by Labour. Partly, this was because the official candidate, Sir Arthur Griffith-Boscawen, was faced by an Independent Conservative supported by Lord Rothermere.[14] The Independent took 12·7 per cent of

[14] For Rothermere's part in this campaign, see entry dated 2 Mar 1923 in Lord Bayford's diary, quoted in Maurice Cowling, *The Impact of Labour, 1920–1924* (1971) p. 257.

the poll, a sufficient level of support to let Labour in, with the Liberals trailing a very poor third, with 15·2 per cent.

In every sense, however, Labour's gain was nothing short of spectacular. Mitcham was hardly the seat to set Socialists dreaming of the promised land.[15] Chuter Ede, the Labour candidate, found on his arrival in the division that the local party consisted of a voluntary secretary and a few scattered trade union branches. This handicap was somewhat reduced by a strong campaign extremely well organised from headquarters – so well organised, in fact, that the local Conservatives were instructed to imitate it.[16] Particular use was made by Labour of the mass canvass; no doubt this was one factor that caused turnout to rise abruptly from 52·7 per cent to 66·2 per cent.

Labour's triumph in Mitcham was followed by two further Conservative losses. In a straight fight the Liberals gained the suburban Willesden East constituency while Labour captured their first ever seat in Liverpool, the marginal Edge Hill division which was won largely on Conservative abstentions (turnout fell from 70·5 per cent to 58·1 per cent).

After this flurry of by-election reverses, the next contests produced little excitement. The death of Sir O. Thomas, the sitting Independent Labour Member, enabled a fairly united Liberal Party in Anglesey to recapture a traditional Liberal stronghold. The very safe Conservative seat of Ludlow produced no excitement. With no organisation whatsoever, Labour's intervention was rewarded with only 7·8 per cent of the poll. As one leading Labour agent bemoaned after the election, virtually every working-class Labour man still continued to vote for the Liberal.[17]

In the Berwick-upon-Tweed by-election, where the sitting National Liberal had been unseated on petition and his wife subsequently stood as an official Conservative in his place, the voting revealed very little change. The intervention of a Labour candidate again hit the Liberal share of the poll, while

[15] For the reluctance of the local Labour Party to contest the seat at all, see R. McKibbin, 'Labour: The Evolution of a National Party', unpublished D.Phil. thesis (Oxford, 1971) p. 410.

[16] *Manchester Guardian*, 28 Feb, 1 Mar 1923.

[17] McKibbin, op. cit., p. 273.

the Conservative vote was almost exactly that polled by the National Liberal the previous November – perfect evidence, if any were needed, of the extent to which nominal National Liberals were so often Conservatives in all but name. As in Ludlow, Labour intervention was probably the cause of the increase in turnout.

With very little comfort from previous by-elections, the Liberals were able to console themselves with a gain in the Tiverton by-election on 21 June 1923. In a very high poll (88·1 per cent), the Conservatives also increased their total vote while the Liberals gained victory by 403 votes. Little of significance can really be interpreted from the result, since whereas Labour had contested the division officially in 1922, the same candidate in 1923 was not officially endorsed and polled only 495 votes.

Much more significant of the standing of the Liberals were the by-elections in Morpeth and Leeds Central. In the mining division of Morpeth, which Labour had won in 1922 on a minority vote, the Conservatives stood down to give the Liberals a clear run. The result was a Labour triumph, with 60·5 per cent of the vote on an increased turnout. It was yet further evidence that the miners had finally deserted the Liberals. Similarly, in Leeds Central, in a three-cornered contest, the Liberal share of the vote in this Conservative-held seat slumped from 22·2 per cent to 11·0 per cent.

The final three contested by-elections (four by-elections were pending at the Dissolution on 16 November 1923) all occurred in safe Conservative territory. A second by-election in Portsmouth South was caused by the appointment of the Rt Hon. L. O. Wilson, the sitting Conservative, as Governor of Bombay. On a very low poll (54·9 per cent), the Conservatives easily retained the seat against Liberal opposition. The Yeovil by-election, on 30 October 1923, was perhaps most significant as an example of Liberal difficulties in recapturing votes that had been lost to Labour. Not having fought the seat in 1922, the Liberals were unable to dislodge Labour from second place at the by-election.

Whereas the Yeovil Liberals were at least attempting to regain lost ground, no such animation stirred what remained of the ranks of the Rutland and Stamford Liberals. No Liberal had contested the division in 1922 and none appeared at the by-election, despite warnings by senior officers of the Eastern Counties Liberal Federation that such lack of action would cause irreparable damage to the future prospects of the party.[18] In a straight fight with Labour, the Conservatives easily retained the seat.

In all, despite the losses suffered by the Conservatives in March, the more recent by-elections had not shown any signs of a major shift of votes against the government. Rather, the significance of the by-elections had been in Labour's ability to consolidate and extend its gains in industrial areas – mainly at the expense of the Liberals – and Labour's slow but definite advance in rural areas, again hitting hardest at the Liberals. Certainly, the by-elections gave little indication of the electoral earthquake that was to come with Baldwin's disastrous tariff election on 6 December 1923, but they had not, in any case, been fought on the tariff question.

[18] Eastern Counties Liberal Federation, Minutes, Executive Committee, 1 Oct 1923.

7 The Coming of the Election

The position of the Liberal Party was transformed almost overnight, and the future of British politics completely altered in October 1923, when Baldwin decided to lead his party into a tariff election. The motives behind Baldwin's decision, and the chronology of events that led to a December election, have now been fairly well established.[1] There is still no substantive evidence to support the view that Baldwin feared Lloyd George was about to launch his own campaign for Preference, although the latest biography of Baldwin still repeats the story.[2] What is clear is that, in Protection, Baldwin saw an issue that would separate for ever the Coalition Conservatives from the Free Trade Coalition Liberals.

In his desire to reunite the Conservative Party, Baldwin achieved a double irony: he split his own party over the issue whilst achieving the goal that had eluded all Liberals – a seeming reconciliation of Lloyd George and Asquith.

The campaign and results of the 1923 election, with the Conservative débâcle in such areas as Lancashire and the widespread Liberal and Labour gains in the country, cannot be rightly interpreted in isolation. They need to be seen against the background of warnings delivered to Baldwin by almost all his senior Cabinet colleagues over the inadequacy of his policy, the tactical errors of an immediate dissolution and the constituency opposition and unpreparedness of his party. All these factors, ignored by Baldwin, were to aid the Liberal Party and make possible the sensation of December

[1] See K. Middlemas and J. Barnes, *Baldwin: A Biography* (1969) pp. 158–77.

[2] H. M. Hyde, *Baldwin* (1973) p. 181. It remains true that J. C. C. Davidson, one of Baldwin's closest confidants, suffered something of a neurosis concerning Lloyd George.

1923. It was not so much Protection which proved the downfall of the Conservatives as Baldwin's method of launching his policy on the country.

Although several leading Conservatives later concurred with Baldwin's plan for an immediate dissolution, every senior Cabinet colleague at one time argued against an early election. Their arguments proved a classic example of wisdom before the event.

The position of Baldwin's most senior colleagues needs to be briefly summarised.

NEVILLE CHAMBERLAIN (CHANCELLOR OF THE EXCHEQUER)

Although an advocate of Protection, Chamberlain advised against an early dissolution. Chamberlain's plan was to go in for a few extra duties in November, then to lead up by an educative campaign to a more thorough-going policy by the time of a general election.[3] Indeed, Chamberlain added his voice to the *Spectator* and *Sunday Times* by suggesting the idea of a referendum. He wrote to Baldwin:

> I must say I think the idea is worth serious consideration . . . . I speak at Leeds tomorrow night. Do you see any objection to my sending up a kite – to test the wind.[4]

Presumably, Baldwin negatived this plan, for it was not mentioned at Leeds.

L. S. AMERY (FIRST LORD OF THE ADMIRALTY)

Amery was widely blamed for the early election. In fact he cautioned strongly against it, writing to Baldwin:

> I am still not sure there is not a good deal to be said for postponing the election until after the introduction of the Budget.[5]

---

[3] See K. Feiling, *Neville Chamberlain* (1946) p. 108.
[4] Baldwin Papers, F35/59, Neville Chamberlain to Baldwin, 4 Nov 1923.
[5] Baldwin Papers, F35/60, Amery to Baldwin, 5 Nov 1923.

He continued:

> Every Free Trader would in fact be put on the defensive to explain by what fresh taxes he is to make the Budget square if he foregoes the tariff revenue.

Amery wrote again to Baldwin three days later:

> I hear there is a great move for an immediate election on the ground that we should then carry the country on the general idea before criticism has become effective. I confess I am very alarmed at that. Criticism can become much more effective in 3 weeks than a constructive policy can be explained.[6]

W. C. BRIDGEMAN (HOME SECRETARY)

Bridgeman supported Protection but warned against a hurried election. He wrote to Baldwin:

> I also feel that there is no need for hurry, as any fiscal change will not help unemployment this winter . . . and I have an idea there is a kind of turn for the better. . . . Good luck to you – but be careful.[7]

Bridgeman went on to warn Baldwin:

> . . . our agricultural and fiscal policy requires more elaboration before we can take the plunge into an election – it will not be enough to go with a general expression of opinion that there should be protection and bounties.

VISCOUNT CAVE (LORD CHANCELLOR)

Cave, like his colleagues, advocated caution. He warned Baldwin:

> Bonar Law, who is a shrewd judge, could not carry the election of last November without a pledge . . . . Is there anything to show that you could do so now, only 11 months later? The English . . . are slow thinkers, and require time to think over a new departure.[8]

[6] Baldwin Papers, F35/71, Amery to Baldwin, 8 Nov 1923. In this letter, Amery delivered a strong warning to Baldwin over the shortcomings of Conservative agricultural policy.

[7] Baldwin Papers, F35/32, Bridgeman to Baldwin, 24 Oct 1923.

[8] Baldwin Papers, F35/37, Cave to Baldwin, 25 Oct 1923.

MARQUESS CURZON (FOREIGN SECRETARY)

Curzon was among the most vociferous critics of the early election. He wrote to his wife of

> the recklessness with which the Government and the country, entirely contrary to the wishes of either, had been plunged into the General Election by the arbitrary fiat of a single weak and ignorant man.[9]

The letter continued:

> Jim Salisbury is talking of resigning . . . . Derby is furious, and says Europe is dominated by two madmen, Poincaré and Mussolini, and England is ruled by a damned idiot, Baldwin.

In addition to these five Cabinet members, holding between them the most important offices of state, there was the group of Free Traders within the Cabinet opposed not only to an early election but to the policy of Protection. This group was made up as follows:

1. VISCOUNT NOVAR (SECRETARY OF STATE FOR SCOTLAND)

Novar was the least influential of this group. He seems to have been consulted only rarely, and his position can be rapidly portrayed in the rather plaintive letter sent to Baldwin:

> We believed . . . that any step so grave as that you now propose entailing an immediate election, would be disclosed to your colleagues and be discussed fully in Cabinet before it was irrevocably made.[10]

Novar's plea for a referendum was not taken up by Baldwin despite the warnings that an election 'may result in handing over the fortunes of the country to the Socialist Party'.[11]

2. LORD ROBERT CECIL (LORD PRIVY SEAL)

Cecil was placed in particular difficulty by the Baldwin policy. Insult was added to injury by the fact that he was not fully

---

[9] Quoted in L. Mosley, *Curzon: The End of an Epoch* (1960) p. 182.
[10] Baldwin Papers, F35/35, Novar to Baldwin, 24 Oct 1923.
[11] Baldwin Papers, F35/79, Novar to Baldwin, 8 Nov 1923.

informed of what was happening. Not surprisingly, Cecil's correspondence with Baldwin was consistently critical. He warned that an election before Christmas would be 'exceedingly bad policy' because of the difficulties the constituencies would face.[12] Cecil's letter continued in stronger vein:

> No one wants a general election. It is very expensive and costs hundreds of thousands of pounds which might be devoted to productive employment . . . . It unsettles men's minds and creates the fear, or hope, of a Labour Government.[13]

3. DUKE OF DEVONSHIRE (COLONIAL SECRETARY)

Devonshire's position was made quite clear to Baldwin in a letter sent the day before the Plymouth speech. Devonshire wrote:

> I fail to see how the far-reaching proposals you made will, to any appreciable extent, relieve unemployment during the coming months. Is there, therefore, any useful purpose to be served by raising the big issues now.[14]

As Devonshire stressed, if 'dumping' was a major problem, then action could be taken by extending the existing Safeguarding of Industries Act.

4. MARQUESS OF SALISBURY (LORD PRESIDENT OF THE COUNCIL)

Like Devonshire, Salisbury was against the policy, although willing to bend over as far as possible to aid Baldwin. Salisbury wrote to Baldwin:

> I go a long way about anti-dumping . . . and might be willing to go further on the existing lines of widening somewhat the customs duties . . . but a regular Protectionist tariff is a much stiffer proposition.[15]

---

[12] Baldwin Papers, F35/65, Lord Robert Cecil to Baldwin, 7 Nov 1923.

[13] Cecil himself deliberately did not seek re-election in Hitchin, asking Baldwin instead for a peerage. See Viscount Cecil of Chelwood, *All the Way* (1949) pp. 179–80.

[14] Baldwin Papers, F35/33, Devonshire to Baldwin, 24 Oct 1923.

[15] Baldwin Papers, F35/22, Salisbury to Baldwin, 19 Oct 1923.

Salisbury went on to suggest a possible alternative course of action, including fiscal retaliation against dumping, the encouragement of emigration and a bounty on wheat cultivation while the agricultural depression lasted.

5.   EARL OF DERBY (SECRETARY OF STATE FOR WAR)

Derby's position was possibly the most unenviable of all. It was hardly surprising that he wrote to Salvidge complaining bitterly that he was sick over the whole election.[16] Derby reflected the opinion of Lancashire Conservatism when he wrote to Stanley Jackson that everybody was united in protesting against an immediate election or even an election next year.[17]

In even stronger terms Derby wrote to Younger:

> I think we really must put our foot down and prevent elections being sprung upon us without any of those who know about election work being consulted: with the Chief Agent of the Party a candidate himself and away the whole time; and with a policy which was only disclosed in brief to the Cabinet 48 hours before it was launched on the public.[18]

The position of the remaining eight members of the Cabinet was again overwhelmingly against an early election. There is evidence in the Baldwin papers that two Ministers, Edward Wood and Sir William Joynson-Hicks, both delivered warnings to Baldwin. Wood, the President of the Board of Education, who acted as mediator between Baldwin and the Free Trade group in the Cabinet, wrote to the Prime Minister:

> There are, no doubt, a good many reasons (January fox-hunting among them) which support having an election, which is inevitable, as early as possible. But I think it is vital we should give Parliament, and through Parliament the country, an adequate

[16] Derby Papers, Derby to Salvidge, 18 Nov 1923.
[17] Derby to Jackson, 9 Nov 1923, quoted in R. Churchill, *Lord Derby: King of Lancashire* (1959) p. 530.
[18] Derby to Younger, 1 Dec 1923, quoted ibid., p. 531.

opportunity of examining the question on which they are asked to pronounce.[19]

He continued:

> ... if this is not consistent with a December election (and making such attempt as I can to forecast dates I can scarcely see how it is) I think we should be acting both unwisely and wrongly, and should aggravate the difficulty of some of our number, if we were to attempt to 'snatch a verdict'.

In similar vein, Joynson-Hicks, the Minister of Health, although in full support of Protection, warned Baldwin of the dangers of his policy. In a lengthy letter, he asked Baldwin to consider the election from the following viewpoint:

(1) It would be most unpopular with our party in the house. They have all paid one thousand pounds to get there and their wives do not want to pay another thousand with a risk of being thrown out.
(2) It would be most unpopular with the City and commercial circles ... they want to be let alone for three years in order to have their promised tranquillity.

Joynson-Hicks went on to point out that the McKenna duties could easily be extended to such depressed industries as lace and tyres without violating Bonar Law's pledge. The letter concluded on a warning note:

> Anything like a General Tariff, for which I admit you want an election – would frighten a great many people, and I am not sure of the result. ... I am a pretty old electioneer, you know.[20]

Like Amery, Sir Philip Lloyd-Greame at the Board of Trade, although an equally convinced Protectionist, was worried over Baldwin's plans. He believed that, with public opinion probably still hostile to tariffs, it was essential to build up to an election by a planned, well-organised campaign on tariffs.[21] This was also the position of Sir Anderson Montague-Barlow, the Minister of Labour, Sir Laming

---

[19] Baldwin Papers, F35/11, Wood to Baldwin, 8 Nov 1923.
[20] Baldwin Papers, F35/30, Joynson-Hicks to Baldwin, 20 Oct 1923.
[21] A. Earl, 'The Political Life of Viscount Swinton, 1918–1938', unpublished MA thesis (Manchester, 1960) pp. 104–7.

Worthington-Evans, the Postmaster-General, and Sir Robert Sanders, the Minister of Agriculture.

The position of the remaining two Ministers is less easy to define. There is no evidence at all for Viscount Peel, the Secretary of State for India, who probably played no major part in these events. Sir Samual Hoare, the Secretary for Air, was an ardent Protectionist and may have encouraged Baldwin in his action. However, firm evidence of this is lacking.

In all, therefore, the overwhelming majority of the Cabinet had at one time or another put forward valid arguments against an immediate dissolution. The fact that Baldwin was able to call an election without cabinet resignations was less significant than the fact that the objections and fears of an early appeal to the country remained.

It was widely reported at the time that Baldwin's immediate election owed much to the advice of the party officials. The evidence does not support this view. The party's Principal Agent, Sir Reginald Hall, advised against an early dissolution, writing to Davidson:

> ... regarding last night; I adhere to my opinion; to rush an election now or in January is a gamble which gives most of the cards to the other side. Safeguarding of Industries – let it run for a year and we ought to be in clover.[22]

Another influential party organiser to advise strongly against an early election was Sir George Younger. He wrote to Baldwin:

> I still hold firmly to the view I expressed to you about not hurrying an appeal. The pitch must be carefully prepared .... Too much haste might be fatal.[23]

Younger added that the prevailing feeling in Scotland was strongly against an immediate election. Younger was also worried over finance for the election. As he wrote to Baldwin:

> I feel certain that many of our men who asked for no help last time will do so for this election, and all who got it last time will want increased grants now. ... I shouldn't wonder if this election was

[22] Davidson Papers, Hall to Davidson, 19 Oct 1923.
[23] Baldwin Papers, F35/67, Younger to Baldwin, 7 Nov 1923.

to cost £150–£160,000. . . it is difficult to see where all the money is to come from unless we can widen our subscription list.

Younger had a further reason to dislike an early election on the tariff question, since he was attempting to negotiate anti-Socialist pacts with the Liberal leaders. As he wrote to Baldwin:

I have gone so far as to discuss this, both with Pringle and Hogge. Now, however, that Asquith is going to make fiscal policy a party question, I suppose all chance of any arrangement has gone.[24]

The position of Stanley Jackson, the Chairman of the Party Organisation, is less easy to classify. There is no evidence that Jackson advised against an early election, although he must have been aware of discontent at the prospect. Derby, for example, had informed Jackson of the opposition in Lancashire.[25]

Another official who might have been expected to be consulted was Salvidge, the leader of Liverpool Conservatism. Salvidge, however, received the information of the election in the daily press. In addition, the Chief Whip, Commander Bolton Eyres-Monsell, protested strongly at the prospects of an imminent dissolution.[26] In fact the protests of Eyres-Monsell were a reflection of the widespread back-bench Conservative hostility, from all sections of the party, at the prospect of an early dissolution.

One such warning came from Colonel John Gretton, the MP for Burton, who wrote to Baldwin:

I would add that a General Election just now would be suicide for the party, and, much worse, the temporary eclipse of a great policy. When the government has acted (and much can be done without breaking the 'pledge') you will be able to ask the country to support your full proposals at a General Election.[27]

---

[24] Ibid.

[25] Derby Papers, Derby to Jackson, 9 Nov 1923.

[26] Churchill, *Lord Derby*, pp. 530–1.

[27] Baldwin Papers, F35/28, Gretton to Baldwin, 24 Oct 1923. Five days earlier, Gretton had strongly advised Baldwin against making his Protection speech at a *party* meeting rather than putting it forward as a national policy.

An even more urgent warning was delivered by Sir Robert Bird, the MP for Wolverhampton West. In a telegram to Jackson, Bird declared:

> My friends and self protest strongly against any declaration by Premier for protective tariffs . . . consider moment not ripe . . . action thus forced prematurely provokes complications additional to those already sufficiently numerous at home and abroad.[28]

A similar strong warning was delivered to Amery by Sir Arthur Steel-Maitland, the MP for Erdington, who wrote that 'over the question of an early General Election, I don't like it a little bit . . . and wish that it could be avoided.[29]

Despite increasing his majority, Sir Charles Wilson, the Member for Leeds Central, wrote to a colleague declaring that the decision to hold a snap election was 'a grave blunder' which 'savoured too much of the act of a dictator'.[30]

This back-bench discontent at an early election was particularly prevalent in Scotland. One Conservative to make no attempt to disguise his opposition was the retiring Member for Dunbarton, who declared that:

> He had no idea a month ago that an election would take place so soon. Speaking generally, and from his heart, he had never seen any necessity for it. He had made that perfectly plain both to his party in the House of Commons and to Colonel Jackson.[31]

Similarly, when the Scottish Liberal, MacCallum Scott, chanced to meet Sir Robert Horne on the train to Glasgow, Scott found Horne 'very much perturbed by Baldwin's action in precipitating an election at this moment'.[32] Horne believed that the government's policy was 'ill-considered and hastily improvised' and that the issue had been put before the country in its crudest form. These were not isolated criticisms.

---

[28] Telegram, dated 23 Oct 1923, Bird to Jackson in West Wolverhampton Conservative Association, Minutes, Executive Committee, 20 Nov 1923.

[29] Baldwin Papers, F35/88, Steel-Maitland to Amery, 10 Nov 1923.

[30] Baldwin Papers, F42/145, Wilson to Wood, 12 Dec 1923.

[31] *Dumbarton Herald*, 21 Nov 1923.

[32] MacCallum Scott diary, entry dated 13 Nov 1923.

Indeed, according to the Liberal Member for Westbury, there was not a single Conservative to be found in the lobby who could understand what Baldwin was aiming for or explain what had driven him into his present course of action.[33]

It is of course quite possible that Baldwin received influential advice from outside the Cabinet, the party chiefs and the back-benchers in favour of an early election. There is, however, no evidence to support this view. On the contrary, such people as Geoffrey Dawson, the editor of *The Times*, W. A. S. Hewins, the influential Tariff Reformer, and William Massey and J. C. Smuts at the Imperial Conference, all warned Baldwin about his proposals.[34]

Indeed, Baldwin not only precipitated an election against the advice of Cabinet colleagues and the party back-benchers, but with the leaders of the national press either positively hostile or at best unenthusiastic.[35]

Ironically, public opinion at the time widely believed that Baldwin, far from having instigated the election, was a mere puppet in the hands of the party hierarchy. Thus, one provincial paper found Baldwin an 'amiable well-meaning man', but lacking 'the ability and strength of character to withstand the hotheads of his party'.[36] Similarly, the *Sunday Times* sought to identify the 'power behind the throne', while the *Daily News* believed that Baldwin had been rashly guided by the 'youngest and most inexperienced members of the Cabinet'.[37] Younger, Hall, Worthington-Evans and Davidson were all mentioned in different journals as the architects of a snap election.[38]

The net result of all these factors was that the Liberal Party entered the election of 1923 on the most favourable of all

[33] Quoted in *Sheffield Daily Telegraph*, 15 Nov 1923.

[34] For Hewins's position, see W. A. S. Hewins, *Apologia of an Imperialist* 2 vols. (1929).

[35] For Dawson's cautious reaction, see J. E. Wrench, *Geoffrey Dawson and our Times* (1955) pp. 222–3.

[36] *Carlisle Journal*, 16 Nov 1923. For a similar accusation, see *Worcestershire Echo*, 13 Nov 1923.

[37] *Daily News*, 8 Dec 1923.

[38] *Daily Express*, 12 Feb 1924; *Essex County Telegraph*, 17 Nov 1923; *Bristol Times and Mirror*, 17 Nov 1923.

8 The Evidence of the Nominations

The revival of Protection, together with the onset of a December election, transformed the position of the Liberal Party. Baldwin succeeded where every Liberal had failed in reuniting the two warring Liberal factions.

Any doubts on Lloyd George's future course of action were resolved when, landing at Southampton on his return from the United States, the former Prime Minister declared himself unreservedly for Free Trade. The road to Liberal reunion lay ahead.

The formal details of reunion were discussed on the morning of 13 November at a meeting attended by Lloyd George, Mond, Asquith and Vivian Phillipps.[1]

As a result of this meeting it was agreed that the election should be fought by the united Liberal forces under a Liberal Campaign Committee. Lloyd George raised the question of the chairmanship, and wanted someone not hitherto associated with either faction. Sir Edward Beauchamp was eventually suggested by Lloyd George. To finance the election, it was agreed to have a united Liberal Campaign Fund, while all candidates were to stand as Liberals 'without suffix or prefix'. Sir William Edge and Sir Alfred Cope for the National Liberals, with Vivian Phillipps and Geoffrey Howard, were deputed to settle rival candidatures.[2] It was agreed there should be no duplication of election literature.

The most interesting discussion centred on the Liberal campaign strategy. Free Trade presented no problems, for Lloyd George spoke as an unqualified Free Trader.

[1] The following account is based on the material in the Gladstone Papers, BM Add. MSS 46,475, F253/259.
[2] In Scotland this task was delegated to Sir Robert Hutchinson and Wood.

Regarding unemployment, Lloyd George suggested the use of national credit during depression, while the Asquithians proposed an extended unemployment insurance scheme. On foreign policy, it was decided to launch a major attack on the government's handling of the Ruhr question and Reparations. These lines of attack, on Free Trade, unemployment and foreign affairs, were to be expected. Nothing very radical or new was proposed. The meeting agreed that nothing corresponding to a 'Newcastle Programme' could or ought to be attempted, but that what was wanted was 'a limited number of bold but effective pronouncements'. A manifesto on these lines was drafted the same evening by Mond and Phillipps. This decision was of vital significance, for the whole Liberal campaign was subsequently to centre on a negative defence of Free Trade.

The ease with which reunion seemed to be accomplished, and a campaign policy agreed on, in fact disguised several factors. It certainly disguised the extent to which Lloyd George retained control not only over his money, but also over his Coalition Liberal organisation.

The financial arrangements soon caused considerable acrimony. At the 13 November meeting, Lloyd George had promised considerable financial support, although no record of the exact amount has survived. It was left to Lord Gladstone to be responsible for collecting Lloyd George's contribution from Sir Alfred Cope. After more discussions, it was agreed that a contribution of £100,000 from the Lloyd George wing and £50,000 from the Independent Liberal headquarters would be sufficient. But actually getting the money out of Lloyd George proved less easy. By 30 November, Gladstone had received only £30,000 and was experiencing extreme difficulty in persuading Cope to fix a meeting with him. When, on 30 November, they at last met, Gladstone told Cope that he was still waiting for a further £70,000. At this, Cope replied that he had no authority to make decisions while the Trustees were away. In this atmosphere the seeds of a future conflict were already present.

Nor did Lloyd George's outwardly complete reunion with the Asquithian Liberals prevent him attending – at Beaverbrook's invitation – a last reunion of the old Coalition leaders at Cherkley on 12 November. In addition to Beaverbrook and Lloyd George, Churchill, Birkenhead and Austen Chamberlain were all present. All were optimistic that the coming election would provide the means of discomfiting Baldwin. The plan agreed at the meeting (although subsequently it miscarried badly and the whole plot failed) was that Birkenhead and Austen Chamberlain would accept Baldwin's overtures to join the government; Birkenhead would then rally Lancashire to the Conservative Free Trade cause, Lloyd George and Churchill would fight the cause as Liberals, Beaverbrook would (rather less neatly) attack Protection and advocate Empire Free Trade in the press. Then, with Baldwin ousted at the polls, the Free Traders of both parties would come together under a new Lloyd George Coalition.

The plot (rather unreal even at the outset) foundered when Arnold Bennett (who had also been at the Cherkley meeting) accidently revealed the plot to a *Daily News* journalist. Baldwin, in alarm, withdrew his offer to Birkenhead and Austen Chamberlain – leaving Birkenhead without any practical alternative to stumping Lancashire anyway. There was, in any case, a deeper cause of the failure of the plot.

Lloyd George, having taken up Free Trade and rejoined the Liberal ranks, had to become Asquith's second. As Beaverbrook expressed it, 'he really had a choice between death and surrender on fairly easy terms'.[3] The Free Trade Liberal Party was in Asquith's control, not Lloyd George's. Lloyd George's position after the election, when his National Liberal followers were decimated, only reinforced this realisation upon Lloyd George.

Nor is it likely that Churchill ever really believed that this plan was a likely starter. It is possible that Churchill saw the 1923 election as a way of reingratiating himself in the Asquithian party at the expense of Lloyd George, whom he (very rightly) believed to be bitterly unpopular in some sections of the party. Certainly, Beaverbrook believed this to be so.

Although rumoured in the press, Lloyd George's reluctance to leave his Coalition past behind him did not mar the

---

[3] A. J. P. Taylor, *Beaverbrook* (1972) p. 219.

galvanising effect of Liberal reunion on constituency morale and activity. Hitherto dormant associations were brought by the onset of Free Trade and a reunited party into hurried activity. The net result was that the Liberals were able to field 457 candidates. The Conservatives increased their total from 482 to 536, a factor which disguised the real decrease in their aggregate vote.

At the Dissolution, the endorsed Labour candidates, including sitting Members, numbered only 239. Within a fortnight nearly 200 additional candidates were placed and Labour entered the election with 427 official candidates, compared with 414 in 1922 and 361 in 1918. In all, 1,446 candidates sought election, an increase of five over the 1922 election.

The ease with which Liberal reunion was achieved at national level was not so easily repeated in the constituencies. Five years of division were not healed overnight. Indeed, in two constituencies rival Liberal candidates were adopted in 1923. In Cardiganshire, the scene of the bitter by-election of February 1921, a rival Independent Liberal, R. H. Morris, successfully contested the seat against the sitting National Liberal.[4] A similar situation arose in the Camborne division where Captain A. H. Moreing, the retiring National Liberal, lost his seat despite the official support of the local Conservative Association.

In addition, in several Scottish constituencies rival Liberal candidatures were only narrowly avoided. As one correspondent found in Roxburgh and Selkirk, the quality of Liberal reunion looked better in a manifesto than it did in real life.[5] In the crofting counties of northern Scotland, Liberal disunity was widespread. In Ross a reunion meeting broke up in disarray and throughout the campaign the Independent Liberals continued a vendetta against Ian Macpherson, the sitting National Liberal.[6] Similarly, in Argyll the National

---

[4] For a detailed discussion, see Kenneth O. Morgan 'Cardiganshire Politics: The Liberal Ascendancy, 1885–1923', *Ceredigion*, V, 4 (1967), pp. 333-7.

[5] *Scotsman*, 22 Nov 1923.

[6] *Glasgow Herald*, 21 Nov 1923. For a similar position in the Western Isles, see *Scotsman*, 19 Nov 1923.

Liberal Member, Sir William Sutherland, was adopted without the knowledge of the 'Wee Frees', who then refused him
active support during the campaign.[7] In Moray and Nairn,
after a stormy reunion meeting, the Independent Liberals
vowed to vote Conservative in order to unseat the National
Liberal. Maybe this threat was fulfilled, for the Conservatives
gained the seat.[8]

Outside Scotland, local reunion was often achieved only
with difficulty. In Pontefract local divisions were healed only
by adopting a candidate with no previous connection with the
constituency, whilst at Barnsley reunion was achieved only at
the last minute of the eleventh hour in the calming atmosphere of the Young Men's Christian Association.[9]

The essential fact of constituency Liberal reunion was that
it came too late for the local associations to rebuild their
electoral organisation. In a sense, it is remarkable that the
Liberals were able to fight on such a wide front as they did in
view of the chronic weakness of party organisation. However,
in this respect the party was saved by the massive injection of
finance from headquarters.

With the rallying cry of Free Trade, many Liberal Associations were restored to a sense of purpose which they had not
known since 1910 or 1906. However, perhaps as important as
those associations revived by the advent of Protection were
those constituencies in which, even in 1923, no candidates
were fielded. They were a significant comment on the extent
to which morale had collapsed.

Thus, at Grimsby the refusal of the local association to
contest the division, even though funds were available,
provoked open discontent among rank-and-file Liberals.[10]
Likewise, in Westmorland, despite a strong feeling in favour

---

[7] *Scotsman*, 22 Nov 1923.

[8] *Scotsman*, 19 Nov 1923. For examples in the Lowlands, see Midlothian
and South Peebles (*Scotsman*, 20 Nov 1923) and Berwick and Haddingtonshire (*The Times*, 22 Nov 1923).

[9] *Yorkshire Post*, 20 Nov 1923; *Sheffield Daily Telegraph*, 19 Nov 1923.

[10] *Yorkshire Post*, 24 Nov 1923.

of fighting the constituency, a meeting of the Liberal Executive at Kendal took no action.[11]

This reluctance to bring forward candidates was particularly noticeable in industrial seats held by Labour. So, in the Durham City division, although the local association had been reorganised since the 1922 election, no action was taken to field a candidate. Similarly, criticism in the Spennymoor division at the lack of a candidate forced the association secretary to pledge that a candidate would be obtained for the next contest. The promise was not fulfilled.[12]

A similar story of inaction can be found in South Wales. In the Ogmore division the Maesteg branch requested a meeting of the constituency Liberal Executive to consider fielding a candidate. Nothing was done, no candidate appeared and Vernon Hartshorn was returned unopposed for Labour, as he was to be again in October 1924.[13]

Several factors explain this lack of activity. It was a mixture of lack of finance, sometimes an unwillingness to split the anti-Labour vote, sometimes a defeatist attitude in a safe seat, but most of all difficulty in attracting candidates. This difficulty in finding candidates was itself explained by a variety of factors. The split in the party and the lack of a radical policy had driven many younger men into the Labour ranks. In addition, one Federation Secretary emphasised the discouraging effect of the electoral system, giving Liberals in industrial seats little prospect of success but the certainty of heavy expenditure.[14]

The net result was that, in such less hopeful areas as Sheffield, the Liberals were engaged in a fruitless search for candidates. Certainly, in the Hillsborough and Brightside divisions the Liberals were still, after a two weeks' search, without a candidate. In the neighbouring Don Valley constituency, despite a decision of the Liberal Executive to field a

[11] *Carlisle Journal*, 23 Nov 1923. When a Liberal appeared in 1929, the first since 1910, he took over 38 per cent of the poll in a three-cornered contest.

[12] *Durham Chronicle*, 17 Nov, 1 Dec 1923.

[13] *Western Mail*, 24 Nov 1923.

[14] Midland Liberal Federation, Minutes, Executive Committee, 2 Feb 1923.

candidate, none could be found.[15] The Liberals were in a similar predicament at Seaham and Wansbeck.[16] This difficulty in attracting candidates was reflected in the large number of Liberals adopted at the last possible moment.[17]

In addition to this symptom of decline, there was also considerable evidence of the party in 1923, particularly in industrial areas, negotiating electoral pacts with the Conservatives.

Indeed, only the resurrection of the Free Trade controversy prevented widespread local anti-Socialist pacts in 1923. As it was, these pacts were still frequent occurrences in areas where Labour had secured victory in 1922.

This was particularly true of Scotland. As the *Scotsman* commented on Glasgow, 'but for the introduction of the fiscal question, there is little doubt that a determined effort would have been made by Unionists and Liberals to combine forces against the Socialists'.[18]

Younger, in fact, had made just such a determined effort. He wrote to Baldwin:

I have been urging some arrangement with the Liberals to avoid three-cornered contests and I have gone so far as to discuss this with both Pringle and Hogge. Now, however, that Asquith is (obviously?) going to make fiscal policy a party question I suppose all chance of any arrangement has gone.[19]

Younger's pessimism was exaggerated, for a variety of local pacts was organised in the Scottish burghs. This was true of Dunfermline, where the Liberals enjoyed the active support of leading Conservatives, while in Stirling and Falkirk the Conservatives refrained from fielding a candidate after seeing a deputation from the Liberals.[20] At Kirkcaldy the co-operation which dated from the by-election of 1921 still continued, while in the double-Member constituency of Dundee the strong faction in the Conservative camp which

[15] *Yorkshire Post*, 19 Nov 1923; *Sheffield Daily Telegraph*, 23 Nov 1923.
[16] *Durham Chronicle*, 24 Nov 1923.
[17] The list of 46 'late' nominations in *The Times*, 24 Nov 1923, contained 36 Liberals, but only 8 Labour and 2 Conservatives.
[18] *Scotsman*, 26 Nov 1923.
[19] Baldwin Papers, F35/67, Younger to Baldwin, 7 Nov 1923.
[20] *Dundee Advertiser*, 15 Nov 1923; *Scotsman*, 24 Nov 1923.

favoured fielding only one candidate was successful.[21] Within
Glasgow, an unofficial Liberal delegation approached the
Tradeston Conservatives, whilst in the Govan division the
Liberals enjoyed the 'benevolent neutrality of the
Unionists'.[22]

It was mentioned earlier that, with the exception of
Nottinghamshire and Derbyshire, the mining areas were,
from an early date, regions in which the Liberals and Conservatives formed tacit anti-Socialist alliances.

This was particularly true in 1924, but there were several
examples in December 1923, especially in South Wales. In
the Aberavon division, which had elected Ramsay Mac-
Donald in 1922 on a minority vote in a three-cornered fight,
negotiations for a pact began. Eventually the Liberal candidate who was already in the field withdrew, while a circular
was sent out by senior members of the Aberavon Liberal
Executive urging their members to vote Conservative. As this
circular explained:

> '. . . we have the assurance of Conservative support in our fight in
> this division . . . the defeat of the Socialist leader on this occasion
> will clear the way for the return of a Liberal when the time
> comes.'[23]

In the Rhondda East division a Conservative candidate,
who was given a clear field in 1923 in return for the straight
fight the National Liberal had enjoyed in 1922, came forward
as a 'Unionist Free Trader and Anti-Socialist', having been
officially adopted by both the Conservative and Liberal
Executives.[24] In the adjacent Rhondda West, similar moves
united both parties behind a Liberal candidate.

---

[21] *Glasgow Herald*, 16 Nov 1923; *Dundee Advertiser*, 21 Nov 1923.

[22] *Glasgow Herald*, 19, 22 Nov 1923. Moves by the Executive committee
of the North Lanarkshire Conservatives for a pact failed to materialise.

[23] *South Wales Daily Post*, 20 Nov 1923; *New Leader*, 14 Dec 1923. In
October 1924 the unsuccessful Conservative candidate in the 1923 election
wrote to the Aberavon Conservatives urging them to honour the pact by
giving the Liberals a straight fight. This was done. *South Wales News*, 14
Oct 1924.

[24] Election Address, Rhondda East.

The Durham coalfield provides a particularly good example of the extent to which the older parties in 1923 avoided splitting the anti-Socialist vote.

In 1924 the Secretary of the Durham County Unionist Association admitted that 'certain arrangements' had been made, on the initiative of the Conservatives, to avoid three-cornered contests.[25] The net result was that, of the eleven county seats in Durham, only one triangular fight took place, in the Bishop Auckland division.

These examples from South Wales and Durham have parallels in other mining areas. Thus, in Mansfield, where the Liberal candidate had enjoyed Conservative support at the last election, similar support was forthcoming in 1923. The Mansfield Conservative Association endorsed his candidature and prominent Conservatives campaigned actively for him.

Outside these mining areas anti-Socialist pacts were organised in several large cities, most particularly in the industrial areas of Bristol and Newcastle. In Bristol South the sitting Liberal, Sir Beddoe Rees, enjoyed the full support of the local Conservative Association.[26] In the industrial Kent division of Dartford a joint election committee of representatives from the Liberal and Conservative Associations was formed to promote George Jarrett's candidature as a Constitutionalist.[27]

Similarly, in Wolverhampton a Liberal was unopposed in the East division, while Sir Robert Bird was faced with only Labour opposition in Wolverhampton West. Close Liberal–Conservative co-operation also appeared in the Pottery towns in such divisions as Burslem, Stoke and Newcastle-under-Lyme.[28]

As in municipal elections, several industrial Lancashire constituencies continued a local anti-Socialist pact. This was

[25] *Yorkshire Post*, 13 Oct 1924. In Consett, Morpeth and Houghton the Liberals received Conservative support.

[26] *Bristol Times and Mirror*, 20 Nov 1923.

[27] *Dartford Chronicle and Kentish Times*, 23 Nov 1923. Jarrett adroitly bridged the fiscal question by declaring that he was neither a doctrinaire Free Trader nor a Tariff Reformer.

[28] *Staffordshire Advertiser*, 17 Nov 1923.

true of Accrington and also of Heywood and Radcliffe, where the local Conservative Association passed a resolution supporting the Liberal.[29] Perhaps the best example was the double-Member constituency of Blackburn, where a Free Trade Conservative and a Liberal ran in harness. In the election the Conservative polled 28,505 votes, the Liberal 31,117. No fewer than 25,518 voters split their ballot paper for the Conservative–Liberal pact.

In addition to these examples, in several cases active negotiations for a pact were undertaken, only to break down over disagreement on some point. In Carlisle, where both the Conservatives and Liberals were sympathetic to a pact, the Carlisle Conservative Executive had gone so far as to appoint a specific deputation to arrange matters with the Liberals. The initiative failed, since no agreement was forthcoming over a suitable candidate.[30]

One sitting Liberal Member to make repeated, though unsuccessful, attempts to retain Conservative support was Brigadier-General Edward Spears in the Loughborough division. At first, the Executive Committee of the Loughborough Conservatives gave him assurances of support. A later meeting rescinded this by 203 votes to 72. Even so, some Conservative councillors took the chair at Liberal meetings, and the Liberal agent thanked those Conservatives who had voted for Spears.[31]

It is a significant comment on the Liberal Party that, at the same time that pacts and unofficial agreements were negotiated with the Conservatives in industrial and mining constituencies, there were still lingering attempts to secure local pacts with Labour in certain areas.

In 1922 the circumstances of the election led to a fair number of local Lib–Lab pacts, usually on an unofficial basis. Thus, it was not unusual to find Liberal and Labour candidates in adjoining constituencies running parallel campaigns. The Labour candidate in Leicester East and the Liberal in Leicester South co-operated unofficially, but did not

[29] *Birmingham Post*, 21 Nov 1923; *Nelson Leader*, 14 Dec 1923.
[30] *Yorkshire Post*, 16 Nov 1923.
[31] *Leicester Mercury*, 19 Nov, 8 Dec 1923.

acknowledge their support openly.[32] However, even in 1922 these local pacts were running into increasing hostilities from divisional Labour Parties eager to contest every seat in their neighbourhood. Thus, even in 1922, Labour support for Liberals in Torquay and Birkenhead East led to dissent within the Labour ranks.

The indecisive Liberal attitude to Labour (and the experiences of the by-elections) all made it less likely in 1923 that these pacts would continue. However, the speed with which the Dissolution was announced and, even more important, Labour's lack of finance in some rural seats led to several examples of co-operation.

In the Eastbourne division a formal agreement gave the Liberals a straight fight against the sitting Conservative.[33] At Newark it was widely reported that a Labour candidate would stand aside if a Liberal sympathetic towards Labour were adopted. There was a similar sentiment within the constituency Liberal Association: in the event, a joint committee was formed and a candidate acceptable to both sides adopted.[34]

In Staffordshire an agreement existed that Labour would not stand in Stone if the Liberals refrained from fielding a candidate in Leek.[35] There was a similar understanding in Shropshire, where Labour left the Liberals a clear field in the Shrewsbury division on the implied understanding that no Liberal intervened in the Wrekin. The result in 1923 was the first ever Liberal victory in Shrewsbury and a Labour victory in the Wrekin. Likewise, in Dorset the Liberals received a free run in the North and Labour in East Dorset.[36]

Much more numerous were those constituencies where, once Labour found itself without sufficient funds or organisation to contest, the local association then gave active and public assistance to the Liberal candidate. At Denbigh the local Labour chairman publicly urged the pledged party

---

[32] Kinnear, *The British Voter*, p. 200.
[33] *The Times*, 21 Nov 1923.
[34] *Yorkshire Post*, 16 Nov 1923.
[35] *Birmingham Post*, 22 Oct 1924.
[36] *Bournemouth Daily Echo*, 14 Nov 1923.

members to vote for Ellis Davies. In Huntingdonshire, where lack of finance had prevented a Labour candidate, the divisional association issued a manifesto calling on all members to vote Liberal, while in such divisions as Finchley and Hemel Hempstead the successful Liberals subsequently thanked Labour for their platform assistance.[37]

Likewise, radical Liberals returned the compliment by urging pledged Liberals to cast their vote for Labour: the Liberal Member for Louth addressed an open letter calling on Liberals to 'vote solid' for the Labour candidate in Holland-with-Boston. Nonconformist Liberal ministers took the chair at Labour meetings.[38] The Mitcham Liberal Association likewise issued a manifesto calling on all members to vote Labour, while at Maldon, a constituency in which for the first time in its history there was no Liberal candidate, Labour received active Liberal platform support.[39] There was similar assistance in South Norfolk.[40]

It was extremely rare, however, for co-operation to continue in the larger boroughs. It is true that in 1922 this had occurred in Rochester, Birkenhead and, possibly, Middlesbrough West.[41] In 1923 an unwritten and unofficial agreement continued in Birkenhead, for in the East division H. G. White, the sitting Liberal, faced no Labour opponent, while in the West division the Labour candidate had a straight fight against the Conservative. In Rochester, however, where there had been straight fights against Conservatives in 1922 in both Chatham and Gillingham, three-cornered contests took place in 1923.

In addition to Birkenhead, the only other borough in which co-operation survived was the double-Member constituency

---

[37] *Peterborough and Huntingdonshire Standard*, 16 Nov, 14 Dec 1923; *Finchley Press*, 14 Dec 1923; *Bedfordshire and Hertfordshire Telegraph*, 24 Nov 1923.

[38] *Lincolnshire Free Press*, 27 Nov, 4 Dec 1923.

[39] *Surrey County Herald*, 17 Nov 1923; *Essex County Telegraph*, 11 Dec 1923.

[40] *Norwich Mercury*, 15 Dec 1923.

[41] Kinnear, *The British Voter*, p. 108.

of Preston. Only one Liberal and one Labour candidate were fielded throughout the elections of the 1920s.[42]

Just as the figure of 457 Liberal candidates disguises a variety of pacts and local arrangements, so the Conservative total hides the considerable number of candidates who stood on a Free Trade platform in 1923. These were to have a significant effect on the unity and cohesion of the Conservative campaign.

If Baldwin had believed he would be able to lead a united party at constituency level into the election, he was much mistaken. Partly, Baldwin's discomfiture was the result of the number of Free Traders returned in November 1922. In that election Lancashire and Cheshire returned 13 avowed Free Traders.[43] Another 9 had been returned elsewhere.[44] In addition to these 22, there were those like the Member for Hexham who, although against a general tariff, favoured major extensions of the Safeguarding of Industries Act.

It soon became apparent that not all these Free Traders would accept this new departure. A first hint of the seriousness of discontent in Lancashire came with the resignation of Lieutenant-Colonel Albert Buckley, the Member for the

[42] In 1923 Labour polled 25,816 votes, the Liberal 25,155 and the Conservative 23,962. Some 21,335 votes were split between Liberal and Labour, while only 962 voted for one Conservative and one Liberal. 831 votes were split between Conservative and Labour.

[13] Kinnear, *The British Voter*, p. 102. These were as follows: C. Ainsworth (Bury), W. Brass (Clitheroe), W. J. H. Briggs (Manchester Blackley), J. B. B. Cohen (Liverpool Fairfield), Sir W. de Frece (Ashton-under-Lyne), D. Halstead (Rossendale), Sir S. H. H. Henn (Blackburn), W. Russell (Bolton), J. E. Singleton (Lancaster), Sir E. F. Stockton (Manchester Exchange), Sir G. Stewart (Wirral), T. Watts (Manchester Withington) and G. D. White (Southport). In addition, Lt. Cdr. F. W. Astbury, in Salford West, can be added to this list, for he was a Free Trader except that he was prepared to see Protection in the dye industry (*Gleanings and Memoranda*, Jan 1923, p. 49).

[44] These were: Lord H. C. Bentinck (Nottingham South), Lord Hugh Cecil (Oxford University), Lord Robert Cecil (Hitchin), R. B. Colvin (Epping), Maj F. H. Fawkes (Pudsey and Otley), Hon. C. James (Bromley), Sir E. Manville (Coventry), R. F. Roundell (Skipton) and D. E. Wallace (Rugby).

Waterloo division, as Parliamentary Secretary to the Department of Overseas Trade.[45]

A second resignation occurred in Clitheroe when Captain W. Brass, the sitting Member, resigned as Parliamentary Private Secretary to Neville Chamberlain. Nonetheless, he was not only readopted, but readopted unanimously, by his local association.[46]

Constituency opposition to Baldwin's departure took on a variety of forms. So, in Southport, the sitting Member, Lt. Col. G. D. White, refused to stand for re-election, explaining that he was an 'honest doubter' on the wisdom of Baldwin's proposals. At Bolton, faction fights developed within the constituency when the Conservative candidate wished to fight as a Free Trader. By a majority decision the Executive Committee adopted a Protectionist and the Free Trader withdrew.[47] In the Mossley division the Conservative Association did not bring forward a candidate, but instead supported the Independent, A. Hopkinson, despite his avowed Free Trade speeches.[48]

Although Lancashire was the centre of opposition to a tariff election, constituency opposition was not confined to that county. In the Tamworth division Sir Percy Newton retired as Conservative MP owing to his inability to stomach Protection, while in the Wrekin, H. S. Button, the sitting Conservative Member, withdrew for similar reasons.[49] An important defection occurred in Croydon South, where Sir Allan Smith was refused permission by the local Executive to stand as a Free Trader. He subsequently stood for the Partick division of Glasgow as a Unionist Free Trader candidate.[50]

[45] *The Times*, 19 Nov 1923.

[46] *Manchester Guardian*, 19 Nov 1923.

[47] *Manchester Guardian*, 20 Nov 1923.

[48] *Wigan Observer*, 6 Nov 1923. The president of the Mossley Conservatives explained that he had come 'within a sheet of paper' of agreeing with Hopkinson.

[49] *Burton Guardian*, 22 Nov 1923; *The Times*, 21 Nov 1923.

[50] *Manchester Guardian*, 15 Nov 1923. Sir Allan Smith was chairman of the Commons Industrial Group and also chairman of the Engineering and National Employers' Federation.

In Wales the Conservative constituency associations displayed little enthusiasm for Protection. One MP, J. C. Gould in Cardiff Central, declared that Protection 'would only serve to intensify the tragic position of the workless'.[51] In fact, the Central Cardiff Conservative Executive invited Gould to stand again, which he was to do, but only after a long interview with Baldwin.[52] Gould was not the only Welsh MP whose fiscal position was uncertain. Neville Chamberlain reported to Baldwin that he had 'brought back the scalps of two doubtful MPs for Cardiff'.[53]

In all, the net result was that over a score of Free Trade Conservatives appeared in 1923. The disruptive effect that they produced on the Conservative campaign was not long in coming.

[51] *South Wales Evening Express*, 16 Nov 1923.
[52] Ibid, 16, 22 Nov 1923.
[53] Baldwin Papers, F35/59, Neville Chamberlain to Baldwin, 4 Nov 1923.

9 Free Trade versus Protection: The Campaign Issues

It was against this background, with scarcely concealed divisions in the Conservative ranks, with a new spirit of unity on the Liberal side, and with Labour fighting on a wide front in spite of financial weakness, that the campaign of 1923 opened.

In a sense, there was little new in the campaign. The argument and the debate had all been heard before. Asquith and Lloyd George were fighting again the battle of 1906.

All the tactical advantages lay with the Free Trade cause. To begin with, the election was unpopular not only with the Conservative back-benchers, but in the country at large. There were numerous official protests against a Christmas election by trade organisations.[1] These protests echoed the general feeling in the provinces.[2]

The consequence of this was that Conservative candidates were immediately forced into a defensive and apologetic campaign. In Hull North-West, for example, the Conservative candidate apologised to his constituents that 'no one can regret more than I do the inconvenience and annoyance of another General Election so soon'.[3] Similar apologies were widespread.[4]

---

[1] For example, the protest delegations from the National Chamber of Trade, the Early Closing Association and the Drapers' Chamber of Trade. *Manchester Guardian*, 14 Nov 1923; *Birmingham Post*, 14 Nov 1923.

[2] For examples of this, see *Northampton Independent*, 10 Nov 1923; for Scotland, see *Dundee Advertiser*, 13 Nov 1923.

[3] Election Address, Hull North-West, Conservative.

[4] See Election Addresses in Bath, Chelmsford and Petersfield.

From the start, Conservative candidates had to stress that the election was vital for the country, and not a snap election for party advantage. After an unsuccessful contest in Hackney Central, the defeated Conservative candidate complained bitterly to Baldwin: 'I wish some of us businessmen could have had a word with you before you came to the decision. . . . I had to make it a first point at every meeting that it was an honest election and not a trick one.'[5] Likewise, Sir Robert Horne commented that no policy would ever be successfully carried if advocated in the shamefaced, half-hearted way that Protection had been put before the country.[6]

The Conservative campaign could possibly have overcome these obstacles had Baldwin, together with the other party leaders, given a firm lead and a well-defined policy. This did not occur. The theme which Baldwin had introduced at Plymouth on 25 October was repeated at Swansea five days later. However, except for appealing for support from the trade unionists for a policy of Protection to conquer unemployment, Baldwin was deafeningly silent on the details of his proposals. It was not until Baldwin's third major speech, in the Free Trade Hall at Manchester on 2 November, that for the first time a more detailed policy was outlined.[7]

The real significance of these speeches was not what Baldwin said. Rather, it was in the detailed proposals left unsaid. This continuing uncertainty over the exact proposals Baldwin intended prevented any chance of the Conservative Party moving on to the attack. There was considerable truth in the indictment of the *Economist* that the country had been asked

> to follow the bad example of our neighbours, not for the sake of some heroic remedy . . . but for a dose of Protection concocted haphazard, of whose effect even its author is uncertain. The Prime Minister has invited the country to sell its birthright for a mess of pottage.[8]

[5] Baldwin Papers, F35/122, D. T. Keymer to Baldwin, 11 Dec 1923.
[6] *Glasgow Herald*, 8 Dec 1923.
[7] For the text of Baldwin's speech, see *The Times*, 3 Nov 1923.
[8] *Economist*, 17 Nov 1923.

The Liberal campaign was additionally helped by the fact that the Conservatives did not merely fight the campaign from a defensive and hesitant position. They also spoke with a divided voice.

In calling an immediate election, Baldwin made a fundamental error in making hardly any attempt to lessen the impact of his fiscal conversion on the sympathies of Free Trade Lancashire. As was seen earlier, neither Derby nor Salvidge had the slightest desire for an election, neither was properly consulted and, not surprisingly, neither was able to bring Lancashire Conservatism properly behind Protection.

Individual MPs were placed in quite impossible positions in attempting to go along with Baldwin. Thus, Major J. B. B. Cohen, the Member for the Fairfield division of Liverpool, had made it clear in November 1922 that, with the exception of the occasional industry, Free Trade must be maintained. A year later, Cohen was explaining to his constituents that he did not mean to fight this election on the arguments of the past.[9]

The occasional Conservative candidate, as in Salford North, was able to solve the dilemma, as Lord Derby himself had, by declaring that abnormal times required abnormal measures.[10] These, however, were isolated examples. For the election of 1923 the Lancashire Conservatives presented a political Pentecost of strange tongues and diverse languages. In the Nelson and Colne division a Protectionist Conservative took the field. In the adjoining Clitheroe division the Conservative rejected Protection and all its works, whilst in the Accrington division no Conservative came forward at all, and the Conservatives openly supported the Liberal.

Everywhere inconsistency and contradiction entered into the Conservative campaign. In the Bury division the Conservative explained that he could not accept Baldwin's proposal for a general tariff. In the nearby Leigh constituency his Conservative colleague denied that any general tariff was even proposed by the Prime Minister.[11]

[9] *Liverpool Post*, 19 Nov 1923.
[10] Election Address, Salford North, Conservative.
[11] Election Addresses, Bury, Leigh, Conservatives.

Lacking any comprehensive, detailed statements from Baldwin, the Conservative campaign rapidly degenerated into a series of local promises. So, in such hat-making centres as Luton, Conservatives stressed the benefits of Protection in the face of rising imports. The Liberals counter-attacked with the accusation that Protection would raise the cost of many essential articles. In reply, the Conservatives retaliated by pledging not to tax such items as straw braid. As one newspaper observed, 'the ordinary individual may be pardoned for not feeling quite sure of his ground'.[12]

A similar involved controversy centred around the fishing industry. When the Conservative candidate in Moray claimed that, under Protection, the fishing in the Firth would benefit, the Liberal replied that nets and gear would all cost more.[13]

These local Conservative pledges frequently became inconsistent with national promises. Thus, in Hull North-West, with its important trawler vote, the Conservative advocated a food tax on fish caught by foreign vessels, despite other Conservative denials that Protection would involve 'stomach taxes'.[14]

It was interesting that, for an election fought on Protection, the Conservatives displayed considerable eagerness to suggest that they were really the Free Trade party – and that only the changed circumstances of the world economic position had forced them to adapt an old and trusted policy. So, in the Hertford division, the Conservative proclaimed that he was the 'REAL Free Trader', while in the Saffron Walden division the Conservative emphasised that he wanted 'Freer Trade', and in Durham his colleague stressed a 'FREE Breakfast table'.[15]

Despite the shortcomings of the Protection campaign, the position of the Conservatives in rural areas might possibly have been saved had the party been able to put forward an attractive and imaginative agricultural policy to counter the discontent among the farming community.

[12] *Stockport County Borough Express*, 6 Dec 1923.
[13] Election Address, Morya and Nairn, Liberal.
[14] Election Address, Hull North-West.
[15] *Hertfordshire Observer*, 24 Nov 1923; Election Addresses, Durham City, Saffron Walden.

Protests at the agricultural depression had resulted in November 1922 in the loss of safe Conservative seats to Independent Liberals. A year later the depression was still continuing. Agricultural prices, which had slumped during 1921 and had continued to fall during 1922, were still declining in 1923.[16] Despite this prolonged agricultural depression, the Conservative Government had formulated no new policy to combat the position. As one county newspaper observed, Conservative candidates had no tangible reason to put forward why they should be supported again.[17]

Not surprisingly, the prospect of an early election in this situation had alarmed leading Conservatives. Bridgeman warned Baldwin that agricultural policy required urgent attention, while Amery warned that 'on every side I hear anxiety about the farmers' point of view'.[18]

Three days later, Amery again warned Baldwin 'if you want an early election, you must *make* sure of the agricultural vote, *Labourers* and *Farmers*'.[19] Baldwin failed to heed these warnings. Not until 9 November was a Cabinet Committee appointed to report on agricultural policy. This committee hastily proposed an agricultural subsidy which was accepted by the full Cabinet on 14 November, although, as Edward Wood warned Baldwin, the proposals had not been fully considered.[20] The net result was that inconsistencies and haste marred the Conservative campaign in the rural constituencies as they had in the boroughs. The results from these areas were to prove disastrous for the Conservatives.

As the campaign drew towards its close, the Conservatives began switching their line of attack from Protection to the dangerous Socialism of the Labour Party. This itself was an indication that the Conservatives sensed their campaign was weakening.

[16] See Kinnear, *The British Voter*, p. 43.
[17] *Bath and Wiltshire Chronicle*, 10 Nov 1923.
[18] Baldwin Papers, F35/32, Bridgeman to Baldwin, 24 Oct 1923; ibid., F35/71, Amery to Baldwin, 8 Nov 1923.
[19] Baldwin Papers, F42/113, Amery to Baldwin, 11 Nov 1923. Amery wrote again the following day suggesting a really low fixed rate for the carriage of agricultural produce as one possible course of action.
[20] Baldwin Papers, F35/113, Wood to Baldwin, 14 Nov 1923.

Even in 1923 several Conservatives attempted to identify the Labour Party with Communism. In the Hartlepools division the Conservative stressed the 'terrible and horrifying example of Russia' as a warning against 'the suicidal proposals of the Labour-Socialist-Communist Party'.[21] This type of accusation was widely used, particularly in mining divisions.[22]

In addition, much campaign propaganda was made from the Labour Party's link with the Second International. This was particularly used in East London. In Hackney Central, for example, the Conservative accused Labour of being 'a party whose policy is directed by the German Socialistische Arbeiter Internationale'.[23]

Although significant as a foretaste of the campaign of October 1924, these 'Red Scare' techniques had little impact in 1923. In all, the Conservative campaign, lacking direction from the top and unity in the constituencies, could hardly have provided Liberal and Labour candidates with an easier target.

It was ironic that much of the Liberal success in 1923 was the result of the party fighting on an essentially conservative policy. During the campaign the Liberals fought as the party of common sense and established right.[24] As one commentator observed of the contest in Leicester West, on this occasion it was the Conservative candidate who desired change and the Liberal who feared it.[25]

The tone of the Liberal campaign was firmly set by Asquith. It was, essentially, the orthodox defence of Free Trade that had been debated twenty years before. Asquith set himself out to establish that Protection would raise food prices and that neither nationalisation nor the capital levy could be introduced without damaging the economic system. If the Liberals had a programme other than this, it was hardly spectacular. Speaking on 23 November, Asquith went on to

[21] Election Address, The Hartlepools, Conservative.

[22] See Election Addresses, Frome, Cannock, Don Valley and South Lanarkshire.

[23] Election Address, Hackney Central. For similar examples, see Islington South, Southwark Central and Wandsworth Central.

[24] Cowling, *The Impact of Labour*, p. 345.

[25] *The Times*, 27 Nov 1923.

outline some other Liberal aims: he called for a remodelling of the Insurance Act, courageous use of national credit, development of Imperial resources and the full operation of the Trade Facilities Act.

Nor, except for occasional remarks by Lloyd George, did the Liberal leadership think they needed anything more radical or constructive in terms of policy. As Cowling observes, although Lloyd George declared that Liberals would be as successful in the future in introducing major social reforms as they had been previously, the details of this future legislation were left to look after themselves.[26] The radicalism of April 1923 had vanished from Lloyd George's speeches. In the campaign, little distinguished Lloyd George, Asquith or Viscount Grey. The emphasis, again and again, was on the negative virtues of Free Trade.[27]

The theme set by the leaders was faithfully repeated in the constituencies. At Wellingborough, only two days before the end of the campaign, the Liberal candidate wrote to Lloyd George that he had disposed of Protection and that he was 'developing a Liberal programme'.[28] It was a perfect example of too little too late. Similarly, in the Northampton division, C. A. McCurdy appealed in an open letter to all Conservatives: 'surely Conservatism stands for resistance to hasty and revolutionary proposals from whatever quarter they come'.[29] Whilst McCurdy's appeal may have attracted Conservative votes, it was significant that Labour won its first ever victory in 1923, having made further inroads into the radical vote.

In areas where the Liberal Party had once been in the vanguard of radicalism, the campaign in 1923 revealed a party that could offer only an anaemic conservatism. This was particularly true of South Wales. The Liberal in Neath, after devoting his main attack to Socialism, could offer the electors only an undefined 'sane, circumspect course'. His colleague in Gower offered little more positive than the old motto 'Peace,

[26] Cowling, *The Impact of Labour*, p. 346

[27] Much the best discussion of the main speeches of the Liberal leaders is to be found in R. Lyman, *The First Labour Government* (1957) pp. 42–52.

[28] Lloyd George Papers, G/18/1/16, G. H. Shakespeare to Lloyd George, 4 Dec 1923.

[29] *Northampton Independent*, 24 Nov 1923.

Retrenchment and Reform', whilst in Pontypool the Liberal stressed that little now separated his party from the Conservatives.[30]

This type of campaign was repeated in industrial Scotland. In such seats as Dunfermline or Stirling and Falkirk the Liberals relied on a negative attack on Socialism to attract Conservative votes.[31] Indeed, in several cases Liberal candidates imitated the Conservatives in accusing the Labour Party of Bolshevism. This was once again particularly common in such London seats as Battersea North and Poplar South.

This negative attack on Protection, Socialism and the capital levy was paralleled in the rural areas by an equally negative attack on the subsidy. It was soon clear that the Liberals had little to offer in the way of definite constructive alternatives.[32] During the campaign Liberals attacked the proposal as ill-considered and unworkable, as well as ridiculing the sudden Conservative conversion to subsidies. This task was made all the easier since leading Conservatives had only recently denounced the possibility of an agricultural subsidy.[33]

Apart from these opportunities, the Liberals in constituencies suffering most from the agricultural depression were on the defensive. Indeed, the *Yorkshire Post* was able to taunt the Liberal leaders for avoiding campaigning in these areas.[34]

[30] For a more detailed discussion of the campaign in Wales, see C. P. Cook, 'Wales and the General Election of 1923', *Welsh History Review*, IV, 4 (1969).

[31] *Scotsman*, 26 Nov 1923.

[32] The Liberal manifesto spoke, in vague terms, of improved credit facilities, co-operative marketing and improved housing for agricultural labourers. This is all the more surprising since, in April 1923, the *Lloyd George Liberal Magazine* had warned that agriculture would be the burning issue of the succeeding months. Lloyd George set up a Rural Policy Committee under Sir Robert Hutchinson in September 1923. The Asquithians had done little or nothing.

[33] In October 1922 Baldwin himself had stated that 'neither agriculture nor any other industry in this country can look to this or any other government for a direct or indirect subsidy of public money' (*The Times*, 29 Oct 1922). Similarly, Sir Robert Sanders had stated that 'heroic measures' such as subsidies could not be considered because of the expense (*Daily Chronicle*, 17 Feb 1923).

[34] *Yorkshire Post*, 24 Nov 1923.

A consequence of the lack of Liberal policy was that several candidates either accepted the Conservative subsidy or proposed similar plans of their own. In Cirencester the Liberal candidate withdrew to support the subsidy and the seat was uncontested by the Liberals.[35] In such divisions as Eye and Penrith, Liberals put forward schemes involving a subsidy.[36]

This negative Liberal defence of Free Trade, together with the inadequacy of the party's agricultural or unemployment policies, had an important effect on the polling. The Conservatives were able to attack the Liberals as a party whose only policy was 'wait and see'. Harold Macmillan fighting Stockton, attacked the Liberals as a party living in the dead past that had not advanced beyond the age of Cobden and Bright. This was not entirely exaggerated. One provincial paper found even committed Liberals uncomfortable because 'as regards any remedy for unemployment thay have no definite policy beyond the old and unpalatable nostrum of wait and see'.[37]

This lack of policy in fact produced the resignations of several important Liberals. The most important of these was Sir William Bulmer, the chairman of the Yorkshire National Liberal Council who resigned declaring that the Liberal Party 'offered no vestige of hope or encouragement to the weary army of unemployed'.[38] The onset of depression in industry was no doubt a factor which caused several former Liberal industrialists to go over to the Conservatives. Typical of these was Sir Donald Horsfall, a prominent Yorkshire millowner and a former president of Skipton Liberal Association.[39]

By far the most significant consequence of this sterile, negative Liberal campaign was not these relatively infrequent defections to the Conservative ranks, but the fact that the party offered nothing to win back the working-class industrial

[35] *Swindon Advertiser*, 21 Nov 1923.

[36] *The Times*, 30 Nov 1923; Election Address, Eye, Liberal.

[37] *Essex County Standard*, 1 Dec 1923.

[38] Letter of Sir William Bulmer to Sir William Edge, quoted in *The Times*, 28 Nov 1923.

[39] A second example was Oswald Sanderson, the managing director of the Ellerman Wilson Line (*The Times*, 21 Nov 1923).

vote which had been captured by Labour. Many times before 1923, radical Liberals had warned of the consequences of fighting without a constructive radical programme. These warnings went unheeded. The result was that in the election Labour made a further substantial inroad in the industrial areas.

It is true, of course, that in 1923 the Labour campaign itself faced the problem of switching the issue from Free Trade to the full Labour programme. Despite the inadequacy of the Labour Party's 'remedy' for unemployment, the fact remains that during the campaign the party was able to portray the Liberals as a sufficiently discredited, effete and ineffective force in industrial seats to make further important gains.

A feature of the campaign that was to have extremely important repercussions was the bitterness with which Labour attacked the Liberals. MacDonald himself took the lead in this. At Manchester, on 24 November, he attacked the 'miserable time-serving' in the Liberal Party and went on (at Neath on 1 December) to declare that the Liberals were occupied 'not with political principle but with mere expediency'.

There was more than mere campaign rhetoric to this, as the events of 1924 were to show. Others followed the lead set by MacDonald. Dorothy Jewson, fighting Norwich, declared that the Liberals were bankrupt of principles; the Liberals 'came with a lie on their lips', stated James Hudson, the Labour candidate at Huddersfield. The party was 'a fraud and a sham' declared Herbert Dunnico at Consett, adding for good measure in his election address that 'Loyalty to principle has been regulated (by the Liberals) to the limbo of forgotten things'. Arthur Greenwood, fighting Nelson, declared that the Liberal Party was now 'a mere miserable negotiating instrument prepared to sacrifice principles for power to damn the Labour Party'. And, added F. W. Pethick-Lawrence at Leicester West, 'not a single principle for which the old Liberalism stood . . . had remained intact'.

So the attack went on: led by MacDonald, willingly continued throughout all levels of the party, it was all yet further evidence of how far Labour's hostility to the Liberals had grown even since October 1922.

During the campaign itself, however, the most immediately evident feature was not Labour's advance at the expense of the Liberals, but the discomfiture of the Conservatives. Without any additional factors, the defects of Baldwin's election strategy and campaign would no doubt have ensured an important reverse at the polls. A Conservative defeat was in fact made a disaster by the almost complete hostility of the national and provincial press to Baldwin's policy. This press opposition was to have direct and vital effects on the nature and extent of the Liberal resurgence in 1923.

Even before the Plymouth speech and the resurrection of Protection, Baldwin had been without firm support in the national press. As one journal commented:

> As far as the cheap popular Conservative papers are concerned, Lord Rothermere and Lord Beaverbrook divide the world between them in unequal proportions . . . we have a great bulk of organised popular power without any political moorings, which may drift at any moment across the bows of the Government.[40]

Similarly, there was speculation that a new Conservative evening paper might well be launched, for there was no evening journal on which the government could at present rely for consistent support.[41] This situation had partly arisen from the demise of the Hulton empire, the bulk of which Rothermere now controlled.[42]

It was against this background that Baldwin forfeited the support of the Conservative Free Trade journals by his Protectionist policy. The *Spectator*, under the editorship of St Loe Strachey, came out strongly in opposition. A bitter article entitled 'How to kill the Unionist Party', having looked back to the position of the Conservative party when Baldwin took over as leader, went on:

[40] *Tatler*, 24 Oct 1923.

[41] For speculation of this sort in the press, see *Bury Guardian*, 20 Oct 1923.

[42] The papers taken into the Rothermere empire included the *Evening Chronicle, Daily Dispatch, Sunday Chronicle, Empire News* and *Daily Sketch*, together with the *Sporting Chronicle, Athletic News* and *Illustrated Sunday Herald*. At the same time, the *Pall Mall Gazette*, owned by Sir John Leigh, had been taken over by Beaverbrook and merged with the *Evening Standard*.

And now look at the party. It is shivering as a ship shivers when she has struck a huge mass of floating wreckage . . . the wreckage of Tariff Reform and the Chamberlain policy. She is not going to founder at once, but no man can say how far the damage has spread.[43]

According to the *Spectator*, Baldwin had split his party both laterally and horizontally on a policy that was ambiguous and dangerous. The path Baldwin had adopted was vividly compared to a walk on a dark cold winter's night through a churchyard, with the spectres of Free Trade hovering around.[44]

Like the *Spectator*, the *Sunday Times* also adopted a hostile attitude to the resurrection of Protection. As the paper stated, however distasteful it might be to oppose one's own party, it had become a lamentable necessity. This was reflected in a series of editorials attacking Baldwin.[45]

The opposition of these journals would not have been particularly damaging if Baldwin had commanded the support of the major dailies. This was not the case.

Although *The Times* did not oppose Protection, the paper echoed Dawson's warnings on the dangers and unpopularity of an early election. The editorial on 20 October warned of the 'unwarrantable risk' of disturbing the stability of the government. Baldwin's Plymouth speech was greeted equally cautiously. The paper warned that a 'process of education' was vital to prepare the nation to accept Protection as a truly national measure.[46]

After Baldwin's speech at Swansea *The Times* again made clear its opposition to an early election, declaring: . . . 'it would be rash as a matter of leadership, and unfair to the electorate, to seek a verdict before the time has come, and before the case in all its bearings has been submitted to those who are to judge it'.[47] During the campaign the paper supported Protection only because it had little option. Although the *Daily Telegraph* likewise supported Protection,

[43] *Spectator*, 3 Nov 1923.
[44] Ibid., 17, 24 Nov 1923.
[45] *Sunday Times*, 18, 25 Nov 1923.
[46] *The Times*, 26 Oct 1923.
[47] *The Times*, 31 Oct 1923.

the paper took this course partly, as the *Daily Herald* observed, because the alternative was support for Socialism.[48]

Much the most devastating setback to Baldwin's campaign was the opposition of the Rothermere and Beaverbrook press. Between them this action effectively removed any major popular press support for the Conservative campaign.

Baldwin had in fact attempted to win over Beaverbrook to a Protection campaign. Beaverbrook, however, was adamant that the only policy he would support was a true Empire policy of Imperial Preference. Beaverbrook's hostility was sincere and unshakeable and went to the extent of refusing to subscribe to the Conservative campaign fund, although when pressed by Younger he agreed to pay the expenses of 'two needy candidates' who were sound Imperialists.[49]

The result was that, in the *Daily Express* and *Sunday Express*, Beaverbrook launched a bitter attack on Baldwin. A blistering onslaught on the election strategy was made on 18 November. Under the headline 'Making the Best of a Bad Election', Beaverbrook attacked the election as 'a grave blunder' which had disturbed the unity of the Conservative Party, reunited the Liberals and exposed the government to serious defeat.[50]

Beaverbrook intensified his attack a week later, charging that the Conservatives had chosen the part of the Chamberlain policy for which the founder cared least. Beaverbrook accused Baldwin of basing his policy not on conviction, but on fear.

It was in this article that Beaverbrook made his extraordinary appeal to his readers to vote, of all things, for the Liberals. Beaverbrook justified this volte-face by declaring:

> At this very time when the Imperial tide seems to have receded in the Tory cabinet, the Liberals have made a great advance . . . the Liberals would appear to be ready to give subsidies on shipping, which would in effect be a substantial preference on Canadian wheat and Australian meat.

[48] *Daily Herald*, 6 Nov 1923.
[49] Beaverbrook Papers, Beaverbrook to Younger, 26 Nov 1923. Beaverbrook paid £1,000 to one candidate and £750 to the other.
[50] *Sunday Express*, 18 Nov 1923.

Beaverbrook continued:

> The Conservatives are only holding back from the full policy because their leader is afraid. . . . The Liberals, on the other hand are advancing steadily towards the conception of Imperial Preference.

Beaverbrook's determination to thwart Baldwin and all his works led him to take the extraordinary step of cabling Rothermere, then in the south of France, to urge that his newspapers in Lancashire support the Free Trade cause. Not surprisingly, Rothermere refused.

The net result of the manoeuvring by Beaverbrook, together with similar attacks on Baldwin by Rothermere in the *Daily Mail*, was to give the Liberal Party an enormous advantage. With virtually all the national press critical of the election, with normally Conservative papers actually urging their readers to vote Liberal or to abstain, the Liberal Party enjoyed a press support it was never again to have.

This advantage was heightened by a similar opposition to Baldwin among the bulk of the provincial press. Almost the only major regional paper to support the election was the *Yorkshire Post*, itself really only a mouthpiece of Stanley Jackson, a director of the paper.[51]

In general, however, these occasional papers supporting Baldwin did so only because they were dragged into the struggle by the hair of their heads.[52] Many papers, like many Conservative backbenchers, were placed in a position of hopeless inconsistency. Thus, the pro-Conservative *Reading Mercury*, which had been stressing the need for 'a period of tranquillity and stability' which must not be disturbed, had then to reconcile this with support for an immediate dissolution.[53]

In addition, the advent of Protection cost the Conservatives the support of those former Liberal papers that had drifted to a more right-wing anti-Socialist position. Typical of these was

[51] *Star*, 15 Nov 1923.
[52] *Fortnightly Review*, Feb 1924, p. 184.
[53] *Reading Mercury*, 3 Nov 1923.

the *Leicester Mercury*. The revival of Protection brought the paper firmly against the Conservatives during the campaign.[54]

As with the Scottish Unionist Party, the press north of the Border welcomed Protection with the eagerness of sheep preparing for the slaughter. Although the *Scotsman* supported Baldwin, the influential *Glasgow Herald* adopted a position of total hostility.[55] Under the headline 'The Political Crisis: A Question of Principle', one editorial warned:

> ... in the event of the authors of the crisis gaining an electoral majority for their Protectionist policy, they will deal a staggering blow to the economic and financial stability of the nation. We believe further that, in the event of failure, the result will be the great and indefinitely prolonged enfeeblement of the Party.

Unlike the *Scotsman*, which denied that the Conservative ranks were divided over Protection, the *Glasgow Herald* believed that the party 'was threatened at the best with division, at worst with catastrophe'.[56]

When the immediate Dissolution was announced, the paper attacked the snap verdict as 'the fitting consummation of a hastily conceived policy ... the rash sequel to an utterly mistaken diagnosis of the country's economic needs'.

An interesting aspect of Baldwin's election campaign was the hopelessly misleading reports on the likely outcome which he received, both from the constituencies and from Conservative Central Office.

Thus, on 16 November, Tom Jones recorded in his diary that William Cope, the Welsh Conservative Whip, had reported on electoral prospects in Wales in euphoric terms, suggesting that Mond would be defeated at Swansea (he was – by Labour) and that Lord Lisburne, fighting Cardiganshire, might get in between the two rival Liberals. In fact, Lisburne came bottom.

Only two days before the election, Jones made another long and interesting entry in his diary on Tuesday, 4 December:

[54] See, for example, the editorial attacking the Plymouth speech, *Leicester Mercury*, 27 Oct 1923.

[55] *Glasgow Herald*, 9 Nov 1923.

[56] *Glasgow Herald*, 13 Nov 1923.

'PM returns from Liverpool and goes to Malvern in his own county. Mr McLachlan, a chief official of the Unionist Central Office, was with the PM when I saw latter at No. 10 just before 4 o'clock. McLachlan's official estimate of the result of the forthcoming poll is:

Conservatives		351
Liberals	114 ⎫	
Labour	145 ⎬	264
Independent	5 ⎭	
Unionist majority		87

PM very cheerful at this prospect and almost his last words to us before going to his train were: I don't want any bands here when I come back'

Jones went on to record that, after addressing a rally at Liverpool, Baldwin moved on to Knowsley, where he received very favourable reports of the progress of the campaign in the North from Derby and Birkenhead.[57]

It was remarkable that, with so much evidence of hostility in the press, and with the Conservative campaign so obviously in disarray, few people (least of all Baldwin and Conservative Central Office) envisaged the likely outcome of the election Baldwin had brought on his party. When the polls closed on 6 December, few if any Conservatives realised the scale of the débâcle that was shortly to face them.

[57] T. Jones, *Whitehall Diary* (Oxford, 1969) vol. I, p. 257.

10 The Results Analysed

From the first results, it was clear that the Conservative Party had fared badly. The first declaration, from the Exchange division of Manchester, showed a swing against the government of 11·8 per cent. This early result from Manchester was followed by a succession of Conservative defeats in Cheshire and Lancashire.

Had these losses been confined to Free Trade Lancashire, the Conservatives might still have retained a working majority. This was not to be. Labour made persistent gains in the large cities, whilst safe rural seats and even safer middle-class suburbs fell to the Liberals.

The scene on the night of 6 December as the first results came in was faithfully and evocatively recorded in Tom Jones's diary:

At 5 to 10 we got the first result in our private sitting-room. Sir Edwin Stockton was knocked out in Manchester – a Unionist Free Trader. Then Wakefield, also a loss to the Government. We pooh-poohed these. They were in the infected North. We made for No. 10 through a thick fog and I remained there until 1.30 a.m. . . . about midnight Davidson and Mrs Davidson arrived from their fight at Hemel Hempstead. We were not very despondent for the first hour or so, as we were reminded of what took place a year ago when Bonar sat there in misery doubtful even about his own election. But as the Liberal and Labour gains continued in an unbroken stream, except for Middleton where Ryland Atkins, a Liberal, was defeated by a Government nominee, our faces grew longer, we saw less and less chance of the home counties putting things right. Bath and Nottingham were a great shock. If Nottingham would not vote for a tariff after all the trouble about foreign competition in the lace trade, who was going to support Baldwin? Bath we put down to folk with fixed incomes who feared soaring prices. Mrs Davidson was almost beside herself with panic for the fate of a country so blind to its best interests as to vote against the one policy which could save it.

I watched the growing tale of Labour victories with undisguised joy amid cries of 'You Bolshevist!'

The nation had spoken decisively against Tariff Reform. However, although the Conservative Party had lost, and lost overwhelmingly, it was less clear whom the electors had favoured in its place. Although the rejection of Protection was emphatic, the national result was peculiarly indecisive. No party had a majority, whilst Labour and Liberal were hardly distinguishable in their aggregate vote. The final verdict of the electors in December 1923 is shown in Table 10.1[1] The Conservatives gained only 20 seats for the loss of 108. Labour gained 63 seats, losing 16, while the Liberals secured 80 gains for the loss of 38 seats.[2]

TABLE 10.1
General Election, 1923

	Total votes	% share	Candidates	MPs elected	Un-opposed returns
Conservative	5,514,541	38·0	536	258	35
Liberal	4,301,481	29·7	457	158	11
Labour	4,439,780	30·7	427	191	3
Communist	39,448	0·2	4	–	–
Nationalist	97,993	0·4	4	3	1
Others	154,452	1·0	18	5	–
	14,547,695	100·0	1,446	615	50

These figures in fact disguised a variety of cross-currents. Although the Liberals gained, on balance, 51 seats from the Conservatives, they made a net loss of eight to Labour.[3]

[1] Craig, *British Parliamentary Election Statistics*, pp. 4–5. The five 'others' elected were: G. M. L. Davies (University of Wales), A. Hopkinson (Mossley), R. H. Morris (Cardiganshire), O. E. Mosley (Harrow) and E. Scrymgeour (Dundee).

[2] In addition, the Communists lost one seat to the Conservatives, Labour gained one seat from a Constitutionalist in Dartford, and a Christian Pacifist gained a Welsh University seat from a Liberal.

[3] The Liberals gained 67 Conservative seats and 13 Labour seats, but lost 16 to the Conservatives and 21 to Labour respectively.

Labour succeeded more evenly, taking 41 seats from the Conservatives for the loss of only three.

The most dramatic feature of the election was the 108 seats lost by the Conservatives, offset by only 20 gains. These 20 gains came, in general, from the Liberals in agricultural constituencies. The only three seats taken from Labour were Mitcham, lost in the by-election of March 1923, the Sedgefield division of Durham, won by a mere 6 votes, and the Cathcart division of Glasgow.[4]

In all, the Conservatives took 16 seats from Liberals. Of these, seven had been held by National Liberals, nine by Asquithians. The great majority of these victories were in rural areas, including four Scottish county seats, three in eastern England, and other equally agricultural territory such as Holderness, West Derbyshire and Penrith.[5]

The 41 Labour gains from the Conservatives were almost exclusively to be found in urban industrial constituencies. Labour won 11 metropolitan borough seats, making its first gain in West London, as well as making inroads into such working-class areas as St Pancras, where the party took two seats. Otherwise the bulk of the Labour gains were in the boroughs of northern England, with occasional exceptions such as Coventry, Ipswich and Cardiff.

Of the county seats won by Labour, only two, South Norfolk and Maldon, could be classed as rural. In neither case was there a Liberal opponent; in each case the local Liberal Association rendered support to the Labour candidate. Otherwise the Labour gains in county constituencies were confined to such mining divisions as the Wrekin, Frome and Barnard Castle, and semi-industrial seats in the London area.[6]

These Labour victories did not contain many surprises, in marked contrast to the 67 Liberal gains at the expense of the Conservatives.

[4] The Conservatives also took the Motherwell division from the sitting Communist Member, J. T. W. Newbold.

[5] The four Scottish seats were Kinross and West Perthshire, Roxburgh and Selkirk, Moray and Nairn, and Kincardine and West Aberdeenshire.

[6] Seats such as Enfield, South-East Essex and Gravesend.

Of these 67 victories, 23 were in borough constituencies, 44 in county divisions. In 1923 the Liberals swept five Manchester seats, together with two Liverpool constituencies, the Wavertree and West Derby divisions, which had never before returned Liberals.[7] As in Manchester and Liverpool, the Liberal borough victories were nearly all in middle-class seats where Labour's challenge was weak. The seats in this category included Bath, Blackpool, Leicester South, Southport and Portsmouth Central; all these were seats with a large business vote. In London the Liberals won four seats, all with a high proportion of fixed-income clerks and office workers, while the only Scottish burgh seat gained, the Edinburgh North division, was a similar constituency.[8]

It was the 44 county divisions, all except one in England, which provided the major area of Liberal advance. The party did particularly well in three areas. In the South-West the Liberals secured twelve gains. The South Midlands and northern Home Counties produced another six victories, while on Lincolnshire and East Anglia Liberals took a further six.

The party also gained a few semi-industrial county divisions with a strong Nonconformist vote. Examples in this group were the Nuneaton division, with its mining villages, the Bosworth division in Leicestershire, Darwen and Royton in Lancashire and Hexham and Cleveland in the North-East.

The Liberals also captured several totally unexpected victories in normally very safe Conservative seats. In this category were such seats as Chichester, Sevenoaks and Newbury. None of them had previously returned Liberals, nor were they ever to abandon the Conservative fold again.

In all, the Liberals held more rural seats after the 1923 election than in any inter-war election: 43 of the 86 most rural constituencies returned Liberals, compared with a mere 11 in 1924 and 26 in the revival of 1929.[9]

[7] In Wavertree the defeated Conservative was Sir Harold Smith, Lord Birkenhead's brother. In West Derby the defeated Conservative was the principal agent of the party, Sir Reginald Hall.

[8] The London seats gained, all dormitory suburbs, were Stoke Newington, Hackney North, Islington East and Brixton.

[9] Kinnear, *The British Voter*, p. 120. Of these 86 seats, the Conservatives won 54 in 1918, 48 in 1922, 38 in 1923, 74 in 1924 and 55 in 1929.

Although the Liberals had won a series of victories from the Conservatives, their success in taking seats from Labour was markedly weaker. The party gained only 13 seats, losing 21 in exchange. In fact, these Liberal gains were almost all the result of local alliances.

This was true of Newcastle East, where a local anti-Socialist pact unseated Arthur Henderson, and also the Newcastle West division, another seat which Labour had won in 1922 in a three-cornered contest. Both seats were regained by Labour in 1924.

Three Liberal gains in Yorkshire, in Dewsbury, Elland and Keighley, were all won in the absence of Conservative opposition.[10] Local pacts were responsible for the Liberal successes in Accrington and Burslem, while both the seats taken from Labour in London, in Battersea North and Bermondsey West, resulted from definite pacts.

The Liberals won only two Labour-held seats in three-conered contests in 1923—Rochdale and Gateshead. In contrast, Labour captured seats from sitting Liberals in a variety of industrial areas.

Liberal losses were particularly heavy in their former strongholds in the industrial Midlands. Northampton, Wellingborough, Mansfield, Lichfield and Leicester East were all lost. The Liberals also lost their few remaining strongholds in London, together with such traditional areas as Bristol and Norwich. Four more Liberal seats in Scotland fell to Labour.

However, despite these losses, the Liberals had still not been dislodged from their working-class territory in the North-East together with a variety of textile towns in Lancashire and Yorkshire. Labour's breakthrough in these areas was to come in October 1924.

Much the best advance for Labour in 1923 was the Greater London area. The number of Members returned leaped from 16 to 37. Otherwise the same areas contributed the bulk of the parliamentary party. Wales and Scotland returned 53 Members, Lancashire and the North-West sent 27, Yorkshire and the North-East 37. In all, these three areas contributed

[10] For a useful discussion of Dewsbury politics, see C. James, *MP for Dewsbury* (Dewsbury, 1970).

61 per cent of the total Labour MPs after 1923, compared with 75 per cent after 1922. Labour was still, as it was to remain until 1945, a party essentially of industrial Britain.

An important consequence of the Liberal gains and losses was the shift in the relative strength of the Lloyd George and Asquith elements in the parliamentary party.

For the former National Liberals the results were an unmitigated disaster. Mond was ousted in Swansea West; Churchill was beaten by Pethick-Lawrence in Leicester West. Hamar Greenwood, Hilton Young and McCurdy were all unsuccessful.

These losses meant a distinct move to the left in the composition of the parliamentary party. Lord Gladstone was not slow to delight at the fate of Lloyd George's supporters. According to his calculations, of 45 National Liberals in the last Parliament, excluding those who were retiring, 25 had been defeated and only 20 returned. Of the 64 Independent Liberals, however, 50 were re-elected and only 14 defeated. In all, Gladstone estimated that no fewer than 118 members of the parliamentary party after 1923 supported Asquith.[11]

Although the seats which changed hands in 1923 provide considerable evidence of the nature of the Liberal revival, much the most important analysis is to be made from an examination of the movement of votes rather than seats. Table 10.2 shows the number of votes cast compared with 1922.

TABLE 10.2

	1922		1923	
	Votes	*%*	*Votes*	*%*
Conservative	5,502,298	(38·5)	5,514,541	(38·0)
Labour	4,237,349	(29·7)	4,439,780	(30·7)
Liberal	2,668,143	(18·9)	4,301,481	(29·7)
National Liberal	1,412,772	(9·4)		
Others	571,768	(3·5)	291,893	(1·6)
	14,392,330	(100·0)	14,547,695	(100·0)

[11] Gladstone Papers, BM Add. MSS 46,480/63–65.

These aggregate voting figures conceal two important factors. First, the increase in the Conservative total poll did not reflect a real rise in support in the country. It was the result of a larger number of candidates. Secondly, the National Liberal vote in 1922 was not really a Liberal vote. In many seats in 1922 National Liberal candidates had received the full backing of the Conservative organisation, and their poll was in many cases very much inflated by Conservative votes.[12]

To compare electoral movement in December 1923 with the election of November 1922, it is essential to analyse only the comparable groups of contests. Despite the complexity of the 1922 election, there are 235 constituencies in which useful statistical comparisons can be made.[13]

The first group of constituencies, the 63 seats fought by Conservative and Liberals only on each occasion, provide a useful indication of the extent of the Liberal revival. The votes cast in these 63 seats are shown in Table 10.3. The swing to the Liberals in these 63 seats averaged 5·8 per cent the Conservative share of the vote falling from 55·1 per cent. to 49·3 per cent. This average swing, however, disguises several important variations. Thus, Stoke Newington swung 16·5 per cent to the Liberals, while Leominster swung by 5·1 per cent to the Conservatives. Likewise, in Scotland, Edinburgh North swung by 17·5 per cent to the Liberals, Central Aberdeenshire by 6·5 per cent to the Conservatives.

There is an important difference in behaviour in these 63 contests between the agricultural seats and the middle-class seats.[14] The position in the 28 agricultural seats is shown in Table 10.4. In the middle-class constituencies the movement of votes was markedly different (Table 10.5). Thus, whereas in the agricultural seats the swing to the Liberals had averaged only 1·2 per cent, in the middle-class seats the swing was 9·1 per cent. Particularly heavy swings against the

[12] For example, such constituencies as Romford, Dartford or Wellingborough.

[13] These were the 94 three-cornered contests, the 53 Conservative–Labour straight fights, the 63 Conservative–Liberal contests and the 25 seats where Liberals faced only Labour opposition.

[14] 'Agricultural' and 'middle-class' seats are defined as in Kinnear, *The British Voter*, p. 119.

TABLE 10.3

	1922		1923	
	Votes	%	Votes	%
Conservative	784,374	(55·1)	726,242	(49·3)
Liberal	640,398	(44·9)	745,641	(50·7)
	1,424,772	(100·0)	1,471,883	(100·0)

TABLE 10.4

	1922		1923	
	Votes	%	Votes	%
Conservative	307,518	(50·5)	306,631	(49·3)
Liberal	301,566	(49·5)	315,635	(50·7)
	609,084	(100·0)	622,266	(100·0)

TABLE 10.5

	1922		1923	
	Votes	%	Votes	%
Conservative	476,856	(58·5)	419,611	(49·4)
Liberal	338,832	(41·5)	430,006	(50·6)
	815,688	(100·0)	849,617	(100·0)

Conservatives occurred in such middle-class constituencies as
Southend (11·7 per cent), the Isle of Thanet (11·1 per cent),
Waterloo (15·7 per cent), Windsor (12·8 per cent) and
Wallasey (12·1 per cent). By contrast, of the 28 agricultural
seats, only eight swung Liberal by more than 2 per cent, while
ten constituencies actually swung Conservative, with quite
definite swings to the Conservatives in Holderness (3·5 per
cent), Taunton (3·9 per cent) and Leominster (5·1 per cent).
The Conservative share of the vote either increased or held

steady in such Scottish county seats as Forfar, Dumfries, East Fife and Central Aberdeenshire.

These 63 seats, though a useful sample, are not representative of the movement of votes in industrial England. For this purpose, the three-cornered contests and the Conservative–Labour straight fights provide the best analysis.

In the 53 seats in which Labour was faced only with Conservative opposition on both occasions, the votes cast are shown in Table 10.6 The swing to Labour in this group of

TABLE 10.6

	1922		1923	
	Votes	%	Votes	%
Conservative	697,581	(53·1)	605,986	(47·9)
Labour	615,876	(46·9)	658,960	(52·1)
	1,313,457	(100·0)	1,264,946	(100·0)

constituencies averaged 5·2 per cent, with Labour's share of the poll rising from 46·9 per cent to 52·1 per cent.

As with the Conservative–Liberal straight fights, it is useful to divide these 53 seats into smaller groups. Excluding the three Scottish contests, 25 of these were in borough constituencies, 25 in counties. In the 25 borough seats the average swing against the Conservatives was 6·0 per cent, whereas in the counties it was only 4·4 per cent. Once again, the more agricultural the seat, the less the swing against the Conservatives.

In the borough constituencies the anti-Conservative swing was most marked in Lancashire and in Greater London. In the eight comparable constituencies in London the swing averaged 8·4 per cent, in the seven Lancashire boroughs the swing reached 9·1 per cent. The anti-Conservative swing was particularly heavy in such dockside seats as Deptford and Birkenhead West.

In contrast to these constituencies, the Conservatives polled relatively well in two areas. The first was the chemical and heavy engineering town of the North-West, such seats as Wigan, Workington and St Helens.[15] A second group occurred in the West Midlands, in Birmingham itself and in neighbouring constituencies such as Wednesbury. In 1923, and again in 1924, the West Midlands remained fairly isolated from the national voting trend.

The 94 seats enjoying three-cornered contests on each occasion provide the most useful sample. The votes cast are shown in Table 10.7. In all, the Conservative share of the vote

TABLE 10.7

	1922		1923		
	Votes	%	Votes	%	%
Conservative	1,079,070	(43·0)	954,123	(38·1)	−4·9
Liberal	676,494	(27·0)	779,695	(31·1)	+4·1
Labour	754,528	(30·0)	771,203	(30·8)	+0·8
	2,510,092	(100·0)	2,505,021	(100·0)	

had fallen by 4·9 per cent, while that of the Liberals had risen by 4·1 per cent and Labour's by 0·8 per cent. Once again, a division of these contests into borough and county constituencies provides different evidence.

For 66 borough constituencies, the figures are shown in Table 10.8.[16] In these 66 seats the Conservative share of the poll fell by 5·5 per cent, with Labour up by 2·4 per cent and the Liberals by 3·1 per cent. In the 28 county constituencies, however, the votes are shown in Table 10.9. Here, the Conservative share of the total vote fell by only 3·6 per cent. Labour's also fell, by 3·2 per cent, while the Liberal share rose by no less than 6·8 per cent.

[15] The swing against the Conservatives in Wigan was only 1·1 per cent, in Workington 1·9 per cent. St Helens actually swung 3·8 per cent to the Conservatives.

[16] The 8 Scottish contests, all in industrial territory, are included in the 66 borough seats.

The conclusion to be reached from these figures is that the Liberals *were* recapturing votes from Labour in rural constituencies. If the Labour vote in urban areas was solid, in rural England it was still open to attack by the old radical party.

TABLE 10.8

	1922		1923	
	Votes	%	Votes	%
Conservative	740,686	(42·5)	643,044	(37·0)
Liberal	440,969	(25·3)	492,264	(28·4)
Labour	559,708	(32·2)	600,672	(34·6)
	1,741,363	(100·0)	1,735,980	(100·0)

TABLE 10.9

	1922		1923	
	Votes	%	Votes	%
Conservative	338,384	(44·0)	311,079	(40·4)
Liberal	235,525	(30·6)	287,431	(37·4)
Labour	194,820	(25·4)	170,531	(22·2)
	768,729	(100·0)	769,041	(100·0)

This was particularly true in rural constituencies with a Nonconformist vote, and where trade union organisation was confined to an occasional branch. Examples of this sort were to be found in Banbury, Oswestry, Wells, the Isle of Ely, Luton, King's Lynn and Tonbridge. In all these seats the Labour percentage of the poll fell more than the Conservative.

It is essential to emphasise, however, that there was virtually no borough constituency in which the Liberals drew more votes from Labour than from the Conservatives, although this was true of a few seats with a mixture of light industry and residential development, such as Watford, Pudsey and South Dorset.

Of this interchange of votes in 1923 Dr Lyman has written:

... while Liberals and Conservatives traded a few voters between themselves, neither seems to have attracted any significant new help, either from Labour or from previously uncultivated areas of the political landscape.[17]

Lyman continued:

... Any additions to the Liberal vote that did not come from Tory Free Traders can be accounted for by Liberals who had refused to vote in the 1922 election because of the internecine warfare then raging in the party.

This view is difficult to sustain, although it is true that, with very few exceptions, Liberals were not recapturing Labour votes in *industrial* areas in 1923.

Additional proof of this latter point can be found in the 25 constituencies, the final sample, in which Liberals and Labour had straight fights in 1922 and 1923. The votes cast on each occasion are shown in Table 10.10. The swing from Liberal to Labour averaged 2·7 per cent. Although only two constituencies in this group were rural (Merionethshire and Caernarvonshire), it is significant that both swung to the Liberals.

TABLE 10.10

	1922		1923	
	Votes	%	Votes	%
Liberal	292,060	(48·1)	277,184	(45·4)
Labour	314,543	(51·9)	333,073	(54·6)
	606,603	(100·0)	610,257	(100·0)

The evidence from these comparable contests can be supplemented by analysing the 114 constituencies in which a major party withdrew or intervened.[18]

---

[17] Lyman, *The First Labour Government*, p. 74.
[18] These 114 seats were the 18 seats in which Labour withdrew, the 13 Conservative withdrawals and the 19 Liberal withdrawals, together with the 19 Labour entries and the 45 Liberal entries.

In the 18 constituencies in which Labour withdrew to leave a straight fight, the voting was as shown in Table 10.11. The Liberal share of the poll rose by exactly 20 per cent, a clear demonstration of the extent to which, without a candidate of their own, Labour supporters would transfer to the Liberal. It is an interesting speculation on the extent to which Liberals would have prospered under a system of the alternative vote.

TABLE 10.11

	1922		1923	
	Votes	%	Votes	%
Conservative	220,738	(47·9)	208,065	(45·7)
Liberal	158,389	(34·3)	247,571	(54·3)
Labour	82,164	(17·8)	–	–
	461,291	(100·0)	455,636	(100·0)

There is a strange irony about these 18 contests in which Labour withdrew, and also the 63 contests in which Conservatives fought Liberals on each occasion. If Labour, with sufficient money and resources, *had* contested these seats, such Labour intervention would have robbed the Liberals of victory: Conservatives would have retained the seats on a minority vote. As a result they could well have secured an overall parliamentary majority. The paradox is that the first Labour Government was, in part at least, the result of the financial weakness and organisational handicap of the party in rural England.

The second group of constituencies, the 13 seats in which the Conservatives withdrew to leave a straight fight between Liberal and Labour, produced the voting figures shown in Table 10.12. The withdrawal of the Conservatives quite clearly benefited the Liberals, whose percentage of the poll rose by 18·6 per cent. In such seats as Accrington and Pontypridd almost the whole Conservative vote seems to have transferred to the Liberal. However, two other factors are equally important. The first is the solidarity of the Labour vote, which rose by 10,000 on a reduced poll. Although the Liberals had gained from the Conservatives, they had failed to regain Labour votes and had probably lost yet more to Labour. The final feature of these contests was the reduction in turnout. Clearly, many Conservatives had simply not voted. A year later, in these constituencies, turnout rose very sharply as Conservatives, who had not seen fit to vote for a Liberal in 1923, did so in October 1924.

In view of the large-scale entry of Labour candidates in 1924, the 19 cases where Labour forced three-cornered contests in seats in which there was a straight fight in 1922 are particularly important. The position is shown in Table 10.13. Much the most significant feature of these contests was that Labour could poll an average 19 per cent of the total vote.

TABLE 10.12

	1922		1923	
	Votes	%	*Votes*	%
Conservative	97,278	(26·5)	–	–
Liberal	109,290	(29·7)	159,695	(48·3)
Labour	161,182	(43·8)	171,204	(51·7)
	367,750	(100·0)	330,899	(100·0)

TABLE 10.13

	1922		1923	
	Votes	%	*Votes*	%
Conservative	256,278	(54·7)	222,261	(45·1)
Liberal	212,505	(45·3)	177,325	(35·9)
Labour	–	–	93,767	(19·0)
	468,783	(100·0)	493,353	(100·0)

This fact, coupled with the well-known determination of Labour to fight on as broad a front as possible, should have served as a warning to the Liberals of the insecurity of their victories in the absence of Labour opposition.

Even in 1923 this intervention was sufficient to deny the Liberals victory. Without Labour intervention, for example, the Liberals could have won Stourbridge on a swing of 1·8 per cent, Chatham on a 1·5 per cent swing and Kelvingrove on a 4·8 per cent swing. They won none of these. In each, Conservatives were returned on a minority vote. In 1923 this Labour intervention was relatively unimportant; in 1924 it helped to seal the fate of the Liberal Party.

Much the most useful evidence from an analysis of the 64 constituencies in which the Liberals entered or withdrew candidates is in answering the question whether Labour or the Conservatives benefited.

In the 19 contests in which Liberals withdrew, the voting was as shown in Table 10.14. The most likely interpreta-

TABLE 10.14

	1922		1923	
	Votes	%	Votes	%
Conservative	192,722	(38·1)	203,834	(44·6)
Labour	227,114	(45·0)	253,542	(55·4)
Liberal	85,201	(16·9)	–	–
	505,037	(100·0)	457,376	(100·0)

tion to be drawn from these figures is that in those seats in which Liberals withdrew, probably as many as half the erstwhile Liberals abstained. In aggregate, taking only the Conservative–Labour two-party poll, excluding the Liberal vote in 1922, the swing to Labour in 1923 in these 19 contests was only 1·3 per cent. The suggestion of these figures is that, in general, the Liberal withdrawal benefited the Conservatives. It must be stressed, however, that 15 of the 19 contests were in industrial seats won by Labour in 1922. In the three more rural seats (Buckingham, Maldon and Holland-with-Boston), using the two-party poll, the swing to Labour was 12·2 per cent, 13·0 per cent and 2·9 per cent, respectively.

Perhaps the most important conclusion is that the effect of Liberal withdrawal varied from seat to seat, depending on the social composition and political tradition of a given constituency. In this respect, generalisations on Liberal withdrawal disguise the variation from constituency to constituency. This fact is of vital importance for analysing the effect of the mass of Liberal withdrawals in 1924.

In similar fashion, the 45 constituencies in which Liberals intervened in 1923 provide evidence on whom the party was drawing votes from. The votes cast are shown in Table 10.15.

TABLE 10.15

	1922		1923	
	Votes	*%*	*Votes*	*%*
Conservative	622,054	(58·3)	476,739	(43·0)
Labour	444,532	(41·7)	362,886	(32·8)
Liberal	–	–	267,905	(24·2)
	1,066,586	(100·0)	1,107,530	(100·0)

It was a significant comment on the voting strength of the Liberals that they could still poll one in four of all the votes cast in constituencies they had not even fought in 1922. Since the Conservative vote fell twice as much as the Labour decrease, evidence suggests that these Liberals were damaging the Conservatives more than Labour – although 40 of the 45 seats in this category in which Liberals intervened were Conservative-held seats.

A further point concerning Liberal strength in 1923 is also worth discussing. Several historians (most notably Trevor Wilson) have stressed that in December 1923 the Liberals won some victories that appeared so freak that they cannot really be taken as evidence of a genuine grass-roots revival. Yet detailed analysis of such seats hardly supports this view.

Bath was one such case.[19] In 1922 the Liberals had fought the seat with no party machinery, no organisation, no ward committee and a 62-year-old agent.[20] Nonetheless, the Liberals polled well, easily taking second place (the figures were: Conservative 13,666, Liberal 8,699, Labour 4,849).

In 1923 Labour stood down and the Liberals won the seat, with the Conservative share of the poll falling only slightly. In 1929 the Conservative share of the vote was *less* than in both 1922 and 1923, but the Labour vote had risen sufficiently to deny the Liberals victory. In other words, given the absence of a Labour candidate in 1923, there was very little 'freak' in the Liberal victory. That victory would probably have been repeated in 1929, but for Labour intervention.

A second example, the Hemel Hempstead division, was another constituency in which the Liberal victory in December 1923 seemed an electoral freak.

The local Liberal Association had collapsed. No candidate was fielded in the 'coupon' election of 1918, in the by-election of November 1920 or in the general election of 1922. The *Morning Post* found Hemel Hempstead to be a constituency in which 'a contest could only make Liberal and Labour appear ridiculous'.[21]

It was against this background that an eleventh-hour Liberal with no constituency organisation behind him was fielded. The Conservatives did not take this Liberal threat very seriously. The appearance of a Liberal candidate, fighting with all the enthusiasm of 1906, transformed the position. The *Star* now found Davidson's position 'far from impregnable', whilst two days before polling, the *Daily Chronicle* could run the headline 'Hemel Hempstead Tory Fort Toppling'.[22] The *Daily Chronicle* proved to be an

---

[19] The constituency in which J. A. Spender observed that there were 'more old tory tabbies in the place than – I should think – in any other single town in the country outside London'. Spender to Gladstone, 3 Mar 1922, quoted in Wilson, *The Downfall of the Liberal Party*, p. 259.

[20] Spender to Miss Stevenson, 25 Nov 1922, in Lloyd George Papers, G/18/9/1.

[21] *Morning Post*, 23 Nov 1923.

[22] *Star*, 23 Nov 1923; *Daily Chronicle*, 4 Dec 1923.

accurate prophet. The Liberal won the seat by 17 votes, with 8,892 to the 8,875 votes of J. C. C. Davidson.

Barbara Hammond was to write of the result to Gilbert Murray: '. . . it is the greatest joke that the Liberal has got in here . . . .Of all constituencies, this was regarded as the most hopeless . . . .'[23] Barbara Hammond's political judgement is open to question. Six years later, in the election of May 1929, a Liberal again came within a narrow margin of victory, only to be robbed by a Labour candidate who lost his deposit. The Conservative in 1923 polled 49·9 per cent; in 1929 he polled 49·8 per cent. The difference in 1929 was that Labour was able to draw off sufficient Liberal votes to return a Conservative on a minority vote.[24]

These constituency examples do not deny that, by 1929, the Liberals were unable to stop the advance of Labour, but they do question whether the Liberal success in 1923 was *so* remarkable.

They lead naturally on to a point which cannot be too strongly over-emphasised. The weakness of the Liberals in the early 1920s was not in winning seats, but in holding them once they had been won. Table 10.16 illustrates this point.[25]

TABLE 10.16
Seats won, 1918–29

Times won	Con.	Lib.	Lab.
5	154	22	49
4	105	19	63
3	76	34	48
2	54	69	53
1	56	137	91
0	157	321	298

[23] Barbara Hammond to Gilbert Murray, 16 Dec 1923, quoted in Wilson, *The Downfall of the Liberal Party*, p. 253.

[24] The figures in 1929 were: Conservative 15,145, Liberal 11,631, Labour 3,624.

[25] Figures are from Kinnear, *The British Voter*, p. 36. The table excludes Northern Ireland (because of boundary changes). If Ulster were included, it would only have re-emphasised Conservative predominance.

Although the Liberals managed to win some 281 seats on different occasions between 1918 and 1929, they won only 22 seats on all five occasions. Labour won 49 seats on every occasion, the Conservatives no fewer than 154. The figures are even more striking if we examine those seats won by the Liberals on three or more occasions. Only 75 seats returned Liberals in at least three general elections, compared with 160 Labour and a massive 335 Conservative.

The real Liberal problem was retaining seats won on a favourable tide. No fewer than 137 constituencies returned a Liberal on a single occasion. If, by organisation, finance and propaganda, these and similar seats could have been made secure, some 200–250 seats could have been within the party's sight.

Much of the evidence from all this electoral analysis lends support to the argument that the Liberals in 1923 enjoyed more popular support than historians have sometimes been willing to admit. However, there are some important qualifications that need to be made concerning this apparent Liberal upsurge.

The first concerns the absolute Conservative vote. Despite the many Liberal victories in rural constituencies, the Conservative vote had often held at its 1922 level. In other words, in these seats it was not so much the Conservatives who had done very badly, but the Liberals who had attracted votes not cast a year before. Three examples in the West of England demonstrate this point. In Devon, a county in which the Liberals won Barnstaple, Tiverton, Torquay and Totnes, the Conservative vote *rose* from 78,034 to 79,721. Similarly, in Wiltshire the Liberals won both Devizes and Salisbury, yet the Conservative vote rose from 40,748 to 41,331.[26] Finally, in Somerset, where the Conservatives lost Bridgwater, Wells and Weston to Liberals, and Frome to Labour, their vote fell only from 62,201 to 61,678.

No doubt these figures owed something to the appeal of the subsidy. Much more significant, they were an indication that,

---

[26] These figures do not include Swindon, which was not a rural seat and where comparisons are marred by a Liberal intervention.

if agricultural prices improved, as they were to do in 1924, the Conservatives would recapture their lost rural votes.

The second qualification on the scale of the Liberal revival concerns the fall in turnout. In England, turnout fell from 72·4 per cent to 70·8 per cent, in Scotland from 70·3 per cent to 67·6 per cent and in Wales from 79·4 per cent to 77·3 per cent.[27] The most useful evidence for the extent of turnout decline can be seen in the 514 constituencies contested on each occasion. Turnout fell in 312 of these and rose in 202. In six out of ten seats fewer people voted than in 1922. The main variations in turnout are shown in Table 10.17. Significantly, in those constituencies fought by the same parties as in 1922, turnout decreased substantially, by over 4 per cent, in 143 seats, but rose substantially in only 59.

TABLE 10.17

		No.	% of total
Increased turnout:	over 8%	15	(2·9)
Increased turnout:	4–8%	44	(8·6)
Increased turnout:	0–4%	143	(27·8)
Decreased turnout:	0–4%	169	(32·9)
Decreased turnout:	4–8%	91	(17·7)
Decreased turnout:	over 8%	52	(10·1)
		514	(100·0)

It is probable that this decrease in turnout was the result of three factors: the apathy of Conservatives in safe seats; the deliberate abstention of those Conservatives not willing to accept Protection but unwilling to vote Labour or Liberal; and finally, the apathy of Labour voters in safe industrial and mining seats.

Certainly, after the election many Conservatives attributed part of their defeat to apathy. Complaints on these grounds were voiced in such divisions as Epsom, Hemel Hempstead

[27] The electorate had increased by 2 per cent on the 1922 figure, from 20,874,456 to 21,283,085.

and Peterborough.[28] This seems to have been particularly prevalent in the middle-class seats of the Home Counties and the South-East.[29] In such safe Conservative territory as Richmond turnout fell by 9·5 per cent and in Hendon by 9·7 per cent. It was not surprising that in Finsbury, for example, the unsuccessful Conservative candidate complained to Baldwin after the election that it was impossible to get Conservatives to the poll.[30]

In addition to the reduction in turnout explained by apathy, which soon vanished with the changed political climate of 1924, many Conservatives in 1923 deliberately abstained rather than desert their party. This was particularly significant since, once Protection had been removed from practical politics, these Free Trade Conservatives could be expected to return to the party fold.

The exact extent of these abstentions is impossible to determine, but contemporary observers believed them to be an important factor. At Bolton, for example, the local press believed that the Conservative Free Trade vote had stayed at home.[31] In Scarborough the press similarly noted that:

> many have abstained from voting because of the fear that a tariff policy would mean an increase in the cost of living. In the minds of the boarding-house keepers of Scarborough and Whitby this has been a very real fear . . . .[32]

Similar views were echoed elsewhere. There is evidence in the voting figures, especially in old Free Trade areas where no Liberal candidate appeared, of abstention on the part of Conservatives.

---

[28] For these complaints in Epsom, see Epsom Conservative Association, Annual Report, 1924. For Hemel Hempstead, see Davidson to Sir T. G. Jones, 17 Dec 1923, in Davidson Papers. For Peterborough, see Peterborough and North Northamptonshire Conservative Association, Minutes, Executive Committee, 26 Jan 1924.

[29] Turnout in Essex averaged 60·3 per cent; in Middlesex, 66·1 per cent; in Surrey and Kent, 62·0 per cent; and in the 11 most residential seats in London only 56·8 per cent.

[30] Baldwin Papers, F35/159, Archer-Shee to Baldwin, Dec 1923.

[31] *Bolton Evening News*, 7 Dec 1923.

[32] *Yorkshire Post*, 8 Dec 1923.

The two North Lincolnshire divisions of Brigg and Grimsby provide useful examples. Neither was contested by Liberals, although these had once been strong Free Trade constituencies. In Brigg the Conservative vote fell by 3,051, the Labour vote rose by only 1,568; turnout fell from 80·3 per cent to 72·8 per cent. Similarly, in Grimsby the Conservative vote fell by 6,149; the Labour vote rose by only 1,732; again, turnout fell heavily from 72·3 per cent to 62·2 per cent.

In this type of constituency with a Free Trade tradition, and with no Liberal candidate, abstention on the tariff issue, especially among women, seems the most probable answer. Certainly, the seats in which turnout fell most were the Conservative–Labour straight fights.

Just as, in 1923, apathy on the part of Conservatives affected turnout, so similar lack of enthusiasm in the Labour ranks also increased this phenomenon.

There were two main areas in which this factor was clearly at work. The first was the region of Labour's spectacular advance in 1922, the Clyde. In Glasgow, for example, turnout fell from over 76 per cent to 69 per cent, with very heavy reductions in such safe Labour seats as Shettleston or Govan.[33] The second group was the mining areas. Turnout fell heavily in every coalfield. In Yorkshire turnout was down by 9 per cent, in Lancashire by 5·7 per cent and in Durham by 6·8 per cent.[34] Possibly the weak Liberal challenge in the coalfields was partly responsible, but probably over-confidence by Labour after its victories in 1922 was more important. In the 'Red Scare' campaign of 1924 turnout increased to exactly its 1922 level.

The significance of these turnout figures is important in assessing the increased turnout in 1924. In 1923 both the Conservatives and Labour had a section of their normal voting strength which, for reasons of apathy or deliberate abstention, had failed to vote. In the changed conditions of

[33] Turnout fell by 12·9 per cent in Shettleston and 12·6 per cent in Govan. In 8 of the 15 seats in Glasgow turnout fell by over 10 per cent.

[34] The turnout figures for each coalfield were: Yorkshire, 64·6 per cent, South Wales, 78·3 per cent; Durham, 71·8 per cent; Nottinghamshire and Derbyshire, 69·9 per cent; Lancashire, 79·3 per cent and Scotland, 72·2 per cent.

1924 these would rally to the party. The Liberals could expect no such bonus.

In explaining their disaster at the polls, the Conservatives certainly blamed the Liberal successes on the dear food issue affecting the women's vote. As one candidate wrote to Baldwin:

> We always thought women were of a conservative nature . . . the Conservatives suddenly brought forward anything but a conservative measure and the women voted true to type which in this case did not apply to the Conservative Party.[35]

In more violent language, Sir Samuel Hoare stressed that 'it was the ignorant opposition and credulity of the women' which was to blame.[36] Many leading Conservative women accepted the truth of the allegation. Thus, the chairman of the Women's Parliamentary Committee for the Eastern Provincial Area stressed the need 'for better organisation to enable us to counter the inaccurate statements on dearer food by our opponents to the women electors'.[37]

In addition to using the 'Dear Food' cry so effectively, the Liberals possessed a support from the press magnates that the party was never to enjoy again. Not surprisingly, the bitterest comments from the Conservatives were reserved for Beaverbrook and Rothermere. Thus, St Loe Strachey consoled Baldwin by stating that he had been 'vilely treated' by the 'malign and ineffable' Beaverbrook.[38] Similarly, one Conservative back-bencher wrote to Baldwin that Rothermere ought to be shot, and Beaverbrook sent back to Canada – where he would be by his compatriots.[39]

In an election in which so many factors favoured the Liberal campaign, the real extent of the revival of the party in 1923 is difficult to determine. However, temporary though some of the factors were in its revival, the fact remained that

[35] Baldwin Papers, F35/122, Keymer to Baldwin, 11 Dec 1923.

[36] Davidson Papers, Hoare to Davidson, 8 Dec 1923.

[37] Women's Parliamentary Council of the Eastern Provincial Area of the National Union of Conservative and Unionist Associations, Minutes, Executive Committee, 31 Dec 1923.

[38] Baldwin Papers, F35/189, St Loe Strachey to Baldwin, Dec 1923.

[39] Baldwin Papers, F35/186, Morrison-Bell to Baldwin, 11 Dec 1923.

the Liberal Party in 1923 could poll as many votes as Labour. The Liberals remained the second largest party in the 230 English county divisions, the second largest party in the Welsh and Scottish boroughs and the largest single party in the Welsh counties. The Liberal Party remained the alternative to the Conservatives in non-industrial England as well as a rival to Labour in such industrial areas as the North-East or Yorkshire.

It is possible that, with this basis of support, if the reunited Liberals *had* been the second largest party in 1923, and formed a minority government, the genius of Lloyd George in office might have launched the party on a new crusade, such as he was to do for the 1929 election, which might have transformed the decline of the party.

This did not happen, but it is not to say it *could* not have happened. As it was, the Liberal revival induced into many Liberal minds an over-euphoric belief that reunited Liberalism was now strong and would grow stronger. As Cowling has written:

> It induced the illusion that Liberals were the arbiters of English politics and that the ideology of 'Free Trade' as the 'Middle Way' between Protection and the Capital Levy could become the basis for a commanding Central party to span the area between the Conservative Right and the Labour Left.[40]

This euphoria disguised the dilemma in which the 1923 results had left the party – whether to maintain Baldwin in office or install a Labour Government. This dilemma – and its consequences – the Liberals never really solved. Within a mere ten months, the hopes of December 1923 had become only a memory. For this drastic reversal of fortunes, the Liberals had in many ways only themselves to blame.

[40] Cowling, *The Impact of Labour*, p. 347.

11 Putting Labour In

Although the results of the 1923 election were indecisive, the decision to put into office a Labour Government proved to be one of the most crucial events in the decline of the Liberal Party. In a sense, the débâcle in the election of October 1924 was a corollary of this decision.

It was ironic that the degree of success achieved in 1923 by the Liberal Party could hardly have been more paradoxical. Had the party done only fractionally better, and become the second largest party, the problems facing the Liberals would have been considerably reduced. The party might probably have formed a government and faced the next election, at a time and on an issue of its own choice, as a united party.

If the Liberals in 1923 had fared worse and the Conservatives returned an overall majority, the party would have been spared the dilemma of putting Labour in. Reunion might have become a reality and the party have faced the next election well prepared and well financed, with Labour still not having had the experience of office. Neither of these events had happened. The Liberal Party had the unenviable choice of maintaining a Conservative Government in office or installing a Labour minority administration.

The dilemma in which the Liberal Party found itself might have been solved had the Conservatives split as a result of the election disaster. In fact, although the seven weeks between 6 December 1923 and 22 January 1924, the day on which Baldwin formally offered his resignation as Prime Minister, were dominated by intrigue and speculation, the Conservative leadership was not precipitated into disastrous action.

It is true that a plot was launched to stampede Baldwin into resignation *before* facing Parliament, with the object of replacing him as Prime Minister by a Conservative such as Austen Chamberlain or Lord Derby. The extent of this plot remains unclear, although it seems to have been confined

mainly to those Conservatives still hankering after a renewed
Coalition.[1] The vital fact was that Baldwin's closest colleagues, Bridgeman and Amery, violently opposed any premature resignation. Bridgeman wrote to Baldwin: '... we
share your responsibility for what has happened .... I know
of no other leader who could hold the party together as you
still can.' He concluded: 'Magna sit veritas et praevalebit.'[2] In
similar vein, Amery wrote to Baldwin: '... if you talk of
resigning the leadership, you break up the party, and you
throw men like Neville, Philip, Wally Bridgeman and myself
on the street.'[3]

The day after writing these letters, Amery and Bridgeman,
along with Davidson, lunched with Baldwin. This would seem
to be the occasion when Baldwin decided to remain. With this
decision to face Parliament, the immediate future was settled.

However, the Liberals might still have been put in a
position to form a government had the various plans hatched
in the Conservative ranks to avoid a Socialist Government
come to fruition – plans that were given considerable encouragement by the more right-wing press. The *English Review*
thought that the 'sun of England seems menaced by final
eclipse', whilst Winston Churchill, who had just been defeated as Liberal candidate for Leicester West, declared that
a Labour Government would be a 'national misfortune such
as has usually befallen a great state only on the morrow of
defeat in war'. In some quarters it was suggested that the best
solution would be to set up a government of 'national
trustees' under some such figure as McKenna, who had
deserted politics for banking.

---

[1] The best account of this event is in Middlemas and Barnes, *Baldwin*, pp.
252–3. The plot seems to have involved Birkenhead, Austen Chamberlain,
Derby, Worthington-Evans, Joynson-Hicks, Beaverbrook and Rothermere.

[2] Baldwin Papers, F35/173, Bridgeman to Baldwin, 8 Dec 1923.

[3] Baldwin Papers, F35/170, Amery to Baldwin, 8 Dec 1923. A colourful
appeal to Baldwin was also made from St Loe Strachey, who urged him to
'save the Unionist Party from Birkenhead, Churchill, Beaverbrook and
Rothermere'. Strachey added: 'Don't leave us alone with such a crew.'
Baldwin Papers, F35/189, St Loe Strachey to Baldwin, undated letter.

One of the more serious schemes on these lines was devised by Younger. Younger suggested to Lord Stamfordham, the King's private secretary, that when Baldwin was defeated in Parliament, the King should send for MacDonald and ask the Labour leader if he could give a firm assurance that he would be able to govern for a reasonable time. Not having consulted the Liberals, MacDonald would presumably not be able to give the required assurance. The King would reply that he must see if Asquith could give the necessary guarantee. At this juncture, the Conservatives would proffer support to a minority Liberal Government and Asquith would become Prime Minister.[4]

A very similar plan was devised by Sir Robert Horne. Horne's object, like Younger's, was to put an Asquith administration into office as quickly as possible. He wrote to Derby suggesting that, if Baldwin was defeated, and MacDonald formed a government, the latter was to be unseated immediately. Not having had an appreciable term in office, the King would be able to refuse MacDonald a dissolution. Asquith would then come in, with the Conservatives offering general support. Horne continued his letter:

> The Liberals could pass legislation to create the alternative vote, and then go to the country after a year of quietness. Such a development would start business again and cheer commerce.[5]

Horne also wrote on these lines to Baldwin, urging a 'working arrangement' with the Liberals. He argued that, if Asquith demanded legislation to provide for the alternative vote, then this would not be any detriment to the Conservative Party.[6] Horne also wrote in similar vein to Lloyd George.[7]

Another Conservative to think, rather more vaguely, of a 'caretaker' government was J. F. Hope, who wrote to Davidson:

---

[4] Younger told Lord Gladstone of this scheme. This account of Younger's plan is derived from the Gladstone Papers, BM Add. MSS 46,474/64. For Gladstone's unsympathetic reaction, see pp. 184–185.

[5] Derby Papers, Horne to Derby, undated letter.

[6] Baldwin Papers, F35/183, Horne to Baldwin, 10 Dec 1923.

[7] Lloyd George Papers, G/10/6/1, Horne to Lloyd George, undated letter.

Let some patriot of repute (Grey?) form a Government of whomsoever he can get . . . but let the leaders, Conservative and Liberal, stand out, keep their party machinery intact and promise support say for a year.[8]

All these plans and schemes, however, never progressed once Baldwin had determined that Ramsay MacDonald should form a government and the Conservatives go into opposition without any collusion or pre-arranged intrigue with the Liberals.

The most outspoken and persistent advocate of a period in opposition was Amery. Of the political crisis, Amery wrote to Baldwin: 'Above all there must be no talk of a Coalition with the Liberals: that would *break up the party* who hate them *much worse than Labour.*'[9]

Amery made abundantly clear in this letter his scorn for Austen Chamberlain's suggestion of a 'moderate' government. He continued:

I see Austen, who is a damn faint-hearted ass if ever there was one, has already begun talking about supporting a 'moderate' government. I have stood up for Austen all I could so far, but I really am fed up with him now.

Amery wrote again to Baldwin against any support for a Liberal Government:

. . . the real healthy and natural division of parties in this country is between constructive Conservatism on the one side and on the other Labour-Socialism. Make it clear we'll never support the Liberals.[10]

According to Amery, the Liberal Party had only one option – to put Labour in. As he bitterly observed, that responsibility would prove the deathbed of the Liberals.

Amery, indeed, held out little hope for the future of the Liberal Party. As he wrote to Geoffrey Dawson of *The Times*:

Surely the right solution is for the Liberal Party to disappear by one section of it gradually joining with and diluting the Labour Party and the other section coming into line with us.[11]

[8] Davidson Papers, Hope to Davidson, 9 Dec 1923.
[9] Baldwin Papers, F35/168, Amery to Baldwin, 8 Dec 1923.
[10] Ibid.
[11] *The Times* Archive, Amery to Geoffrey Dawson, 9 Jan 1924.

In addition to Amery's determined opposition to any collusion with the Liberals, several Conservatives were far-sighted enough to realise the eventual benefit the party might reap from the impact of a Labour Government. As H. A. Gwynne, the editor of the *Morning Post*, wrote to Baldwin of the prospect: 'The City would be horribly afraid of it, but I am not sure that a shock like that would not do the country a lot of good.'[12]

There was also a general feeling among Conservatives that, with unemployment so high and the position in Europe unsettled, whoever formed a government in the next few months would have an unenviable task.[13]

The net result of these factors was that the decision on whether to install a Labour Government was placed firmly in the Liberal camp. It was a critical moment for the Liberals.

The Liberal Party, and most particularly its leadership, was completely divided over its course of action. On the one extreme was the clear declaration for complete independence from the *Liberal Magazine:*

> There are no conceivable circumstances in which the Liberal Party could enter into a Coalition, alliance, partnership or other collusive arrangement . . . with the Conservative Party. Liberals are not separated from Conservatives merely by a difference in the way of doing things . . . They are separated in their fundamental aims, in thought, in idea, in principle; and there is neither any event nor any formula that can ever bridge this gulf.[14]

A representative of this radical wing was Lord Gladstone. Younger, on holiday in Nice, chanced to meet Gladstone and informed him of his plan to thwart MacDonald. Gladstone, not impressed, wrote to Maclean that although it was a 'pretty scheme on paper', it was 'all wrong and based on no intelligible principle'. Gladstone argued that it would be fatal, since

---

[12] Baldwin Papers, F35/164, Gwynne to Baldwin, 7 Dec 1923.

[13] For arguments on these lines, see Baldwin Papers, F35/179, Younger to Baldwin, 8 Dec 1923.

[14] *Liberal Magazine*, Jan 1924.

the party would be acting merely as a warming-pan for the Conservatives.[15]

At the opposite extreme to Gladstone were such determinedly anti-Socialist Liberals as Churchill, Hamar Greenwood and Guest. Although a relatively small group, they were influential and an embarrassment to the rest of the party.[16]

Lloyd George well summarised this division in the party when he wrote to C. P. Scott on the question of voting Labour into office:

> Quite a number of the 'important and influential' emphatically dislike it, but if Ramsay were tactful and conciliatory I feel certain that the Party as a whole would support him in an advanced Radical programme.[17]

At the centre of the dilemma now facing the Liberals was Asquith. Of the position in which Asquith was now placed, Roy Jenkins has written:

> Almost any Government would have been possible in this Parliament, but Asquith, who was clearly the pivotal figure, seems to have decided at an early stage that it had better be a Labour one.[18]

He continues:

> Furthermore, he was anxious that the Labour Party should not be soured by the opposition of a 'bourgeois' alliance. And he was able to comfort the conservative part of his conscience with the reflection that if a Labour Government was ever to be tried in this country, as it would be sooner or later, it could hardly be tried under safer conditions.

The evidence from the Lloyd George papers does not support this interpretation. It would seem that Asquith was

---

[15] Gladstone Papers, BM Add. MSS 46,474/64, Gladstone to Maclean, 12 Jan 1924.

[16] Lloyd George, for example, found Guest 'busily seducing the Independent Liberals in the lobbies' in January 1924. See ibid., Maclean to Gladstone, 22 Jan 1924.

[17] Lloyd George Papers, G/17/11/8, Lloyd George to Scott, 27 Dec 1923.

[18] R. Jenkins *Asquith* (1964) pp. 499–500.

not the pivotal figure, nor was he originally in favour of installing Labour.

To understand the action of the Liberal leaders in December 1923, it is absolutely essential to realise the distrust and suspicion with which the Asquithians viewed Lloyd George. It is no exaggeration to say that such people as Sir Robert Hudson, the party treasurer, or Gladstone were far more concerned about what Lloyd George might be plotting than what Ramsay MacDonald might do.

During the campaign Hudson had written to Gladstone rejoicing that 'Lloyd George's stock is slumping, just as ours is rising'.[19] After the election Gladstone thought it necessary to warn Maclean that Asquith was 'not Lloyd George proof by any means' and must not be left alone with him any more than could be helped.[20] The next day, Gladstone wrote again:

> The General Election was a triumph for H. H. A. L. G. knows that he cannot possibly claim any material share in our successes . . . . His only asset is his fund and he will use this for terms . . . . I am afraid it is all a dirty business and I shrink from it.[21]

This bitterness was not confined to attacks on Lloyd George but extended to a denigration of the campaign efforts of former National Liberals.[22] It was against this background of suspicion and distrust that the Liberal leaders met to decide on their course of action.[23] At this meeting, Asquith's own plan, strongly supported by Simon, was to turn the Conservatives out as soon as possible but then to do the same to Labour, 'as speedily as possible by a combination with the

[19] Gladstone Papers, BM Add. MSS 46,475, Hudson to Gladstone, 4 Nov 1923. Of the reunion of the Liberal leaders at Paisley, Hudson wrote cynically: 'I read of Margot almost hugging Lloyd George. I observe Violet walking warily and cleverly (ibid., 26 Nov 1923).

[20] Gladstone Papers, BM Add. MSS 46,474/51, Gladstone to Maclean, 29 Dec 1923.

[21] Ibid., 30 Dec 1923.

[22] Gladstone, for example, attacked Sir William Edge, who had unsuccessfully defended his Bolton seat, as 'one of the least useful and indeed positively unhelpful forces in Lancashire'. Gladstone Papers, BM Add. MSS 46,474/60, Gladstone to Simon, 10 Jan 1924.

[23] The following account is based on the entry in C. P. Scott's diary dated 5–6 Jan 1924, in Scott Papers, BM Add. MSS 50,907.

Tories'. According to Asquith's reasoning, the Liberals would then be called upon to take office.

Lloyd George immediately came out against this plan, demanding to know from Asquith what any such Liberal Government, totally dependent on Conservative support, would be able to achieve. In the debate which ensued, the feeling of the meeting went against Lloyd George, who then proposed an adjournment. Asquith, always ready to adjourn anything, agreed. The Liberal leaders duly met again. By this time Asquith had changed his views and now favoured a policy of total independence. There was to be no collusion with the Conservatives, who were to be turned out of office at the earliest opportunity. The Liberals would then adopt a non-committal attitude to the Labour Government. Lloyd George accepted this change on Asquith's part as a first step in the right direction. A later entry in Scott's diary (this time dated 2–3 February 1924) confirms the same story. Scott's diary recorded:

> I asked him a little more about the meeting of Liberal party leaders held just after the election. It was on the Sunday after the results of the election were known. There were present – besides himself and Asquith – Simon, Mond, Macnamara and McCurdy. On that day McCurdy alone supported George in the policy of co-operation. The rest were in favour of themselves taking office, with Conservative support. (A paradoxical situation. George, the Coalitionist, against a virtual coalition, the Independent Liberals, its sworn antagonists, in favour.) It was not till the adjourned meeting that Asquith propounded his policy, announced at the National Liberal Club, of the half-way house, or holding the balance, which George accepted as a step in the right direction and which Asquith afterwards, in his famous speech on the Address, developed into one of frank co-operation [with Labour].

As Scott himself noted, it was indeed paradoxical that the only two persons wanting to give Labour a fair chance were the old Coalitionists – Lloyd George and McCurdy.

Certainly, however, the second thoughts of Asquith and the others at the later meeting prevailed. On 18 December, Asquith made it clear, in a speech to the Liberal Parliamentary Party, that the Liberals would not keep the

Conservatives in office or join in any combination to keep Labour out. If a Labour Government were ever to be tried, Asquith declared, 'it could hardly be tried under safer conditions'. Asquith went on to add that, whoever might be in office, 'it is we, if we really understand our business, who really control the situation'.[24]

Even after this speech, however, speculation continued on what Asquith's real motives were. Tom Jones certainly believed that Asquith had not abandoned hopes of unseating MacDonald and becoming Premier himself. He wrote to a colleague:

> Yesterday Asquith declared war on the Government in the National Liberal Club with the united blessing of L. G. and Sir John Simon. It is, therefore, practically certain that we shall have a Labour Government before the end of January. It is equally certain, I think, that the heavens will not fall and that the Capital Levy will not appear in the next budget. I believe the idea is to give the Labour Party a fair chance for some months at any rate and then possibly bring the Liberals into power without a dissolution.[25]

Asquith's private correspondence – even in January – reveals him still uncertain that it was wise for either Baldwin to go or MacDonald to replace him. Asquith wrote to Pringle:

> It . . . would seem that the immediate future is now settled: that Baldwin is to resign and Ramsay to come in. I doubt whether either of them is right. Baldwin could easily have snapped his fingers at a no-confidence amendment and announced that, as leader of the largest section of the House, he had better moral authority than anyone else to carry on the King's Government until he was absolutely blocked. And Ramsay might well have declined to start the first Labour Government under impossible Parliamentary conditions.[26]

If Asquith continued to doubt and waver, there is little reason to doubt the sincerity of Lloyd George's enthusiasm for the

---

[24] For the text of this speech, see *The Times*, 19 Dec 1923.
[25] *Whitehall Diary*, p. 260, Tom Jones to Sir John Chancellor, 20 Dec 1923.
[26] Asquith MSS, Asquith to Pringle, 10 Jan 1924.

experiment of a Labour Government. Thus, on 27 December 1923, Lloyd George wrote to Scott:

> I am very anxious to have a talk with you about the interesting situation which is developing in the new Parliament. I am entirely in accord with the line you have taken in the *Manchester Guardian*. The Liberal Party is very divided on the question of supporting Labour. Quite a number of the 'important and influential' emphatically dislike it, but if Ramsay were tactful and conciliatory I feel certain that the Party as a whole would support him in an advanced Radical programme.

Similarly, Scott's diary entry for 5 January 1924 gives an interesting picture of Lloyd George:

> Met Lloyd George in London at his request and drove with him to his new house at Churt. All our talk on the way was of the new position of parties and the relations to be established between the Liberal and Labour parties. He was in great spirits and exploded with joy at his final escape from Tory trammels. He did not confess to the immense mistake of that entanglement, but I think it was clearly in his mind.

Scott's diary went on:

> He repeated the view he had indicated when he wrote to me (he then said he entirely agreed with the line taken by the *Manchester Guardian*) that the only possible course, under present conditions, for the Liberal party was to back the Labour party wholeheartedly to the full extent open to it, and in concert with it to reap a full harvest of Radical reform.

However, Lloyd George was not without his worries. As he explained to Scott, Liberal support for Labour could not be mere paper support. There would have to be constant co-operation in the lobbies. Scott's diary entry recorded:

> But, if there was to be co-operation for common purposes with Labour, there must be consultation. It was not merely occasional support that the Labour Government would require in divisions: the support must be continuous. The Liberal whips would have to 'keep a House' for Labour, that is some 60 Liberals would have to be constantly in reserve. It was no use for the Labour leaders to

---

[26] Asquith MSS, Asquith to Pringle, 10 Jan 1924.

say that they would ignore snap divisions; they might ignore them now and again, but no Government could afford to be placed constantly in a minority – the conduct of business would become impossible and the Government would be discredited. Yet if the Liberals simply failed to attend this must be the consequence. Co-operation to be of use must be complete and it must be concerted.

At no time was there any suggestion of worry by Lloyd George that MacDonald might deliberately reject harmonious relations. Rather, Lloyd George's concern at this stage was with his fellow Liberals. Lloyd George went on to explain to Scott:

There will of course be opposition to this on the Liberal side. Simon in particular remains entirely hostile. At the party meeting at the National Liberal Club soon after, Asquith adhered rigidly to his purely non-committal policy and evidently had still in mind the ulterior aim of upsetting and superseding Labour. I went to the meeting (said Lloyd George) prepared to speak, but after hearing Asquith, I determined to be silent. I should have advocated co-operation and that would have introduced disharmony. So I held my peace.

Afterwards, Lloyd George went on to discuss possible areas of collaboration. Again, Scott's diary is exceedingly informative:

As to policy he saw no difficulty. There was an ample field common to the two parties. The danger, to his mind, was not that Labour would go too fast and far, but that it would not go fast and far enough and perish of inanition. It must be prepared to take risks and Liberalism should back it in a courageous policy. The line of advance would, however, have to be carefully selected. Thus if an advance were to be made in the direction of nationalisation it would be well to begin with the easiest matter – Electricity. Electrification was not a local affair and could not be dealt with locally. It was national and so was specially adapted to [national] treatment.... The railways should come next as being also non-local and amalgamation had already prepared the way. Mines were a good deal more difficult.

Thus, by 18 December, the Liberal die had been cast. Asquith (albeit reluctantly) had decided that Labour should have its chance to govern. But would Labour accept this opportunity?

In this situation everything depended on the attitude of the Labour Party. The immediate reaction of the Labour leadership to the results of 6 December was a mixture of sheer disbelief, followed by elation and then considerable apprehension. Over the weekend, when it still seemed possible that Baldwin would resign in the next few days, Sydney Arnold and H. B. Lees-Smith advised MacDonald not to take office, on the grounds that a Labour Government would be bound to fail and that the party would then be 'overwhelmed'.

Gradually, however, MacDonald and his closest colleagues became convinced that if they were given the opportunity to form a government it would be completely mistaken to turn it down. On 9 December, as well as talking to Arnold and Lees-Smith, MacDonald discussed the situation with J. A. Hobson and J. H. Thomas.[27] Both were in favour of taking office, the same course that was forming in MacDonald's own mind.

By 10 December the decision was almost made. MacDonald had received assurances indirectly (through McKenna) that there would be no panic in the City at a Labour Government. MacDonald had also secured Haldane's acceptance of the post of Lord Chancellor, and had calculated that even the difficult posts in the Lords could be filled. MacDonald was clear in his own mind that it was necessary for the party to take office to prove its capability to govern. The whole position was confirmed at an important dinner held at the Webb's on Monday 11 December. Beatrice Webb's diary recorded the scene:

> On Monday we had a dinner here of leaders; J. R. M., Henderson, Clynes, Thomas and Snowden – to discuss taking office and what exactly they would do if they did. Sidney reports that they have all, except Henderson, 'cold feet' at the thought of taking office, though all of them believe that J. R. M. ought not to refuse.[28]

[27] I am indebted to Mr David Marquand, MP, for his great help in establishing the sequence of events that led to MacDonald taking office as the first Labour Prime Minister.

[28] M. I. Cole (ed.), *Beatrice Webb's Diaries, 1912–24* (1952) pp. 255–6, entry dated 12 Dec 1923.

In the next two days the position was considered, in turn, by the Labour Party National Executive, by a joint meeting of the National Executive and the TUC General Council, and by the Executive of the Parliamentary Labour Party. At each of these meetings MacDonald pointed out that if the Labour Party were to refuse office after defeating the government, and if Asquith were then to form a government instead, the Liberals would sit on the government benches. The opposition front bench, and most of the other opposition benches as well, would be occupied by the Conservatives. The Labour Party would be relegated to the position of a group, and would probably sit below the gangway on the Liberal side of the House. When the Liberals were defeated, as they would be in due course, it would be they, and not the Labour party, who would take the opposition front bench. By refusing office, Labour would lose all the parliamentary advantages it had gained by becoming the official opposition in 1922; its position in the country might be put back by a decade. These arguments proved conclusive. On 12 December the National Executive resolved that 'should the necessity for forming a Labour Government arise, the Parliamentary Party should at once accept full responsibility for the Government of the country without compromising itself with any form of coalition'.

The following day (13 December) the joint meeting of the National Executive and the General Council arrived at a similar decision. The same afternoon, the Executive of the Parliamentary Labour Party did the same.

Whilst a minority of Labour back-benchers – mainly on the left wing – were still opposed to forming a government, nonetheless the almost complete unity within the higher echelons of the Labour Party removed any last chance of the Liberals avoiding the delicate task of voting Labour into office.[29]

[29] Among those opposing any minority government were Pethick-Lawrence, Robert Smillie, David Kirkwood and George Lansbury. See Lyman, *The First Labour Government*, p. 88. For Lansbury's position, see *Workers' Weekly* 21 Dec 1923. Such people as James Maxton and Tom Johnston favoured forming a minority government which would immediately go to the country on a Socialist policy.

Against this background of events in January 1924, it is interesting to speculate whether the Liberal Party could have pursued any other course of action which might have avoided the fate the party faced in 1924.

Several Conservatives argued, perhaps very naturally, that the Liberals' most advantageous action would have been to have maintained a Baldwin administration in office. Bridgeman wrote on these lines in his diary:

> When the Liberals took the very foolish course of turning us out to put the Socialists in, I was much relieved – if they had kept us in at the end of a tether they could have prevented us from carrying out any effective measures, and chosen their own moment for turning us out with little to show to our credit, and making a very advantageous ground for their own appeal to the country.

He continued:

> If they had followed the wiser course the result of the next election might well have been to secure for the Liberal Party the triumph which their short-sighted action eventually gave to us.

In retrospect, Bridgeman's argument was strong. In the circumstances of December 1923, however, having fought a campaign almost exclusively on Free Trade, the course of maintaining a Baldwin administration was not really within the realm of practical politics. No major Liberal leader is known to have advocated this course.

A more interesting question is whether the Liberals, in return for installing Labour into office and, say, guaranteeing a fixed period of support, could have persuaded Labour to offer electoral reform and, in addition, to put through legislation acceptable to the Liberals. It is by no means certain that the Parliamentary Labour Party would have rejected electoral reform, if this had been strongly pressed in the crucial period before 21 January 1924, at a time when, as Beatrice Webb's diary recorded, the Labour leadership had 'cold feet'.[31] Even if the results were negative, an approach by the

[30] Bridgeman Papers, entry in Bridgeman's diary, Nov 1924, p. 103.

[31] In a debate in March 1923 in the House of Commons to introduce an Alternative Vote Bill, 102 Labour men voted in favour, only 5 against. The division was lost by 180 votes to 209.

Liberals for preliminary discussions on the possibilities of limited co-operation would have forced MacDonald into a definite position of friendship or hostility.

After the fall of the first labour Government, Lloyd George confessed to C. P. Scott what he believed had been the Liberals' great mistake:

> Looking back he said he felt that the real mistake of the past session had been not the putting of Labour into office but doing so without any understanding or conditions. I confess, he said, it never occurred to me that we could be treated as we were treated. I took for granted that the relations of the two parties would be analogous to those between the Irish and Liberal parties in the Home Rule period. Even as it was I should have put the proposal of co-operation a little differently at the [first] Party meeting and I had come with notes of a speech in my pocket. But Asquith did not consult me beforehand and after he had spoken I felt there was nothing for me to do but to put back my notes into my pocket and briefly to concur.[32]

Apart from the lack of consultation between Asquith and Lloyd George, there is little doubt that the Liberals should have taken more heed of MacDonald's bitterness towards their party during the previous campaign. This was in itself remarkable, for, as was seen earlier, the 1923 election campaign had clearly shown an increasing bitterness by Labour towards the Liberals. The *Liberal Magazine* quite rightly declared that during the campaign, MacDonald had personally been 'full of neurotic complaints and suspicions' about the Liberals.[33] Even after 6 December these attacks continued. In the *New Leader* MacDonald launched a bitter attack on the 'petty nastiness' and 'dirtiest hitting' of the Liberals.[34]

And yet these warnings went unheeded. No Liberal leader really took stock of the possibility that the party, though supporting Labour in Parliament, might find itself constantly under attack in the constituencies.

---

[32] C. P. Scott's diary, Scott Papers, BM Add. MSS 50,907, entry dated 27 Nov 1924.
[33] *Liberal Magazine*, Jan 1924.
[34] *New Leader*, 14 Dec 1923.

The net result of all this was that the Liberals voted Labour into office without ever having considered how they would fare if Labour refused to co-operate. In this vital respect, Asquith's policy was without reality from the start. The Liberal Party would *not* be able to judge Labour on its merits. Either the Liberals would have to support Labour measures or vote against them. To vote against meant an election which the Liberals could not, for financial reasons, contemplate. It was to prove to be a policy without room to manoeuvre. Thus, by late December, the lines of battle had been drawn up. Parliament actually assembled on 8 January, and on 15 January the Debate on the Address began in the Commons. Two days later, on 17 January, a Labour amendment to the Address was moved by J. R. Clynes. After a heated debate, in which Austen Chamberlain made his speech declaring that if Asquith voted Labour into office, it would be the swansong of the Liberal Party, the vote was taken on 21 January. The Address, as amended, was carried by 328 votes to 256. The voting was as shown in Table 11.1.

TABLE 11.1

		Con.	Lib.	Lab.	Ind.	Total
Ayes		–	138	186	4	328
Tellers		–	–	2	–	2
Noes		245	10	–	1	256
Tellers		2	–	–	–	2
Total		247	148	188	5	588
Speaker		–	1	–	–	1
Vacancies		1	–	–	–	1
Absent:	Paired	7	3	3	1	14
	Unpaired	3	7	–	1	11
Grand total		258	159	191	7	615

The prospect of a Labour Government had finally become reality. Yet even at its very moment of birth, the Liberal Party had been divided in bringing it into existence. Ten Liberals had defied the party line by voting with the Conservatives.[35] In addition, a total of seven Liberal MPs did not vote and were not 'paired'.[36] Much to the indignation of the Conservatives – both nationally and locally – ten Liberals who had won in straight fights against Labour (and therefore won on Conservative votes) actually voted for the Labour amendment.[37]

At the next election these Liberals were to be the subject of particularly hostile attacks from the Conservatives. In January 1924, however, the next election was not a thought uppermost in people's minds. The question that remained to be answered was how well the experiment of a Labour Government would work. On 22 January, Baldwin tendered his resignation to the King. Shortly afterwards, following a meeting of the Privy Council, at which MacDonald was sworn a member, the King invited Ramsay MacDonald to form a government. The first Labour Government had arrived. With its advent, the Liberal party was about to be launched on the disastrous course which culminated in the débâcle of October 1924.

[35] They were: J. Duckworth, J. H. Edwards, Col. A. England, Sir E. Griffith, H. C. Hogbin, W. A. Jenkins, Sir W. B. Rees, Sir T. Robinson, W. E. Robinson and J. L. Sturrock.

[36] They were: Sir C. J. Cory, Sir R. N. Kay, Sir M. Macdonald, Brig.-Gen. E. L. Spears, Sir W. Sutherland, Sir R. J. Thomas and Lt-Col. J. Ward.

[37] They were: Sir R. W. Aske, Capt. W. Benn, Sir G. Collins, T. E. Harvey, R. M. Kedward, Sir G. McCrae, Major G. Owen, R. R. Pilkington, Capt. C. B. Ramage and W. T. Thomson.

Part Three

The Liberal Dilemma: The Politics of the First Labour Government

12 Labour: The Politics of Moderation

In January 1924 the imminence of a Labour Government – albeit dependent on Liberal votes – was a prospect that filled Conservatives with deep foreboding and the Labour movement with a mixture of elation and apprehension.

The dominant personality during the lifetime of the first Labour Government proved to be its Prime Minister, Ramsay MacDonald. The personality, the political prejudices and the path that MacDonald set himself are vital to an understanding of the politics of these months. Within the space of five short years MacDonald had risen from the abyss to the pinnacle: from the defeat and humiliation of the 'coupon' election to the invitation from Buckingham Palace. A mere three years earlier, in the Woolwich East by-election of 2 March 1921, his whole parliamentary career had seemed in ruins. Now he was Prime Minister of the first Labour Government and, at 58, at the peak of his powers.

The varied fortunes of these years had left an imprint on MacDonald that was to shape the course of the 1924 government. MacDonald was ambitious, but his ambition was tempered by a complex mixture of self-consciousness, shyness and a search for respectability that made for a difficult personality. He was vain; he worked too hard; and he was utterly incapable of delegating even the merest matter of detail.

Both to opponents and colleagues alike, the personality and peculiar vanity of MacDonald gave rise to early fears. Thus, Scott recorded in his diary a talk he had had with Lloyd George about the advent of a Labour Government. Scott wrote afterwards:

> The great danger to a Labour party was its extreme inexperience and consequent timidity. He expressed some doubts as to

MacDonald's own qualities as a leader. He had had no experience of administration, even of a trades union, and he was extremely vain. (This was strongly confirmed by Mrs Snowden at dinner. He had courage but lacked persistence. This also was confirmed at dinner by H. A. L. Fisher. They had been in India together on an Education Enquiry Commission and you never could depend on MacDonald to stick to an opinion for a week together.)

Earlier, when Scott saw MacDonald himself, some interesting points came to light. When Scott spoke to MacDonald about Liberal co-operation, MacDonald replied:

The difficulty was the strong feeling of hostility toward Lloyd George throughout the party, and the people I referred to – such he presumed as [Arthur] Ponsonby and [E. D.] Morel – hated him even more than the rest. They felt they could not trust him. His own experience bore this out in a small way. Before he went to Russia Lloyd George promised to see him through, but when the pinch came he did nothing. I said there must surely be someone less hard-bitten who could serve the purpose and he promised to find one.

One thing he was clear about – there must be an end to the flaunting of Labour's dependence [on the Liberals]. It might be tolerated once, it might be tolerated twice, but after that, if repeated, he should speak out strongly. He showed a curious sensitiveness on this and spoke with feeling, as though this were a matter of deep importance. Probably it is the matter on which his own party feels most and on which he would be most exposed to attack.

A great difficulty he said for him and his party was that they had been taken entirely by surprise and as they had not the least expectation of being called upon to take office, so they were quite unprepared for it. I expressed surprise as the possibility had been very present to our own minds.

The circumstances of the first Labour Government gave a massive importance to these personal traits. By taking on the Foreign Office in addition to the Premiership, MacDonald's inclination to overwork led him to a near-breakdown. Its effects were to be seen in the 1924 election campaign and in his handling of the Zinoviev letter. Similarly, having set himself out to reduce the Liberal Party to parliamentary impotence, MacDonald's vanity would brook of no moderation or compromise. MacDonald could have escaped the

Campbell censure. He preferred not to. The short lifetime of the first Labour Government was as much the fault of MacDonald as anyone else.

MacDonald was conspicuous as a Premier by his solitude. He made his decisions alone; consultation was not a habit that came easily to him. Of his Cabinet colleagues, only Thomas was really close to MacDonald. Snowden, who had been a bitter critic of MacDonald prior to 1914, was much less close. Not surprisingly, Clynes, Webb and Henderson – all of them pro-war in 1914 – never really enjoyed the leader's confidence.

MacDonald had accepted that Labour should form a government after December 1923 primarily for one reason: to prove that Labour could actually govern. The political strategy that underlay MacDonald's thinking was centred on this point. To MacDonald, the 1923 election demonstrated that there was still a mass of middle-class, middle-of-the-road voters who must be won to Labour. To do this, Labour must establish itself as the natural alternative to the Conservatives. To this end, Labour must govern not as a caretaker government satisfying no party, but as a government of studied moderation carrying out useful and widespread reforms. MacDonald, rather than Asquith or Lloyd George, must become the natural leader of the old radical tradition.

In such a political strategy as this, only one factor marred the equation – the Liberal Party. From the first, MacDonald determined to have no truck with the Liberals. He personally detested Lloyd George and, whilst admitting that Asquith was the best of a singularly bad bunch, bitterly objected to Asquith's patronising and condescending tone. In this climate – whose temperature neither Lloyd George nor Asquith ever accurately gauged – there could be no deals, no *quid pro quo* on proportional representation or similar legislation. If the Liberals liked Labour measures, they could duly vote in the lobbies. If they objected, then they could face the consequences of a general election as soon as they wished. MacDonald would govern on his own terms or he would not govern at all. And the longer MacDonald was in office, the more he hoped to capture the old Liberal vote in a programme of moderate, respectable reform. At the same time, the more his personal dislike of Asquith and Lloyd George grew.

Respectability was soon in evidence in the composition of MacDonald's Cabinet. After 18 December, when Asquith's pronouncement made a minority Labour Government a real probability, considerable speculation centred on the likely composition of a Labour Cabinet. From the start, it was clear that not only would MacDonald be Prime Minister, but he would also enjoy considerable freedom in his choice of colleagues.

In the event, the final choice of Cabinet presented a curious mixture. The first Cabinet of a Labour Government contained two Conservatives (Lords Parmoor and Chelmsford) and no fewer than five ex-Liberals (Haldane, Buxton, Henderson, Trevelyan and Wedgwood). In the major offices, MacDonald (after first wanting J. H. Thomas) eventually took the Foreign Secretaryship himself. Haldane was probably MacDonald's best single 'catch'. With Haldane on the Woolsack, Parmoor as Lord President of the Council, and Chelmsford (a former Viceroy of India and lifelong Conservative) at the Admiralty, the claims of respectability had been well satisfied.

The tone of the new government was well set by MacDonald at the Albert Hall rally on 8 January. MacDonald, whilst referring again and again to the cause of utopian Socialism that was their ultimate goal, emphasised that this minority government would set its target in pragmatic, moderate, realistic legislation. With this speech – and the eminently unrevolutionary composition of the Labour Cabinet – the hysteria that had grown up rapidly receded. After weeks of election campaigning, then manoeuvring, the political turmoil had subsided. In relative quiescence, Ramsay MacDonald took over the reins of government.

MacDonald's determination to steer a moderate course was evidenced in three directions: in the legislative programme put before Parliament; in the conduct of foreign affairs; and in his handling of trade union disputes.

Until the end of February, the government, for the first few weeks, might have seemed merely to be playing itself in. But by the end of February both Conservative and Liberal opponents were noticing that it showed 'day by day at question time' that the new Ministers took 'practically the same view of things as the late Capitalist government'.[1]

Nor were these judgements wrong. In the first few months of office the government carried out those few policies which MacDonald had authorised before Baldwin resigned. The capital levy was postponed. In unemployment, Sidney Webb, who was President of the Board of Trade and chairman of the Cabinet Committee on Housing and Unemployment, hardly upheld the claims which the Labour Party had campaigned on in 1923 – that a Labour Government was uniquely qualified to deal with unemployment. As Maurice Cowling has written, the outcome of Webb's efforts

> was a statement that 'the most helpful solution of the unemployment problem lies in the re-establishment of normal peaceful conditions throughout the world', the adoption of dilution in the building industry . . . and an increase in the amount to be spent through the Trade Facilities, Export Credits, Trunk Road, Empire Development, Housing, Drainage and Afforestation programmes, all of which had been inherited.[2]

Of the government's legislation in early 1924, very little was new and even less was radical. No Bill was introduced to nationalise the mines, and the Cabinet decided it would be inexpedient to introduce one. The only mining legislation introduced was a Coal Mines (Washing and Drying Accommodation) Bill. Railway nationalisation was similarly ignored. In agriculture, Noel Buxton's policy statement early in February proposed the strengthening of County Agricultural Committees, urged more agricultural co-operatives on the lines of the Linlithgow Report and suggested the restoration of Wages Boards. A few minor reforms were made in the area of unemployment insurance: the gap in the receipt of unemployment insurance was abolished; weekly benefit was increased and the unemployment insurance scheme was extended to juveniles. Meanwhile, in education, a number of

[1] L. S. Amery diary, 20 Feb 1924, quoted in Cowling, *The Impact of Labour*, p. 372.
[2] Ibid., p. 375.

useful reforms were introduced, inspired in part by the Hadow Report.

The only exception to this relatively minor legislation came with a major piece of housing legislation – the Wheatley Act. When forming his government, MacDonald had allocated a strong ministerial team to the Ministry of Health. John Wheatley, the lone Clydesider in the Cabinet, was Minister of Health, and had an able Parliamentary Secretary in Arthur Greenwood. The Wheatley Housing Act did not receive the Royal Assent until 7 August 1924, but both in its drafting and in the preliminary discussions with all the parties involved, as well as in actually piloting the Bill through difficult times at Westminster, Wheatley earned himself a personal triumph.[3] The *Nation* declared that Wheatley was 'the one conspicuous success in the new Parliament' and that in him the House had found a new favourite.[4] Under the Conservative Government that resumed office in November 1924 the Housing Act went on to do useful work. E. D. Simon, a Liberal expert on housing (and a stern critic of the Bill during its passage), gave it credit for the expansion in house-building from 86,210 houses built in 1923–4 to 238,914 in 1927–8.[5]

With the exception of Wheatley's Housing Act, many of the decisions of the Labour Government seemed almost to have as their object a demonstration of the government's Liberal credentials. Thus, on 17 March, the Cabinet instructed Wheatley to negotiate an agreed all-party measure of Poor Law Reform on the basis of the Maclean Committee report.[6] The reduction of the cruiser programme gave similar pleasure to many Liberals. The move to reverse the decision to build a major naval base at Singapore was presented as a move to strengthen international co-operation and the League of Nations.

In a sense, the apex of the government's desire to prove its Liberal (and especially Free Trade) credentials came with

---

[3] For the details of the background of the Bill and its specific proposals, see Lyman, *The First Labour Government*, pp. 110–30.

[4] Quoted in Lucy Masterman, *G. F. G. Masterman* (1939) p. 341.

[5] Lyman, *The First Labour Government*, p. 121.

[6] Cowling, *The Impact of Labour*, p. 376.

Snowden's Budget of April 1924. The Labour Chancellor received widespread praise for his Budget (which he modestly described as 'the greatest step ever towards the Radical idea of the free breakfast table'). Among its provisions were the reduction on sugar duty from 2¾d. per pound to 1¼d; the halving of the duties on tea, cocoa, coffee and chicory, lowering of the entertainment tax and, more important, the abolition of the McKenna duties. In all, indirect taxes were cut by £29 million and direct taxes by £145 million.[7]

The reaction in Labour circles to what was hardly even the most mildly Socialist of Budgets was jubilant. *Forward* declared that 'the housewife knows this week that the Labour Government is in earnest and means business', whilst the *Socialist Review* found Snowden to be the 'hero of the month' who had 'swept the Liberals off their feet'. Even Beatrice Webb rescinded her harsh judgement of Snowden and applauded his triumph.[8]

The Budget met with equal acclamation from the Liberals. In the Commons on 29 April, Asquith expressed on behalf of himself and his colleagues 'extreme satisfaction' with the Budget, adding: 'There is nothing in the Budget, so far as I know, in which principle is concerned, to which a single one of us sitting on these benches will not heartily subscribe.' On the following day, 30 April, the Parliamentary Liberal Party also gave warm approval to the Budget. The Liberal press was equally enthusiastic. 'A good Free Trade Budget, safe, sound and practical' was the verdict of the *Daily News*. 'The Liberal ideal of the free breakfast table is brought almost to realisation by this admirable Budget' declared the *Star*. 'A Liberal Budget in the best sense' stated the *Manchester Guardian*. Similar praise came from the *Westminster Gazette*, the *Daily Chronicle* and the Liberal *Yorkshire Observer*.

The success of Labour's studied moderation in domestic matters was accompanied by a diplomatic triumph for MacDonald in foreign affairs. Foreign policy was the government's greatest success, although it was in many ways a

---

[7] Lyman, *The First Labour Government*, pp. 145–9, has an excellent detailed discussion of the Budget.

[8] Ibid., p. 148.

personal triumph for MacDonald. MacDonald's diplomatic efforts towards a reconciliation of Germany and France bore fruit in the London Conference. As Cowling has written, the London Conference was the sort of milestone Lloyd George had hoped to reach at Genoa in 1922 and Baldwin had unsuccessfully sought in 1923.[9] At the conference (in July 1924) MacDonald presented himself as the presiding practitioner of a Liberal foreign policy, a natural successor to Grey. It was perhaps ironic that foreign affairs, which was MacDonald's triumph, should also, in the episode of the Russian Treaties, have been his downfall.

In foreign affairs, in fiscal and trade matters, and in a variety of domestic reforms, the minority Labour Government had begun to establish itself as the natural heir of the Liberal tradition. As leader of a minority government, MacDonald was exposed to defeat in Parliament. Yet although, by 21 July, the Labour Government had been defeated on no fewer than ten different occasions, none of these defeats (except the Rent Restriction Bill) was on an important issue, as the following list illustrates:

GOVERNMENT DEFEATS IN THE HOUSE OF COMMONS 1924

1. 13 March. The supporters of the Labour Government were loath to surrender private Members' time, and in consequence the government proposed to suspend the eleven o'clock rule in order to facilitate the conclusion of finance business before the end of the financial year. The opposition were prepared to give up private Members' time to this end, and could see no reason why Labour private Members should not make equal sacrifice. The government was defeated by 234 votes to 207.
2. 7 April. The Second Reading of the government's Rent Restriction Bill was defeated by 221 votes to 212, and the government was compelled to abandon its policy.
3. 7 April. This second defeat on the same day was on a motion in connection with the War Charges Validity Bill.

[9] Cowling, *The Impact of Labour*, p. 379.

4. 16 June. A defeat on the Report stage of the London Traffic Bill.
5. 23 June. The government was defeated by 315 votes to 175 in resisting a motion that Wheatley's Housing Bill be considered by a Committee of the whole House.
6. 24 June. This was a second defeat on the Report stage of the London Traffic Bill.
7. 30 June. This defeat was on the Committee stage of the Finance Bill, when the government refused to accept a Conservative amendment to exempt from the entertainments duty entertainments where the profits are devoted to philanthropic, charitable or educational purposes. The vote against the government was 220 to 165.
8. 18 July. This defeat, by 171 votes to 149, took place during the Report stage of the Unemployment Insurance Bill, on the question of 'contracting out'.
9. 21 July. On the Housing Bill, the Health Minister declined to make retrospective the subsidy to private persons who undertook to build. An amendment moved by Sir Charles Starmer, which made the subsidy retrospective, was carried by 201 votes to 155.
10. 21 July. This second defeat on the same day was also on the Housing Bill. T. Williams moved a new clause to prevent the ejection of a tenant from a house into which he had removed as a condition of employment on ceasing to work for the owners of the house. Wheatley accepted the clause, but on a division it was rejected by 137 votes to 119.

On no occasion had the Labour Government been defeated by the Liberals or Conservatives for introducing a Socialist measure. The reason was not hard to find. MacDonald had determined that no such contentious measure would be introduced. There was to be no popular 'People's Budget' or nationalisation on which Labour would seek an early dissolution. The politics of moderation allowed for no such tactics.

The moderate image created by the government was further strengthened by the attitude adopted by MacDonald and his Cabinet towards the trade unions.

The government's first test came in February when the Transport and General Workers' Union called a national dock strike. The Cabinet made it clear that it was willing, if necessary, to proclaim a state of emergency under the 1920 Emergency Powers Act. Josiah Wedgwood, the Chancellor of the Duchy of Lancaster, privately warned the union that the government was prepared if necessary to use troops to move essential supplies. In the event, the strike ended without an open conflict with the government, since the Court of Inquiry (to which the dispute had been referred) found in favour of the dockers.

A more serious dispute occurred on 21 March, when the London tram drivers came out on strike. The Court of Inquiry ruled in favour of the tram drivers, but at the same time stated that the employers would not be able to afford to pay unless the government introduced a Bill to co-ordinate London's fragmented transport services. At this juncture, on 26 March, the union (the TGWU again) announced that it would call out the London Underground drivers. On 27 March, MacDonald answered this threat by telling the House of Commons that a state of emergency had been declared. At the same time, a London Traffic Bill was introduced and a compromise settlement of the wage claim agreed (much to the opposition of Herbert Morrison and other London Labour Members). Henceforth, relations with the unions caused relatively little trouble.

Despite the success of MacDonald in foreign affairs, and despite the appearance of moderate legislation and firmness with the unions, the first Labour Government's course was not entirely harmonious.

MacDonald's own conduct estranged him more and more from his colleagues. Partly, indeed, this lay behind the fiasco of the Rent Eviction Bill. Prior to this event, Beatrice Webb noted in her diary that the parliamentary party was 'drifting', that Clynes was incompetent, and that the 'dullheaded miners' in the Whips' office did not earn their salaries of £1,000 a year.[10] According to Beatrice Webb, neither Henderson nor Clynes found MacDonald approachable. MacDonald, added Beatrice Webb in her diary, 'remains the

---

[10] This view of Clynes was shared by Tom Jones: Clynes's appointment as Leader of the House was, according to Jones, 'a great risk' since Clynes was 'so negligible a personality'.

"mystery man" to all his colleagues – who know little of his thinkings and doings'.

Meanwhile the politics of chaos, in terms of indiscipline in the lobbies, was not confined to the Liberal benches. Mac-Donald was faced with frequent discontent from his own back-benchers, in particular the ILP group. Such opposition was hardly surprising. A strong undercurrent in the ILP had been against taking office. Those in favour of accepting office had seen this as a matter of tactics; in office, the ILP wanted nothing less than a bold full-blooded Socialist policy.[11] Such people as Clifford Allen argued that if Labour's plans were thwarted, there should be an immediate 'appeal to the country and fight on the issue of Labour versus the Rest'.[12] The studied moderation of MacDonald soon caused a sharp reaction. This disillusion was voiced when in March a number of ILP Members, led by W. H. Ayles, an ILP pacifist, voted against the government on the Service estimates, and *Forward* launched a bitter attack on Chelmsford and Earl Beatty, the First Sea Lord. Later the same month, 45 Labour MPs abstained from voting on the government's Trade Facilities Bill.

Distress at what appeared to be the temporising policy of MacDonald's government spread rapidly. In March 1924, H. N. Brailsford (who was not on the left of the ILP) wrote in the *New Leader* that the last impression that the ILP wished to make on public opinion was to be seen as a somewhat fresher alternative Liberal team.[13]

At the meeting of the ILP National Administrative Council on 17 May, considerable criticism was voiced at Labour's handling of the unemployment question. By August 1924 the *New Leader* was stating that 'There is no disguising that the Labour Movement is disappointed at the Government's failure to tackle the unemployment problem.[14] Further

[11] For a detailed discussion of relations between the Labour Government and the Independent Labour Party, see R. E. Dowse, *Left in the Centre* (1966) pp. 102–16.
[12] *New Leader*, 14 Dec 1923.
[13] *New Leader*, 28 Mar 1924.
[14] *New Leader*, 8 Aug 1924.

criticism centred around government policy towards Europe and the Empire.[15]

If the ILP was becoming increasingly irritated by Labour's timidity, the Labour Government was becoming equally annoyed at ILP behaviour. Ponsonby angrily accused the ILP rank and file of behaving like an opposition. MacDonald's correspondence with Clifford Allen revealed his growing irritation. On 16 September, MacDonald wrote to Allen:

> Were I to say that from the moment I took office to now I have not had a particle of support from the ILP I should be unfair, but it would only be an exaggeration, not an invention.[16]

MacDonald's annoyance was understandable. On 7 August, Clifford Sharp, the editor of the *New Statesman*, had launched a bitter attack on Labour's record. He wrote in the *Evening Standard*:

> The obvious answer to the question 'Can Labour Govern?' as afforded by the Parliamentary history of the past six months, is 'No' . . . .
>
> The actual achievements of the Labour Government have not been substantial. It has not attempted to carry out, or even to introduce, any single one of those items in its programme which distinguished it from other parties, and its left wing is seriously disgruntled.

Whether these attacks from the Left did MacDonald any harm is unlikely. In a sense, they all enhanced his politics of moderation. What better way was there to achieve respectability than to isolate the men from the Clyde? In one area, however, ILP attacks did hit home. This was over the question of unemployment. A variety of Labour complaints on this score were given wide publicity. Thus, F. H. Rose, the MP for Aberdeen North, wrote in the *Clarion*:

> The simple truth is that our loudly-trumpeted professions, that we alone had the precious elixir of industrial health and life, were based upon sheer pretence, and were at best nothing but plausible political gags . . . . Political Labour has no remedy for unemployment.[17]

[15] See Dowse, *Left in the Centre*, pp. 107 ff.
[16] MacDonald to Allen, 16 Sep 1924, quoted ibid., p. 107.
[17] *Clarion*, 23 May 1924.

Others were less extreme, but no less critical. R. C. Wallhead, the MP for Merthyr Tydfil, stated in Parliament:

> We on these benches are entitled to express dissatisfaction with the smallness of achievement of the Labour Government . . . . I am quite sure I am voicing the opinions of a large number of my colleagues when I say that we are not satisfied.[18]

Hugh Dalton added his own criticism:

> It would be idle to pretend that the Government's policy on unemployment as a whole inspires complete confidence in its supporters. There is very little to show as yet, so far as the provision of new work is concerned.[19]

Undoubtedly unemployment – the 'intractable million' – was Labour's least successful area. Their attempts to alleviate unemployment were utterly orthodox and unconvincing, and their failure dogged the subsequent election campaign.[20] The party emerged little wiser from the 1924 experience and the full price of this failure was to be paid in 1931.

With the exception of unemployment, there can be little doubt that MacDonald's policy of moderation was reaping dividends. At the beginning of March, Ponsonby noted the government's growing prestige in the country, largely due to MacDonald's powers and personality. By the end of April, MacDonald himself believed that the country was accepting a Labour Government splendidly. The by-elections also seemed to deliver the same message, with Henderson's convincing victory at Burnley and a Labour gain at Liverpool West Toxteth.[21]

The politics of moderation had paid off in another sense also. Labour had used the months of 1924 to expand its organisation into rural and residential areas in which previously there had been no party activity, and to concentrate on improving both membership and morale.

---

[18] *H. C. Deb*, 29 May 1924.

[19] *New Leader*, 30 May 1924.

[20] For a detailed discussion of Labour and the unemployment problem, see Lyman, *The First Labour Government*, pp. 131–56, and R. Skidelsky, *Politicians and the Slump* (1967) *passim*.

[21] The by-elections are discussed on pp. 261–262.

One impact of the formation of a Labour Government had been to generate increased interest in the movement. It was reflected in increased space in the national journals and increased circulation figures for the *Daily Herald*. After a long period in which party membership nationally had been falling, the advent of a Labour Government at last reversed that trend (see Table 12.1). This small increase in membership was hardly a fair indication of a rapid spread of Labour organisation into new areas. By mid-1924 there were 2,967 divisional and local branches, an increase of 300 in twelve months. In the women's sector the total of branches rose to 1,332 and membership reached 150,000.

TABLE 12.1
Labour Party Membership Statistics

1921	4,010,361
1922	3,311,036
1923	3,155,911
1924	3,194,399

A parallel stimulus was given to the propaganda work of the Independent Labour Party by the electoral success of December 1923. The total number of branches rose from 635 in February 1923 to 772 a year later. It was noted at the annual conference at York in April 1924 that no fewer than 131 branches had been formed in the last five months. The increase of branches in the period 1923–5 was particularly great in Scotland (up from 171 to 307), London and the Home Counties (from 80 to 166) and Lancashire (from 100 to 136).

The most vital consequence of this extension of constituency Labour organisation, even though rudimentary, was that the party was able to field parliamentary candidates in areas in which previously only the Liberals had provided an alternative to the Conservatives.

The first Labour Government survived only until October 1924. This had hardly been a long time to inaugurate even relatively moderate reforms. Some items which Labour inherited, such as the military estimates, it was virtually impossible to change. There was further delay in acclimatising to new offices and growing accustomed to Civil Service routine. At an early stage, MacDonald had ruled out such controversial issues as the Capital Levy. And yet, given all the restraints of inexperience, lack of time and MacDonald's insistence on moderate measures, the government was able to enact some useful, if in the main unexciting, legislation.

And yet, even though its legislative achievement was so limited, the first Labour Government had vindicated Mac-Donald's strategy. It had proved, to his party and to the people, that Labour could and would govern. The party of opposition had become the party of government. Even more important, MacDonald's strategy in occupying the middle ground of politics – and thereby removing the *raison d'être* of the Liberals – was succeeding. In an age preceding opinion polls, precise judgements of popular opinion are difficult. But from every type of source during 1924 the evidence was that MacDonald's policy of moderation was paying off. As early as February 1924, Sir Edward Grigg wrote:

> Ramsay MacDonald is definitely established as the national leader of the Left. . . . I have very little doubt that if his health stands him in good stead, he will take with him a very large section of the Liberal party when next he goes to the country.[22]

The general election of October 1924 was to prove his judgement correct.

[22] Altrincham MSS, Grigg to Bailey, 28 Feb 1924.

13 A Party Divided: Liberal Leadership and Policy

The decision to install a Labour Government was both vital and crucial for the Liberal Party. For such a decision to succeed, it was imperative for the Liberals, while the minority Labour Government remained in power, to achieve several targets. To begin with, strong leadership was essential. And this meant a complete healing of the Asquith–Lloyd George split, as opposed to the hurried coming together that Baldwin's tariff election had brought about.

Secondly, it was imperative to use the coming months to develop constructive proposals – in social reform, industry, unemployment and foreign affairs – so that in any subsequent general election the Liberals could offer a distinctive, constructive and wide-ranging manifesto. Moreover, so that the party could fight on as broad a front as possible, derelict constituencies would have to be revived, candidates recruited and finance made available.

United and purposeful leadership was the prerequisite for new policies, revived organisation and sustained morale. It was essential if, in the changed order of British politics after the advent of Labour to office, the Liberals were to have a powerful and central position on the political stage. It was to be the fate of the Liberal party that, during the crucial months of the first Labour Government, they were to be granted none of these gifts.

In name, the party was united. In reality, it remained as divided as ever. The nearer one came to the centre of Liberal power, the greater the divisions that were evident.

Nor, perhaps, was this so surprising. The reunion brought on by the tariff election had been both sudden and incomplete. During the election campaign Lloyd George's Coalition Liberal headquarters was still operating, and was not finally disbanded until February 1924.[1] Moreover, many Asquithians found it difficult to accept the return of the Prodigal Son with his hankerings after Coalitionism so recently buried. Indeed, to a large extent it was not so much personal animosity between Lloyd George and Asquith (Lloyd George insisted he could get on well with 'the old man') which marred reunion, but the bitter distrust of Asquith's close colleagues such as Maclean, Gladstone, Phillipps and Hudson – to say nothing of Margot.

However, the real cause of suspicion and distrust during 1924 centred much more on the realities of political power rather than on lingering personal animosities – although personalities exacerbated the problem. The root of the problem lay in the weakened position of Lloyd George and his supporters after the results of 1923 were known. During the campaign Lloyd George had very much played second fiddle to Asquith – not because he wanted to, but because there was no alternative. The results of 1923, as were seen earlier, had decimated the ranks of the former Coalition Liberals. Among Lloyd George's closest supporters such figures as McCurdy, Mond and Churchill were all defeated. The balance of power within the new Liberal Party was undeniably in Asquith's favour. Yet Lloyd George retained one asset of unrivalled value – his Fund. Virtually bankrupted by two successive general elections almost within one year, the Independent Liberal organisation was desperate for funds. Without money, it simply could not wage a general election on a broad front. This fact Lloyd George knew only too well. It was the one card he had left to play.

However, more than simply an internal power game between Asquith and Lloyd George divided the two men in 1924. They were both divided on the tactics to be adopted towards Labour.

Asquith's position is easier to understand, because it remained more stable. Once Asquith had decided that Labour should be given its chance to govern, he seems to have

[1] *Daily News*, 31 Jan 1924.

hoped (with the condescension that so infuriated Mac-
Donald) that before long it would make such a mess of affairs
that MacDonald would resign, the King would send for
Asquith and all would be right again with the world. In the
meantime the Liberals would support Labour, while repair-
ing their own party machine. Time would also give the
Liberals a chance to raise money.

Having decided on this general course, the early months of
1924 were characterised by a total lack of positive leadership
by Asquith, whether in Parliament or the country. His
attitude, once again, was that the best plan was to 'wait and
see'. Before very long, his lack of leadership (made more
noticeable by an illness in March) was producing widespread
discontent within the Liberal ranks in the country. This
became particularly strong after the Abbey by-election of 19
March 1924. At no stage did Asquith (or Lloyd George)
envisage the hostile treatment that Labour would mete out.
When it came, Asquith was both bewildered and impotent.

Lloyd George's stance during the period from January
to July 1924 is more difficult to follow. Lloyd George, in a
position rather like a caged animal unused to its loss of
freedom, adopted a series of positions. In the very early days
of December 1923 and January 1924 (if Lloyd George is to
be believed, and if Scott's diary is a reliable testimony) Lloyd
George hoped to see a period in which, in constructive
partnership, the Labour Party, supported by the Liberals,
would put a series of radical, reforming measures on the
statute book. How long (given MacDonald's only too obviously hostile attitude) Lloyd George held to these views is
unclear. By early February, however, other doubts had
already begun to set in. When C. P. Scott saw Lloyd George at
Churt on the evening of Saturday 2 February (and again the
next morning) he noted in his diary:

> . . . evidently George was still much exercised in his own mind as
> to how the thing should be worked out. He kept coming back on
> its difficulties from the party point of view. If Labour succeeds
> they get all the credit; if it fails we get the blame for putting them
> in power. Then again to be safe from day to day in the House they
> will need to be able to rely on the support of at least 120 Liberals.
> If 50 seceded their majority would be gone. Already, on the vote

of want of confidence, there was a secession of 10 and the number will grow. How can you expect Liberals to go on continuously supporting Labour with no share in the Government?[2]

Lloyd George was clearly seeking advice, for Scott's diary continued:

> One of the last things he said to me was 'Well, what am I to do?' I could only suggest that, in a strange and tangled situation, we should go right ahead on the simple line we had taken and make all possible allowance for the section of the party which, having been in direct conflict with Labour at the election, found it hardest to co-operate with it afterwards. The present alignment of parties was obviously unreal and there would have to be readjustments.

Tom Jones saw Lloyd George at approximately the same time, and again found him rather subdued, 'relapsing very much into the position of a Private Member'. Jones went on:

> [Cope] thinks that very little would turn L. G. into a country gentleman, living quietly in retirement at Churt, but I think this must be a misjudgment and that L. G. is just loafing after the terrific outburst of energy in America and in the General Election.[3]

Useful evidence on Lloyd George's position at this time comes in a letter he himself wrote to his daughter Megan:

> What changes are taking place. A socialist govt. actually in power. But don't get uneasy about your investments or your antiques. Nothing will be removed or abstracted. They have come in like a lamb. Will they go out like a lion? Who knows? For the present 'their tameness is shocking to me'.
>
> They are all engaged in looking as respectable as lather and blather will make them. They are out to soothe ruffled nerves. When you return you will find England quite unchanged. Ramsay is just a fussy Baldwin – and no more.
>
> The Liberals were bound to turn Baldwin out and the King was bound to call Ramsay in and we are all bound to give him a chance. That is the situation.[4]

[2] C. P. Scott's diary, entry dated 2–3 Feb 1924, quoted in Wilson, *The Downfall of the Liberal Party*, p. 455.

[3] *Whitehall Diary, Vol. I* p. 271.

[4] Lloyd George to Megan Lloyd George, 4 Feb 1924, quoted in *Lloyd George: Family Letters* p. 202.

Clearly, in early February, Lloyd George's early enthusiasm for Labour was waning. MacDonald was a mere 'fussy Baldwin'. Lloyd George was perhaps, if not almost bored with politics, at least having doubts on the radical experiment of Liberal–Labour co-operation he had hoped to see.

However, by the following month a new event on the political scene turned Lloyd George's mind back towards the old Coalition. This was the decision of Churchill to contest the Westminster Abbey division as an Independent Constitutionalist. Although Lloyd George played no part in the by-election (he had 'too heavy commitments' to find time to speak on behalf of Scott Duckers, the Liberal candidate), he was watching events, closely and suspiciously, to see if the by-election might herald a revival of Coalitionism.[5]

The dismal Liberal performance, both in Abbey and in subsequent by-elections, was not lost on Lloyd George. He realised the party was in dire straits, but he had no intention yet of acting. As he wrote later in March to Megan:

> Here the situation is growing more and more difficult . . . . I am not sure how it is going to work out. The Liberals are in a tight place and for the moment things are not going too well for them. I am lying low – deliberately – but the time will come . . . .[6]

Meanwhile the growing lack of harmony between Asquith and Lloyd George was not hidden from the Parliamentary Liberal Party. As early as 20 March 1924, Grigg wrote of the political situation:

> There is no sign at present of any real understanding between Asquith and L.G. Asquith has been ill lately and has hardly been in the House of Commons at all. L.G. also has been away and seems to be keeping himself to himself to a very large extent. On the whole this is much the best line and I am glad that he is following it. He ought not to mortgage himself and his funds in any way to the Wee Free organisation. They have no desire except to strangle him at the earliest possible opportunity.[7]

[5] Altrincham MSS, Grigg to Bailey, 20 Mar 1924.
[6] Lloyd George to Megan Lloyd George, 25 Mar 1924, quoted in *Lloyd George Family Letters*.
[7] Altrincham MSS, Grigg to Bailey, 20 Mar 1924.

At the same time that the Liberal leaders vied for power in the party, the growing Labour attack on the sitting Liberal MPs (by the adoption of Labour candidates) was causing more and more concern. It was vital, both to restore morale and to instil a sense of purpose, that the Liberal leadership act on this issue. At a meeting of the Parliamentary Liberal Party on 25 March, at which Asquith presided, the following official communiqué was issued:

> A discussion took place on the Parliamentary position, in the course of which attention was drawn to the fact that while the Liberal Party was giving general support to a Labour Government in the House so long as its policy was consistent with Liberal principles, yet Liberal members were being increasingly subjected to Labour attacks in their constituencies. Several members indicated that if these conditions continued they might find it their primary duty to devote their time and energy to counteracting this propaganda in the country.

The communiqué, though reflecting increasing back-bench frustration, suggested little in the way of positive action. Not surprisingly, at a further Parliamentary Liberal Party meeting on 15 April, tempers began to fray. Unofficial accounts of this meeting appeared the following day.

In the Liberal *Daily News* the Lobby Correspondent reported that it had been decided to hold a special meeting of the party early in May to consider the question of the relations between Liberals and the Labour Government. This decision was 'an indication of the growing resentment with which the Government's attitude towards Liberals is regarded by those who sit below the gangway'.[8] The *Daily News* account added:

> Liberals feel that outside the House of Commons the Government's tactics are dominated by the desire to exterminate politically the party without whose votes the Government cannot live for another day inside the House of Commons. Moreover, they consider that in the House itself the Government loses no opportunity of abusing Liberal leaders, and heaping contempt upon the party generally. Yet all the time, the Government looks to the Liberal benches to provide it with a Parliamentary majority at all hours of the day and night.

[8] *Daily News*, 16 Apr 1924.

At this meeting Lloyd George bitterly attacked the contemptuous Labour attitude to the Liberals. Asquith, agreeing with Lloyd George, proposed that a special meeting of the parliamentary party be held to discuss this. To add further heat to the meeting, F. E. Guest (who had won Stroud in 1923) declared that he would not contest the seat again as a Liberal.

Meanwhile (since no official report of this meeting was released) a variety of fanciful newspaper accounts added further confusion. Vivian Phillipps, the Liberal Chief Whip, was subsequently forced to issue a denial that Asquith and Lloyd George had differed in their attitude towards the Labour Government. Phillipps's statement came too late; the damage had been done. Rumours and doubt were now rife that revolt was brewing in the party. Once again the divisions between Lloyd George and Asquith, and a general lack of either consultation or ability to take stock of the position of the party, had led to nothing constructive being done.

During April and May, Lloyd George grew increasingly worried about the Labour threat in the constituencies (particularly after a Labour candidate was adopted against him in Caernarvon Boroughs) and about the bad relations in Parliament (which Lloyd George partly blamed on the two Whips, Vivian Phillipps and Ben Spoor). After one long conversation with Lloyd George, Tom Jones noted in his diary:

> He began by telling me of his visit to his constituents in Caernarvonshire. Excellent meetings, lots of young people, and a growing opposition to Labour among the Liberals. Throughout our talk he was plainly preoccupied with the relations of the Liberal Party in the House and in the country to the Labour Party, and clearly willing to be on good terms with Labour. He did not want office – he had had his fling – but he was out to help. The Labour programme was more timid and prudent than his own pre-War campaign. They were doing nothing about the land, and they would muddle Housing.[9]

Grigg also had a long private talk with Lloyd George a little earlier, and formed very much the same opinion. Grigg wrote:

[9] Entry dated 27 Apr 1924, quoted in *Whitehall Diary*, Vol. I p. 277.

In the last few weeks Labour has put up a candidate against him in his own constituency in Wales and is making a dead set there to cause him difficulty. There is nothing like action of this kind for giving leaders a stimulus in the way they should go, and L.G. is now beginning to realise, I think, that co-operation with Labour is absolutely illusory as a goal for sensible Liberals. For the moment this makes his position even more difficult than before since the hostility against him by a number – probably a large number – of the Conservatives is unabated.[10]

A month later, the parliamentary prospects of the Liberals had become desperate. The one hope they had come to see as their salvation – the introduction of proportional representation (or at least some measure of electoral reform) – had gone (see p. 261). Throughout May, Lloyd George adopted a progressively more hostile view towards Labour. This was reflected in his speeches to the National Liberal Federation at Brighton.

The conviction was growing in Lloyd George's mind that a moment of decision was approaching. Lloyd George was determined to counter the Labour attack, and at the end of May an opportunity arose. The Conservatives launched a strong attack on the government's overt failure to reduce the high level of unemployment. This was an issue on which the Liberals in general, and Lloyd George in particular, were willing to do battle. They had counted without Asquith's inability to act. On 27 May, at a meeting of the Liberal Shadow Cabinet, Lloyd George (with the support of Pringle, Phillipps, Simon and Howard) took a tough line, arguing that the Liberals should vote against Labour on this. Asquith refused to face a crisis that might precipitate a general election. Instead, Asquith proposed that a decision on this issue should be put before a general meeting of the Parliamentary Liberal Party. Here – as Asquith had no doubt anticipated – the general tone was more moderate. Reports of the meeting[11] stressed the fear in the minds of many Liberal MPs (particularly those with small majorities) that to precipi-

[10] Altrincham MSS, Grigg to Bailey, 27 Mar 1924.
[11] For reports of the meeting, see *Manchester Guardian*, 30 May 1924, and *Glasgow Herald*, 30 May 1924.

tate an election would be disastrous. Asquith estimated that the feeling of the meeting was 7 to 3 against defeating Labour on this issue.[12] Grigg echoed the feeling of many Liberals when he described the meeting as 'a desperate farce'. As he wrote afterwards of the gathering:

> If you put the question of facing a general election at any time to a party meeting of precariously placed and highly impoverished Members of Parliament, there is really no question about their answer. We are therefore pottering on, supporting the Government and yet criticising it. The time must, however, come soon for taking our lives in our hands, and I am quite certain that L.G. means to give a lead when he sees an opportunity.[13]

Grigg was right. Lloyd George was more than ever concerned to force a showdown. In the debate on the government's record on unemployment, Lloyd George refused to support the official Liberal line (i.e. going into the government lobby) and indicated that he would abstain.

With the opening of the London Conference[14] in July, Lloyd George sensed that a new opportunity had arisen to try and force the Labour Government to come to terms. Lloyd George calculated that MacDonald would be willing to make sacrifices or come to a compromise rather than forfeit his growing stature in foreign affairs and his role as a European peacemaker. Lloyd George also sensed that Asquith's patience was at last exhausted. Certainly, by July, even Asquith's pronouncements against Labour had taken on some force. Speaking at Norwich on 11 July, Asquith had launched one of his strongest attacks:

> The path of the Government, as we in the House of Commons know only too well, their path week by week and almost day by day, is strewed with unfulfilled pledges and broken promises. In their legislative projects, so far as they are directed for dealing with urgent social problems, while they have enjoyed, I say

[12] H. A. L. Fisher's diary, 29 May 1924.

[13] Grigg to Bailey, 5 June 1924, quoted in Wilson, *The Downfall of the Liberal Party*, p. 275.

[14] A conference in London attended by the Prime Ministers of Britain, France, Belgium and Italy, and later by the German Chancellor. France agreed to evacuate the Ruhr.

without hesitation, almost unexampled tolerance, and no lack either of goodwill, or even of helpful co-operation, they have shown a singular and unequalled lack of constructive legislation.[15]

Even now, Asquith was not prepared to translate words into action. Lloyd George urged Asquith to take up again the issue of Labour's failure over unemployment. Scott's diary records Lloyd George's version of this July episode:

> Later I tried to force an understanding and in July I proposed to hold up the Labour Party on the Unemployment question. MacDonald dared not then have dissolved; he was too keen about the London Conference and foreign affairs. But I was overruled and the party would not take the risk[16]

This last attempt to force a showdown was wrecked by Asquith's refusal to go to the brink.

Whether Lloyd George was right will never be known. His policy was overruled and the Liberal Party refused to take the risk. Had it done so, the party could hardly have fared worse than in October, most particularly as the Conservatives were less prepared and Labour would have been defending its weakest point, its failure to reduce unemployment.

As it was, the summer recess arrived with relations between the Liberal and Labour parties at their most embittered level, and with no sign of any coming together of Asquith and Lloyd George. The crucial months from January to July 1924 had found the Liberals leaderless and lost.

The consequences of this divided leadership in the party were made worse by the attitude of those below Asquith and Lloyd George who might, by positive and constructive leads, have helped fill the vacuum. None was to succeed. Churchill, defeated in Leicester West in December 1923, and bitterly hostile to the decision to install Labour, had already deserted the Liberals. By March, with the Abbey by-election in Westminster, the break was final. Guest was occupied in trying to organise a right-wing breakaway. Simon, who might have filled such a vacuum, was bent on a negative anti-Socialist campaign. Maclean and Gladstone were too busy

---

[15] *Eastern Daily Press*, 12 July 1924.
[16] Scott Papers, BM Add. MSS 50,907, C. P. Scott's diary, 27 Nov 1924.

fighting Lloyd George, whilst Pringle was devoting his energies to carping criticism of Labour in general and MacDonald
in particular.

Thus, not merely the personal differences of Asquith and
Lloyd George, but a deeper failing of personalities in the
upper echelons of the party, accentuated the failure of
leadership. Yet, having emphasised the place of personalities
in 1924, in a sense this emphasis can be overdone. Even if the
Liberal Party had not been so deeply split in 1924, it would
still have needed to make a major adjustment to the advent of
a Labour Government by taking some fundamental decisions
on its basic philosophy, policy and programme.

By 1924 it was difficult to determine exactly what the
Liberal Party stood for. Was it a party of radicals? Or
anti-Socialists? Or had it become a loose Free Trade moderate Centre Party? The Asquithian Liberals had made few
attempts to answer that question. And, in large measure, the
blame lay with Asquith. In the period after the Paisley
by-election of 12 February 1920 and the Leamington conference of May 1920, vital years went by (particularly in the
run-up to the 1922 election) with the Liberal leader giving
neither lead, direction nor policy. Asquith, who was 70 in
1922, was becoming a shadow of his former self.

Meanwhile, even when advanced radical ideas were discussed, such adventures ended disastrously. Thus, when some
radical Liberals flirted with the idea of nationalisation early in
1920, the party immediately witnessed yet another split. A
'Liberal Anti-Nationalisation Committee' (consisting largely
of the wealthier Liberal industrialists) ran a scare campaign
that their party was proposing a 'state tobacco industry' and
that cigarettes would soon, like French cigarettes, contain
socks, gloves, nails and even mice.[17] As Kinnear comments,
such internal disputes over economic policy would not, in
normal times, have greatly hurt the party – they were indeed a
healthy sign of intellectual debate – but occurring as they did
in a divided and leaderless party they assumed an importance
out of all proportion.

[17] Quoted in Kinnear, *The Fall of Lloyd George*, p. 31.

Lack of positive leadership over policy from Asquith was clearly one factor. Another – allied with it – was the fact that, even before 1918, dissident radical Liberals could now look for an alternative party in Labour. This process had begun during the war; several Liberal MPs and candidates, including such figures as Ponsonby, Trevelyan and Buxton, were to desert to Labour. Some of these seceders might have returned to the Liberal fold if Asquith had adopted a constructive and radical programme. As it was, the long-term effect was to siphon off many advanced social reformers and make the party perhaps less open to radical ideas.

Given the political situation after the 1923 general election, and the advent of a Labour minority government, it was doubly important that the Liberal Party should adopt a positive and constructive policy – and a distinctive one – that would set it aside from both Conservatives and Socialists in the eyes of the electorate. Without it, radical Liberals would increasingly feel that little separated them from moderate Labour, whilst the right-wing Liberals (to say nothing of those electors who had voted for Free Trade against Protection in 1923) would become increasingly tempted to rally to the Conservatives in the face of a Socialist (albeit moderate) government.

The abysmal leadership and divided counsels of Asquith, Lloyd George and the other leaders had done little to help the party. This factor, however, might have been righted had the party used the months of 1924 to produce a constructive policy on such issues as unemployment, housing and industry with which to appeal with a bold policy in any subsequent general election.

The circumstances of the 1923 election – in particular the dominant role played by Free Trade in the campaign – had disguised the lack of distinctive policies held by the Liberals. Admittedly, Labour had attacked the Liberals on their lack of a social reform programme (and Conservatives had asked what Liberal policies would aid unemployment), but in general the campaign had been on favourable ground in 1923.

Now all the factors in the equation had changed. The Conservatives, having buried Protection, were once again the party of the *status quo*. More than any other party, they could simply fight on a negative anti-Socialist policy, and wait for the electors, frightened by the outcome of 1923, to rejoin their cause. Labour had an equally straightforward task. Ramsay MacDonald's dual aim was to show the respectability of his party and prove that it could govern. Labour, as was seen earlier, was intent on achieving the politics of moderation, if necessary with men and measures little different from orthodox Liberalism.

The first – and basic – task for the Liberal Party was to decide where it stood in relation to Labour. This, in the six years after 1918, Asquith and his supporters never established. As Kinnear has written, Asquith himself declared that he was 'not in the least alarmed by the Red Spectre', whilst Simon (not even on the left wing of the party) had stated that Labour ought not to be treated as the common enemy.[18] Yet these declarations were oddly at variance with the *Liberal Magazine* (the official Asquithian journal).

These contradictions had not been resolved, either in the 1922 general election or subsequently. In the months preceding the formation of the first Labour Government it was almost impossible to determine where the Liberal Party stood in relation to Labour. The dilemma carried on into 1924.

On the major topics of the day – on economic policy, social reform, on industry and nationalisation – Liberal policy was equally unclear or non-existent. This was particularly true of economic policy. As Kinnear has written:

> Compounding this problem was the fact that Asquith did not seem to have a policy of his own on economic matters. Lloyd George's epithet of 'stale flapdoodle' was unfair in the sense that Asquith based his programme on a melange of ideas produced by the numerous Liberal workshops on economics. However the uninspiring way in which Asquith presented this mixture shows that he was more interested in the mainly political issues, such as Home Rule and the supremacy of the Commons, which had been the chief concern of his previous career.[19]

---

[18] Kinnear, *The Fall of Lloyd George*, p. 201.
[19] Ibid., p. 216.

This is not to say that the Liberals lacked economic thinkers. Such figures as Ramsay Muir, Keynes and Beveridge all found a home in the Liberal ranks. But the fruition of their ideas came when Lloyd George, not Asquith, was at the helm after 1926.

In 1924, on such key issues emanating from economic questions as nationalisation and unemployment, Liberal policy was difficult to determine. An example of this was to be seen on 27 May 1924, when the Labour MP, Ben Turner, asked leave of the House to introduce a Public Ownership of National Resources Bill, a measure 'to restore to the nation all land, minerals, streams and tributaries'. Hardly unexpectedly, the motion was lost by 176 votes to 164. The left wing of the Liberal Party voted for the measure, exposing the divisions within their ranks yet again. The 29 Liberals who voted with the Bill constituted the main core of radicals in the party.

On unemployment, the Liberal remedy appeared to be made up of a three-pronged mixture of Free Trade, the restoration of peace in Europe, and the extension of the schemes of National Insurance. By the summer, the party had not advanced in any bolder fashion. At the Liberal Summer School held in Oxford in August 1924, C. F. G. Masterman gave a lecture on a constructive policy towards unemployment. It was hardly a success. The Liberal *Daily Chronicle* declared that his lecture 'was in violent contrast to the scientific method . . . . It was an ordinary party polemic with the loose analysis and broad sweeping assertions that pass muster on party Platforms'. He was also rebuked by the *Daily News*, which described the lecture as 'an aggressive and highly personal political speech, and the School is neither suited nor intended for developing that aspect of politics'.

Nor was Liberal policy much further advanced in terms of social welfare or in the field of education. In education, a Liberal Education group secured the services of an advisory committee during 1924 in an attempt to draw up a Liberal policy on this subject and to offer counsel to the group when education matters were discussed. Despite a distinguished committee, under the chairmanship of Sir Robert Blair (former Education Officer of the London County Council), little or nothing was achieved in the short period before the general election.[20]

The whole area of social policy was hardly any better. As Scott wrote late in 1924 to Sir Charles Hobhouse: 'What we need of course above all is a sane but courageous social policy. There is not one of the party leaders who can be trusted to supply it. It will have to come from the body of the party – from people like yourself.'[21] Indeed, Scott's letter to Hobhouse had been prompted by a highly gloomy but extremely accurate account of the lack of Liberal policy in 1924. Hobhouse had written of the Liberal party:

> I doubt if it any longer stands for anything distinctive. My reasons are on the one side that moderate Labour – Labour in office – has on the whole represented essential Liberalism, not without mistakes and defects, but better than the organised party since Campbell-Bannerman's death. On the other side the Liberal party, however you divide it up, never seems any better agreed within on essentials. Of the present fragment part leans to the Tories, part to Labour, part has nothing distinctive, but is a kind of Free Trade Unionist group. The deduction I draw is that the distinction between that kind of Labour man who does not go whole hog for nationalisation on the one side and the Liberal who wants social progress on the other is obsolete.[22]

He continued:

> But tradition and class distinctions kept many good Liberals outside Labour. Now Labour has grown so much that it tends to absorb them and to leave only the 'bad' Liberals who incline to the Tories and a mass of traditional Liberals who can't desert a party of that name.

His judgement, delivered in November 1924, was absolutely correct.

---

[20] *Morning Post*, 26 July 1924. The committee included Dr Cyril Maude (Headmaster of Marlborough), J. R. M. Butler (a former Member for Cambridge University), A. Pincombe (Secretary of the London Teachers' Association) and Frank Roscoe (Secretary of the Teachers' Registration Council).

[21] Scott Papers, Scott to Hobhouse, 19 Nov 1924.

[22] Scott Papers, Hobhouse to Scott, 7 Nov 1924.

Despite the patent lack of party policy, and despite the warnings given by such radicals as Scott or Masterman, the Liberals (with the notable exception of Lloyd George) made little attempt to rectify this situation. Perhaps the most useful insight into Liberal philosophy at this time can be seen in an analysis of the agenda and resolutions of the 41st annual meeting of the National Liberal Federation, held at Brighton on 22–3 May 1924. Here was an opportunity for the leadership to voice new proposals, and for the delegates to set to work preparing the bones of a party manifesto.

After the business of electing officials,[23] the main resolutions debated by the delegates can be summarised as follows:

Subject	Main Points of Resolution
Free Trade	Welcomed Labour decision to abolish McKenna duties and urged further repeal of Safeguarding of Industries Act and Dyestuffs Act.
Russia	Sir George Paish asked the conference to record the opinion that the restoration of Russia was essential to European prosperity and to call for the sincere and active co-operation of the British Government and of the British people. The resolution was carried, with the addition of a proviso that Russia should recognise her obligations and that any loans which may come from this country should be applied not to military but only to productive purposes.
Land values	Resolution in favour of taxation of land values passed almost unanimously.
Electoral reform	Resolution called on the party to redouble its effort for proportional representation or, failing this, the alternative vote.
Industrial policy	Sir John Simon opened the discussion on 'The Security of the Worker' by moving a resolution which deplored the long-continued existence of abnormal unemployment and industrial unrest, and stressed that unemployment could be

[23] Sir Donald Maclean was re-elected President and Sir Robert Hudson, Treasurer.

Subject	*Main Points of Resolution*

prevented by the adoption of an industrial programme, and particularly by pressing forward the Liberal policy of security through insurance. He strongly advocated the development of the system of National Insurance so as to cover adequately the economic risks that arise from unemployment, sickness, industrial accident, old age and death; it pledged itself to make every effort in support of the principle of this policy, and recommended the Executive Committee to appoint a special committee for the examination of detailed schemes.

An amendment to add to the resolution words expressing the importance of the establishment of a policy of peace and limitation of armaments throughout the world as necessary for a return to prosperity was carried.

The resolution was further amended by a demand that the Liberal leaders in Parliament should introduce without delay a Bill embodying the necessary amendments to the various Insurance Acts to carry out the policy outlined in the motion; and by a temperance amendment calling attention to the harm caused by the enormous expenditure on intoxicating liquor.

Taxation

The Federation decided to ask the party to survey the whole position of the incidence of taxation, locally and nationally.

Agriculture

Sir Harry Verney moved a resolution which expressed opposition to the policy of subsidies and to the imposition of protective duties, and urged the desirability of re-establishing district wages boards, of removing the hardships in connection with the tied cottage system and of securing on all farms such reforms as the labourers' weekly half-holiday and the payment of overtime wages for Sunday work. The motion declared that financial relief should be given to farmers not by Treasury subsidies but by a thorough reform of the rating system. The resolution was carried, with an added reference to the need for the modification of existing railway rates.

There was very little that was either exciting or indeed new in these resolutions. Electoral reform received more prominence than hitherto, but this was an issue whose greatest appeal would be to the party faithful. Whilst Free Trade and the taxation of land values received their customary emphasis, there was little to capture the imagination in industrial policy except the extension of National Insurance that had been put forward in the December 1923 campaign. A bold social policy was conspicuously absent.

Asquith's keynote speech to the Brighton conference, on 23 May, hardly gave any added inspiration. It was devoted to two themes: security of livelihood for workers 'by co-ordination and completion of social insurance against the risks of sickness, accident, old age and widowhood', and the development of national production. Asquith stressed, however, that with schemes of national development 'we do not ask that the work should be done by the State at the cost of the taxpayer'.

Neither the conference nor the leadership gave the delegates gathered at Brighton the sort of rallying call that the party so urgently needed.

The irony of the position after the Brighton conference was that the only positive move towards giving new and radical policies was coming from Lloyd George. The dilemma of Lloyd George was noticed by the observant Scott.

> Lloyd George's immediate position is obviously difficult. He is nothing if not a Radical yet circumstances have made him appear as the leader of the right wing of the party – of the 'bad Liberals'. I put it to him that he had really nothing in common with these people and that the only course open to him was to lead the Radicals. That is what he wants to do, but meanwhile his supporters in the party are on the Right and his opponents on the Left. Asquith who is really a Whig is accepted as a better Liberal than he.[24]

Scott observed thus in his diary after the 1924 election. But it was equally true in the early summer of 1924. Scott talked of the need for a constructive policy with Lloyd George in July

[24] Scott's diary, entry dated 8 Nov 1924.

1924, and found Lloyd George already taking the initiative. Scott recorded in his diary:

> I suggested that what the Liberal Party needed was a coherent constructive policy which could be distinguished from Socialism and Toryism. He said that a number of Committees were at work shaping out such a policy, and after lunch he gave me a Memorandum by Philip Kerr, written for one of these Committees, in which P.K. urged nationalisation of minerals and a substantial increase in the workers' participation in the control of the industry. There is a Committee on Electrification also. 'But', he went on, 'the trouble is that when you have got a policy ready and Asquith launches it, it will freeze on his lips; all kindling warmth and hope will die out of it; he will present it accurately, but without sympathy.' He liked Asquith, worked cordially with him, but as a leader he was too coldly intellectual.

Perhaps the most positive moves during 1924 were instigated by Lloyd George towards formulating a radical land programme. On 12 July 1924, in a speech at King's Langley, Lloyd George announced his intention of following up his inquiry into coal and electricity by an investigation of the system of land tenure.[25]

Earlier, Lloyd George's ideas for a major campaign were outlined in a speech to the London Liberal Federation in May. According to Lloyd George, the solution was to raise the banner of a new crusade: a crusade for the creation of greater wealth, from the land, the mines and electricity; and a crusade against the vested interests which were hampering the nation's development. In the two months following this speech – and almost entirely at his own instigation – Lloyd George launched a 'Great Liberal Campaign' throughout the country. This culminated in a massive rally at Belle Vue, Manchester.

---

[25] *Daily Chronicle*, 14 July 1924. It would appear that Lloyd George's ideas for reforming agriculture included a form of land nationalisation: agricultural land (other than that owned by the person who farmed it) was to be taken over by the state and leased on 'cultivating tenure'. This tenure would give security of occupation and even some right of bequest, but only if the tenant's standard of farming satisfied the supervision of a local committee. If it did not, he could be displaced. Wilson, *The Downfall of the Liberal Party*, p. 285.

The manner in which Lloyd George went about this campaign, in particular the obvious disregard he had for the official leadership, did not endear him to supporters of Asquith. The publication of Lloyd George's first major report – a book entitled *Coal and Power* – was only endorsed by Asquith *after* it had already been printed. Similarly, there were widespread complaints from Liberal MPs that they had not been consulted. Lloyd George, in fact, was not interested in Asquith, the parliamentary party or even a close associate like Mond (who disagreed with him on the land question). Lloyd George's new-found radicalism – and the results of his various committees of inquiry – were for his own use to further his own motives. Maybe he was seeking to restore his radical image to prepare for the succession. In this, he was to some extent succeeding. Former embittered enemies such as Masterman and Acland had to admit Lloyd George's genius for ideas and propaganda, and post-war radicals such as Ramsay Muir and E. D. Simon found themselves being drawn into his camp.[26] When Asquith was leader during 1924, the only radical ideas came from Lloyd George. And when Lloyd George became leader, and put his ideas in a crusade to the country, the ideas were too late to retrieve the fallen position of the party. With the sweeping programme of 1926, and the bold policies contained in *We Can Conquer Unemployment*, Lloyd George proved yet again that he had both ideas and the skill to propagate them. Sadly for the Liberal Party, these ideas came too late. They came when, after 1924, the party was no longer seen as a realistic alternative government. To this extent, the irony was that the ideas of advanced Liberalism, the theories of Keynes and the Welfare State of Beveridge, came when parliamentary and electoral Liberal support was at its lowest ebb.

Meanwhile, as the months of 1924 progressed, this double Liberal failing – of leadership and policy – was exposed in a variety of ways. It was seen in the chaotic indiscipline of the party in the lobbies at Westminster; it was to be seen in the disintegrating morale and organisation of the party in the constituencies; and it was to be witnessed in the important series of by-elections that occurred during the first Labour Government.

[26] Ibid., p. 286.

14 The Politics of Chaos: Liberals and Labour at Westminster

To some extent, the continued divisions in the Liberal leadership, the harangue over finance, and the more fundamental divisions over policy, might all have been disguised had the parliamentary party adopted a united, constructive and positive stance in Parliament. Sadly, it cut if anything a more abject figure than the leaders themselves. In the lobbies the party presented a picture of total confusion and inconsistency.

Liberal dissillusion with the tactics of the minority Labour Government was not long coming. Most of the party entered the first session of 1924 believing that, at least in the short term, Liberals and Labour together could enjoy relatively happy and easy relationships as the twin parties of the Left. From the start, the Labour Government made it fairly abundantly clear that it was not in the least interested in establishing harmonious relations with the Liberals, on whose votes it depended to stay in office. As a result, it lacked the two most powerful weapons which are normally at the disposal of any government – control of the parliamentary timetable, and an automatic majority for government business. Ministers were condemned to live from hand to mouth, with no way of knowing whether they would survive from one week to the next.

Difficult though this made the position of the Labour Members, it was infinitely worse for the Liberals. If the Parliamentary Liberal Party had realised it would not always receive sweetness and light from Ramsay MacDonald, it hardly, even in its worst moments, had expected constant abuse, vituperation and enmity.

Even without this hostility, the Liberal Whips in the Commons would have faced a difficult situation. There was growing concern that the group of Liberals who had voted to maintain a Conservative Government would rapidly be joined by other right-of-centre colleagues. Equally, there was a danger that the radical Left of the party might be tempted into the arms of a moderate Labour party. Firm leadership was essential to reduce these dangers of a three-way split. Firm leadership was exactly the ingredient lacking in 1924. Asquith, as we have seen, was waiting on events: at best, half-hearted; at worst, supine. Lloyd George was conspicuously absent from the division lobbies. Guest (and Churchill outside Parliament) were fomenting right-wing revolts.

To make matters worse, the Liberal Chief Whip, Vivian Phillipps, was in some ways an unfortunate choice. He had been appointed to the post by Asquith in 1923 (against many more obvious choices). He was so closely linked to the circle of Asquithians (such as Lord Gladstone and Sir Donald Maclean) that he saw Lloyd George's intriguing designs in the most harmless of events. Certainly, Scott took a poor view of Phillipps. Talking with Lloyd George of Liberal–Labour co-operation in parliament, Scott's diary recorded:

> As to the actual business of co-operation I said a great deal would of course depend on the Whips and I was afraid Vivian Phillipps, as Chief Whip, would be a serious obstacle. My own experience of him, of which I gave him the particulars, had been highly unfavourable. . . . He said his impression also was unfavourable. We went through the list of the Liberal Whips and found them a poorish lot (with a relatively bright spot in the person of Lloyd George's own son!).[1]

Given this leadership, and the incipient breakaway trends already evident in the parliamentary party, it was not long before the first serious evidence of disunity occurred. The occasion was the Poplar debate.

Immediately on coming into office, the Labour Minister of Health, John Wheatley, rescinded the earlier order preventing the Poplar Board of Guardians from exceeding a pre-scribed scale of outdoor relief. This action provoked Asquith

[1] Scott's diary, entry dated Feb 1924.

into an attack in which he declared that unless the government reconsidered the matter, their action stood no chance of receiving approval by the Commons. Asquith's rush of blood was followed by more sober reflection. If the Labour Government refused to back down in the face of these warnings (and it soon became clear they had no intention of doing so), then Liberal action would precipitate both a government defeat and a general election. The last thing Asquith wanted was to force a political crisis. Certainly, neither the party organisation nor the workers in the constituencies were remotely ready for an election. Nor was this point lost on Labour. As Grigg wrote as late as April, 'Labour knows only too well that the Liberals do not want an election at the present time'.[2]

Asquith was now in a difficult position. He had uttered a threat which he did not really mean and which his party could not deliver. The only way out was to retreat. Asquith, having declared himself satisfied with a statement from Wheatley and MacDonald that they had no intention of countenancing 'Poplarism' among local authorities, then brought the Liberals into the lobby to vote *with* the government against the closure, in order to prevent their own motion coming to a vote.[3] Here, indeed, were the politics of chaos.

Having already lost considerable face by this obvious retreat, the Liberals were further humiliated by a three-way split in the lobbies. The analysis of the vote in Table 14.1 shows these divisions. Whilst 117 Liberals voted with the Government, 13 broke ranks to vote with the Conservatives, and the relatively large number of 28 were absent unpaired.[4]

[2] Altrincham MSS, Grigg to Bailey, 24 Apr 1924, The *Daily Chronicle* (on 21 Oct 1924) stated that 'the Liberals' disinclination to enter upon an early struggle was well-known to all politicians'.

[3] The Liberal motion was worded: 'That this house regards the action of the Minister of Health in cancelling the Poplar Order, and in remitting any surcharge that might be made under it, as calculated to encourage illegality and extravagance, and urges that the real remedy for the difficulties of necessitous areas is to be found in the reform of London Government and of the Poor Law system'.

[4] The Liberals to vote with the Conservatives were: Sir C. Barrie, Sir C. Cory, J. Duckworth, C. R. Dudgeon, Col. A. England, A. Harbord, H. C. Hogbin, J. M. Hogge, W. A. Jenkins, R. M. Kedward, Capt. J. T. Rees, Sir W. Rees and Sir R. Winfrey.

TABLE 14.1

	Con	Lib.	Lab.	Ind.	Total
For closure	214	13	–	1	228
Tellers	2	–	–	–	2
Against closure	–	117	176	2	295
Tellers	–	–	2	–	2
Total	216	130	178	3	527
Speaker	–	1	–	–	1
Vacancies	1	–	1	–	2
Absent: paired	6	–	5	1	12
unpaired	35	28	8	2	73
Grand total	258	159	192	6	615

Thus, the outcome of the Poplar debate, particularly since it came so early in the session, was a significant triumph for Labour (and Wheatley in particular) and a heavy blow at the credibility of Liberal threats. As one provincial paper bitterly commented: 'When next the Liberal Party proposes to stage a formal protest against a Government irregularity let us hope its backbone will prove equal to the occasion.'[5] Such right-wing Liberals as Grigg were even more furious, particularly since once MacDonald knew that the Liberal bluff had been called, Labour could afford to be both valiant and unapologetic.[6]

The important Poplar debate followed hard on the heels of a similar Liberal split over the decision, announced in the Commons on 21 February, to undertake the construction of five new cruisers and two destroyers, provided parliamentary sanction was given. This proposal immediately produced opposition, not merely from the Liberals, but from Mac-Donald's own left-wing back-benchers. When the matter was raised at Question Time on 21 February, W. M. R. Pringle, Liberal MP for Penistone and a persistent left-wing critic of

[5] *Glasgow Herald*, 27 Feb 1924, quoted in Wilson, *The Downfall of the Liberal Party*, p. 271.
[6] Altrincham MSS, Grigg to Bailey, 28 Feb 1924.

MacDonald, rose to move the adjournment. Pringle recalled the declaration of the Labour Party with regard to disarmament and the reduction of naval and military expenditure. MacDonald replied very moderately, arguing that this was no new departure, merely speeding up work to prevent imminent unemployment in certain naval dockyards. The outcome of the adjournment debate was a government majority of 299. The Liberals, as the division list in Table 14.2 shows,

TABLE 14.2

	Con.	Lib.	Lab.	Ind.	Nat.	Total
Noes	182	30	159	1	–	372
Tellers	–	–	2	–	–	2
Ayes	–	71	1	1	–	73
Tellers	–	2	–	–	–	2
Total	182	103	162	2	–	449
Speaker	–	1	–	–	–	1
Vacancies	1	–	1	–	–	2
Absent	75	55	28	3	2	163
Grand total	258	159	191	5	2	615

were completely split. Whilst 73 Liberals supported Pringle's amendment, no fewer than 30 voted with the Conservatives and 55 were absent unpaired. Whereas Pringle received the support of such Liberals as Sir John Simon, Francis Acland and Geoffrey Howard, others such as Rt. Hon. J. I. MacPherson, John Seely and T. J. Macnamara joined with the Conservatives. Neither Asquith nor Lloyd George voted on the adjournment.

This adjournment debate was far from the end of the matter. At a meeting of the Parliamentary Labour Party on 27 February, a discussion took place on the government's proposal to proceed with the construction of five new cruisers. The Prime Minister explained the grounds upon which the government had come to its decision and, according to an official report, his explanation was accepted.[7] In fact, this

[7] *The Times*, 27 Feb 1924.

seeming healing of the Labour split did not survive the resurrection of the issue in the Commons. On 18 March, on a motion in connection with the Navy estimates, the Liberal H. Seely (seconded by H. Johnstone) moved an amendment that

in the opinion of this house, the proposed construction of five new cruisers is not justified either on the ground of relieving unemployment or of providing for the naval needs of the Empire, and is calculated to increase competition in armaments.

It was clear from the support the amendment received from such Labour MPs as Ben Turner that the government would be hard pressed to keep its ranks intact. The voting on the Liberal amendment was as shown in Table 14.3. Although

TABLE 14.3

	Cons.	Lib.	Lab.	Ind.	Nat.	Total
Against	153	24	127	–	–	304
Tellers	–	–	2	–	–	2
For	–	93	18	2	1	114
Tellers	–	2	–	–	–	2
Total	153	119	147	2	1	422
Speaker	–	1	–	–	–	1
Vacancies	1	–	–	–	–	1
Absent	104	39	45	2	1	191
Grand total	258	159	192	4	2	615

the amendment was easily defeated by 304 votes to 114, an analysis of the division lists gave little comfort either to MacDonald or the Liberal leaders.

No fewer than 18 Labour Members voted against the government, while a further 45 were absent.[8] Among the more notable Labour absentees were several Ministers,

[8] The 18 Labour Members who voted against the government were: W. H. Ayles, T. Dickson, Rev. H. Dunnico, J. P. Gardiner, W. Gorman, T. E. Groves, G. D. Hardie, J. H. Hudson, Miss D. Jewson, T. Johnston, G. Lansbury, W. H. P. Martin, R. Nichol, J. Schurr, E. Thurtle, B. Turner, C. H. Wilson and W. Windsor.

including Ben Spoor, the Chief Whip (who was ill), Sidney Webb and Tom Griffiths.

The Liberal ranks presented an even more divided spectacle. The number of Liberals defying the party line and voting with the Conservatives had grown to 24.[9] As Lloyd George had foreseen, the original nucleus of a dozen or so right-wing Liberals, centred on Grigg, Guest, Beddoe Rees and Spears, was rapidly attracting new recruits. Not, perhaps, that Lloyd George was conspicuous by his positive action in this division: as on the former occasion when the question was discussed, Lloyd George took no part in the debate or the division.

Meanwhile, further evidence of this total Liberal disunity was seen in the debate in the House on 6 March, on the reduction of the levy on imported German goods from 26 per cent to 5 per cent under the German Reparation (Recovery) Act. This was marked by divergent views expressed by leading members of the Liberal party. While Sir John Simon, although seeking explanation upon certain points, declared it was to the credit of the Socialist Government that they had lost no time in making a new arrangement, Lloyd George considered that the government had given away a valuable instrument for getting reparations, and said that if the attitude assumed by the Chancellor of the Exchequer represented the spirit in which the government was going into the London Conference, British interests would be completely surrendered.

Although the outcome of the debate was a comfortable victory for the government (by 240 votes to 170), there was little comfort for the Liberals. The division lists were as shown in Table 14.4. Once again, a right-wing coterie of seven Liberals voted with the Conservatives.[10] As before, Lloyd

---

[9] The following 24 Liberals voted against the majority of their party: Sir R. W. Aske, Sir T. Bramsdon, Major J. Burnie, J. Duckworth, C. R. Dudgeon, Col. A. England, Lt-Cdr. R. T. Fletcher, I. Foot, G. Lloyd George, J. D. Gilbert, Sir E. Grigg, F. E. Guest, H. C. Hogbin, W. A. Jenkins, T. J. Macnamara, Capt. C. B. Ramage, Sir T. Robinson, Maj.-Gen. J. Seely, Sir A. Sinclair, Brig.-Gen. E. L. Spears, J. L. Sturrock, Lt-Col. J. Ward and A. Williams.

[10] They were: W. A. Jenkins, Col. A. England, Sir W. B. Rees, Capt. J. T. Rees, Dr G. E. Spero, Lt-Col. J. Ward and H. C. Hogbin.

TABLE 14.4

	Con.	Lib.	Lab.	Ind.	Nat.	Total
Ayes	163	7	–	–	–	170
Tellers	2	–	–	–	–	2
Noes	–	85	152	2	1	240
Tellers	–	–	2	–	–	2
Total	165	92	154	2	1	414
Speaker	–	1	–	–	–	1
Vacancies	1	–	–	–	–	1
Absent	92	66	38	2	1	199
Grand total	258	159	192	4	2	615

George failed to take part in the division – one of a total of 66
Liberals who abstained. Admittedly, the issue was a relatively
unimportant one, but it was indicative of the growing lack of
unity and cohesion in the Liberal Party. Its seriousness was
revealed only three weeks later in an important debate over
the Singapore naval base.

The decision by the Labour Government to abandon the
development of the Singapore naval base produced a major

TABLE 14.5

	Con.	Lib.	Lab.	Ind.	Total
Against amendment	–	118	167	2	287
Tellers	–	–	2	–	2
For amendment	201	9	–	1	211
Tellers	2	–	–	–	2
Total	203	127	169	3	502
Speaker	–	1	–	–	1
Vacancies	–	–	–	–	–
Absent: paired	24	8	16	–	48
unpaired	31	23	7	3	64
Grand total	258	159	192	6	615

political storm.[11] In the House of Commons on 25 March, Sir Robert Horne voiced Conservative protests by moving an amendment to the Navy estimates. On division, the amendment was negative by 287 to 211. The division is analysed in Table 14.5. Once again, the Liberals were embarrassed by Grigg, Guest, Beddoe Rees and their supporters voting with the Conservatives.[12] Similarly, a total of 23 unpaired Liberal absentees was not evidence of good lobby discipline. The image of the party improved a little at the beginning of April when a Conservative MP, Lieutenant-Colonel W. E. Guinness, introduced a motion condemning the principle of a capital levy.[13] Since MacDonald had already made it clear that no capital levy would be enacted during the present Parliament, the motion was as much designed to embarrass the Liberals as anyone else. In the event, the resolution against the capital levy was carried by 324 votes to 160, a majority of 164. Some 121 Liberals voted for the motion, only one (J. M. Hogge) against – although J. M. Kenworthy, the radical Liberal MP for Hull Central, was also paired in favour of the levy.

The relative ease with which the capital levy resolution was dealt with came in very marked contrast to the chaos that ensued over the government's Rent Bill in early April. With this measure, the Labour Government was as much responsible for the ensuing chaos as the divided Liberal opposition. The following timetable outlines the main events leading to the first major parliamentary clash on 7 April:

[11] The proposal for a major naval base at Singapore had been approved in principle by Lloyd George's Cabinet in 1921, and subsequently confirmed by the Imperial Conference in 1923. In February 1924 the new MacDonald Cabinet appointed a committee to re-examine the question (and also to inquire into the naval building programme). The Admiralty won on the building programme, but not on Singapore.

[12] The nine Liberals who voted with the Conservatives in favour of Singapore were: J. H. Edwards, Col. A. England, Sir E. Grigg, F. E. Guest, A. Harbord, H. C. Hogbin, Sir W. B. Rees, Sir T. Robinson and Lt-Col. J. Ward.

[13] The exact text of the resolution was: 'That this House is of the opinion that what is needed is not the destruction of enterprise but its encouragement, not the frightening away of capital but its fruitful use, and that a Capital Levy would therefore prove disastrous to employment.'

21 March   Bill introduced by the Minister of Health included a provision to allow unemployed to live rent free at the expense of their landlords.

2 April   Government agreed to the substitution of a clause which would throw upon public funds the cost of maintaining the distressed tenant in his home.

4 April   Government proposed to take steps to secure that the Poor Law authorities, both in England and Scotland, when granting relief, should give such relief as may be necessary to protect the tenant from eviction.

4 April   David Kirkwood (Lab.) demanded a guarantee that the state should bear the burden. Thereupon the government disclaimed opposition to the policy of recouping the local authorities from state funds.

7 April   Government proposed to amend the Bill so that no eviction order should be issued until the tenant had had a reasonable time to apply to the local Poor Law authorities for relief and the authority had had an opportunity of considering the application.

It was at this juncture, when J. H. Thomas, for the government, said that there could be no question of

TABLE 14.6

	Con.	Lib.	Lab.	Ind.	Total
For the Bill	–	53	158	1	212
Tellers	–	–	2	–	2
Against the Bill	198	22	–	1	221
Tellers	2	–	–	–	2
Total	200	75	160	2	437
Speaker	–	1	–	–	1
Vacancies	–	–	1	–	1
Absent: paired	11	–	11	–	22
unpaired	47	83	21	3	154
Grand total	258	159	193	5	615

withdrawing this clause, that a division was taken. The Bill was narrowly defeated by 221 votes to 212, a majority of 9. The votes were cast as shown in Table 14.6. On an issue on which the government had suffered a defeat (and consequently a vote which produced considerable press comment), the Liberals could hardly have appeared in a worse light. Whilst 53 had voted for the Government, 22 had gone into the lobbies with the Conservatives and no fewer than 83 (more than half the parliamentary party) had simply abstained. The Liberal chaos was accentuated by the action of the party leaders. Among those to abstain were Asquith, Lloyd George, Acland, H. A. L. Fisher, Grigg, Guest, Lambert, Simon, Ramsay Muir and Phillipps, the Chief Whip.

Lloyd George later defended the Liberal action by declaring that the party had been determined to support the Bill but for the statement in the debate by Ramsay MacDonald which had so confused the issue that the Whips had decided to ask Liberals to abstain. This statement failed to explain why, if the Whips had decided on abstention, 75 Liberals voted in the debate. In all, it was a disastrous Liberal performance, from which Ramsay MacDonald was not slow to make capital. In an interview quoted in the *New Leader* he attacked the Liberals for abandoning 'ordinary decency in Parliament' and declared that he had never known 'all my life such a meaningless factious attitude'. MacDonald went on to say that he was grateful that the majority of those Liberals who had voted had 'flouted the little-minded appeals of their Leaders'. He concluded a bitter interview by hoping that 'the friends of Labour were watching very carefully recent actions in the House of Commons and would see that from every platform in the land the truth about Monday's discreditable performance is told'.[14]

If the Labour Government was after revenge on the Liberals for the defeat of the Rent Bill, its moment came at the beginning of May with the defeat of the Representation of

[14] *New Leader*, 11 Apr 1924. The following day, MacDonald announced that the rejection of Wheatley's Bill made it impossible to introduce another Bill on similar lines during that session. The government therefore proposed to support a private Member's Bill on the same subject which had been introduced earlier in the session by Sir John Simon.

the People Act (1918) Amendment Bill. The Liberals had to endure many bitter and humiliating Parliamentary rebuffs during 1924, but none hurt their feelings and aspirations more than the fate of this Bill, which had been introduced on 18 January 1924 by A. Rendall (Liberal MP for Thornbury), and was backed by three Conservatives, two Labour and five other Liberals.[15]

The outcome of this Bill was of extreme importance for Liberal morale, for any measure of electoral reform was likely to benefit the party enormously. When the Parliamentary Liberal Party met on 30 April, Asquith urged Lloyd George, Ramsay Muir, Isaac Foot and the others who wanted a nationwide campaign to revive party morale to await the outcome of this measure. The meeting 'unanimously decided that the party should support the Second Reading, and that the Government should be invited to give the Bill official support, and grant facilities for its passage into law this session'.[16] The following day the Parliamentary Labour Party held a special meeting to consider its attitude. It decided, by a very large majority, that no facilities of any kind should be afforded by the government. It was agreed that the question should be left to a free vote of the House. Thus, when the debate on the Second Reading was inaugurated by Rendall on 2 May, it was clear that it would face a difficult passage. In the event, the Bill was defeated on its Second Reading by 238 votes to 144. Some 107 Liberals, 28 Labour and 8 Conservatives were among those voting for the Bill. Only one Liberal (Sir G. C. Marks) voted against, but he was joined by 146 Conservatives and 91 Labour. Over 40 Liberals were absent from the debate. Although MacDonald did not vote, the Bill

---

[15] The main provisions of the Bill can be summarised thus: The Bill provided that at a contested election for a parliamentary constituency each elector should have one transferable vote, and that where there were two or more Members to be elected, the election should be according to proportional representation (Clause 1).

Commissioners were to be appointed for the purpose of preparing a scheme to provide for certain constituencies being combined into single constituencies returning not fewer than three nor more than seven Members. Further, the scheme was to be laid before Parliament, which retained powers of amending the scheme (Clause 2).

[16] *Daily News*, 1 May 1924.

was supported by Snowden, Thomas, C. P. Trevelyan, W. Leach, C. G. Ammon and Emanuel Shinwell.

The defeat of this Bill was a shattering blow to Liberal hopes. They were now left with the stark choice of supporting Labour in Parliament – come what may – or facing a general election with all prospect of electoral reform gone.

After this vote, the remaining debates in Parliament before the summer recess intervened to give both Labour and Liberal a respite centred around unemployment, Imperial Preference and agriculture. None of the debates was to give any joy to the Liberals.

On 22 May an amendment was moved by Sir William Joynson-Hicks to reduce by £100 that part of the Vote for the salaries and expenses of the Ministry of Labour which provided for the salary of the Minister himself (i.e. an attempt to spotlight the Minister's failure to reduce unemployment). Though such Liberals as Macnamara and Masterman had denounced the record of the government in dealing with unemployment, the bulk of the Liberals present voted with the government to prevent the closure from being applied in order that a direct vote on Tom Shaw's salary might be taken. The outcome of the vote on closure is shown in Table 14.7. No fewer than 61 Liberals were absent unpaired, 16 voted with the Conservatives, whilst 74 helped to save Labour from facing the Conservative amendment.

On 29 May this matter of the Ministry of Labour Vote was again debated. On this occasion Sir Robert Horne moved to reduce Tom Shaw's salary by £100. By the help of the Liberals the government was again saved from defeat. A division took place on Sir Robert Horne's amendment, which was lost by 252 votes to 300. In this vote, the Liberal ranks had been assembled a little more firmly. However, although 117 Liberals voted with Labour against the Conservative amendment, 31 were still absent unpaired and 8 voted for the Conservatives.[17]

These divisions were once again apparent during the debates on 17–18 June on the question of Imperial

[17] The eight were the same familiar names of C. R. Dudgeon, Col. A. England, F. E. Guest, H. C. Hughes, Sir W. B. Rees, Sir T. Robinson, Dr G. E. Spero and Sir R. J. Thomas.

TABLE 14.7

	Con.	Lib.	Lab.	Ind.	Total
For closure	193	16	–	1	210
Tellers	2	–	–	–	2
Against closure	–	74	167	3	244
Tellers	–	–	2	–	2
Total	195	90	169	4	458
Speaker	–	1	–	–	1
Chairman of Committee	–	–	1	–	1
Dep. Chairman of Committee	–	1	–	–	1
Vacancies	2	1	1	–	4
Absent: paired	23	5	18	–	46
unpaired	38	61	4	1	104
Grand total	258	159	193	5	615

Preference. Whilst the Labour Government had made it quite clear that it disagreed with any proposals of this sort, it agreed, in conformity with pledges given on 15 January 1924 by MacDonald, that the recommendations of the Imperial Economic Conference of 1923 should be submitted to Parliament. As a result, Baldwin put a series of resolutions in favour of Imperial Preference for different commodities on the Order paper. It was agreed that, if the first four were all defeated, no further divisions would take place.[18]

[18] The first four resolutions were:
1. *Dried fruits* now subject to duty (figs, raisins, plums and currants) should, if of Empire origin, be free of import duties.
2. The rate of duty on *tobacco* of Empire origin should be reduced from five-sixths to three-quarters of the duty charged on tobacco imported from other countries.
3. The rate of duty charged on *wines* produced within the Empire should be reduced from 4s. to 2s. a gallon (strength between 30° and 42°); the preferential rate on the surtax of 12s.6d. a gallon sparkling wines to be increased from 30 to 50 per cent.
4. For a period of ten years, the preference on *sugar* produced within the Empire should be kept at ½d. a lb., so long as the duty on foreign sugar should not fall below that level.

TABLE 14.8

Motion	Liberals who support	Liberals who vote against	Liberals absent unpaired
1. Dried fruits	19	110	24
2. Tobacco	19	111	23
3. Wines	17	111	25
4. Sugar	12	117	24

After two days' debate, divisions were taken on these resolutions. On each of them, as Table 14.8 shows, a persistent small Liberal split occurred.

At least, in these four divisions, the Liberal split was relatively consistent. These resolutions on Imperial Preference were relatively insignificant compared with a renewal of criticism from both the Conservative and Liberal benches at the end of July on the unemployment question. Once again, the Conservatives moved a resolution calling for a reduction in the salary of Tom Shaw, the Minister of Labour, in order to add point to their general criticism. When the division was taken on the amendment, the Liberals resumed their role of the 'patient oxen'. The Conservative amendment was lost by 204 votes to 254. An analysis of the division is given in Table 14.9. Among the 60 Liberals absent unpaired were Asquith, Lloyd George, Mond and Simon. Phillipps, the Chief Whip, voted with the 85 Liberals supporting Labour. If this conduct was hardly likely to win the Liberals much positive support in the urban areas, on the same day the Liberals did nothing to endear themselves to the agricultural workers by their conduct over the Labour Bill for the establishment of Agricultural Wages Committees. The general behaviour of the Liberal Party in connection with the Bill was commented upon by R. B. Walker, general secretary of the National Union of Agricultural Workers. He wrote in the *Daily Herald*:

> The whole conduct of the Liberals during the Committee stage of the Bill was dictated by one motive – to make Party capital. Throughout, they have been as slippery as eels, and have disgusted Labour and Tory alike, for no one has been able to be

TABLE 14.9

	Con.	Lib.	Lab.	Ind.	Total
For amendment	193	10	–	1	204
Tellers	2	–	–	–	2
Against amendment	–	85	168	1	254
Tellers	–	–	2	–	2
Total	195	95	170	2	462
Speaker	–	1	–	–	1
Chairman of Committee	–	–	1	–	1
Vacancies	1	1	1	–	3
Absent: paired	17	1	16	–	34
unpaired	45	60	6	3	114
Grand total	258	158	194	5	615

sure that on any one day they will be where they were during the previous twenty-four hours.[19]

These two debates, on unemployment and agriculture, were perhaps an appropriate end to one of the most disheartening sessions the Liberal Party had ever had to endure.

When Parliament rose for the summer recess, it was clear to everyone that, at Westminster at least, the Liberals had appeared as no less than a pathetic, disorganised and leaderless group. The chaotic indiscipline of the Liberal Party at Westminster caused Maclean to write to Lord Gladstone: 'I don't know what our opponents think of our Parliamentary generals, but they terrified me'.[20] It was an appropriate comment. And yet the session need not have developed the way it did. On the surface there was no fundamental reason why the experiment of a minority Labour Government holding office with Liberal support should not have succeeded. On such issues as housing, foreign policy, unemployment and certain areas of social policy the two parties had much in common. The experiment failed for two main

[19] *Daily Herald*, 30 July 1924.
[20] Gladstone Papers, BM Add. MSS 46,474/74, Maclean to Gladstone, 3 Aug 1924.

reasons. On the Liberal side, indiscipline and lack of leadership, linked with Asquith's condescending attitude and Lloyd George's maverick intrigues, did not augur well for co-operation. But a much greater reason was MacDonald's personal bitterness and vanity. This fact was not lost either on Liberals or Labour. As Lloyd George wrote in the *Daily Chronicle* after Labour had fallen from office: 'How could [Asquith] have conjectured that the Leader of a great party would have behaved like a jealous, vain, suspicious, ill-tempered actress of the second rank?'[21] And, as Trevor Wilson notes, even some Labour supporters asked the same question. The *New Statesman* referred to MacDonald's 'lack of courtesy' to the Liberals and his 'vanity and easily wounded pride', and went on:

> If he had treated his Liberal allies with even common courtesy he might have remained in power not merely until 1925, but for some years to come, possibly even for a decade.
> But instead he has missed no opportunity of insulting and deriding those who placed him in power.[22]

---

[21] *Daily Chronicle*, 1 Nov 1924.
[22] *New Statesman*, 11 Oct 1924, quoted in Wilson, *The Downfall of the Liberal Party*, p. 269.

15 A Party Losing Faith: Liberal Organisation, Finance and Morale

The Liberal failure in Parliament was made worse by the fate that was overtaking the party in the country. The long-term dangers that might result from the Liberal decision to install a Labour Government without conditions were hardly realised by the constituency associations in January 1924. The immediate reaction at constituency and federation level to Asquith's decision was almost universally favourable. Such constituency associations as Harborough passed unanimous resolutions of support.[1] The Yorkshire Liberal Federation gave enthusiastic support to the motion that 'only in the full exercise of freedom and independence can the Liberal Party continue to advance the cause of Liberalism'.[2]

That this was the general feeling of the party workers can be seen in the case of the Midland Liberal Federation. The Executive Committee met on 14 December to debate their action as a result of the indeterminate election returns. The committee decided that the Liberal party should not enter into an alliance with either of the other parties in the House of Commons but, in the event of Labour being called upon to form a government, should give friendly support as long as the policy pursued was in accordance with Liberal policy. When the annual meeting of the Midland Liberal Federation took place in February, the decision of the Executive Committee was warmly supported.[3]

[1] Harborough Division Liberal and Radical Association, Minutes, Executive Committee, 9 Feb 1924.

[2] Yorkshire Liberal Federation, Minutes, Executive Committee, 17 Jan 1924.

[3] Midland Liberal Federation, Minutes, Executive Committee, 14 Dec 1923, 28 Mar 1924.

The only real opposition to this decision came from such individuals as Churchill and Guest, whose activities were seen earlier. Their opposition to this policy was reflected, as might be expected, in those few Liberal constituency associations whose Members were dependent on Conservative votes. Thus, Sir Beddoe Rees, the Liberal Member for Bristol South, wrote to one constituent:

> The election in Bristol South was fought on the one question of Socialism, and by a substantial majority Socialism was defeated . . . . That being so, I have no hesitation in saying that . . . I shall vote with the Government, and against the amendment because, if the amendment is carried the inevitable result will be the setting up of a Socialist Ministry.[4]

Similarly, Brigadier-General Spears wrote that, since the party had fought Socialism as much as Tariff Reform,

> I have notified the leaders of the party that I could under no circumstances support a Labour amendment. I for one refuse to be responsible for bringing into power a Socialist Government.[5]

Although a vocal influence, these right-wing constituency associations were relatively few in number in the early days of 1924.

Although the Liberal party had remained relatively united in putting Labour into office, the period from January to October 1924 was a time of lost opportunity in the constituencies for the Liberals. Nationally the party drifted without firm purpose or policy until an election arrived which found it dismally unprepared both in terms of policy and leadership. At constituency level, in organisation, finance, candidates and morale, the party had fared even worse.

This need not have been so, for in parts of the country local associations responded vigorously to the unexpected victories of 1923. A useful example of this relationship between electoral success and party morale can be found in the Home Counties Liberal Federation. The 15 Liberal MPs returned within the Federation in December 1923 were the most numerous since the *annus mirabilis* of 1906. The Federation

---

[4] *Daily News*, 21 Jan 1924.
[5] Ibid.

Annual Report, presented at Chelmsford in May 1924, waxed lyrical:

> All through our areas the revival of Liberalism continues.... Political activity is greater than at any time since the outbreak of the Great War .... Liberalism has never been more active in this area except in the years preceding the landslide of 1906.[6]

An example of this was to be found in Hampshire, where a new County Organisation had been established and, for the first time, a full-time paid women's organiser was at work.

A similar position was to be found in the Eastern Counties. In March 1924 the Federation Secretary reported to his Executive Committee:

> At the dissolution ... we were not in a state of preparedness for an election. We then held seven seats out of 28, and three others only had secured candidates. Since the election there has been renewed activity in the constituencies .... Before the election we had eleven agents on the ground, today we have sixteen.[7]

The Secretary went on to report that, in the eight seats uncontested in 1923, new associations had been formed in Grimsby, Ipswich, Bury St Edmunds and South-West Norfolk.[8]

However, despite this improved organisation, finance presented a major problem, for the Federation Secretary had already received a letter from Lord Gladstone at Headquarters, warning:

> It must be realised at once that Headquarters which has had to bear the burden of two General Elections and now has a third in prospect, is not in a position to undertake any exceptional expenditure in connection with organisation work, however desirable.[9]

Consequently, the Federation Secretary reported to his Executive:

[6] Home Counties Liberal Federation, Annual Report, 1923–4.
[7] Eastern Counties Liberal Federation, Minutes, Executive Committee, 27 Mar 1924.
[8] Leaving only Brigg, North Norfolk and South Norfolk still unorganised.
[9] Eastern Counties Liberal Federation, Minutes, Executive Committee, 27 Mar 1924.

Our great difficulty is finance. In most of the constituencies it is impossible to raise sufficient income to pay an agent and working expenses, and consequently the work of re-organisation is retarded . . . . With adequate funds the outlook for the future would be greatly improved.[10]

Finance was indeed the great difficulty. A key to the Liberal débâcle in October 1924 lay in the acute and parlous financial state of the party nationally. There were three factors in the equation: the constituencies (and indeed the federations) were dependent, in most cases, on subsidies from party headquarters in London. But party headquarters (or rather the Asquithians) were themselves nearly bankrupt. By January 1924, all available resources at Liberal Headquarters had been exhausted. In that month, Gladstone warned the party that £30,000 was required for urgent organisational work to prepare for a general election. In addition, a firm guarantee of £100,000 would be needed for the election itself. As Gladstone concluded, two elections within twelve months had absolutely exhausted the financial reserves.[11]

The only large amount of money available in Liberal circles belonged to Lloyd George. His Fund could have solved – at a stroke – all Liberal financial needs in the short or even the medium term. Its value was not lost on Lloyd George: it was his last remaining weapon. And he meant to use it to its fullest extent.

Thus the outcome of constituency reorganisation was itself dependent on the outcome of the protracted discussions over the Fund between November 1923 and October 1924. Even during the 1923 election campaign, the issue of finance had caused considerable acrimony. Once the election was over – and the position of Asquith in the party very much strengthened – the attempt to get hold of Lloyd George's money really began in earnest. From the Asquithian viewpoint, it was essential to get financial backing from Lloyd George without allowing him any real share in running the

[10] Ibid.
[11] Gladstone Papers, BM Add. MSS 46,480/129, memorandum 'Reflections and Suggestions on the General Organisation of the Liberal Party', 18 Nov 1924.

party or any opportunity to establish a claim to become leader when Asquith died or retired.

On 19 December there were preliminary discussions between Phillipps and Howard for the Asquithians and Guest and Sir William Edge as representatives of Lloyd George. These, however, started off on a particularly bad footing.[12] It was eventually decided that negotiations would in future be conducted by Hudson and Maclean for the Asquithians and by Davies for Lloyd George.

A succession of attempts was made in the early months of 1924 to settle the financial question with Lloyd George, but by the beginning of April three months had been wasted with nothing settled.[13] As Hudson wrote to Gladstone, 'the situation as regards Lloyd George and his money-bags is thoroughly unsatisfactory'.[14]

On 15 April, at Maclean's request, a second interview was arranged between Maclean and Davies. On this occasion Lloyd George raised the objection that he was not being consulted with regard to the policy and strategy of the party. Until this state of affairs was remedied, Lloyd George would undertake no contributions. No further progress occurred until both Maclean and Hudson saw Lloyd George on 1 July.[15]

Lloyd George used this occasion to launch a bitter attack on the party, declaring that its organisation was 'rotten' with 'constituencies and Federations all looking to the centre for

[12] Maclean refused to permit negotiation with Guest and Edge, despite Guest's part in collecting the Lloyd George Fund, because he knew that Guest and Churchill were trying to negotiate joint entry into the Conservative Party. Since he did not trust Asquith to be sharp enough with Lloyd George, he asked that he should negotiate with Mond, Fisher, A. H. Illingworth or Hilton Young.

[13] The occasions on which Maclean saw Lloyd George were 10, 17 and 22 January and 5 March 1924.

[14] Gladstone Papers, BM Add. MSS 46,475, Hudson to Gladstone, 17 Jan 1924.

[15] Except that Maclean attempted to make concessions to Lloyd George over Wales. One result was that Henry Gladstone, the brother of Lord Gladstone and President of the Welsh Liberal Federation, consented to step down and share the Vice-Presidency with Lord St Davids, thereby allowing Lloyd George to become President. Gladstone Papers, BM Add. MSS 46,480/207.

funds'. The remedy, according to Lloyd George, was that the Federations should be made self-supporting. As a means to this end, Lloyd George suggested the appointment of 'collectors' on a 5 per cent commission basis. Following this up, Lloyd George proposed a meeting of the Federation chairmen to study reorganisation. Meanwhile, despite a request by Hudson, Lloyd George refused to give any assurance of financial help; or rather, to use Gladstone's phrase, anything 'sufficiently definite for the purpose of bank credit'.

Just how bitter the feeling had become was revealed in a letter Hudson wrote to Gladstone after this meeting:

> As to your resolution, 'D——d Lloyd George', I beg to second. Our 40 minutes talk with him was so poisonous that I took to my bed with a temperature the next afternoon. . . . Such are the consequences apparently of being shut up in a small room with a Goat.[16]

Whatever Lloyd George's real motives, his request for a meeting of Federation chairmen was granted. This took place on 23 July, only to prove a complete fiasco. Lloyd George, not mentioning his earlier charge on Liberal organisation, accused the Federations of being 'spoonfed' by Headquarters. Gladstone observed that 'the talk was all over the place' and nothing materialised except the proposal that there should be a Committee of Inquiry.

It was hardly surprising that, after this meeting, Gladstone was brought to a point of despair, writing to Asquith that he could undertake no further commitments until definite financial guarantees were forthcoming. Asquith forwarded Gladstone's letter to Lloyd George, adding 'some fairly plain language' of his own. Lloyd George replied, insisting that reorganisation must come first. Nothing further developed until September.

The effect of the inability of the party to support the Federations with grants to aid constituencies was nothing short of disastrous. Thus, in the Midland Federation, another area where 1923 results had acted as a much needed tonic, by

---

[16] Gladstone Papers, BM Add. MSS 46,475/125, Hudson to Gladstone, 4 July 1924.

the spring of 1924 the effect was seen in the fact that a mere
nine prospective candidates were in the field for 76 constituencies within the Federation.[17]

Even winnable seats were not preparing for the future. In
the Dudley division, where the Liberal was only 1,717 votes
behind the Conservative, no move towards adopting a candidate was made until July. Although the Federation offered
the names of potential candidates, nothing had been settled
by October, and in the event no Liberal fought the election.[18]

Dudley was not an isolated example. By October, only
occasional additions had been made to the total of prospective candidates.[19] As one correspondent observed in October,
literally scores of candidates were needed in the West Midlands before the Liberals could attempt to launch an effective
challenge.[20]

This difficulty in finding candidates was the result not
merely of financial weakness but of a serious disintegration in
party morale. Throughout 1924 depressing reports came in of
former Liberals defecting to Conservative or Labour.[21]

Compared with some parts of the country, the Midland
Liberals actually enjoyed relative health. Perhaps the worst
cases were to be found in Wales and Scotland. Of the sad
position of Welsh Liberal organisation, one paper commented:

> Welsh Liberals have allowed things to drift . . . have postponed
> decisive action . . . have been preoccupied with their own pet-
> tifogging differences, while the enemy massed his forces at the
> gate. Now, when the attack is sounded, we are without
> defenders.[22]

The Liberals were indeed without defenders. As late as
September 1924 the party was without a single prospective

[17] Midland Liberal Federation, Minutes, Executive Committee, 28 Mar
1924.
[18] *Birmingham Post*, 10, 13 Oct 1924.
[19] Midland Liberal Federation, Minutes, Executive Committee, 19 Sep
1924.
[20] *Birmingham Post*, 10 Oct 1924.
[21] For example, A. J. Bennett and C. G. L. Du Cann, both Liberal
candidates in 1923, joined the Conservatives.
[22] *South Wales News*, 10 Oct 1924.

candidate in Cardiff, Swansea, Newport and Merthyr, whilst there were only three candidates ready at the Dissolution in the whole of Wales.[23] In Cardiff East it had still not been decided who should replace the sitting Liberal, for both Sir Donald Maclean and Emlyn Jones had rejected invitations. Nor had reorganisation taken place in the many mining valleys where organisation had totally collapsed.

In Scotland the party was equally disorganised. Even in constituencies in which the party stood a distinct chance of success, no preparatory work was being undertaken. Thus, in the West Perthshire division the prospective Liberal candidate for the constituency refused to stand in 1924, explaining that

> Since his adoption very little effort had been made by some of the prominent Liberals in the constituency to place the organisation . . . in such a condition as to enable their candidate to contest the seat with any reasonable success.[24]

A similar lethargic association in Moray and Nairn resulted in a seat which had returned a National Liberal unopposed in June 1922 going uncontested in 1924.

Indeed, Lord Londonderry's remark, that all the electricity in the world would be required to galvanise the Liberal Party into life, was certainly true of industrial Scotland. At the end of September only one prospective Liberal candidate was ready for the 15 seats in Glasgow; the Conservatives had 13 already placed.[25] In the whole of Scotland the Liberals had only 8 candidates apart from their 23 sitting MPs. The Conservatives, defending only 16 seats, had 33 other candidates already fixed.[26] With this inactivity and lethargy, the morale of party supporters was slumping. In a disturbing account of party morale in Scotland, one Liberal wrote to Maclean that 'hundreds of Liberals now are going to vote, not

---

[23] *Manchester Guardian*, 13 Oct 1924; *South Wales News*, 10 Oct 1924.
[24] *Scotsman*, 13 Oct 1924.
[25] *Glasgow Herald*, 10 Oct 1924; *Scotsman*, 13 Oct 1924.
[26] *Glasgow Herald*, 9 Oct 1924.

on a party ticket, but country before party . . . every Labour man I meet is determined to slay the Liberal Party'.[27]

The phenomenon was not confined to Scotland. Throughout the country the morale of party activists was declining. In Lancashire the *Liverpool Courier*'s correspondent found Liberals in the country 'in the doldrums' with officials reporting that Labour was gaining converts.[28] This increasing lack of morale was reflected in a growing unwillingness on the part of Liberals to commit themselves as candidates. In this respect, Gladstone's interview with Sir Walter Essex was typical. Gladstone found Essex 'sound in the faith, but rather reluctant'. Similarly, after seeing another potential candidate in late March, Gladstone noted in his diary: 'Not inclined to stand now. But after longish talk think he might come on if the Liberal situation improved about July'.[29] As the Secretary of the Midland Liberal Federation explained on behalf of Headquarters to his organisation, it had become 'a very formidable thing' since the war to secure candidates

> 'because in dark times like these when there are so few decent chances to offer a candidate it has become exceedingly difficult to find men and women who are prepared to face a contest and provide all the money.[30]

This lack of finance was a heavy burden. Even worse for its effect on party morale was the onslaught launched by Labour in Liberal-held constituencies. The bitterness of this attack at the grass roots, coming at the very time when Liberals were maintaining MacDonald in office, left Liberals bewildered and stunned. This was a development they had not expected.

To some extent, the Liberals had only themselves to blame for their political blindness. The signs had been there during the 1923 campaign. In his report on the election to Gladstone, the Secretary of the Midland Liberal Federation

---

[27] Gladstone Papers, BM Add. MSS 46,474/87, James Wood to Maclean, 26 Apr 1924.

[28] *Liverpool Courier*, 27 Mar 1924.

[29] Gladstone Papers, BM Add. MSS 46,486, entry dated 25 Mar 1924, in Lord Gladstone's political notebook.

[30] Asquith Papers, W. Finnemore to A. Andrews, 5 Sep 1925.

declared that he had never seen Labour so bitter towards the Liberals.[31]

The Labour attack was all the more serious because it did not discriminate between Liberals of the right wing of the party or the left. Thus, Philip Oliver, the Liberal Member for Blackley, complained bitterly that, after faithfully supporting the government in the lobbies, he found a Labour candidate adopted against him.[32] Nor did even the most unlikely territory daunt Labour's efforts to spread organisation and propaganda. Among the unlikely constituencies in which Labour candidates appeared in March were Henley, St Marylebone and Bedford.[33]

Nor did a tradition of Liberal–Labour co-operation in a constituency prevent Labour disturbing the old order. Such a change occurred in the Harborough division, a constituency in which, as recently as February 1923, the local Labour Party had been willing to support a Liberal candidate in return for a *quid pro quo* elsewhere.[34] In addition, the Liberal MP, Alderman J. W. Black, was a firm radical. He had once declared that the only objection between his political faith and that of the Labour Party was his opposition to the nationalisation of all the means of production and distribution, although he supported land nationalisation.[35]

As late as May 1924, a delegate to the Liberal Executive Committee again raised the question of a possible arrangement with the Labour Party. The President stalled, by declaring that it was 'not advisable to do anything at present'. The opportunity had gone. By September 1924 a Labour candidate was already in the field, and in the subsequent election the Liberal lost his seat.[36]

---

[31] Gladstone Papers, BM Add. MSS 46,480, Midland Liberal Federation Report on 1923 election.

[32] *Manchester Guardian*, 8 Apr 1924.

[33] *Daily Herald*, 4, 7, 8 Mar 1924.

[34] See Midland Liberal Federation, Minutes, Executive Committee, 8 Feb 1923.

[35] Harborough Division Liberal and Radical Association, Annual Report, 1919–20.

[36] Harborough Division Liberal and Radical Association, Minutes, Executive Committee, 17 May 1924.

Just how far the position in the constituencies had changed in two months can be seen by comparing the rapid change in the attitude of Phillipps, the Liberal Chief Whip, to Labour. Early in February, Phillipps declared that 'With goodwill and consideration not only in Parliament but in the constituencies, the two parties could march together a long way before their paths need diverge'.[37] Two months later, speaking in Edinburgh West, Phillipps complained that, despite Liberal help at Westminster, 'The Prime Minister's only response is to mobilise his machine in the constituencies against the very men who are sacrificing their time and health in the House of Commons in order to keep him in office'.[38]

Against this dark, foreboding scene one hope kept the constituency associations alive: the hope that the debate on electoral reform shortly to take place in Parliament might produce favourable results. It did not. The last hope that Labour might support electoral reform vanished when the government refused to give facilities for the proportional representation Bill.

From this moment, whether in Parliament or in the constituencies, the Liberals had nowhere to turn. There was now not the remotest chance of co-operating with Labour on dignified terms. The Liberals at constituency level had now to fight back. They had neither the resources, the money nor the morale to do so. Even in their own territory, when by-elections fell vacant, their impotence was only too clearly demonstrated.

The record of the Liberals in the ten by-elections that occurred during the lifetime of the first Labour Government was as dismal as the part played by the party at Westminster.

None of these by-elections provided any degree of comfort for Liberals. At Dover, the by-election failed to instil any breath of life into the dormant Liberal Association, whilst in the City of London the Liberal candidate who came forward had earlier sought the Conservative nomination.[39]

---

[37] *Glasgow Herald*, 10 Feb 1924.
[38] *The Times*, 22 Apr 1924.
[39] *Dover and County Chronicle*, 8, 15 Mar 1924; Maclean to Gladstone, Gladstone Papers BM Add. MSS 46,474/74.

The story of the more important by-elections of this period – in particular the contests at Burnley, the Abbey division of Westminster, Glasgow Kelvingrove and Oxford – has recently been recounted in detail elsewhere.[40] It is worthwhile, however, attempting a brief summary of the significance of these by-elections in the context of the minority Labour Government.

Diverse though these by-elections had been, in the political situation of 1924 these contests lent themselves to a very definite interpretation. The lesson of the by-elections for the Liberal Party should have been clear. In every contest the party had polled a worse vote than in 1923: this was true from such Liberal-held seats as Oxford and Carmarthen through to Kelvingrove. Where the party had intervened (as in Lewes) there had been little impact. Equally disturbing was the ability of Labour to deny the Liberals victory in Oxford, and to advance in areas as diverse as Carmarthen or Abbey.

Beyond the poor – at times disastrous – showing of the Liberals goes a more fundamental meaning of these by-elections. Three factors together demonstrate that these by-elections in many ways foreshadowed the general election of 1924: the ability of Labour to increase its vote even in strongly entrenched Liberal areas (e.g. Carmarthen and Oxford); the ability of the Conservatives to rouse the electorate against the Socialist threat (as at Kelvingrove and Lewes); thirdly, and finally, the extent to which, long before the Russian Treaty and the Zinoviev letter, turnout was increasing and the campaigns becoming increasingly centred on the 'Bolshevist' nature of the Labour Party, even in such areas as Holland-with-Boston. It was significant that turnout increased in every by-election except for Burnley and Oxford. Even here, turnout was very high, at 82·4 per cent and 80·3 per cent respectively.

Even though, no doubt, the course of events during the 1924 election campaign accentuated the difficulties facing a sorely tried Liberal Party, long before Campbell or Zinoviev the writing was to some extent already on the wall.

---

[40] For a detailed discussion of the by-elections of this period, see Cook, C. and Ramsden, J. *By-Elections in British Politics*, pp. 44–71.

Part Four

The Liberal Agony:
The General Election of
October 1924

16   The Fall of the Labour Government

There had been no shortage of predictions during the first Labour Government that its life would be a short one. These forecasts, which had tended to fade a little after Snowden's Budget and the London Conference, were realised in October 1924 with comparative suddenness. When Parliament prepared to depart for the summer recess, three major problems had been left outstanding: the Irish boundary dispute, the Russian Treaty and the Campbell case. It was over these two latter issues that the minority Labour Government was to fall.

As a minority government, Labour had risked constant defeat in Parliament (and indeed on relatively unimportant issues, had actually *been* defeated). It had survived because the Liberals had not dared to bring it down and the Conservatives had not particularly wanted to. By the autumn of 1924 the Conservatives had recovered rapidly from their election disaster. This changed position in the Conservative ranks not only ended the lifetime of the Labour Government but was also to affect the degree of Conservative success in the subsequent election. As such, it needs to be briefly examined.

The Conservative mood in September 1924 was in marked contrast to the shock and demoralisation that had followed the disaster of 6 December 1923. The reaction of the Conservative Party to defeat at the polls and the formation of the Labour Government had followed a predictable pattern. The reaction was one of a party determined to put its house in order, determined to perfect organisation, increase membership and prepare for a contest which could not be very long delayed. However, in the immediate term there had been a short, if bitter, inquest. In the immediate wake of the election disaster, criticism was widespread at the folly and lack of preparation with which Baldwin had called the election. Not surprisingly, the bitterest comments came from Lancashire.[1] This criticism was not confined to that county, however. Thus, the Eastern Provincial Council of the National Union, after a lively meeting of the Executive, passed a motion declaring that 'this meeting . . . desires to express its regret that steps were not taken to ascertain by consultation with the divisions the views of the different constituencies . . . prior to the election'.[2]

The Conservative agents themselves were particularly vocal in their criticism of the election strategy. At a meeting in mid-January, the chairman of the National Society of Conservative and Unionist Agents protested strongly at the methods which had led to the December débâcle. When the agents for the Home Counties met to discuss the position, a heated controversy was clearly expected. They met behind closed doors, and no report of their discussions was issued except to state that the meeting had indulged in 'straight talking'[3]

Outside such centres of Free Trade as Lancashire and Cheshire, it is quite clear that, in explaining their electoral defeat, the Conservative rank and file were not complaining over the actual *policy* of Protection, but rather at the way it was introduced. Thus, the same Executive meeting of the Eastern Provincial Division which had protested at the lack of consultation carried unanimously a motion urging that tariff reform, provided it did not involve the taxation of food, should be retained as an integral part of Conservative policy.[4] In a very similar way, the party was urged to retain the agricultural subsidy.

After this initial inquest on the reasons for the electoral disaster, a surprising feature of the mood of local associations was the unanimity with which motions of loyalty to Baldwin

[1] The 'Lancashire Plot' is well detailed in R. T. McKenzie, *British Political Parties* (1955) pp. 114–5, 238–40.

[2] Eastern Provincial Division of the National Union of Conservative and Unionist Associations, Minutes, Executive Committee, 8 Jan 1924.

[3] *Conservative Agents' Journal*, Feb 1924, p. 21.

[4] Eastern Provincial Division, Minutes, Executive Committee, 8 Jan 1924. For letters in similar vein urging the party to retain tariff reform, see Baldwin Papers, F35/120, Spender Clay to Baldwin, 6 Dec 1923; ibid., F35/125, McInnes Shaw to Waterhouse, 14 Dec 1923.

were passed. Examples of this sort could be seen in Oxford and Derby.[5] Much of the bitterness towards Baldwin was confined to defeated candidates and passed relatively swiftly.

Once the decision to install a Labour Government had been taken, Baldwin's main task during 1924 was to rebuild his party. To do this, it was essential that Protection be dropped from the programme of the party. This was done at the party meeting at the Hotel Cecil on 11 February. Here, Baldwin made his statement that

> I do not feel justified in advising the Party again to submit the proposal for a general tariff to the country, except on the clear evidence that on this matter public opinion is disposed to reconsider its judgment of two months ago[6]

Having buried Protection, Baldwin's speech then moved on to the attack. The party would be reorganised. The Labour Government would be opposed – not with a policy of tranquillity, but with a programme of constructive social reform. Party committees, aided by outside experts, would be set up to work out detailed policies for different subjects, beginning with agriculture. Baldwin's Hotel Cecil speech was well received. It captured the mood of the party. Baldwin went on to secure his position by recruiting the former Coalitionists to work with him, in particular Austen Chamberlain and Birkenhead.

Having abandoned Protection at the Hotel Cecil, and with Austen Chamberlain and the ex-Coalitionists reunited to the party, Baldwin's next move was to reorganise Conservative Central Office. Sir Reginald Hall (whom many had blamed for the election disaster) was replaced as Chief Agent by Herbert Blain, a Liverpool man and formerly general manager of London's public transport system. At the same time, Baldwin instituted the nucleus of a Shadow Cabinet with a Policy Secretariat based in Palace Chambers. The Secretariat was headed by Colonel Lancelot Storr, assisted by such new blood as Geoffrey Lloyd and Robert Boothby.

[5] Derby Conservative Association, Minutes, Executive Committee, 17 Dec 1923; Oxford Conservative Association, Minutes, Annual General Meeting, 1 Feb 1924.

[6] *The Times*, 12 Feb 1924.

Meanwhile, Baldwin found himself being pressed by many people in the party to adopt more positive policies. Baldwin grew rather irritated by these demands. Tom Jones recorded a talk with Baldwin in his diary on 9 April:

> He had some troublesome followers who were clamouring for a positive policy without being able to suggest one. The one he had offered had been rejected. There was nothing for it but to await events, and he imagined that that was what L.G. was doing.[7]

Baldwin, however, did not quite live up to his words. By the end of April he had decided on his next move. On 2 May, in a major speech at the Albert Hall, Baldwin put forward his own version of Disraelian Conservatism with an appeal for a constructive national policy that would not be a mere anti-Labour campaign.

During May and June, Baldwin delivered a series of ten major speeches, all on the theme of Tory Democracy, which received widespread publicity. At times, Baldwin departed from this theme to attack Labour's record over unemployment and its decision to abandon the Singapore naval base.

Thus, by the autumn of 1924, the Conservatives were eager and willing to force an election. They could not have wished for a better subject than Labour's proposed Russian Treaty.

On assuming office, MacDonald had formally recognised the Soviet Government. And, as part of his plan for a general reconciliation in Europe, he was keen to negotiate a trade agreement with Russia and thus restore normal commercial ties. In February, MacDonald had informed the Commons that negotiations with the Soviet Union to settle all outstanding differences would begin as soon as possible. They actually began in April.[8]

The negotiations did not run particularly smoothly, in particular over the position of British bondholders whose claims on the Tsarist regime had been repudiated by the Soviet Government. All along, the Russians demanded a loan

---

[7] *Whitehall Diary*, p. 275. It was on this occasion that Baldwin told Tom Jones that he thought Asquith too far gone 'even to be Master of Balliol'.

[8] Although MacDonald chaired the first meeting, the real conduct of the negotiations was left to Arthur Ponsonby, MacDonald's Parliamentary Secretary.

as part of any commercial treaty settling the payment of these pre-revolutionary debts. On 5 August negotiations broke down. This caused considerable unhappiness on the left wing of the Labour Party. After ILP intervention and much pressure, these negotiations were resumed. At last a complicated compromise was reached, and a 'treaty' between the Russian and British delegates signed in August 1924. In fact there were two treaties, not one.[9] The general treaty – which was not strictly a treaty in the real sense of the word, but a vague agreement that might in the future lead on to a substantive treaty – nonetheless provoked intense Conservative opposition.

At Conservative insistence, the Labour Government agreed that there should be a delay of 21 parliamentary days between signature and ratification. Hence, the treaty would not be ratified until after the end of the summer recess.

At this juncture, several possibilities remained open. In the face of Conservative opposition, Labour could make a tactical withdrawal, rather than risk an all-out battle. Alternatively, the government could wait and sense the Liberal attitude, and then manoeuvre accordingly. Or the government could stick to its guns and risk defeat. Clearly, the outcome depended largely on two factors: the attitude of MacDonald, and the position adopted by the Liberal Party.

During August and September the evidence of the Mac-Donald papers makes it quite clear that there was no thought of retreat in his mind.[10] On 13 August, MacDonald wrote to Ponsonby:

> We shall have a fight to get it through, but we shall face the House of Commons in a fighting spirit and defy them to turn it down. The great thing is – keep your fighting spirit up and no surrender.

[9] The commercial treaty was fairly straightforward. The wider general treaty proposed further negotiations between the bondholders and the Soviet Government. Only if the outcome of these subsequent negotiations had the approval of the bondholders (or, to be more precise, holders of at least 50 per cent of the total capital value of the bonds in question), and only if the remaining outstanding differences were settled, would a third treaty be signed, after which the British Government would actually guarantee a loan.

[10] I am extremely indebted to David Marquand, MP, for allowing me to consult the relevant chapter of his forthcoming life of Ramsay MacDonald.

MacDonald's position, at least, was clear. And, as September approached, the attitude of the Liberal leadership hardened over the issue. Earlier on, during August, the party had been as divided on this issue as on most others. These divisions were perfectly reflected in the Liberal press. On 8 August the *Daily News* stated:

> It is difficult to explain, except on the assumption of rather paltry motives, the heat of the outcry against the signing of the Russian Treaty. The Prime Minister's speech yesterday seems to us a very reasonable and sensible appeal.

Earlier, the *Westminster Gazette* had supported MacDonald, declaring that 'the Prime Minister was well within his rights in insisting on signing the Treaty at once'.[11]

The *Daily Chronicle*, however, had no such sympathy. On 8 August it declared:

> The text of the two new Russian treaties thoroughly justifies Mr Lloyd George's description of them as a fake. . . The only ground on which one might justify Mr MacDonald's action in signing the treaties (contrary to his pledge) before Parliament has had a proper chance to consider them is that they are sham documents for shopwindow use only.

The *Daily Chronicle*, of course, was simply reflecting Lloyd George's views. There is considerable evidence to suggest – as MacDonald himself believed – that Lloyd George intended to force an election over the Russian Treaties. On 2 October, for example, Lloyd George wrote that

> It looks now as if we are in for another General Election. I have done my best to precipitate it. Labour had its chance and with a little more wisdom and what the old Puritans sagely called 'Grace of God' they could have remained in another three years and formed a working alliance with Liberalism that would have ensured a progressive administration of this country for 20 years. But they lost their heads as men and women will from sudden elevation. Hence their fall.[12]

[11] *Westminster Gazette*, 8 July 1924.
[12] Lloyd George to Megan Lloyd George, 2 Oct 1924, quoted in *Lloyd George: Family Letters*.

Scott's diary corroborates Lloyd George's desire to have done with MacDonald's government. Scott recorded:

> When it came to the autumn his patience, I gathered, was exhausted. He certainly meant and the party meant to reject the Russian Treaty, but whether he meant to do this unconditionally or would have been ready to make terms did not clearly appear. When I said there seemed no reason why we should not have accepted the Treaty in a modified form he merely replied 'Well, why did they not try'. But in an earlier conversation he said something which indicated that he did not want them to get as far as to bring in a Budget in which, he said, there would have been proposals for the taxation of land.[13]

Lloyd George's antipathy to the treaty probably reflected the majority view of the party. Whilst a radical element, that included Kenworthy and Hogge, gave support to the treaty, most of the left wing Liberals lined up with the right. The Manchester Liberal Federation condemned the treaty; E. A. Lessing, a Liberal expert on Russia and often sympathetic to the Soviet Government, wrote a pamphlet that was exceptionally hostile.[14] Masterman later claimed that the party was practically solid against a proposal to loan the Russians money in order to persuade them to pay back some of what they already owed.[15]

The clamour against the treaty, led by Lloyd George, rapidly gained the support of Simon, Runciman, Grey, Mond, Maclean and Masterman. Possibly the Carmarthen by-election of 14 August also encouraged the Liberals to take a firmer line. On 3 September the Liberal Party publication department produced a pamphlet entitled *A Sham Treaty*. On 8 September the *Daily Chronicle* followed up the attack with a series of articles entitled *'In Darkest Russia'*.

Much, however, would depend in the last resort on Asquith's attitude. Asquith, who was ill at the time, does not seem to have made his position clear in these early days.

---

[13] Scott's diary, entry dated 9 Nov 1924, quoted in Wilson, *The Downfall of the Liberal Party*, p. 472.

[14] Ibid., p. 276.

[15] *Nation*, 4 Oct 1924.

Gradually, however, he seems to have moved over towards the Lloyd George position. When Lloyd George saw Asquith early in September, he found him 'quite firm' in opposing the treaty.[16] In a letter to *The Times* on 22 September, Asquith attacked the Russian Treaties as 'crude experiments in nursery diplomacy' and urged Parliament not to accept 'a loan of undefined amount, upon unspecified conditions'. However, at the same time, Asquith seemed to be urging the Liberals not to reject the treaties totally, but to amend them. Once again, Asquith was appearing both to leave his position uncertain and also to be attempting to gain the best of both possible worlds.

Whatever purpose Asquith had in mind in hinting that the treaties might be amended, MacDonald ensured that it came to nothing. When the Cabinet tentatively discussed the idea of a deal with the Liberals, MacDonald violently opposed it. MacDonald's papers reveal only too clearly that not only did he see Liberal tactics becoming more and more dishonest, but that if Asquith wanted an election he was more than welcome to have it.

In a major speech at Derby on 27 September, MacDonald made it perfectly clear that, although minor details of the loan might be subject to change, the government would not compromise on the principle of a guaranteed loan. He left no doubt that Labour would fight an election over the issue.

MacDonald had made his position clear. Four days later, as Parliament reassembled on 1 October, the Parliamentary Liberal Party supported a hard line. With only a handful of dissenters, the meeting passed a motion rejecting the idea of a guaranteed loan. It was, as the *Glasgow Herald* commented, notice on the Labour Government to quit.[17] Yet the Liberals were in an invidious position.

If they stuck to their guns, a Labour defeat was inevitable. Yet was the issue of the Russian Treaty a good ground on which to do battle? Kenworthy had warned the party meeting

[16] H. A. L. Fisher Papers, Fisher's diary, 16 Sep 1923, quoted in Wilson, *The Downfall of the Liberal Party*, p. 276.

[17] Glasgow Herald, 9 Oct 1924.

on 1 October that an election on this issue would be a disaster. The *Manchester Guardian* was also worried on that score, arguing that on any anti-Russian campaign the Conservatives would benefit, but that neither Labour nor Liberals stood to gain anything.[18]

The Russian Treaty had another tactical disadvantage for the Liberals. They occupied a dangerous middle ground; for whatever the party might think of a guaranteed loan, there was a considerable desire to improve relations with Russia.[19] For a Liberal Party needing an easily identifiable position, any campaign on the Russian Treaties was clearly fraught with dangers. The Liberals were in fact caught in their own trap. They could not compromise w.th Labour, because Labour would not compromise. They had to face an election, or abandon their posture that they were keeping Labour to a safe moderate course. Yet the party was in no shape to face an election.

In fact, at this eleventh hour, the Liberal dilemma was resolved in a way which had not been expected. Labour chose to accept defeat, not on the issue of the Russian Treaties, but over the Campbell case.

As with the Russian Treaties, the origins of the Campbell case dated from before the summer recess. The article in the *Workers' Weekly* on which the subsequent prosecution was based appeared on 25 July. On 5 August the offices of the *Workers' Weekly* were raided by the police and Campbell arrested. The affair really came to light at Question Time in the Commons on 6 August. Replying to a question from John Scurr, an ILP backbencher, Sir Patrick Hastings (the Attorney-General) stated:

> My attention was called by the Director of Public Prosecutions to an article in the *Workers' Weekly* which, in my opinion, constituted a breach of the law. In consequence, the Director of Public Prosecutions has been engaged in the necessary steps to ascertain the identity of the persons responsible for the article. The editor has accepted responsibility and has been arrested.

[18] *Manchester Guardian*, 8 Oct 1924.
[19] See, for example, the speech of Lord Beauchamp at Nuneaton (*The Times*, 13 Sep 1924).

This reply raised a storm of angry questions from the Labour back-benchers. On 13 August the government abandoned the prosecution of Campbell, the Treasury counsel stating in court that 'the article in question was not an endeavour to seduce men in the fighting forces from their duty' but 'it was a comment upon armed military force being used by the State to repress industrial disputes'.[20]

At the end of September, when Parliament met in a special session to consider the Irish boundary dispute, the Conservatives were on the attack. On 20 September *The Times* reported that Sir Kingsley Wood was tabling a question to Hastings to ask why the Campbell prosecution was being dropped, and a further question to MacDonald to ask if he had sanctioned the withdrawal of the prosecution. Four days later, on 24 September, Simon also joined the attack with a speech implying that the government had acted improperly.

Meanwhile, MacDonald's reaction to these events was largely predictable. The McVitie & Price affair had already made him particularly sensitive to personal criticism. Now, in a different and potentially even more serious way, his political good faith was again under attack.

In addition, MacDonald's health was not good. On 27 September, although he fulfilled a speaking engagement at Derby, he had a heavy cold and felt wretched. MacDonald was still tired and unwell when both he and Hastings had to answer Sir Kingsley Wood's private notice questions on 30 September. Hastings gave a reasoned and carefully phrased reply. The prosecution had been dropped because inquiries concerning Campbell's character and responsibility had indicated that such a prosecution might well fail. Hastings went on to deny that any 'representations' of the sort implied in Wood's question had been made. He added that 'no member of His Majesty's Government suggested or even knew of the proposal until I myself informed them of it'.

Hastings's reply produced a series of Conservative supplementary questions, but he had survived skilfully. MacDonald's reply to Wood was neither skilful nor true (a bloody

[20] Lyman, *The First Labour Government* p. 237.

lie' was how Sir Maurice Hankey, Clerk of the Privy Council, afterwards called it). MacDonald stated:

> I was not consulted regarding either the institution or the subsequent withdrawal of these proceedings. The first notice of the prosecution which came to my knowledge was in the Press. I never advised its withdrawal, but left the whole matter to the discretion of the Law Officers, where that discretion properly rests.[21]

This untrue reply (which MacDonald excused later by saying that he had been so incensed with Kingsley Wood that he had misunderstood part of the question) transformed an embarrassing incident into a political crisis. MacDonald's ingenuous remark may in fact be quite near the truth. There can be little doubt that the emotion uppermost in MacDonald at this moment was anger. MacDonald was badly rattled by the whole affair and was in a mood to hit back first and think afterwards. In particular, he was in a fury at what he saw as the petty spite and smugness of Sir John Simon and Sir Douglas Hogg. Certainly, it is hard to believe that MacDonald's answer had been carefully calculated, since he had far more to gain by telling the truth than by risking an attempt to mislead the House, for the government's handling had not been unconstitutional, even though it had been inept.

As it was, MacDonald's statement led the Conservatives to put down a motion censuring the government for its handling of the Campbell case. MacDonald seems to have welcomed this censure, since it paved the path for a dissolution which might have been difficult if the Conservatives had singled out the action of the Attorney-General alone. MacDonald, however, was overtaken by moves made by the Liberals. On 1 October, at the same meeting at which the Parliamentary Liberal Party decided to oppose the Russian Treaties, Asquith stated that his party would support 'a reasonable motion' on the Campbell affair. On 2 October the Liberals put down an amendment to the Conservative motion of censure, calling for the establishment of a Select Committee to inquire into the matter.

[21] *The Times*, 1 Oct 1924.

Meanwhile, although the *Manchester Guardian* pleaded that there was no need for the crisis to lead to a dissolution, speculation over an election rapidly mounted. MacDonald added to this by declaring that the only select committee whose judgement he would accept was the twenty million electors of Great Britain.

Even at this late juncture, however, the Labour Government could have quite easily avoided defeat by accepting a compromise. At the Cabinet meeting on 6 October, any such compromise was ruled out. It was decided that the censure motion and the Liberal amendment should both be treated as motions of censure, and that if either were carried, Mac-Donald should ask for a dissolution.[22]

At the same time, the Cabinet meeting agreed on what appeared to be a neat way out of the trap. When the first motion was moved from the chair (i.e. the motion to allow the Liberal amendment), Labour Members would either support the Conservative original motion or abstain. In either event, the Liberal amendment would not succeed. Then, when the substantive Conservative motion came to a vote, Labour would vote with the Liberals (who did not like it) to defeat the Conservatives. This somewhat Lloyd Georgian manoeuvre (in which Labour would first vote with the Conservatives to defeat the Liberals and then with the Liberals to defeat the Conservatives) came to nothing. At the end of the debate on 8 October, Baldwin announced that the Conservatives would vote for the Liberal amendment and not for their own motion.[23] This effectively sealed the fate of the Labour Government.

The Liberal amendment was subsequently carried by 364 votes to 199. Fourteen Liberals, on the left wing of the party, voted against the amendment proposed by their own party.

[22] Hastings dissenting, the Cabinet also decided that the government should not offer a less partisan form of inquiry, by a Royal Commission, by the Judicial Committee of the Privy Council or by a judge.

[23] For the course of the debate, in which little new was revealed, see Lyman, *The First Labour Government*, op. cit. The Liberal amendment read: 'That a Select Committee be appointed to investigate and report upon the circumstances leading up to the withdrawal of the proceedings recently instituted by the Director of Public Prosecutions against Mr Campbell'.

They included Hogge, Kenworthy, Percy Harris and Jowett.[24] The two Conservatives to vote with Labour were R. M. Banks and C. Hughes.

Only ten months after the party had first accepted office, Labour was seeking a dissolution. Or rather, MacDonald was insisting on an election against the advice of many senior colleagues. Scott wrote of the events of early October in his diary:

> Neither Lloyd George nor the other party leaders had wished to turn the Government out on the Campbell case and he thought it was a mistake on their part to have proposed an amendment. They ought simply to have voted against the Conservative motion. Asquith did his utmost to make retreat easy for the Government by the modification in the terms of the amendment proposed in the course of the debate, and the Government were divided as to whether to accept it. [Vernon] Hartshorn told me, said Lloyd George, that when Thomas began by proposing that they should consider the new situation MacDonald instantly rounded on him and asked what there was to consider. Then Henderson (with his usual blundering stupidity) chimed in with an indignant 'Are we then to go back on our decision', and finally MacDonald had his way. But there was great dissatisfaction among the other Ministers with MacDonald's leadership.

Scott continued:

> According to Hartshorn MacDonald had really broken down in nerve after about six months of office and had gone on from bad to worse until his palpable and disastrous collapse at the close (in connection with the Zinoviev letter. Lloyd George was clear that this had a tremendous effect on the result of the election). They would not re-elect him now, but for the difficulty of finding any one else to take his place. His egotism said Lloyd George has become a disease and affects his mental stability.

It is hard to disagree with the comment made by Violet Bonham Carter many years after the events of 8 October 1924.

[24] The full list was: T. R. Ackroyd, R. Alstead, Capt. R. C. Berkeley, P. Harris, A. E. Hillary, Lt-Col. J. P. Hodge, J. M. Hogge, W. A. Jowett, Lt-Cdr. J. M. Kenworthy, H. Maden, J. J. O'Neill, A. Rendall, Dr G. E. Spero, and Mrs M. Wintringham.

In the end Ramsay MacDonald committed hari-kari quite wantonly and unnecessarily on the Liberal demand for an inquiry into the Campbell case. He did not fall on his sword – he impaled himself wantonly on a mere bodkin. It was an inglorious end for the first Labour Government, and it had disastrous consequences for the Liberal Party.[25]

[25] *New Outlook*, Feb 1966.

17 Preparing for the Election: Candidates and the Nominations

The end of the experiment of a Labour Government was never far away after Parliament reassembled in the autumn of 1924. After the defeat of the MacDonald government on the Campbell case, events moved swiftly. Parliament was dissolved on 9 October. The closing day for nominations was to be 18 October. The election itself was fixed for Wednesday 29 October. The three parties faced the coming election with considerably different feelings and forebodings.

Labour entered the 1924 election campaign in a mood of challenge and optimism. Partly this was because Labour faced the election in a stronger position than in any previous campaign. For the first time, it fought as an outgoing government, with all the prestige and publicity of MacDonald as Prime Minister.

In addition, the by-elections during 1924, particularly the results in West Toxteth and Kelvingrove, had given the party considerable cause for optimism. The party had also gained two recruits to its ranks: G. M. L. Davies in the University of Wales constituency and Oswald Mosley in Harrow had both accepted the party whip. Mosley, the son-in-law of Curzon, seemed a particularly good catch.

The extension of Labour organisation into many hitherto unorganised rural constituencies also meant the party was fighting on a far wider front than ever before. In the 1924 election Labour was able to make a dramatic increase in the number of its candidates in many areas that had seen intensive propaganda work in 1924. In the South-West the number of Labour candidates rose from 21 to 39, in Southern England from 27 to 40 and in Scotland from 50 to 63. In addition, there was a marked increase in Lancashire and the North-West, from 54 to 71.

In all, Labour intervened in 101 seats in 1924 that it had not contested at the previous general election. Only finance and organisation prevented the party fielding an even greater number of candidates.[1] In 50 of these 101, Labour was fighting the seat for the first time. Even seats unopposed in 1923 were not sufficient to deter a Labour candidate – 14 Conservatives and 5 Liberals in this position in 1923 faced Labour intervention in October 1924. It was hardly surprising that the large number of Labour candidates appearing in seats narrowly held by Liberals (and already being strongly attacked by Conservative candidates) gave rise to Liberal charges of wrecking tactics on the part of Labour.

In only a very few cases were radical Liberal MPs able to dissuade Labour from fielding a candidate against them. Such considerations may have prevented the threat of Labour candidates in the Liberal-held seats of Altrincham, Sevenoaks and Manchester Moss Side, although in all these seats weak Labour organisation was probably an equally strong factor.[2]

Labour also benefited at the outset of the 1924 campaign by the removal of a series of local rival candidatures that had marred their chances in 1923. The split at Paisley was healed when Hugh Guthrie resigned as Co-operative candidate, owing to ill-health. At the ensuing election a united party was able to devote its full energies to the defeat of Asquith. A split in the rock-solid Labour seat of West Fife was also healed, whilst rumours of Co-operative–Labour rivalry in the Sparkbrook and King's Norton seats of Birmingham were soon proved to be unfounded.[3] In fact, 1924 proved to be one of Labour's best contests in terms of dissident unofficial Labour candidatures.[4]

[1] And also accidents: in Bodmin the Labour candidate arrived too late to hand in his nomination papers owing to a car accident (*Western Evening Herald*, 18 Oct 1924).

[2] *Manchester Guardian*, 14 Oct 1924; *Daily Telegraph*, 22 Oct 1924.

[3] *Co-operative News*, 27 Sep 1924.

[4] Those that did come forward were of little more than nuisance value (as, for example, M. R. Richardson in Acton, who stood on behalf of the Acton Democratic Labour Party).

In the 1924 general election, Labour withdrew from very few seats contested by the party in 1923. Only 14 of the 427 seats fought ten months previously were abandoned, and in four of these the withdrawal was due to the Communist problem.[5] Elsewhere Labour fielded only one candidate (as opposed to two previously) in each of the double-Member seats of Brighton and Sunderland. Otherwise (with the exception of Middlesbrough West, a Liberal stronghold) the Labour withdrawals were in safe Conservative-held rural seats such as Warwick and Leamington (where the Countess of Warwick had been Labour's standard-bearer in 1923) and Daventry.

Despite Labour's intensified challenge, it was still the agricultural seats that presented most problems for a Labour candidate. Of the 28 seats in which 40 per cent or more of the working population was engaged in agriculture, Labour fought only half (compared with three-quarters of the 48 seats where agriculture counted for only 20 per cent or above).

The net result of Labour's greatly strengthened field of candidates in 1924 could be seen most clearly in Scotland and Wales. In 1923 Labour fought 27 of the 35 Welsh seats; in 1924 it fought all but two. In Scotland, Labour fought no fewer than 63 of the 71 seats in 1924, having put up candidates on a scale not seen before in the rural and Highland areas. Labour's attack, however, still remained exceptionally weak in rural Cheshire, in the rural areas along the Welsh border and in parts of the East and North Ridings of Yorkshire.[6]

Even more than with Labour, the Conservatives faced the election of 1924 sensing that, on this occasion, the mood of the country was behind them. As was seen in the last chapter, after an initial bout of inquest and recrimination, Baldwin's position had rapidly been consolidated during 1924. The plots and intrigues against him were of no consequence by the

[5] These four seats were: Manchester Rusholme, Battersea North, Bethnal Green South-West and Birmingham West.

[6] It was perhaps symbolic of Labour weakness in the Welsh border areas that no Labour candidate ever appeared in Leominster until 1950, when Labour had already completed three terms of office.

autumn. Changes had been made in the party machinery. Protection had been dropped.

Certainly, compared with the deep divisions the party had suffered only twelve months previously, the Conservatives in October 1924 presented a united and confident party. Apart from the wounds reopened by Churchill's candidature in the Abbey division, the by-elections had indicated a considerable groundswell of support in their favour. The unity and confidence of the party was witnessed during the 52nd Annual Conference of the National Union which opened on 2 October. The business of the conference ran so smoothly that no vote was needed on any contentious issue.

Even before the campaign started, the by-elections had indicated that a fair proportion of the Liberal vote at the preceding general election might well be captured by the Conservatives. This feeling was reinforced by the enthusiasm and eagerness coming from the constituencies. Indeed, a feature of Conservative activity at the grass roots during 1924 was the speed with which candidates were readopted for the next fight. J. C. C. Davidson, in the Hemel Hempstead division, had been readopted on 29 December 1923. At Oxford, where only three weeks before the December election the association had been without a candidate, an adoption was made early in January.[7]

This early selection of candidates was a reflection of an increased activity and interest at constituency level which meant that the Conservatives were in a high state of preparedness by October 1924.

The Peterborough Conservative Association provides a good example. The Executive Committee saw in the 1923 election 'the danger and result of apathy'. In similar vein, the constituency Organising Secretary had spoken of 'the prevalence of apathy amongst some of our supporters'. By April, however, the secretary could report 'a revival of interest consequent upon the existence of a Socialist Government'.[8]

[7] Oxford Conservative Association, Minutes, Executive Committee, 9 Jan 1924.

[8] Peterborough and North Northamptonshire Conservative Association, Minutes, Executive Committee, 26 Jan, 23 Feb, 12 Apr 1924.

Earlier, the Peterborough association had complained of the difficulty of persuading party members to take an active part in constituency work. As 1924 progressed, this was no longer true. The mood among the Conservative rank and file was one of enthusiam and optimism. Similar enthusiasm was to be found almost everywhere. Bridgeman, the former Home Secretary, declared that he had never seen the party workers in his Oswestry constituency so keen and willing.[9] At Derby, the constituency chairman echoed the enthusiasm of the local association by declaring that there had rarely been better prospects for the party.[10]

A perfect reflection of the extent to which constituency morale had revived can be seen in the extension of women's organisation. By May 1924, 476 new branches had been added to the 3,600 in existence twelve months earlier. In mid-1923, 303 constituencies possessed women's branches; by May 1924 this total had reached 355, and by May 1925 stood at 401.[11] Membership figures showed a similar increase. Total membership rose by 152,700 in the twelve months after early 1924, an increase equal to twice the total membership of the Women's Liberal Organisation. No fewer than 20,000 new members were enrolled in the South-East area alone. Throughout 1924 the women's branches conducted systematic canvassing and house-to-house membership recruiting.

In very similar fashion, the professional Conservative agents had reacted vigorously in response to the 1923 defeat. Whatever the substance of the complaints that the agents were partly responsible for the December disaster, throughout 1924 the numbers of full-time agents increased and there was considerable moving around of existing agents. No fewer than 80 agents moved constituency, compared with 23 in 1922, 33 in 1923 and 28 in 1925. Similarly, no fewer than 214 agents either began service or retired in 1924, compared with

---

[9] Bridgeman papers, Bridgeman's diary, entry dated Nov 1924, p. 103.

[10] Derby Conservative Association, Minutes, Executive Committee, 13 Oct 1924.

[11] Figures compiled from Annual Conference Reports, 1923–5, of the Woman's Unionist Organisation.

69 in 1922, 117 in 1923, 102 in 1925 and 96 in 1926.[12] It was this reorganisation and reshuffling that was more significant than the net increase of 26 in the total number of agents.

The net result of this constituency reorganisation and activity was that the Conservatives entered the 1924 election better prepared and better equipped than for at least a decade. In part, their electoral success was connected with this. Like Labour, the Conservatives were also fortunate in 1924 to have virtually no Independent Conservative candidates to complicate the scene.[13]

Both Conservatives and Labour entered the 1924 campaign eager for the fray. Both sensed that this election presented an unrivalled opportunity to attack the rapidly fading fortunes of the Liberal party. Subsequent events proved them only too accurate.

Of the Liberal Party in October 1924 one fact was only too apparent. The advent of the election found the party, like the army of Napoleon which recrossed the Berezina in 1812, a demoralised and disorganised host.

The most pressing problem was finance. Even the imminence of the Dissolution had not ended the protracted question of the disposal of part of the Lloyd George Fund to help headquarters to finance candidates. The last weeks of September had found Lloyd George insisting on a committee of inquiry into the organisation of 21 Abingdon Street. This demand was met, and a committee established on 30 September. Its report merely confirmed that all that could be done was to fix candidates as rapidly as possible.

With a general election now imminent, Asquith wrote to Lloyd George suggesting that a Special Election Committee be established.[14] The next day Maclean went to see Lloyd George at Churt. At this meeting, Maclean informed Lloyd George that, including all the sitting Liberal MPs, the party

---

[12] These statistics have been compiled from the *Conservative Agents' Journal*, 1921–6.

[13] Two nuisance candidates appeared in Londonderry and Manchester Withington. A potentially more serious split was averted in Richmond (*Morning Advertiser*, 27 Sep 1924).

[14] Gladstone Papers, BM Add. MSS 46,480/159, Asquith to Lloyd George, 3 Oct 1924.

had candidates fixed in only 280 constituencies. Within a day, the number could be increased to 300, but Maclean stressed that 450 was the minimum total with which to wage an effective campaign.[15]

Lloyd George reacted to this information quite unexpectedly. He refuted the necessity of fielding more than 300 candidates, at the same time giving Maclean a letter containing a bitter attack on the recently constituted 'committee of inquiry'. Maclean refused to accept the letter, returning it 'for further and better consideration'.

To Maclean, such conduct by Lloyd George was inexplicable, and he could only speculate that perhaps Lloyd George would not be too worried if the Liberal Party fared badly. Whatever the motives of Lloyd George, the position of the Liberal Party when the Dissolution was announced was, in terms of finance, already critical.

With the election actually upon the party, Lloyd George consented to give £50,000.[16] This, according to Gladstone, was the final death-blow. Apart from this donation, only another £72,202 was spent on the campaign. Independent Liberal Headquarters contributed £25,000; £9,900 was realised from the sale of bonds. Otherwise, the contributors were the same faithful few: Lord Cowdray contributed £10,000, Lord Forteviot and Sir James Hill (President of the Yorkshire Liberal Federation) each subscribed £2,000, Harcourt Johnstone gave £1,500 and Lord Beauchamp £1,000. The position was aggravated by those wealthy Liberals, such as Lord Inchcape, who refused to contribute at all, partly no doubt in reaction to the Liberal decision to vote a Labour Government into office.[17]

This lack of finance from headquarters had an immediate and traumatic effect in the constituencies. Liberal candidates had consistently spent more fighting an election than Labour

[15] This account is derived from Maclean's report to Asquith, in Gladstone Papers, BM Add. MSS 46,480/161–2.

[16] In addition Lloyd George made a contribution to the campaign in Wales.

[17] For Inchcape's position, see Gladstone Papers, Inchcape to Gladstone, 15 Oct 1924.

candidates.[18] With grants from headquarters no longer forth-coming, many associations were paralysed. This handicap was particularly serious in the Home Counties and Greater London area. The average headquarters grant per constit-uency in 1923 in London was £503 and in the Home Counties £572.

An attempt to raise £15,000 for a 'Win London for Liberalism' campaign had raised only £3,214 six days before the poll. Even traditional Liberal seats in Lancashire found themselves in similar difficulties. The prospective Liberal candidate in Bolton only discovered early in October that his association had no funds to fight a campaign.[19] Frequently, where a Liberal Association found itself without a grant from headquarters, any desire to contest the seat was abandoned. So the Ipswich Liberals, when informed that no finance would be forthcoming, abandoned the idea of contesting the seat. Leading local Liberals turned their efforts to returning the sitting Conservative, Sir John Ganzoni.[20]

Lack of funds, however, was only part of the explanation behind the massive reduction in seats contested by Liberals. In October 1924 there was simply no will to fight even in some seats where ample funds existed. Thus, in Cambridgeshire, the Liberal Executive passed a resolution endorsing its conviction in the ultimate success of Liberalism, but deciding not to contest the seat on this occasion. As the agent explained, 'We are keeping our powder dry and our money in our pockets.'[21]

A similar turn of events occurred in Aberdeen. When a resolution was put to the Aberdeen Liberal Executive to fight both divisions in the city, only four of the committee were in favour. A resolution to fight only one seat was carried by 18 votes to 4. A few days later this decision was rescinded, and

[18] Even in 1924, the average expenditure by each Conservative candidate was £841, and each Liberal spent £764. On average, Labour candidates spent only £442.

[19] Bolton Liberal Association, Minutes, Executive Committee, 7 Oct 1924, quoted in Wilson, *The Downfall of the Liberal Party*, p. 323.

[20] *The Times*, 15 Oct 1924.

[21] *The Times*, 17 Oct 1924.

no Liberal at all fought Aberdeen.[22] Liberal Associations in Scotland were particularly prone to this course of action.[23]

This lack of any desire to force a contest was evident even in seats in which the Liberals were near to victory in 1923. Seats in this category, in which Liberals withdrew to leave a straight fight between Conservative and Labour, were Penrith and Cockermouth (the Liberals polled 49·1 per cent of the votes cast in 1923), Waterloo (48·4 per cent), Kinross and West Perthshire, Windsor, Wallasey, and Moray and Nairn. In some of these constituencies, as in Waterloo, Wallasey and Moray and Nairn, the Liberal Association claimed great difficulty in finding candidates.[24] In other potentially winnable seats, such as Fylde, the Liberal decision not to contest the seat gave the Conservative an unopposed victory.[25]

Even more significant in reducing the numbers of Liberal candidates fielded was the arrangement of local anti-Socialist pacts by Liberals at constituency level. This, as much as any other factor, helped set the seal on the Liberal fate in the election.

The debates within the constituencies on whether to agree to an anti-Socialist pact left most Liberal Associations divided, uncertain and demoralised. Like the Liberal lobby record, this was three-way politics again. Some associations would whole-heartedly reject a pact; others would embrace it with equal enthusiasm. Others would simply be divided, deciding nothing.

Rotherham provides a perfect example of a constituency Liberal Association split down the centre. After a heated debate, the association gave its support to the Conservative candidate, the Executive Committee voting 11–10 in favour.[26] This situation was paralleled in the Durham mining

[22] *Scotsman*, 15, 17 Oct 1924.

[23] In Ayr Burghs, for example, despite the urging of Scottish Liberal headquarters to field a candidate, the seat went uncontested (*Scotsman*, 17 Oct 1924).

[24] For Moray and Nairn, see *Scotsman*, 16 Oct 1924; for Waterloo, see *Liverpool Post*, 20 Oct 1924; for Wallasey, see *Manchester Guardian*, 11 Oct 1924.

[25] For Fylde, see *Manchester Guardian*, 15 Oct 1924.

[26] *Daily Herald*, 24 Oct 1924.

seats. In Consett, for example, the Liberals had made a tacit agreement with the Conservatives in 1923 not to run a candidate at the next election. During 1924 the Liberals decided to field a candidate. The association then began to divide on the issue, and eventually one of the joint secretaries resigned and went to speak on the Conservative platform.[27] Neighbouring Morpeth produced a similar state of affairs.[28]

Despite Labour accusations to the contrary, electoral pacts between Conservatives and Liberals were not arranged by any national agreement. The only pact to cover an important area was that arranged in the 25 or so constituencies in Glasgow, Paisley and the West of Scotland. The agreement covered such seats outside Glasgow as Renfrewshire, Greenock, Dunbartonshire, West Stirlingshire and parts of Lanarkshire.

This pact stemmed partly from the weak showing of the Liberals in Glasgow in 1923 (only two of the ten Liberal candidates in the city polled over 30 per cent of the vote, and in every three-cornered fight the Liberals had come bottom), and partly from the need to secure Asquith's seat at Paisley. The Liberals, negotiating with the Conservatives from a position of weakness, withdrew their candidates in 19 seats fought in 1923. Only two Conservative candidates withdrew – in Glasgow St Rollox and Paisley (where the prospective Tory candidate moved to West Renfrewshire).

Although, on the surface, the pact was arranged with a neat precision (every Labour candidate in Glasgow's 15 seats faced a straight fight), it worked out less well in practice. Local Conservatives in Tradeston were opposed to the pact.[29] There was even greater Conservative opposition in Paisley.[30] On the Liberal side, the associations in Govan and Hillhead adopted a position of neutrality rather than urge their supporters to vote Conservative – unlike such associations as Bridgeton, Partick or Hamilton which called on their members to vote Conservative.

---

[27] *Newcastle Daily Journal*, 11 Oct 1924.
[28] *Yorkshire Post*, 13 Oct 1924.
[29] *Scotsman*, 14 Oct 1924.
[30] *Daily Herald*, 20 Oct 1924.

The West of Scotland pact, however, certainly did not extend to the rural areas or to Edinburgh. In such seats as Roxburgh and Selkirk, or Berwick and Haddingtonshire, the very idea of a pact was frozen out of court at first sight.[31] The same was true of Edinburgh. Two of the sitting Liberal Members, Vivian Phillipps and J. M. Hogge, were both radicals. No attempt was possible here for an anti-Socialist agreement.[32] Indeed, in parts of Scotland, Conservatives extended their attack to Liberals who had been unopposed a year before. This was true of Galloway and Banffshire, where both seats fell to the Conservatives.

A very similar position to Scotland developed in South Wales. In the mining seats, almost without exception, Labour faced only a single opponent. Anti-Socialist pacts were organised at Aberavon, where the Liberal candidate had an enthusiastic reception when he addressed the Aberavon Conservative Executive. In Pontypridd complete agreement was reached after a meeting of Liberals and Conservatives. The Liberal candidate withdrew, and subsequently Liberals helped the Conservatives with platform appearances.[33]

In South Wales the usual arrangement was that, if one of the anti-Socialist parties was already in the field, the other party failed to produce a rival challenge. Thus, in the Gower division, where the Conservatives had taken advantage of Liberal apathy by putting a candidate in the field, no Liberal came forward in 1924. The net result was that in Monmouthshire no three-cornered fight occurred, and only one took place in Glamorgan (in the Llandaff and Barry constituency). Outside Cardiff, the only three-cornered borough contest was in Swansea West.

In rural Wales, however, the position was radically different. A Conservative candidate attacked a Liberal, unopposed in 1923, in Brecon and Radnor. In North Wales the Provincial Council of the National Unionist Association left

---

[31] *Scotsman*, 20 Oct 1924.

[32] *The Times*, 15 Oct 1924. One exception in East Scotland was Kirkcaldy, where the co-operation of Conservatives and Liberals, which dated from the 1921 by-election, was continued (*Scotsman*, 13 Oct 1924).

[33] *South Wales News*, 17, 20 Oct 1924. A split in the Liberal ranks in Merthyr resulted in no Liberal candidate being fielded (ibid., 17 Oct 1924).

individual Conservative Associations free to decide their own course of action. Most Liberals in North Wales subsequently enjoyed straight fights. In general, this was evidence of Conservative weakness rather than any sudden love for the Liberal Party.[34]

In 1924 the correlation between municipal anti-Socialist pacts and agreements at parliamentary level was particularly in evidence. This was especially true of industrial Lancashire. In the Nelson and Colne division a definite pact was agreed in which the Liberal was given a straight fight against Labour, with the official approval of the Conservative Executive, in return for guaranteeing similar support for the Conservative at the next general election.[35] Equally formal local pacts were organised in Blackburn, Accrington, and Heywood and Radcliffe.[36] After some difficulties with his Executive, Grigg was able to organise a pact in Oldham. In such towns as Manchester, however, with little local municipal co-operation, three-cornered contests still occurred in 1924. In the adjoining Cheshire constituencies the correlation was even more perfect. Crewe produced a parliamentary pact but, as in municipal politics, no agreement was reached in Macclesfield or Chester.

Outside Lancashire, parliamentary anti-Socialist pacts following in the wake of long municipal co-operation were organised in such towns as Bradford and Wolverhampton. In Bradford, for example, pacts were organised in the Central and East divisions but, as in municipal contests, not in the North constituency.[37] Similarly, the local municipal co-operation in Wolverhampton West was extended to the general election when the Liberal leader, Alderman Bantock, wrote to the press calling on all Liberals to vote Conservative. In the East Midlands, both Nottingham and Leicester witnessed pacts in the industrial divisions.[38]

[34] *Daily Telegraph*, 14 Oct 1924.

[35] *Manchester Guardian*, 24 Oct 1924.

[36] In Heywood and Radcliffe, and also in Accrington, joint 'Constitutionalist' candidates were fielded.

[37] *Manchester Guardian*, 17 Oct 1924.

[38] *Wolverhampton Express and Star*, 17 Oct 1924. For Leicester, see Leicester Labour Party, Annual Report, 1924. The closest co-operation in Nottingham occurred in the West division.

No doubt this correlation can be exaggerated, and certainly there are towns where, despite municipal co-operation, rivalry persisted in 1924.[39] Nonetheless, it seems quite clear that local municipal alliances had, in general, served as a step towards open alignment with the Conservatives in 1924.

A further blow to Liberal morale was the number of former Liberals who offered themselves to the electors as 'Constitutionalists'. With some, their reasons for deserting the Liberals were a little illogical. Thus, Sir Hamar Greenwood rejected an invitation to fight a Cardiff seat for the Liberals on the grounds that he did not want to split the anti-Socialist vote, yet he accepted an invitation to fight Walthamstow East as a Constitutionalist even though a Liberal candidate was already in the field.[40] Of the twelve 'Constitutionalists' who came forward, six were ex-Liberals who were now Conservatives in all but name.[41] The other six were Liberals whose names were included in the official list of Liberal candidates.[42]

In those seats in which Liberals and Conservatives united behind a 'Constitutionalist', there was frequently a virtual amalgamation in the constituency.[43] This was true of such seats as Accrington, where the Liberals were accused of having become a mere wing of the reactionary party. A similar position occurred in Stoke.[44]

Similar examples of very close co-operation occurred in the seats covered by the West of Scotland pact. In such seats as Bothwell and Hamilton co-operation had proceeded to the extent of joint candidate selection and a real pooling of

---

[39] In Coventry, for example, negotiations for a pact failed, although subsequently one prominent Liberal councillor urged all Liberals to vote Conservative despite the presence of a Liberal candidate.

[40] *Manchester Guardian*, 20 Oct 1924.

[41] These were: W. Churchill (Epping), J. Davis (Consett), Sir H. Greenwood (Walthamstow East), C. E. Loseby (Nottingham West), A. H. Moreing (Camborne) and J. L. Sturrock (Tottenham North).

[42] These were: W. Allen (Burslem), J. H. Edwards (Accrington), Col. A. England (Heywood and Radcliffe), H. C. Hogbin (Battersea North), Sir T. Robinson (Stretford) and Lt-Col. J. Ward (Stoke).

[43] For example, the co-operation in Heywood and Radcliffe and in Stretford (*Manchester Guardian*, 15, 16 Oct 1924).

[44] *Birmingham Post*, 13 Oct 1924; *Scotsman*, 14 Oct 1924.

resources. Even outside these areas, co-operation had reached the stage of virtual amalgamation in such centres as Bristol. This town, as was seen earlier, boasted one of the closest and longest-enduring 'Citizens' Associations' in England. Even in 1923, parliamentary co-operation had continued in every constituency except Bristol North – where a three-cornered contest had resulted in a Labour victory on a minority vote. The lesson of this defeat was not lost. Fighting Bristol North as a Liberal in 1924, F. E. Guest was adopted by the Liberal Association, and his candidature endorsed by the Conservatives.[45] Guest's own election address was almost indistinguishable from the official Conservative platform, and after his election Guest wanted to receive both the Liberal and Conservative whips. Likewise, the Liberal candidate for Bristol East was a Liberal in name only, or rather, hardly even that, since the description 'Liberal' found no mention in his election address, in which he stood simply as 'Anti-Socialist'.[46]

Although Bristol was exceptional as a centre of coalition, nonetheless, in varying degrees, less intimate assistance was forthcoming from many Liberal Associations.

Frequently, the Liberal Association Executive would issue a resolution or manifesto calling on all Liberals to vote for the Conservative candidate.[47] A similar form of assistance consisted of a public letter of support to the Conservative candidate from a prominent local Liberal official. Thus, the chairman of the Folkestone Liberal Association sent a public letter to Sir Philip Sassoon, the Conservative Member for Hythe, declaring that it was the duty of all Liberals in the division to support the anti-Socialist.[48]

Sheffield provides a particularly good example of this. With not a single Liberal candidate in the city, letters urging Liberals to vote Conservative were sent by Sir William Clegg, the leader of Sheffield Liberalism, and by the former Liberal

[45] Election Address, Bristol North.
[46] Election Address, Bristol East.
[47] See, for example, these forms of assistance in Frome (*The Times*, 28 Oct 1924) and Reading (*Daily Telegraph*, 18 Oct 1924).
[48] *The Times*, 28 Oct 1924.

candidate in Sheffield Central.[49] There were numerous examples (as in Twickenham) of Liberal candidates who had stood in 1923 sending similar letters of support for Conservatives – an interesting comment on the type of candidate attracted to fight the old issue of Free Trade.

It should be remembered, however, that the formation of local anti-Socialist pacts was not only the work of Liberals. In several cases the initiative came from the Conservatives, but was actually rejected by the Liberals. In Chesterfield, for example, the Conservative Association offered to give their formal support to the sitting Liberal, Barnet Kenyon, provided he would give a guarantee 'to support the Unionist interests in the House of Commons and on no account support a Socialist Government as he did after the last election'. Barnet Kenyon refused this pledge and, with no candidate of their own in the field, many of the Conservatives subsequently abstained. Similarly in Bermondsey, although the Conservatives in Bermondsey West stood down in favour of the Liberal, the Rotherhithe Liberals refused reciprocal action.[50] The Doncaster Liberals similarly rejected Conservative overtures.[51]

Although some Liberal Associations fielded an active candidate with adequate funds, it was perhaps not surprising that Liberals fought only 25 seats in 1924 which they had not fought in December 1923. A few of these, such as Glasgow St Rollox, could be explained by the Liberal–Conservative pact. In others, such as North Norfolk and Brentford and Chiswick, organisation had been revived during the year. Most, however, were rather intended to spite Labour (as in Clynes's seat in Manchester Platting) rather than serious contests; 12 of the seats had not been contested since 1910.

Unlike 1923, it was extremely difficult in October 1924 to find signs of any lingering Liberal–Labour co-operation. Only in Preston was a formal Lib.–Lab. pact maintained – and even here problems arose. The Preston Liberal Association split over the issue, with the chairman, treasurer and both

[49] *Sheffield Independent*, 25 Oct 1924.
[50] *South London Press*, 17 Oct 1924.
[51] *Yorkshire Post*, 17 Oct 1924.

secretaries resigning in protest.[52] In a few seats, local Liberals urged support for Labour, but these were isolated and unrepresentative cases.[53]

In October 1924 the Liberals at least managed one improvement on the previous election. No rival Liberals stood in opposition. However, in Wales, progress towards reunion had taken considerably longer than across the border. A conference at Llandrindod Wells on 14 June 1924 had attempted to arrange a union of the two rival Welsh Liberal organisations, but final reunion was not completed until 1925. The June conference had arranged that R. H. Morris should be the official Liberal candidate in the election in Cardiganshire, but this had not finally ended the matter. A group of ex-Coalition Liberals wanted to run Sir Richard Mathies (a National Liberal candidate in Merthyr in 1922) against Morris, but the plan was eventually abandoned.[54]

The overall result of Liberal lack of money, pacts with the Conservatives, a general disinclination to fight and problems in finding candidates was tremendous. The Liberals abandoned 136 seats fought in 1923 – no fewer than 96 in former three-cornered contests (55 in Conservative-held seats). At the close of nominations, on Saturday 18 October, 1,428 candidates had come forward. The Conservatives, with 534 candidates, fielded the largest challenge. Labour fielded 514, an increase of 87 over December 1923. The Liberal total had slumped from 457 to 340.

It cannot be stressed too strongly that this massive reduction of the Liberal challenge, together with the anti-Socialist pacts and the increased Labour field of candidates, virtually decided the main lines of the result before the campaign proper began. The events of the campaign did nothing to improve Liberal or Labour prospects.

[52] *Manchester Guardian*, 15 Oct 1924.
[53] See Windsor (*Morning Post*, 29 Oct 1924) or Penrith and Cockermouth (*Manchester Guardian*, 9 Oct 1924).
[54] *South Wales News*, 18 Oct 1924; *Western Mail*, 15 Oct 1924, Nor was unity very complete in the University of Wales seat. The problem here was resolved when neither of the defeated Liberals in 1923 stood again.

18 The Campaign and the Issues

The campaign which followed the defeat of the first Labour Government was soon to become one of the most heated in British election history. Although, as the party of government, the initiative lay with Labour, the government was soon forced on to the defensive as the campaign developed.

At the outset, however, MacDonald's confident and challenging speech to the Annual Conference (assembled at Queen's Hall, London) provided a convenient occasion to launch the election campaign. MacDonald lost no time in singling out the Liberals for their 'hypocritical and devious ways'.

Labour's election manifesto produced few surprises, although its emphasis was somewhat curious. The manifesto went out of its way (in a section headed 'What the Liberals and Tories Combined to Stop') to emphasise what the party *would* have done in the ensuing months, rather than defend its record since January 1924. Since the only two measures of any significance in the parliamentary pipeline were a Factory Acts Amendment Bill and a measure to prevent profiteering in building materials, this emphasis was somewhat strange. In the longer term, however, the Labour manifesto went on to promise reorganisation in the mining industry, taxation of land values, a national electricity generating system and a Royal Commission to investigate the licensing laws – a somewhat uncoordinated mixture. Of its record in office, Labour paid most attention to its effort in restoring peace in Europe, Wheatley's Housing Act, Snowden's Free Trade Budget and reforms in education.[1]

The main points of Labour's manifesto were repeated very much without exception in the election addresses of Labour

[1] For the text of the Labour manifesto, see *Daily Herald*, 17 Oct 1924.

candidates. Space devoted to individual topics is shown in Table 18.1.[2] These six issues between them dominated the Labour constituency campaigns. Not surprisingly, such issues as the Campbell prosecution were given relatively little space (it was only the seventeenth most frequently mentioned item).

TABLE 18.1

Issue	% of space in election address
Labour's social welfare policy	9·2
Benefits of the Russian Treaty	8·3
Labour's European diplomacy	7·8
Wheatley's Housing Act	6·2
Labour's concern for unemployed	5·9
Reforms in education	5·5

The Conservative manifesto, like Labour's, produced very few surprises. Its main attack on Labour was skilfully directed against those points on which Labour seemed weakest. The government was accused of risking an election on an issue that was hardly even a matter of principle. The Russian Treaties were similarly attacked, with the Conservative manifesto arguing that the government was asking for a loan which, on past experience, the Communists would not repay. Much the main target of the Conservative attack, however, was centred on the government's failure to tackle unemployment and in particular its repeal of the McKenna duties.

After the heavy Conservative losses in December 1923 in rural areas, agriculture featured prominently in the Conservative campaign. Among specific Conservative pledges were relief for agricultural rates, the development of the

[2] These figures have been calculated on a sample 10 per cent of the election addresses of Labour candidates. A similar sample was undertaken for Conservative and Liberal candidates and is discussed later.

sugar-beet industry and extended credit for efficient co-operative enterprises. The Conservative manifesto reflected the 'constructive alternative' to Labour that Baldwin's summer speeches had outlined. Apart from agriculture, the manifesto promised advances in education, a major extension of national insurance, and was extremely guarded in attacking the Wheatley Act. The Conservative manifesto concluded with what was perhaps its most effective single appeal – for a strong government with an overall majority.

The election addresses of Conservative candidates differed in their emphasis. No less than 11·6 per cent of all space was devoted to the Russian Treaties. This was followed by housing (7·2 per cent), the need for stable government (6·8 per cent), development of the Empire (6·7 per cent), the handling of the Campbell case (6·6 per cent), the need for anti-dumping laws (5·0 per cent) and Labour's failure over unemployment (4·9 per cent). In addition, a significant number of candidates laid emphasis on the need for Imperial Preference.

No doubt the amount of space devoted to housing was designed to counter the appeal of the Wheatley Act. Otherwise, even at the outset of the campaign, the Conservatives in the constituencies had as their targets the Campbell case, Russia, and the need for firm government. As the campaign progressed, this concentration on Russia and the Bolsheviks became increasingly pronounced.

The Liberal manifesto bore many similarities to the Conservative. Its difference was one of degree and priority rather than of fundamentals. Whilst Liberal emphasis on Free Trade and temperance differed from the Conservative platform, on such topics as education, pensions and national insurance it was hard to detect any essential difference. A large part of the Liberal manifesto was devoted to land – no doubt reflecting Lloyd George's preoccupation.[3] During the campaign, however, Asquith rarely mentioned it. Similarly, a radical

---

[3] The Liberal land programme envisaged a major reform of the leasehold system, legislation to enable the occupiers of dwellings to purchase freeholds at a fair price, and wider powers for local authorities to acquire land.

programme to develop coal and power (a further brainchild of Lloyd George) not only stood in marked contrast to the conservative emphasis of the manifesto but was again ignored in the campaign. The weakest section of the Liberal manifesto, however, was its appeal to the electors to put the Liberals in office. With 340 candidates, this was simply not the politics of the possible.[4]

Liberals in the constituencies generally reiterated these points. The five issues most stressed in Liberal election addresses were Free Trade (11·1 per cent of all space was devoted to this theme), land reform and site value rating (6·2 per cent), the Russian Treaty (5·6 per cent), the need to develop national resources (4·7 per cent) and the role of the Liberals as a 'safe' middle party. Issues less heavily stressed were Labour's unemployment record (4·2 per cent), the need to support the League of Nations (4·1 per cent) and the anti-Socialism of the party (3·4 per cent). The lack of a distinctive Liberal policy – and the paucity of candidates – crippled the subsequent campaign.

The optimism and confidence with which the Labour campaign opened was relatively short-lived. The party found itself for the first time on the defensive, fighting on its record in government. It also soon became apparent that the issues of the Russian Treaties and the Campbell case were easily used by the Conservatives as the basis for a Red Scare campaign. Labour's answer to these problems was Mac-Donald. The Prime Minister led and dominated the Labour campaign. His campaign was centred around two massive speaking tours, which left him utterly exhausted. Indeed, MacDonald's health had been failing prior to the Dissolution and he had exhibited signs of fatigue. For a man already prone to erratic decisions, the campaign speeches of the election further exhausted him.

MacDonald's tour began on Monday morning, 13 October, at Euston. Meetings were addressed the same day at Rugby, Crewe and Glasgow. By lunchtime the following day, no

---

[4] Much emphasis was placed by the Conservatives during the campaign on the fact that, to win a majority of seats, the Conservatives needed to gain only 70 seats, Labour a massive 135 and the Liberals an impossible 170.

fewer than nine speeches had been delivered in a single morning. By 1.30 he was speaking in Edinburgh; five more speeches followed that afternoon, culminating in a rally at Newcastle in the evening. The next day followed the same intensive programme. The pace continued until, on 17 October at Cardiff, MacDonald's voice failed him. By that evening he was mentally and physically exhausted. After a weekend in his Aberavon constituency, a further speaking tour took him to Leicester, Sheffield, Gloucester, Bristol, back north to Bassetlaw and finally back to Aberavon on 23 October.

During the early speeches, MacDonald concentrated on the Russian Treaties and the Campbell case, before realising that this emphasis was playing into the hands of both Conservatives and Liberals.[5] Similarly, in the early part of the campaign, MacDonald reserved much of his attack for the Liberals. The *Manchester Guardian* noted MacDonald's 'entangling obsession about the Liberal–Tory intrigue to destroy him'.[6] Gradually, MacDonald realised that the best way to attract Liberal votes was to appeal for them, not denigrate everyone who had voted Liberal. On 16 October, at Birmingham, MacDonald appealed to his 'Liberal friends' to vote for a progressive Labour Government. On 21 October, MacDonald urged 'the great body of Nonconformist Liberals' to join the Labour crusade. At the same time, MacDonald tried to switch the emphasis away from Russia and on to Labour's record in housing and in reducing taxation. Four days later, on Saturday 25 October, the *Daily Mail* published the Zinoviev letter.

Meanwhile, the Conservative campaign led by Baldwin was, at least at national level, predictable and unexciting. Baldwin, unopposed in his Bewdley constituency, was free to tour the country – but at a more leisurely pace than MacDonald. The Conservative leader shrewdly finished his campaign in Lancashire, where the party had been routed the previous year. His speeches emphasised stable government,

---

[5] Labour's policy was also wearing thin on the Russian Treaties. Both Wheatley and A. A. Purcell (the Labour MP for Coventry) were reported as saying that, even if the loan was *not* repaid, it would benefit the country.

[6] *Manchester Guardian*, 14 Oct 1924.

Labour's unemployment failure and the disadvantages of the Russian Treaty. The tone of the campaign set by the leader was not, however, faithfully followed in the constituencies.

Baldwin's relative moderation – and the emphasis in the Conservative manifesto on the need to improve social conditions – were both swamped by the rabid and emotional anti-Communist campaign that developed in the constituencies. To such people as St Loe Strachey, this type of campaign led him to write sadly that he had never seen less chance 'for the men of light and leading or for sound ideals'.[7] The notorious 'Red Scare' campaign was not confined to a few Conservative constituency backwoodsmen. The Duke of Devonshire declared that the Labour Government was subject to marching orders from Moscow, whilst Curzon described MacDonald as the secret slave of the Communist Party.[8] Birkenhead, Churchill and Joynson-Hicks all revelled in this type of accusation, frequently mentioning MacDonald's pacifism in the war.

These tactics were most frequently pursued in speeches and leaflets designed for the women voters. Thus, in Workington, the wife of the Conservative candidate declared that under Bolshevism women were of less value than cattle and that marriage was easier than the purchase of a broadcasting licence.[9]

Again and again, Conservatives stressed that if the Socialists were returned, religion and family life would be destroyed. As the Peckham Conservative candidate observed, the destruction of all morality and religion was the first plank in the policy of the Communist Party, which was but the left wing of the Labour Party.[10] Elsewhere women were warned to beware of Communist spies who came disguised as health visitors. Even *The Times* added its own note of reason by

[7] Strachey Papers, St Loe Strachey to Roxburgh, 11 Oct 1924.

[8] *Birmingham Post*, 27 Oct 1924. For similar attacks by Birkenhead, see *Aberdeen Journal*, 25 Oct 1924.

[9] Election Address, Workington, Conservative.

[10] Election Address, Peckham, Conservative. A collection of leaflets in similar vein, published by the National Unionist Association, is available in the library of Transport House. See also *Socialist Review*, Nov 1924, pp. 197–203, for quotations from them.

observing of Labour's proposal to set up a national system of electricity generating stations that 'some such project was dear to Lenin'. The publication of the Zinoviev letter (discussed later in this chapter) came as a culmination of this campaign.

Against this background, the lack of any real or distinctive Liberal policy was a calamity. Essentially the 1924 election campaign was fought on three issues: Russia; the need for stable government; and the record of Labour in office, particularly in respect of housing and unemployment. All three were topics on which the Liberals had nothing to contribute. Or rather, the Liberals said nothing not being said already by Labour and Conservatives. As Violet Bonham Carter commented ruefully on the campaign:

> The Campbell case and the Russian Treaty were short commons on which to feed a hungry electorate . . . . Father and I used to fling ourselves on the papers every morning in the wild hope of finding some utterance . . . which might form a peg on which to hang one of the many speeches which had to be delivered before nightfall.[11]

Asquith's difficulties were compounded by the need to campaign desperately to save his own seat in Paisley. Consequently, the press tended to pay more attention to those Liberal leaders free to roam the country – in particular Lloyd George and Mond and, to a lesser extent, Simon. Mond, with no Conservative opposition against him in Carmarthen, received much publicity in the Tory press for his anti-Socialist speeches, especially his attacks on Labour at Hackney (21 October), Wisbech (23 October) and at Norwich the following day. Lloyd George's tirade against Labour and the Red Peril (his colourful language rivalled some of the die-hard Conservative Right) was in curious contrast to the radical ideas on land, coal and power that he had insisted be included in the manifesto. Meanwhile, to add to the Liberal disarray, Simon spent much of his time stressing Free Trade – the only Liberal leader to do so.[12]

[11] Quoted in R. Jenkins, *Asquith* (1964) p. 503. Asquith, unlike Lloyd George, was restrained in his attacks on the Russian Treaty.
[12] *Manchester Guardian*, 3 Nov 1924.

In the constituencies, the Liberals resorted much more (especially in Lancashire and the Home Counties) to the simple expedient of fighting again the Free Trade battle of 1923. This was particularly true of Manchester. Masterman, in the Exchange division, centred his campaign on Free Trade, while the spectre of food taxes was widely raised in neighbouring divisions.

Despite unequivocal pledges by Baldwin that there would be no taxation of food,[13] this theme was constantly used by Liberals. Typical of this line of campaign was the circular issued by the Stoke Newington Liberals, declaring that 'The Tories are out to tax your food, and under a full tariff scheme fourpence will have to be paid in every shilling by the people'. Reports of similar Liberal tactics were widespread in the West Country and elsewhere in the Home Counties.[14]

Prior to the election, Mond had warned Lloyd George that it was imperative that the party should go to the country 'with definite ideas and a big programme'.[15] The Liberals offered neither in 1924. It was perhaps hardly surprising that one Liberal candidate found himself interrupted by a hostile audience singing 'Tell me the old, old story'. It was a justifiable comment on the Liberal campaign. In a sense, the campaign fell hardest on the radical Liberals. Apart from Kenworthy, most radical Liberal MPs avoided the Russian Treaty, seeing that there were no votes in the issue. But with little positive in the Liberal manifesto, and with Lloyd George and Mond on an anti-Red witch-hunt, they had little to offer the electors.

The radical Liberals also found themselves highly embarrassed by Conservative–Liberal pacts. This anxiety was reflected by Stuart Hodgson, the editor of the *Daily News*, who wrote to Lord Gladstone urging 'the absolute necessity of some official contradiction'.[16] There were frequent protests

---

[13] For Baldwin's speech at Gravesend pledging no food taxes, see *The Times*, 24 Oct 1924.

[14] In addition the provincial Liberal press, especially in such areas as Newcastle, Hull and Worcester, concentrated on reviving the Free Trade issue.

[15] Lloyd George Papers, G/14/5/13, Mond to Lloyd George, 7 Oct 1924.

[16] Gladstone Papers, Hodgson to Gladstone, 23 Oct 1924.

from the Left on these accommodations and on the lack of radical policy in the party manifesto. The protest of MacCullum Scott at these pacts was representative of the radical viewpoint.[17] Others went further: T. G. Adams, a former vice-chairman of the Northern Liberal Federation, wrote a letter of resignation to Walter Runciman, explaining that he was joining Labour because there was 'only one party for radicals today'.[18]

Not only did these local alliances produce division and demoralisation in the Liberal ranks, but they also provided MacDonald and other Labour leaders with perfect ammunition with which to attack the Liberals. The opportunity was not lost. In many respects, Labour was undoubtedly fighting the Liberal Party as a greater enemy than the Conservatives in 1924. The *Manchester Guardian* noted that the brunt of the Labour attack was directed at the Liberals, whilst another paper found that Labour's real bitterness was also pointed at the party.[19] Not surprisingly, Pringle, the Liberal Member for Penistone, found in the 1924 election MacDonald's plot to destroy the Liberal Party.[20] Equally vehemently, Vivian Phillipps wrote to Lloyd George after the election stating that MacDonald's conduct had been 'disgusting to the last degree'.[21]

Meanwhile, to add even more to the difficulties of the Liberal campaign, the party found itself faced with a very changed press compared with December 1923. On that occasion, many normally faithful Conservative journals had not supported Baldwin over Protection. Others had criticised the timing or need for an election. In 1924 the ranks of the Conservative press were united. *The Times* followed Baldwin's line fairly faithfully, although occasionally indulging in

[17] See MacCullum Scott's letter of protest to Asquith, dated 17 Oct 1924, quoted in *The Times*, 18 Oct 1924.

[18] Letter of T. G. Adams to Runciman, in *Newcastle Daily Journal*, 11 Oct 1924. He was immediately adopted as Labour candidate for the West Derby division of Liverpool.

[19] *Manchester Guardian*, 15 Oct 1924; *Birmingham Post*, 10 Oct 1924.

[20] *Manchester Guardian*, 13 Oct 1924.

[21] Lloyd George Papers, G/16/5/5, Phillipps to Lloyd George, 1 Nov 1924.

some Red Scare tactics. The *Morning Post* led the field, in terms of the higher-class newspapers, indulging in the anti-Russian hysteria. It was the Rothermere press which saw the worst extremes of mass hysteria against Labour. The *Daily Mail*'s campaign was nothing less than rabid reaction at its most demagogic. Only slightly less so were the *Evening News* and *Weekly Dispatch*.

Curiously, whilst all these papers attacked the Liberals almost as vehemently as Labour, the Beaverbrook press adopted a different line. Beaverbrook made clear in an article on 5 October that he was against an early general election.[22] When the campaign was under way, Beaverbrook became a determined advocate of Conservative–Liberal cooperation. The 'Red Scare' featured far less in the Beaverbrook press than in the *Daily Mail* or *Morning Post*. The *Daily Express* urged Liberals and Conservatives to concentrate on those areas in which their parties agreed. Clearly, Beaverbrook wanted to preserve a reasonably strong Liberal Party after the election, no doubt seeing in this one possible way to re-create the old Coalition and restore Lloyd George.

Apart from the Beaverbrook papers, the Liberals enjoyed little support elsewhere in the press. This position was made worse by the divided counsels of the main Liberal organs – the *Daily News, Westminster Gazette, Daily Chronicle* and *Manchester Guardian*. Lloyd George's own paper, the *Daily Chronicle*, reflected the anti-Labour tirade of his speeches: its editorial content was almost wholly devoted to the failures and shortcomings of MacDonald and his government. Virtually no mention was made of the Conservatives, and relatively little space was devoted to the constructive radical proposals on land or coal that Lloyd George had insisted be included in the manifesto.[23]

The *Westminster Gazette* offered unexciting reading. In this, if nothing else, it faithfully reported Asquith and Simon. Its editorials, following Asquith's own line, attacked Labour

[22] See article entitled 'No General Election', *Sunday Express*, 5 Oct 1924.

[23] The *Daily Chronicle* also argued strongly for 'mutual support' between Conservatives and Liberals in the constituencies (see, for example, issue dated 29 Oct 1924).

over the Campbell case and the Russian Treaties and were even more scathing over unemployment and housing: indeed, Asquith's criticism of the Wheatley Act far exceeded Baldwin's. As the campaign progressed, the *Westminster Gazette* tended to emphasise Free Trade more and more – no doubt because it had little else to put forward.

The radical wing of the Liberals was represented by the *Daily News* and the *Star*. Both tended to play down the Russian Treaties. Electoral 'arrangements' with Conservative candidates were attacked and the Conservatives were treated as the major enemy. The *Daily News* advised Liberals in constituencies where no Liberal candidate was standing to vote Labour. In general terms, the *Manchester Guardian* took this radical position, although it never actually advised its readers to vote Labour. The *Manchester Guardian* was also more critical of MacDonald himself – no doubt reflecting Scott's bitter disappointment that Labour had treated the Liberals so badly during 1924. In all, these divisions in the Liberal press did nothing to improve the rapidly fading Liberal campaign.

Meanwhile, against this background of a growing hysteria in the Rothermere press, and a groundswell of anti-Bolshevik propaganda by both Conservatives and right-wing Liberals in the constituencies, the *Daily Mail* published its sensational story of the Zinoviev letter on Saturday 25 October.[24] This letter, dated 15 September, purporting to be signed by G. E. Zinoviev, the President of the Soviet Praesidium, and by Arthur McManus of the British Communist Party, contained a series of subversive instructions to the party in Britain. On 10 October a copy of it came into the possession of the Foreign Office, who forwarded it to MacDonald. The Prime Minister, however, was away on his election tour and the letter either did not reach him or lay idle for a week. On 16 October, MacDonald asked the Foreign Office to obtain proof of its authenticity. Meanwhile the draft of a protest to

[24] The fullest discussion of the letter is to be found in L. Chester, S. Fay and H. Young, *The Zinoviev Letter* (1967). See also the useful article by R. D. Warth, 'The Mystery of the Zinoviev Letter', *South Atlantic Quarterly*, Oct 1950. I am again indebted to Mr David Marquand for his assistance on certain points surrounding the controversy.

be sent to the Soviet Government was forwarded to Mac-
Donald by the Foreign Office. This MacDonald returned,
largely rewritten, but not signed, on 24 October. In the
meantime another copy of the letter reached the *Daily Mail*,
who threatened to publish it. Faced with this prospect, the
Foreign Office immediately published the protest – although
MacDonald had said that he wanted to see his revised draft
again before publication.

This combination of circumstances could hardly have been
more damaging to MacDonald and the Labour cause. The
letter was published on Saturday 25 October. MacDonald
made no public statement on the matter until his speech at
Cardiff on Monday 27 October. During the weekend the
other Labour leaders, left without firm guidance from Mac-
Donald, made a bad position even worse.

Labours leaders reacted in a variety of ways: Trevelyan
attacked the letter as 'the usual white lie from Russia'.
Ponsonby, the Under-Secretary of State at the Foreign
Office, thought it 'not unlikely that the letter was a forgery'.
Stephen Walsh, the War Minister, declared that it did not
matter if the letter was a forgery or not.[25] At the other
extreme were such people as Clynes, who declared that the
letter, 'if authentic, would imperil any arrangement with
Russia'. Thomas, Wedgwood and Snowden all tended to
stress how quickly the British Government had acted to pull
up the Russians.

Against this background, MacDonald's Cardiff speech only
added to the confusion. MacDonald, like Thomas and Snowden, seemed to go out of his way to convince his audience that
the government had acted with commendable speed. After
attacking the handling of the issue by the press, he then
concluded by explaining how he had expected to have his
draft returned with proof of the authenticity of the letter. The
implication of MacDonald's statement was that he had been
duped by his civil servants.

The Conservative press rose to the attack: MacDonald had
added insult to injury by blaming his civil servants for
premature   publication   (even   though   in   his   speech

[25] Chester *et al.*, *The Zinoviev Letter*, pp. 131–2.

MacDonald had emphasised that he believed his civil servants acted on the honest belief that the letter was genuine). MacDonald's Cardiff speech proved, in fact, to be a major political blunder. Its major inconsistency was pointed out in the *Manchester Guardian* editorial on Tuesday 28 October – namely that MacDonald was claiming that the Foreign Office had failed to prove the authenticity of the letter before officially sanctioning its release, yet he was simultaneously boasting that the government had acted with greater decision than either a Tory or Liberal administration would have done.

The damage was done. In retrospect, it is hard to see what else MacDonald could have said. Privately, he suspected the letter to be a forgery, but he could hardly state that without proof. Nor does MacDonald seem to have realised the potential electoral repercussions of Zinoviev. He knew he had to break his silence at Cardiff. The only explanation available was the truth; but the truth only made his position seem even more open to attack.

It was an exposed position that the press attacked with fury and hysteria. The disclosures made by MacDonald were 'a staggering blow to himself and his party', declared the *Daily Express*. MacDonald was simultaneously saying the Foreign Office believed the letter to be genuine, while he himself spoke of a 'mares' nest' and 'another Guy Fawkes plot'. The *Daily Mail* declared that MacDonald's policy had been 'to hint and insinuate', while *The Times* declared that never in modern experience had a Minister of the Crown descended so low as to attack the Civil Service.[26]

Meanwhile, the Liberals attacked MacDonald with equal bitterness. Speaking at Paisley, Asquith declared that he had never read 'more dislocated, incoherent and unilluminating statements'.[27] Simon was even more vehement:

I am afraid the truth of the matter is that this episode, like the Campbell case, shows that Mr Ramsay MacDonald, as a Prime Minister, cannot give a simple straightforward account of a grave

[26] *The Times*, 28 Oct 1924.
[27] *Paisley Daily Express*, 28 Oct 1924.

matter, and that is why I say the suspicion that the Government has capitulated to the extremists has become a certainty.[28]

In this sense, the Zinoviev letter had come as a fitting climax to an emotional and heated election campaign. The lifetime of the Labour Government had witnessed the politics of moderation. In the 1924 general election the politics of extremism had come out on top. Curiously, considering the nature of the campaign and the importance of the election, it was surprising that only relatively few predictions of the result were given. On 29 October the *Manchester Guardian* reported that the Conservative estimate of the result was: Conservative 286, Labour 200, Liberals 100. This forecast was near to that made by Beatrice Webb, acting on 'inside information' from Conservative Central Office. The estimate here, in the same party order, was 298, 215 and 95. The most elaborate forecast of the result was given to its readers by the *Daily Express*.[29] An unspecified source from each party was asked to estimate the result. The forecasts are as shown in table 18.2.

TABLE 18.2

	Conservative forecast	Labour forecast	Liberal forecast
Conservatives	311	290	291
Labour	205	235	195
Liberals	93	85	124
Others	6	5	5
	615	615	615

Although the exact figures can only have been guesswork, it is interesting that every forecast (in the *Daily Express* and elsewhere) showed both Conservative *and* Labour picking up seats at the expense of the Liberals. Even the Liberal forecast

[28] *Yorkshire Observer*, 29 Oct 1924.
[29] *Daily Express*, 29 Oct 1924.

in the *Daily Express* showed the pessimism prevalent in the party. Yet even the worst Liberal showing (85 seats in the Labour forecast) was twice what the party actually achieved. Whether this was due to the Zinoviev letter, or whether (as is discussed later) the Liberals were guilty of unjustified optimism, can be seen in an analysis of the voting.

19   The Results Analysed

Unlike the verdict in 1923, the results in October 1924 were unmistakably decisive. From the first declared result (a Conservative gain from Labour in Salford South) it was clear that there was a major and decisive trend to the Conservatives. The first six results all showed Conservative gains – and all from those same northern industrial constituencies which had deserted Baldwin in 1923.[1] By the early hours of 30 October, when the morning papers went to press, the state of the parties read: Conservative 167, Labour 76, and a mere 21

TABLE 19.1
General Election, 1924

	Total votes	% share	MPs elected
Conservative	7,854,523	46·8	412
Liberal	2,931,380	17·8	40[2]
Labour	5,489,087	33·3	151
Communist	55,346	0·3	1
Constitutionalist	185,075	1·2	7[3]
Others	124,868	0·6	4[4]
	16,640,279	100·0	615

[1] These seats were: Salford South, Manchester Exchange, Wakefield, Salford West, Salford North and Stockton-on-Tees (this latter won by Harold Macmillan).

[2] This figure includes F. E. Guest (Bristol North), whose name was originally given in the list of Constitutionalist candidates.

[3] Those elected were: (Conservatives) W. Churchill, Sir H. Greenwood and Capt. A. H. Moreing; (Liberals) J. H. Edwards, Lt-Col. A. England, Sir T. Robinson and Lt-Col. J. Ward.

[4] Namely Dr E. G. G. Graham-Little (London University), A. Hopkinson (Mossley), E. Scrymgeour (Dundee) and T. P. O'Connor (Liverpool Scotland).

Liberal. The results when counting resumed in the rural areas showed an even greater Conservative landslide as the Liberals were swept aside in the counties. The net result was that the Conservatives were returned to power with 412 seats, Labour were reduced to 151, whilst the Liberals could elect only 40 Members (see Table 19.1).

The Conservatives gained 162 seats for the loss of only 7, taking 105 seats from the Liberals, 55 from Labour and 2 from the Irish Nationalists.[5] Labour gained 22 seats, 16 of them from the Liberals, but lost 64. The Liberals gained only 9 seats for the loss of 123.

The Liberal Party failed to take a single seat from the Conservatives. Although they wrested nine from Labour, all except Swansea West were the result of electoral pacts. In Swansea West, lost by Sir Alfred Mond in 1923 by 115 votes, the seat was recaptured for the Liberals by Walter Runciman. Although the Conservatives ran a candidate, the local party was divided, and this may well have aided the Liberals.[6]

A striking feature of the 64 Labour losses was that in only 12 cases did the Labour vote actually *decrease*. In these 64 seats the Labour vote *rose* by 99,871.

In addition, of the 55 Conservative gains from Labour, 40 occurred in straight fights, but only 15 in three-cornered contests. Nearly all these gains were in seats won by Labour in 1923.

Despite their losses, Labour secured 22 gains, several of which were of a remarkable character. All these gains were in industrial constituencies. Twelve of the 22 were in constituencies that had previously been held by Labour. Of the other ten constituencies, the most remarkable gain came in Edinburgh East, a Liberal seat not previously contested by Labour.

---

[5] The Nationalist losses were in the double-Member constituency of Fermanagh and Tyrone, where the retiring Members did not seek re-election. The Ulster Unionists were consequently faced only with Republican opposition.

[6] A resolution to stand down was put by a dissident group of Conservatives at an association meeting but was lost (*South Wales News*, 15 Oct 1924).

The most outstanding victory was in Paisley, where Asquith was defeated in a straight fight by 2,228 votes.[7] The irony was that the pivot of the Conservative–Liberal pact in the West of Scotland was to protect Asquith. In fact, many local Conservatives were hostile to the pact and may even have voted Labour to oust the Liberal.

Five of the 16 Labour gains from Liberals can be explained by the breakdown of Conservative–Liberal pacts which had operated in 1923. Ben Riley regained Dewsbury for Labour. Two other seats in Yorkshire, Elland and Keighley, were similarly recaptured.

Labour also captured two Newcastle seats because the Conservatives indignantly refused to give a free run to sitting Liberals who had voted Labour into office. 'Twice bitten, thrice shy' was the motto of Newcastle Conservatism.[8] So, in the West division, Conservative intervention put the sitting Liberal at the foot of the poll, while in Newcastle East, where the pact had defeated Henderson in 1923, the Liberal was narrowly defeated.

Of these 16 Labour gains, 13 were made in Yorkshire, the North-East and Scotland. In the North-East, Labour captured Middlesbrough East and Gateshead, both in three-cornered contests. Bradford South, Rochdale and Penistone completed these Labour victories in northern England.

To complete the tally of Labour gains, the party won the mining division of Burslem, where the sitting Liberal did not defend the seat and was replaced by a Constitutionalist, together with two London divisions, Bermondsey West and Southwark Central.[9]

Compared with these 16 gains from the Liberals, Labour captured only six seats held by Conservatives. Most of these could be explained by exceptional local factors. The victory at Lincoln, won in a three-cornered contest, resulted partly

---

[7] The figures in 1923 were: Liberal 9,723, Labour/Co-op. 7,977, Conservative 7,758, Independent Labour 3,685. In 1924 the result was: Labour 17,057, Liberal 14,829.

[8] *Newcastle Daily Journal*, 13 Oct 1924.

[9] The Liberals in Bermondsey West had won in 1923, partly by distributing free turkeys to the electors. See F. Brockway, *Bermondsey Story* (1949) p. 118; see also *South London Press*, 4 Jan 1924.

from the local appeal of the Russian Treaty, with the increased exports of agricultural machinery likely to result.[10] In the Peckham division of Camberwell, won by Hugh Dalton for Labour, the retiring Conservative Member had voted with Labour over the Campbell amendment, and did not seek re-election. The new Conservative candidate, Sir Martin Archer-Shee, soon alienated the considerable Irish minority.[11]

The Labour gain in Barrow-in-Furness could largely be explained by the withdrawal of a Liberal. The Barrow Liberals were of the radical wing, and prominent members publicly urged support for the Labour candidate.[12] The Labour victory at Motherwell could again be explained by local circumstances. In 1923 J. T. W. Newbold had fought as a Communist candidate, although having the support (by 36 votes to 5) of the Motherwell and Wishaw Trades Council. In 1924, in a straight fight against a Conservative, a moderate Labour man, James Barr, a minister of the United Free Church, captured the seat, very probably taking the bulk of the Liberal vote.

The statistics of seats won and lost by Labour in fact disguised the improvement the party had made in certain areas of the country. Thus, in the West Midlands area the whole region actually witnessed a fractional swing to Labour. Labour did exceptionally well in Bilston, Walsall (a 5 per cent swing) and Dudley – where Oliver Baldwin secured a 17·8 per cent swing to Labour. There were good results in the Potteries (where, as we have seen, Burslem was gained) and in such rural areas as Stone and Rugby. A second area in which Labour did far better than average was in Merseyside. The party held on to its by-election gain in Liverpool and improved its position substantially in such seats as Bootle and Wallasey.

A less noticeable feature of Labour's position after 1924 was the number of safe seats Labour had secured in the industrial areas. Table 19.2 compares the relative strength of the parties in seats with a majority of over 2,000. Labour

[10] *Yorkshire Post*, 15 Oct 1924.
[11] Dalton, *Call Back Yesterday*, p. 153.
[12] *Daily Herald*, 11 Oct 1924; *Manchester Guardian*, 17 Oct 1924.

TABLE 19.2
Safe Seats after 1924 Election

Majority	Lab.	Con.	Lib.
10,000 +	4	64	3
5,000 +	25	128	7
4,000 +	17	38	4
3,000 +	18	43	2
2,000 +	21	50	4

secured 46 seats in 1924 with a majority of over 4,000; the Liberals managed 14. In no fewer than 76 seats, Labour was 10 per cent ahead of its nearest rival.

Labour's worst results in 1924 came in London (especially the suburbs) and Scotland (where 12 seats were lost). Partly this was due to the large number of Liberal withdrawals in such suburban areas of London as Upton and Tottenham South. In the main, however, the swing against Labour was heaviest in the most middle-class areas – the suburbs which had voted for Free Trade in 1923 and in which the Rothermere press was widely read.

Labour, despite its loss of seats, had several causes for satisfaction after 1924. As is argued later, its real increase in strength was far more than its increased aggregate vote would suggest. Even after 1924, however, its strength in many constituencies was still only embryonic. In 204 seats it polled less than 25 per cent of the vote. However, these seats were overwhelmingly rural. By 1924 Labour was effectively challenging for power in the major towns; only in Hull and, to a lesser extent, in parts of Manchester were there constituencies in which the fight still lay between Conservative and Liberal. Even in the rural areas where Labour was weak, the 1924 election demonstrated its ability to intervene and destroy the Liberals. In the 62 seats where Labour intervened in 1924, Labour *won* Edinburgh East and forced Liberals to third place in 13 others.[13]

[13] 44 of these 62 seats were held by Liberals at the Dissolution. The Liberals failed to retain any.

Indeed, in the long term the most important single event of the 1924 election was the virtual destruction of the Liberal Party. Only 35 of the 158 seats the Liberals were defending survived the massacre. In England, only 17 out of 122 were saved. Even in their worst moments, few Liberals could have dreamed of the electoral massacre that was to occur. And virtually no area of the country escaped. In the English counties the Liberals lost all but four of the 67 seats they were defending. In the South-East, Greater London and East Anglia not a single seat the Liberals were defending was retained. In South Wales the only seat to return a Liberal was Swansea West. In Scotland, although the Highland Liberal strongholds remained faithful (perhaps because three of the five seats here were uncontested), outside this Celtic fringe not a single other county constituency returned a Liberal.

If the counties had deserted the Liberals, even worse was the almost total annihilation of the party in the boroughs.

The extent to which the Liberals had disappeared is set out for the 11 largest towns in Table 19.3. In these 139 constituencies the Liberals had elected only six Members, while only Percy Harris, in Bethnal Green South-West, had faced Conservative opposition.

TABLE 19.3

	Seats	Con.	Lab.	Lib.	Other
London	62	39	19	3	1
Glasgow	15	7	8	–	–
Birmingham	12	11	1	–	–
Liverpool	11	8	2	–	1
Manchester	10	6	4	–	–
Sheffield	7	4	3	–	–
Edinburgh	5	3	2	–	–
Bristol	5	2	1	2	–
Bradford	4	2	1	1	–
Newcastle	4	1	3	–	–
Nottingham	4	3	1	–	–
	139	86	45	6	2

Throughout the country, only seven Liberals managed to secure election in three-cornered contests. Even these survived only by the narrowest of margins: Lambeth North had a majority of only 29 and Bethnal Green South-West a majority of 212. Only a single Liberal took over 50 per cent of the poll in a three-cornered contest (in the Western Isles division, with 54·8 per cent).[14]

Of the 40 Liberals who survived the massacre, only perhaps 15 could be said to have won their seats unaided by Conservative or Labour votes. Of these, seven were in Wales and four in Scotland. To those Liberals who had voted with Labour over the Campbell affair there could seem little justice in politics, for only two survived the election.

The size of the Liberal débâcle could not be measured simply in terms of seats lost. In many cases, sitting Liberal MPs found themselves suddenly at the foot of the poll. No fewer than 31 Liberal candidates defending Liberal-held seats finished third. They included such figures as Pringle (in Penistone) and Hogge in Edinburgh. In 26 seats the Liberal share of the vote fell by over 15 per cent, with Bootle showing the most calamitous result of all (the Liberal share of the vote was down from 44·1 per cent to 19·8 per cent). To make matters even worse, of the five unopposed Liberal seats in 1923 which were contested in 1924, only one was retained.[15]

Hardly any Liberal leaders (except Lloyd George, Mond and Simon) escaped the massacre. Asquith lost his seat, and his fate was shared by Macnamara, Seely, Pringle, George Lambert (who had represented South Molton since 1891), Leif Jones, Geoffrey Howard, Isaac Foot and Spears. It was perhaps a fitting comment on Liberal discipline in the lobbies earlier in 1924 that every single member of the Liberal

---

[14] In contrast, the Conservatives found themselves bottom of the poll in three-cornered contests in only eight constituencies throughout the country. These seats were: Lambeth North, Southwark Central, Southwark North, Bethnal Green South-West, Rochdale, Swansea West, Merioneth and Newcastle East.

[15] Wolverhampton East. The Liberals lost Banff, Galloway, Brecon and Radnor, and South Molton.

Whips' Office lost his seat – Vivian Phillipps, Walter Rea, Mackenzie Wood, Gwilym Lloyd George, Maxwell Thornton and A. J. Bonwick.

The dimensions of the Liberal disaster have a twofold significance. They marked the effective end of the Liberal Party as an alternative government to the Conservatives. More subtly, they marked a vital stage in the alignment of British politics and the evolution of a national Labour Party. This latter point needs examining in detail.

Whilst historians have accepted the dimensions of the Liberal disaster, it is much rarer to find a historian willing to emphasise that the real victor, in the long term, of the 1924 election was Labour. To demonstrate this point, it is essential to realise that Labour, even on a perfect campaign, could not have won in 1924. The following statistics provide a useful starting-point for analysis on this theme.[16]

From 1922 to 1929 inclusive, there were 176 seats won by Conservatives on all four occasions, 107 such Labour seats, but only 16 seats won at every election by Liberals. In addition, from 1923 to 1929 there were a further 9 Conservative and 4 Liberal seats. In all, this totals 312 seats either held by Labour in 1924 or where Labour stood little chance of victory. In addition to their 107 safe seats, Labour won 44 other seats in 1924. Adding this figure to 312 brings the total of seats either held by Labour in 1924 or not within their grasp to 356. Putting aside these 356 seats, this leaves 259 seats in which Labour were the challengers in 1924.

In these remaining 259 seats Labour stood little hope of making gains. In 119 of these 259 Labour's challenge was negligible or non-existent. In 48 Labour were without a candidate; in another 48 Labour was either fighting for the first time, or after a lapse. In the remaining 23 the Labour vote was either at, or below, deposit level.

Of these 119 seats, 96 had been won by the Liberals in December 1923. 92 of these 96 victories were lost in October 1924 to the Conservatives. In the English county divisions alone, Liberals lost 55 seats. The paradox was that these

[16] Derived from S. Graubard, *British Labour and the Russian Revolution* (Cambridge, Mass., 1956) pp. 281–8.

defeats, although accentuated by the disunity and mistakes of the Liberals in 1924, were equally the result of the increased number of Labour candidates in hitherto straight fights. Had Labour chosen a more popular electoral appeal, and succeeded in detaching even more former Liberal voters, the result would have been merely to give even more former Liberal seats to the Conservatives.

Leaving aside these 119 seats, the Labour prospects in the remaining 140 constituencies complete this argument. Labour lost 62 of these seats which it had held at the Dissolution. In addition, the party failed to make inroads in the remaining 78 seats, 52 of them held by the Conservatives, 23 by Liberals and 3 by Independents.

The electoral position in these seats once again explains why Labour gains were virtually precluded even before the campaign began.

In the 52 Conservative-held seats, 27 possessed majorities of over 2,000, and a further 10 had majorities of between 1,200 and 2,000. Thus, Labour were attacking only 15 seats with majorities under 1,200. A substantial pro-Labour swing would be needed to capture more than the occasional seat.

The 23 Liberal-held seats presented a similarly barren prospect for Labour. In 13 of these Labour was in third place behind both Conservative and Liberal. In these seats, the better Labour fared in capturing the radical Liberal vote, the more certain it was that the Conservative would capture the seat. This fact is vital to an appreciation of Labour's performance in 1924. The electoral success of the Conservative Party in this category of seats was an inescapable part of the process of alignment in British politics. It virtually precluded the possibility of a Labour victory in October 1924.

Of the ten Liberal-held seats not examined, three were particularly unlikely territory for Labour. In Chesterfield the veteran Barnet Kenyon, who was returned unopposed in 1918 and 1922, possessed a 6,000 majority. He still retained much mining support, while the absence of a Conservative in 1924 also increased his prospects.[17] In South Shields, Labour faced a Liberal majority of 7,200 with no Conservative

[17] Williams, *The Derbyshire Miners*, p. 826.

candidate fielded. In the double-Member constituency of Blackburn, Labour's prospects were hit by the continuation of a Conservative–Liberal pact.[18] Finally, in a further three Lancashire seats sitting Liberal Members were adopted as 'Constitutionalists', making a full Conservative vote in their favour more likely.[19]

All these factors made a dramatic increase in Labour support in 1924 quite impossible. A reduction in Labour representation was made yet more likely by the insecure nature of the seats the party had won in 1923. In four seats Labour achieved victory in the tariff election but never again during the inter-war period.[20] In addition, five other seats won by Labour in 1923 possessed majorities of less than 500.[21]

The real danger to Labour representation in 1924, however, was the formation of local anti-Socialist pacts. Although, in the long-term, the Liberals suffered most, in the short-term the pacts resulted in seats lost by Labour. The party lost 27 seats, won in three-cornered contests in 1923, to a single opponent in 1924. In each case, Labour increased its percentage share of the poll.

All these factors combined to produce the result that in 1924 Labour could increase their parliamentary strength only by an enormous electoral shift in their favour. In complete contrast, only a small shift of Liberal votes to the Conservatives would produce very many Conservative gains, while Liberal voters who moved to Labour would produce the paradox of Conservative victories.

In addition to misunderstanding the virtual impossibility of a Labour breakthrough in 1924, the extent of the Conservative victory has been exaggerated by historians who have

[18] The closeness of the pact is demonstrated by the fact that, of 31,612 votes cast for the Liberal, 28,586 had been split with Henn, the Conservative candidate. Only 1,665 were split with Labour; 1,361 'plump' votes went to the Liberal.

[19] These seats were Accrington, Stretford, and Heywood and Radcliffe.

[20] The Labour victory at Maldon, for example, was the result of the absence of a Liberal candidate. In 1924, urged on by a telegram from Gladstone, the Maldon Liberals fielded a candidate (*The Times*, 27 Oct 1924).

[21] These constituencies were: Berwick and Haddington (68), Swansea West (115), Lanark (230), East Ham North (416) and Cardiff South (426).

ignored two distorting factors in the election: the fall in the number of unopposed returns and the position in Ulster.

In 1923, only three contested elections occurred in Ulster. In 1924, all except two were fought as Sinn Fein candidates entered the field.[22] The results, in such constituencies as Antrim and Londonderry, were overwhelming landslides for the Ulster Unionist.[23] The enormous poll for the Unionists can be seen from Table 19.4. In all, the change in Ulster had inflated the aggregate Conservative poll by 335,000 votes.

TABLE 19.4
Votes cast in Ulster 1923–4

	1923		1924	
	Votes	%	*Votes*	%
Ulster Unionists	117,161	(49·4)	451,278	(83·8)
Nationalist⎫ Sinn Fein⎭	87,671	(27·3)	46,457	(9·9)
Others	37,426	(23·3)	21,639	(6·3)
	242,258	(100·0)	519,374	(100·0)

The Conservatives received a similar artificial bonus from the fall in unopposed returns. In 1923, 35 Conservatives had been returned without opposition. In 1924, only 16 Conservatives enjoyed this luxury.[24] Excluding Ulster and the University seats, there were 24 constituencies in which Conservatives, unopposed in 1923, faced Labour opposition. In these seats the Conservatives polled 245,271 votes and Labour 96,290.[25] In all, this distorted the real increase in Conservative support in 1924 by perhaps 150,000 votes.

[22] The only seats not fought in Ulster in 1924 were the East and South divisions of Belfast.

[23] In Antrim the result was: Ulster Unionist 60,868, Ulster Unionist 60,764 (both elected), Republican 2,514.

[24] This was part of a general trend to fewer unopposed returns. Unopposed returns fell as follows: 1922 (57), 1923 (50), 1924 (32), 1929 (7). The percentage of the electorate in uncontested seats fell similarly: 1918 (14·4 per cent), 1922 (9·3 per cent), 1923 (7·8 per cent), 1924 (5·0 per cent), 1929 (1·2 per cent).

[25] Liberal candidates appeared in only two of these seats, the Toxteth and Walton divisions of Liverpool.

The position was further distorted by a *rise* in the number of unopposed Labour returns, from three in 1923 to nine a year later.[26] In the six seats in which Labour had faced opposition in 1923 Labour had polled 110,000 votes, the Conservatives a mere 12,000 votes and the Liberals 29,000. These seats artificially *reduced* Labour's real strength by perhaps 100,000 votes in relation to the Conservative poll.

Combining all these factors, the real increase in Conservative strength in 1924, relative to Labour, had been exaggerated by over half a million votes. In other words, although the Conservatives had won a major victory, its size and extent have been exaggerated.

In similar vein, a close analysis of the nature of the Liberal disaster and the increase in Labour support produces a different conclusion on the 1924 election than is usually accepted. In all, there were 265 constituencies fought by the same parties on each occasion which provide useful evidence for comparison.[27]

In the first category, the 39 constituencies fought only by Conservatives and Liberals, the votes cast were as shown in Table 19.5. Nationally, there had been a swing to the

TABLE 19.5

	1923		1924	
	Votes	%	*Votes*	%
Conservative	438,093	(48·6)	560,045	(57·7)
Liberal	462,591	(51·4)	410,321	(42·3)
	900,684	(100·0)	970,366	(100·0)

Conservatives of 9·1 per cent. In fact, a closer analysis of the votes reveals that, although the Conservative vote rose by 121,952, the Liberal fell by only 52,270. The conclusion

[26] The only Labour seats unopposed on each occasion were Ogmore, Abertillery and Wentworth.

[27] These 265 constituencies were made up as follows: the 39 Conservative–Liberal contests, the 80 Conservative–Labour straight fights, the 123 three-cornered contests and the 23 Liberal–Labour straight fights. These figures exclude the University seats.

suggests that the Conservative landslide was caused as much by the increased turnout as by the defection of Liberals. It would also seem that the Conservatives did substantially better in the middle-class, residential areas than in the farming areas. In the 22 'rural' seats the swing from the Liberals was 7·5 per cent. In the remaining 17 seats the swing against them was 10·7 per cent.

The 80 Conservative–Labour straight fights were particularly important. In these contests the voting was as shown in Table 19.6. In these contests there had been a swing of 4·5 per

TABLE 19.6

| | 1923 | | 1924 | |
	Votes	%	Votes	%
Conservative	903,616	(46·7)	1,151,007	(51·2)
Labour	1,031,236	(53·3)	1,097,449	(48·8)
	1,934,852	(100·0)	2,248,456	(100·0)

cent from Labour. This 'swing', however, needs two qualifications. First, the Labour vote in 1924 was in fact higher than in 1923, although the Conservatives vote had increased by a massive 27 per cent. The most likely explanation is not that former Labour voters defected to the Conservatives, but that the Conservatives gained the majority of their new votes from those who had not polled in 1923.

Secondly, the size of the 'swing' to the Conservatives was far from uniform. Seven constituencies swung Labour, 28 swung Conservative by less than 4 per cent, 34 swung Conservative by 4 per cent to 8 per cent, while 11 swung Conservative by over 8 per cent.[28]

It is possible, by reallocating these 80 constituencies into certain major occupational and social groupings, to look

[28] The constituencies to swing to Labour were: Birmingham Erdington (6·5 per cent), Birmingham Deritend (4·6 per cent), Birmingham Yardley (0·3 per cent), Liverpool Everton (3·0 per cent), Liverpool West Toxteth (0·9 per cent), Rotherham (0·7 per cent).

TABLE 19.7

| | 1923 | | 1924 | |
	Votes	%	Votes	%
Conservative	243,697	(39·9)	301,491	(43·6)
Labour	367,639	(60·1)	390,253	(56·4)
	611,336	(100·0)	691,744	(100·0)

more closely at those areas where 'swing' was particularly high or low. For this purpose, two subdivisions are useful: the mining seats, and the seats with a high proportion of middle-class voters.

The position in the 24 mining seats is shown in Table 19.7. In these 24 contests the swing against Labour was kept down to only 3·7 per cent. In fact, Labour had increased their total vote by 6·2 per cent, although the aggregate Conservative poll rose by 23·7 per cent.

By contrast, the group of middle-class constituencies polled on the two occasions as shown in Table 19.8. In these 20 constituencies the swing to the Conservatives averaged 7·2 per cent, double the swing in the mining areas. Whilst the Labour vote remained stationary, the Conservative poll had increased by 36·0 per cent. These figures suggest that Labour did substantially worse in middle-class than in working-class territory. Or, expressed differently, it was the *reaction* of the middle class that explains the high anti-Labour swing.

This same phenomenon was quite clearly at work in the 123 three-cornered contests. In this group the votes cast were as shown in Table 19.9. Whilst the Conservatives had increased

TABLE 19.8

| | 1923 | | 1924 | |
	Votes	%	Votes	%
Conservative	268,193	(56·5)	364,853	(63·7)
Labour	206,902	(43·5)	207,606	(36·3)
	475,095	(100·0)	572,459	(100·0)

their share of the poll by 8·6 per cent, and Labour by a more moderate 2·7 per cent, the Liberal share had collapsed disastrously by 11·3 per cent. However, the corollary of this was *not* that the Liberal decline had necessarily benefited the Conservatives. On the basis of the two-party poll, the swing from Labour to Conservative was only 2·6 per cent, the Conservative share of the vote rising from 58·3 per cent to 60·9 per cent.

TABLE 19.9

| | 1923 | | 1924 | |
	Votes	%	Votes	%
Conservative	1,259,085	(38·3)	1,736,757	(46·9)
Labour	900,847	(27·4)	1,116,950	(30·1)
Liberal	1,129,800	(34·3)	850,156	(23·0)
	3,289,732	(100·0)	3,703,863	(100·0)

This analysis produces the important evidence that the average swing to the Conservatives was *less* in these 123 three-cornered contests than in the 80 constituencies in which Labour enjoyed a straight fight with the Conservatives on each occasion.

This evidence suggests that the Liberal collapse did *not* benefit the Conservatives as much as has often been suggested. Indeed, if the three-cornered contests are divided into regional groups, in only one area, London, was there a heavy swing to the Conservatives (Table 19.10). Outside London, in no case was there a swing of above 2 per cent to the Conservatives.[29] In other words, the evidence rather suggests that the Liberal collapse benefited both Conservative and Labour in fairly equal proportions, with 72 of these constituencies showing a swing to the Conservatives and 51 to Labour.

These three-cornered contests provide no evidence that Liberals were able to capture Labour votes in 1924. Indeed,

[29] And in London the very large increase in turnout was probably the most important factor behind the Conservative 'swing'.

TABLE 19.10
Three-Cornered Contests by Social Group

	No. of constituencies	% swing to Con.
Greater London	24	9·3
Middle-class boroughs	21	1·3
Other boroughs	27	0·7
Rural divisions	23	0·5
Mixed urban/rural	24	0·1

even in the constituencies in which Liberals enjoyed straight fights with Labour on each occasion, Labour in fact strengthened their position. The 23 seats in this category polled as shown in Table 19.11. Despite, in most cases,

TABLE 19.11

	1923		1924	
	Votes	%	Votes	%
Liberal	261,788	(47·5)	289,757	(46·8)
Labour	289,490	(52·5)	329,874	(53·2)
	551,278	(100·0)	619,631	(100·0)

Conservative support for the Liberal candidates, their share of the poll had fallen by 0·7 per cent. No fewer than 13 of the 23 constituencies swung to Labour. This swing was consistent in such industrial London seats as Whitechapel and Bermondsey West, and in a variety of mining seats.[30]

In addition to these 23 contests, in six cases Labour faced a single 'Constitutionalist' candidate in 1924 where they had faced Conservative or Liberal opposition in 1923. Four of these six seats swung to Labour.[31] These constituencies all

---

[30] Examples of constituencies in mining areas to swing to Labour were Aberdare, Broxtowe, Dunfermline, and Clackmannan and East Stirlingshire.

[31] The four seats to swing to Labour were Burslem, Accrington, Battersea North and Consett.

confirmed that, unlike the Conservatives, the Liberals failed to benefit from the 'Red Scare' campaign of the election.

Further evidence of the extent to which Labour was at last inheriting the radical portion of the old Liberal vote was to be seen in the 96 constituencies in which Liberal candidates withdrew in 1924 from seats that had been contested in December 1923 (Table 19.12). Whereas the Conservative

TABLE 19.12
The 96 Liberal Withdrawals in 1924

| | 1923 | | 1924 | |
	Votes	%	Votes	%
Conservative	974,624	(40·4)	1,480,192	(56·0)
Labour	932,530	(38·7)	1,163,255	(44·0)
Liberal	504,070	(20·9)	–	–
	2,411,224	(100·0)	2,643,447	(100·0)

vote had increased by over 500,000, the Labour vote was up by 230,000. Calculated according to the two-party poll, the Conservatives had increased their share of the poll by 4·9 per cent, from 51·1 per cent to 56·0 per cent. In all, 78 of the 96 constituencies swung Conservative in varying degrees.

Once again, however, an analysis of these contests by regions produces significant evidence (Table 19.13). These figures well reveal the extent to which Scotland, with its right-wing anti-Socialist Liberalism, stood out from the rest

TABLE 19.13
Swing to Conservatives by Region of the 96 Liberal Withdrawals

Area	No. of seats	Two-party swing to Con.
Greater London	22	4·4
Non-London boroughs	31	3·0
County seats	23	4·1
Scotland	20	9·2
	96	4·9

of the country. Excluding the 20 Scottish contests, the average swing to the Conservatives in the remaining 76 seats was 3·8 per cent. These figures strongly suggest that, in the non-London boroughs and in the rural areas, although there was a swing to the Conservatives, this was of a very similar level to the Conservative–Labour straight fights. The conclusion is again that Liberal withdrawal, *in many areas*, helped Labour as much as the Conservatives.

In two groups of constituencies the former Liberal vote clearly went in quite opposite directions. In the boroughs with a tradition of Liberal–Conservative municipal co-operation, there was a very heavy swing to the Conservatives. There were at least ten open anti-Socialist pacts in boroughs of this type in 1924.[32] At the opposite extreme were those rural or semi-rural constituencies with a strong Nonconformist tradition. Examples of this sort were to be seen in the swing to Labour in Bilston, Macclesfield or Banbury. Two regions in which Labour benefited from the Liberal collapse were the North Midlands coalfield and the North-East.[33] An analysis of the Liberal vote strongly suggests that the Nonconformist working-class former radical vote went Labour, but in the towns with a tradition of co-operation with the Conservatives to thwart Labour, the Liberal vote moved to the right.

The most misleading interpretation is to believe that, because a Liberal Association or a prominent party member urged Liberals to vote Conservative, this advice was necessarily heeded. Indeed, Liberal officials were not blind to this fact. Thus, when the Secretary of the Durham Conservatives urged

[32] These ten seats, with the size of the swing against Labour, were as follows: Barnsley (13·1 per cent), Bradford Central (11·1 per cent), Bradford East (13·0 per cent), Bristol North (13·4 per cent), Crewe (18·1 per cent), Leicester East (12·2 per cent), Leicester West (9·1 per cent), Leigh (10·3 per cent), Nelson and Colne (10·9 per cent) and Norwich (11·1 per cent).

[33] Examples of constituencies in the Nottinghamshire and Derbyshire coalfield swinging to Labour were Derbyshire South (2·0 per cent), Derbyshire North-East (1·9 per cent) and Bassetlaw (6·9 per cent). As the Executive of the Derbyshire Miners' Association observed, the election had demonstrated that the Derbyshire coalfield was coming more into line with other areas. Derbyshire Miners' Association, Minutes, 8 Nov 1924, quoted in Williams, *The Derbyshire Miners*, p. 829.

his opposite number in the Northern Liberal Federation to advise his members to vote Conservative, the Federation Secretary replied that such advice would merely cause Liberals to vote Labour.[34]

This warning proved accurate. The Liberal vote was cast, not because a wealthy Liberal Association chairman or an old style Whig urged Liberals to vote against some alleged 'Red Plot', but according to the social composition and political leanings of the rank-and-file Liberals in each constituency. Certainly, contemporary observations that the Liberal vote overwhelmingly helped the Conservatives cannot be upheld.

The impact of the Zinoviev letter on the election has been the subject of much myth and exaggeration. To contemporaries in the Labour movement, the Zinoviev letter ruined Labour's electoral prospects in 1924. It was stated by the *Daily Herald* and echoed by the *New Leader* and *Forward*. Margaret Bondfield claimed that the letter 'had a disastrous effect' and 'lost us the election'. Sir James Sexton repeated the assertion in his autobiography. Francis Williams and G. D. H. Cole also came to the same conclusion. Other writers have echoed their views.

Even the Cabinet seemed convinced that it was the Zinoviev letter that had led to the Conservative triumph. Tom Jones noted in his diary on 31 October of the Labour Cabinet meeting that morning:

> One gathered a general impression of everyone trying to maintain a cheerful countenance and determined to say nothing unpleasant about anybody or anything. We sat down, and the PM began with a reference to Jowett, 'the one defeated member of our little company'. The Cabinet then plunged into a discussion of the Election. One had expected an increase of twenty Labour Members, another had expected more. J. H. Thomas said he was 'frankly disappointed'. All agreed that up to Friday night all was going well with the Party prospects; but with the publication on Saturday morning of the Zinoviev letter there was a slump, 'the people lost confidence in us; the women were frightened; speakers felt paralysed'.

[34] *Yorkshire Post*, 15 Oct 1924.

The exact electoral consequences of Zinoviev will never be finally known. Contrary to contemporary opinion, however, the letter probably did no more and no less than accentuate trends already well developed. This view was taken by such people as Hamilton Fyfe, the editor of the *Daily Herald*.

It did not produce a Conservative victory, though it perhaps gave the Conservatives a greater majority. It did not destroy Labour's chances, though in persuading a few more Conservatives to go to the poll it may have swayed the result in a few constituencies. If the Zinoviev letter had an impact on any party, it was on the Liberals, for it made the Liberal case yet more irrelevant.[35] There is very little evidence that it affected the morale of convinced Labour voters.[36]

It is possible that the Zinoviev letter helped produce the large increase in turnout. Even this effect, however, needs a very substantial qualification. Although turnout rose by 5·9 per cent, from 70·9 per cent to 76·8 per cent, there was a variety of reasons in addition to the letter to account for this increase. As was seen earlier, the interest aroused by a Labour Government, together with the hasty repentance of Conservatives who had abstained on the Free Trade issue, had already caused turnout to rise during the by-elections of the 1924 Parliament. In addition, it was seen in 1923 that the introduction of Labour candidates into constituencies not previously contested produced an increase in turnout. This was another contributory factor. A further minor factor helping towards an increased turnout was the fact that the electoral register was only four and a half months old in October 1924 (compared with six months in December 1923). Similarly, it must be remembered that turnout had fallen substantially in 1923 in those mining seats won by Labour with large majorities in 1922. This, no doubt, was the product of apathy and over-confidence. In 1924 turnout rose by almost exactly the amount it had fallen the previous year.

[35] For a contemporary assertion that the letter decided the Liberals in the election, see Home Counties Liberal Federation, Report, Executive Committee, May 1925.
[36] One Liberal candidate in a working-class constituency believed that, rather than destroy morale, the letter led to a greater resolve in the Labour ranks. See F. Gray, *Confessions of a Candidate* (1925) pp. 113–6.

Thus, in the Yorkshire coalfields, turnout fell by 9 per cent in 1923 to rise by 9·2 per cent in 1924; in Lancashire, turnout fell by 5·7 per cent in 1923 and rose by 6·4 per cent in 1924.

Having made these qualifications, it is important to examine in more detail the areas of turnout increase. Nationally, the increase is set out in Table 19.14. Scotland showed the

TABLE 19.14

	1923 %	1924 %	% change
England	70·8	77·2	+6·4
Wales	77·3	80·0	+2·7
Scotland	67·6	75·0	+7·4
Ulster	76·3	65·6	−7·7
Universities	72·6	66·9	−5·7
	70·9	76·8	+5·9

largest increase (7·4 per cent), closely followed by England (6·4 per cent), with Wales a very modest 2·7 per cent. Special conditions (i.e. extreme Republicans in ultra-safe Unionist areas) account for the 7·7 per cent fall in Ulster. The variation in turnout can best be seen by comparing the 524 constituencies fought on both occasions (Table 19.15). These figures reveal some important statistics: in 51·5 per cent of these 524 seats, turnout *rose* by between 6 per cent and 18 per cent. In no less than 92·7 per cent of all seats, turnout rose compared with 1923. These figures disguise, however, the variations in turnout increase in different parts of the country. An area of particularly heavy increase was metropolitan London. Of the 55 seats contested on each occasion, no fewer than 47 showed an increase of over 8 per cent, while 34 increased by more than 10 per cent. Not a single constituency revealed a turnout increase of less than 6 per cent. A similar very large increase occurred in those constituencies where the 'middle-class' vote was most significant. In the 38 seats fought on each occasion in which the proportion of 'middle-class' voters exceeded 35 per cent, turnout rose by 8·5 per cent from 66·3 per cent in 1923 to 74·8 per cent in 1924. In the 23 seats in this group in the London area, turnout rose by 11·0 per cent. In other words, the increase in turnout was most marked among middle-class voters, particularly middle-class voters in the London suburbs. If the Zinoviev letter had any substantial impact, it was among the middle-class voters rather than the working-class.

TABLE 19.15

	Change in turnout	No.	%
Decrease	6%–12%	5	1·0
	0%–6%	33	6·3
Increase	0%–6%	210	40·1
	6%–12%	209	39·9
	12%–18%	61	11·6
	18%–24%	6	1·1
		524	100·0

If, with few exceptions, Labour blamed the Zinoviev letter for their defeat, the Liberals had little option but to blame themselves for their débâcle.

The Liberals were afterwards to admit that probably the single most powerful factor working against them was their limited field of candidates. As one Federation Secretary wrote after the election: 'The result was lamentable. The Liberal Party was practically defeated before the first shot was fired, owing to the paucity of candidates to carry the flag'.[37] As another Federation report observed, the small field of Liberal candidates effectively left the contest between

[37] Midland Liberal Federation, Report on 1924 General Election in Minutes, Executive Committee, 21 Nov 1924.

Toryism and Socialism.[38] For those in search of a stable government, the Liberal Party was not a serious contender. As Lord Gladstone noted, this fact constituted the real death-blow of the party.[39]

In addition, many Liberals blamed electoral pacts with the Conservatives. As one speaker at the Conference of Liberal Trade Unionists in April 1925 accurately observed, pacts, when contracted against Labour, had the inevitable result of driving industrial Liberals into the ranks of Labour.[40] Similarly, as one provincial paper commented, the very idea of Liberals joining hands with their traditional opponents not only discouraged the rank and file but produced untold harm and little advantage.[41] In such areas as London, Labour claimed that these electoral pacts were their strongest electioneering weapon.[42] The Labour candidate in Leicester West echoed this view.[43] In the last resort, however, most Liberals realised that the extent of their disaster had largely been brought upon the party by its own failings. As Lloyd George wrote after the election, the party had entered the battle hopelessly unprepared in a condition resembling a disorganised rabble.[44] This view was shared by Vivian Phillipps, who wrote in an unpublished autobiography:

> The result was what had been foreseen. From the start we were ruled out as serious competitors. The electors were not going to waste their votes on a party which was allowing nearly half the seats in the country to go uncontested.[45]

This view was not based merely on hindsight. Phillipps's autobiography went on to recall that

[38] Home Counties Liberal Federation, Annual Report, 1925.

[39] Gladstone Papers, BM Add. MSS 46,480/238, Memorandum on Party Organisation, July 1925.

[40] Secretary's report, Conference of Liberal Trade Unionists, in Midland Liberal Federation, Minutes, Executive Committee, 25 Apr 1925.

[41] Birmingham Post, 31 Oct 1924.

[42] Manchester Guardian, 21 Oct 1924.

[43] See F. W. Pethick-Lawrence, Fate Has Been Kind, (1953) p. 139.

[44] Lloyd George Papers, G/30/3/34, Lloyd George to Inchcape, 5 Nov 1924.

[45] V. Phillipps, 'My Days and Ways' (unpublished autobiography, n.d.) pp. 116–8.

on the night of the Dissolution, I walked home with Geoffrey Howard. Neither of us had any illusions as to what was in store for us. Geoffrey said 'he (i.e. Lloyd George) has sent us to the shambles'.

Howard's forecast was to come true with a vengeance.

20   Epilogue and Conclusions

The general election of October 1924 had returned Baldwin to power with a massive majority. Labour had confirmed and consolidated its position as a national party that was now the obvious alternative to the Conservatives.

What future was there for the Liberals? During the period from November 1924 to October 1926, the last phase when Asquith was leader of the party, the future looked bleak indeed. The old problems remained for the party – of finance, candidates, organisation and morale. For Asquith (now removed to the House of Lords as the Earl of Oxford and Asquith) the election disaster added a new problem. In 1923 the election results had decimated the former Coalition Liberals and greatly increased the numbers of Asquith's followers. During 1924 the Parliamentary Liberal Party was overwhelmingly Asquithian. After October 1924, over half of the small band of Liberals were former Coalition Liberal MPs or candidates.

On 2 December, Lloyd George secured his election as chairman of the Parliamentary Liberal Party, by 26 votes to 7, with 7 abstentions. Meanwhile, a group of 9 MPs who refused to acknowledge Lloyd George formed themselves into a 'Radical Group' under Runciman. Only weeks after a disastrous election, the Liberals were again an openly divided party. As Scott wrote to Hobhouse, there was now 'a subterranean conflict going on all the time between Lloyd George and Asquith'.[1]

Meanwhile the attempt to restore the finances of the party (through the 'Million Fund', launched at a major Liberal convention in January 1925) had also begun to collapse. As

[1] Scott Papers, Scott to Hobhouse, 7 Nov 1924.

Trevor Wilson has written, by the end of 1925 the attempt to restore Liberal finances through an appeal to the ordinary supporter had foundered.[2]

At the same time, organisation was collapsing further as agents left and money was not forthcoming. As Lloyd George bitterly observed, whatever the decay of agriculture might have been, it was nothing to that which had fallen upon the Liberal organisations in a very large number of constituencies throughout the country.[3] Candidates were equally unobtainable. By May 1926 the Yorkshire Liberal Federation had only 16 candidates (including sitting MPs) in the field for 54 constituencies.

Even in by-elections the tide went against the Liberals. In March 1926 the party lost a seat in the Combined English Universities to the Conservatives. Perhaps the worst humiliation came on 29 November 1926 when J. M. Kenworthy, the Liberal MP for Hull Central, defected to Labour. In the ensuing by-election, Kenworthy was re-elected with 52·9 per cent of the poll, the Liberal taking a mere 9·5 per cent.

Relations between Asquith and Lloyd George deteriorated even further during 1925 and the first months of 1926. They finally came to a head over the General Strike, when Lloyd George argued a case for negotiation and Asquith firmly supported the government's hard line.[4] Asquith, in poor health and unable to get the Liberals to censure Lloyd George, at last resigned the leadership of the party in October 1926.

The accession of Lloyd George as leader of the Liberal Party brought a final attempt at revival. As so often when Lloyd George was at the helm, his old dynamism and energy brought a new sense of purpose. Sir Herbert Samuel, the newly appointed head of the party machinery, worked miracles with organisation in the constituencies. A bold and imaginative plan to tackle unemployment was launched.

---

[2] Wilson, *The Downfall of the Liberal Party*, p. 318.

[3] See Lloyd George's speech at the National Liberal Club, 5 Apr 1927, quoted ibid., p. 315.

[4] This last dispute of Asquith and Lloyd George is well discussed in Wilson, ibid., pp. 313–36.

Ideas, energy and, above all, money were poured into the party by Lloyd George. Within six months of his return, it seemed that at long last a real recovery was at hand. On 28 March 1927 the Liberals gained Southwark North from Labour. A series of by-election victories followed: Bosworth was won on 31 May 1927, Lancaster fell on 9 February 1928 and St Ives a month later, on 6 March. On 20 March 1929 Eddisbury fell to the Liberals, and the following day Holland-with-Boston was also gained. All these gains were from Conservatives and, with the partial exception of Bosworth, were in rural, agricultural areas. Had the Liberals been able to follow up their initial victories in Southwark North and Bosworth with a gain in the Westbury by-election of June 1927 (which the Conservatives retained by a mere 149 votes), the revival might have gathered even further momentum.

As it was, in the spring of 1928 optimism ran very high. Lord Rothermere wrote to Lloyd George on 10 April 1928: 'You are back to where the Liberal Party was at the election of 1923 . . . . In my opinion, an election today would give you just about the same number of followers'.[5] He went on: 'Continue as you are doing and I think you and I will agree . . . that there is almost a certainty that the Liberals will be the second party in the next House. This would give you the Premiership beyond any question'. While Rothermere's political judgement does not have to be taken too seriously, nonetheless the Liberals were doing undeniably well, as the figures in Table 20.1 indicate.[6]

TABLE 20.1

Average Vote in By-Election Contests, May 1926–General Election 1929
(Three-party Contests Only)

	No.	Con. %	Lab. %	Lib. %
May 1926–end 1927	10	37·9	33·6	28·5
Jan–Dec 1928	15	39·8	30·5	29·7
1929 (to Gen. Elec.)	5	33·6	44·6	21·8

[5] Lloyd George Papers, Rothermere to Lloyd George, 10 Apr 1928.
[6] D. E. Butler, *The Electoral System in Britain since 1918*, 2nd ed. (Oxford, 1963) p. 181.

However, even at the height of Liberal success in 1928, Lloyd George himself realised that Liberal by-election victories would not necessarily mean gains at a general election. He wrote to J. L. Garvin of the *Observer* in October 1928: 'I have followed your analysis of the by-election figures. I am convinced that "the triangle" will enable Labour to sweep the industrial constituencies next time'.[7] Lloyd George had written in similar vein to Philip Snowden: '. . . . owing to the fact that Liberal and Labour candidates are fighting each other, there are 170 seats which will go to the Conservatives which in straight fights would have been either Labour or Liberal.'[8] Lloyd George's judgement was nearer the mark.

Labour was, indeed, the Achilles' heel of the Liberal party. Although the Liberals succeeded in winning a series of rural seats from the Conservatives, Labour was continuing to be the main beneficiary of Conservative unpopularity. On 17 September 1925 Labour gained its first by-election victory since the general election, at Stockport. During 1926 seats began to change hands more rapidly. Labour took Darlington from the Conservatives on 17 February, East Ham North on 29 April and Hammersmith North a month later, on 28 May. Even when the Liberal resurgence was at its height, Labour successes continued. In February 1927 Labour gained Stourbridge from the Conservatives; in January 1928 Labour won Northampton, followed by Linlithgowshire in April, Halifax in July (a Liberal seat unopposed in 1924) and Ashton-under-Lyne in October.

Labour completed their successes prior to the 1929 general election by gaining three more seats early in 1929: Midlothian and North Peebleshire (29 January), Battersea South (7 February) and North Lanarkshire (21 March), all from Conservatives. The by-elections of 1924 to 1929 in this respect proved to be accurate pointers to the subsequent general election. The general election of May 1929 proved a bitter disappointment for the Liberal Party. It was, as the *Liberal Magazine* sadly admitted, 'a lost battle in view of our

---

[7] Lloyd George Papers, Lloyd George to Garvin, 31 Oct 1928.
[8] Lloyd George to Snowden, 3 Oct 1928. Lloyd George estimated that, of these 170 seats, 108 would have been gained by Labour and 62 by Liberals.

TABLE 20.2

	Total votes	% share	Candi- dates	MPs elected
Conservative	8,656,225	38·1	590	260
Liberal	5,308,738	23·6	513	59
Labour	8,370,417	37·1	569	287
Others	312,995	1·2	58	9
	22,648,375	100·0	1,730	615

hopes and aims'.[9] The result is shown in Table 20.2.

Labour was once more in office, although – as in 1924 – still without a majority. Labour won 287 seats, the Conservatives 260 and the Liberals only 59. Although the Liberals had polled 5,308,738 votes (23·6 per cent of the total), they had won only 35 seats not captured in 1924 and lost 19. Of these 19 losses, 17 were to Labour. These figures demonstrated only too clearly Liberal inability to recapture industrial seats: indeed, the party lost further ground to Labour in the North-East, Yorkshire, Lancashire and the East End of London.

Virtually all the 35 Liberal victories came in rural areas, some with no vestige of a Liberal tradition.[10] The main Liberal victories were secured in the traditional areas of Liberal support: rural Scotland and Wales (where 7 seats were captured), East Anglia (9 Liberal gains) and Cornwall (5 Liberal gains). Apart from these traditional areas, no other part of the country returned a solid phalanx of Liberal MPs.

This was not to deny, however, that the Liberals had polled well in a variety of areas. In the 203 constituencies which all three major parties contested in 1924 and 1929, the Liberal share of the poll increased from 24·8 per cent to 29·0 per cent.[11] Yet, whichever way the Liberals argued, either in terms of seats or votes, they had lost the election. No change

[9] *Liberal Magazine*, Sep 1929.

[10] Thus, the Liberals won Ashford – a Conservative seat even in the 1906 landslide.

[11] Wilson, *The Downfall of the Liberal Party*, pp. 349–50.

in the voting system would have given them a majority. They were now destined to a position of a third party, holding an uncomfortable and unenviable balance between Labour and Conservative. The explanation was twofold. In 1929, after the events of 1924, the Liberals had slipped too far back to be thought of as an effective alternative government. Secondly, the events of 1922 to 1924 had enabled Labour to deny the Liberals victory. The figures in Table 20.3 – produced by an examination of the voting in 1929 in the 45 county seats gained by Liberals in 1923 – demonstrate the point.

TABLE 20.3

	Total votes	% share	MPs elected	Candi- dates
		1923		
Conservative	505,027	43·4	–	45
Liberal	585,899	50·4	45	45
Labour	71,728	6·2	–	16
	1,162,654	100·0	45	106
		1929		
Conservative	723,379	42·5	33	45
Liberal	608,732	35·7	8	45
Labour	370,852	21·8	4	44
	1,702,963	100·0	45	134

The significance of these figures lies in the redistribution of the radical vote. The Liberals failed to win more than eight of these seats in 1929, not because the Conservative share of the vote had improved, but because Labour had attracted suffi- cient Liberal votes to let the Conservatives in. In the urban areas, this process of alignment had gone further. The elections of 1923 and 1924 had, in varying degrees, removed the Liberals from their industrial bases. The 1929 general election completed this period of alignment and confirmed the new order of two major parties and a third, smaller, Liberal Party.

The general election of 1929 was not the end of the road for the Liberal Party. But it was certainly the end of an era. Not until March 1958 at Torrington was the Liberal Party again to win a by-election. Although the party survived the Liberal National split of the 1930s, and even survived the election of 1951 with a tiny group of 6 MPs, its position as an effective third force was lost for a generation. The party was briefly revived at Orpington in March 1962 and again seemed poised for revival in mid-1973 with sensational victories in Ripon and Ely, only to be rewarded with a mere 14 seats in February 1974. Thus, 1929 had marked the effective end of the era of three-party politics. In so doing it confirmed the judgement of October 1924. Not even the genius of Lloyd George was able to reverse that verdict. Paradoxically, the 1924 disaster had occurred in the wake of the most successful Liberal performance of the inter-war period – the general election of December 1923. But that opportunity had been let slip.

The conclusions of this book, with its examination of constituency politics and electoral change in the period from October 1922 to the fall of the first Labour Government, do not lend themselves to any startling or dramatic new theory to explain the fate that overtook the party. However, the electoral evidence of the period from 1918 to 1929 does emphasise certain factors that have, as yet, not figured fully in the historiography of this subject.

The first is the material provided by an examination of the constituency associations and municipal election results. The evidence here suggests that the decline of the Liberal Party in the constituencies was a more complex and fragmented process than historians have been willing to accept.

Indeed, it would seem to be a fundamental mistake to attempt to chart this constituency decline as a single process. Rather, it is essential to contrast the relatively sudden and overwhelming collapse of the party in the majority of the large cities (and mining areas) with the persistent strength of the Liberal Party elsewhere. In 1923, in voting behaviour, Britain was essentially divided into two nations, the urban and the rural. The chronology, the extent and the speed of the Liberal decline were quite different in each.

Secondly, it is essential to make the distinction between the *decline* of the Liberal Party and its *downfall*. In mid-1923, after the débâcle of the 'coupon' election, the limited recovery in 1922, and the sad state of constituency organisation, no one could doubt that the party was in serious difficulties. Nonetheless, when the election came in 1923, the Liberals were still thought of as a potential party of government, but not really so in 1924, and certainly not in 1929.

Conceivably, if the Liberals *had* become the second largest party in 1923, their subsequent history would have been very different. As it was, although the Liberals achieved a major revival, it was all to no purpose. By a strange paradox, it was this revival which, leaving the party holding the balance of power, led directly to the downfall of the party. Whether the Liberal Party could have come to terms with Labour in January 1924 was doubtful. What is clear, however, is that the party could not possibly have cleared its own path to destruction with more determination during 1924 – both in Parliament and in the constituencies.

The outcome of the crucial 1924 election was the virtual annihilation of the party. After this débâcle, with the Liberals reduced to a parliamentary rump, the party was never really again to be considered as a party of government. This factor underlay Lloyd George's failure in 1929. After 1923, Labour had arrived – and arrived to stay. With that arrival, there was increasingly no room for a Liberal Party divided on leadership and with fundamental divisions of policy.

The election of 1923, rather than the 'split' of 1916, the 1918 'coupon' election, or any earlier date, was perhaps the crucial moment when the Liberal decline became its downfall.

Having stressed this vital distinction between the decline and the downfall of the Liberals as a potential party of government, it is equally true that, in many industrial areas, the Liberals had almost ceased to count as a major political force long before 1923. The municipal evidence from the provincial boroughs amply demonstrates this point.

Quite clearly, this municipal evidence hardly substantiates the school of Liberal historians who argue that the fall of the party was an accident. The municipal malaise stemmed, not from the split of Asquith and Lloyd George, but from fundamental and long-term characteristics in the structure, social composition and outlook of the party in the major industrial and mining areas.

This weakness was reflected in the inability of an essentially middle-class party to accommodate working-class candidates, or to formulate a relevant radical industrial policy. The result was the series of municipal anti-Socialist alliances and increasingly negative attacks on Socialism. Perhaps the war and the split of 1916 accelerated and aggravated these factors, but they were quite clearly at work *before* 1914. To this extent, Trevor Wilson's thesis, with its emphasis on the war as the 'rampant omnibus' which struck the Liberal Party, is not wholly satisfactory in this respect.

Criticism of Dr Wilson's chronology and interpretation of the Liberal decline has also been rightly levelled by Henry Pelling, who has written:

> ... the decline of Liberalism was not due to a sordid intrigue between Lloyd George and a few Conservative leaders and press lords, as many widely read historians of the present day would have us believe. ... Rather it was the result of long-term social and economic changes which were simultaneously uniting Britain geographically and dividing her inhabitants in terms of class.[12]

The municipal evidence of this thesis lends support to this view. However, though *part* of the explanation, social and economic forces were not solely responsible for the Liberal downfall. Rather, it was a succession of political blows coming on top of the changing social structure that reduced the Liberal Party from supremacy to impotence.

The most important of these body-blows were the split of 1916; the débâcle of the 'coupon' election; the inability to regain the position of second largest party in December 1923; and finally, the folly of the Liberal course of action in the months of 1924.

In addition to all these factors must be added the organisational reasons – albeit not permanent or irreversible – behind

[12] H. Pelling, *Popular Politics and Society in Late Victorian England* (1968) pp. 101–120.

the Liberal decline. These included the system, or rather lack of system, that left the constituencies dependent on finance from headquarters. The result of this was the inability to maintain agents or adopt prospective candidates.

The conclusion from this thesis is that there was not a single date when the Liberal Party declined. Rather, it was a long-term phenomenon which varied, both in time and degree, from area to area. In such regions as industrial Scotland, East Lancashire or London the Liberals were in serious difficulties before 1914. Yet in such areas as rural Cheshire, North Wales or rural Scotland, the real challenge of Labour was not significant until 1924 or even 1929. The Liberal decline resembled the pictures of a kaleidoscope, changing from constituency to constituency, with all the complexity of a Seurat landscape.

By 1923, despite the collapse of so much constituency organisation, the process of decline had *not* reached the stage when recovery was impossible. A year later, it was difficult to deny that the Liberal decline had passed the point of no return. Ten months had witnessed, if not the destruction of a party, at least a débâcle that made total recovery almost an impossibility.

In this sense the tariff election, the advent of a Labour Government and the general election of 1924 marked a great divide in British politics. The Labour Party had tasted power, however briefly, for the first time. The Liberal Party had ensured that almost certainly it would never assume power in its own right again. For these reasons, the political spectrum was different in kind and in degree in October 1924 than in November 1922. These two years had constituted a period of alignment in British politics in which the position of the Liberal Party had changed so that it was never again to succeed in winning power.

Select Bibliography

A PRIMARY SOURCES

1. *Private Papers*

Asquith MSS, the papers of the Earl of Oxford and Asquith in the Bodleian Library, Oxford.

Baldwin MSS, the papers of the 1st Earl Baldwin of Bewdley in the University Library, Cambridge.

Beaverbrook MSS, the papers of Lord Beaverbrook, in the Beaverbrook Library, London, quoted by permission of the First Beaverbrook Foundation.

Bridgeman MSS, the diary of the 1st Viscount Bridgeman, seen by kind permission of the 2nd Viscount Bridgeman.

Davidson MSS, the papers of Viscount Davidson, in the Beaverbrook Library, London.

Derby MSS, the papers of the 17th Earl of Derby, in the possession of his grandson, the 18th Earl of Derby.

Fisher MSS, the papers of H. A. L. Fisher in the Bodleian Library, Oxford.

Gladstone MSS, the papers of Herbert Gladstone in the British Library.

Bonar Law MSS, the papers of Bonar Law in the Beaverbrook Library, quoted by permission of the First Beaverbrook Foundation.

Lloyd George MSS, the papers of Earl Lloyd George of Dwyfor in the Beaverbrook Library, quoted by permission of the First Beaverbrook Foundation.

Donald Maclean MSS, in the Bodleian Library, Oxford.

C. P. Scott MSS, the diary of C. P. Scott, editor of the *Manchester Guardian*, in the British Library.

A. MacCallum Scott MSS, the diary of Alexander MacCallum Scott, M.P., seen by kind permission of his son.

Spender MSS, the papers of J. A. Spender in the British Library.

Strachey MSS, the St Loe Strachey papers in the Beaverbrook Library, quoted by permission of *The Spectator*.

2. *Party Archives*

Except where stated the papers are in the office of the association or federation.

Birmingham Liberal Federation, the minute books and accounts of the Federation, in the possession of the secretary.

Bradford Conservative Association, the papers of the association, deposited in Bradford Central Library.

Camborne Conservative Association, the minute books of the association, in the possession of the secretary.

Cambridgeshire Labour Party, the papers and accounts of the association, deposited in Cambridgeshire County Record Office.

Coventry Liberal Municipal Committee, the minutes of the committee, deposited in Coventry Public Library.

Derby Conservative Association, the minute books of the association, in the possession of the secretary.

Eastern Counties Liberal Federation, the annual reports and minute books of the Federation, in the possession of the secretary.

Eastern Provincial Division of the National Union, the papers of the association in the possession of the secretary.

Epsom Conservative Association, the annual reports and minute books of the association, in the possession of the secretary.

Harborough Conservative Association, the minute books and accounts of the association, in the possession of the secretary.

Harborough Division Liberal and Radical Association, the minute books of the association, in the possession of the secretary.

Home Counties Liberal Federation, a few annual reports of the Federation deposited in the National Liberal Club.

Lancashire, Cheshire and North Western Liberal Federation, the minute books of the Federation, in the possession of the secretary.

Leeds Conservative Association, the annual reports and minute books of the association, deposited in Leeds Public Library (Sheepscar Branch).

Leeds Liberal Federation, the papers of the Federation, deposited in Leeds Public Library (Sheepscar Branch).

Leicester Labour Party, the annual reports of the association, in the possession of the secretary.

Leicester Liberal Federation, the papers of the Federation (until 1923 only), deposited in the Leicester City Museum.

London Labour Party, the annual reports, minutes and correspondence of the association, in the possession of the secretary.

Manchester Liberal Federation, the papers of the Federation, in the possession of the secretary.

Midland Liberal Federation, the papers of the Federation, deposited in the Library, University of Birmingham.

National Union of Conservative and Unionist Associations, the annual conference reports of the National Union, in Conservative Central Office.

Oxford Conservative Association, the minute books of the association, in the possession of the secretary.

Peterborough Conservative Association, the minute books of the association, in the possession of the secretary.

Scottish Council of the Labour Party, the annual reports of the council, deposited in Transport House.

Scottish Liberal Federation, the minutes of the Executive, the General Council and the Area Council meetings of the Federation, deposited in the Library, University of Edinburgh, and examined by courtesy of the Scottish Liberal Party.

Sheffield Municipal Elections Committee of the Sheffield Federation of Conservative and Unionist Associations, the papers of the committee, in the office of Sheffield Conservative Association.

Society of Certificated and Associated Liberal Agents, the annual reports, minute books and account books of the society, deposited in Leeds Public Library, (Sheepscar Branch).

Wolverhampton West Conservative Association, the minute books and press cuttings of the association, in the possession of Dr G. W. Jones.

Women's National Liberal Federation, the annual reports of the Federation, in the possession of the Librarian, the National Liberal Club.

Women's Unionist Organisation, the annual conference reports of the organisation, in Conservative Central Office.

Yorkshire Liberal Federation, the papers of the Federation, deposited in Leeds Public Library (Sheepscar Branch).

B   SECONDARY SOURCES

1. *Newspapers and Journals*

(*a*) *Party*

Conservative Agents' Journal, Fabian News, Gleanings and Memoranda, Home and Politics, Labour Organiser, Labour Research Department: Monthly Circular, Liberal Magazine, Lloyd George Liberal Magazine, London Labour Chronicle, New Leader, Socialist Magazine.

(*b*) *National*

Daily Chronicle, Daily Express, Daily Mail, Daily News, Daily Telegraph, Economist, Fortnightly Review, Manchester Guardian, Morning Post, Nation, National Review, New Statesman, Saturday Review, Spectator, Star, Sunday Express, Sunday Times, Times, Westminster Gazette.

(*c*) *Provincial*

[The following newspapers have been extensively consulted. The many local papers used only briefly have not been included in this list.]

Birmingham Post, Bolton Evening News, Bradford Pioneer, Bristol Times and Mirror, Cambridge Daily News, Derby Mercury, Dundee Advertiser, Essex County Standard, Glamorgan Free Press, Glasgow Herald, Gloucester Journal, Huddersfield Examiner,

Leicester Mercury, Liverpool Post, Norwich Mercury, Northampton Independent, Nottingham Guardian, Oxford Times, St Helens Examiner, Scotsman, Sheffield Daily Telegraph, South London Press, South Wales News, Western Mail, Yorkshire Post.

2. *Official Documents, Annual Reports, Yearbooks and Reference Works*

Annual Register, 1918–1925
Constitutional Year Book, 1918–1930
Dictionary of National Biography 1901–1950 (5 vols, London, 1912–1959)
Dod's Parliamentary Companion, 1918–1929
House of Commons Debates
Independent Labour Party, *Reports of the Annual Conference*, 1921–1925
Labour Party, *Reports of the Annual Conference*, 1918–1926
Liberal Year Book, 1918–1929
Who Was Who, 1897–1960 (5 vols London, 1920–1961)
Craig, F. W. S., *British Parliamentary Election Results*, 1918–1949 (Glasgow, 1969)
Craig, F. W. S., *British Parliamentary Election Statistics*, 1918–1968 (Glasgow, 1968)

3. *Autobiographies, Memoirs and Biographies*

[The number of biographies and similar works for the period of this book is enormous. The following list is restricted to those found most directly useful.]

Amery, L. S., *My Political Life* (3 vols, London. 1953–55)
Anderson, M., *Noel Buxton: A Life* (London, 1952)
Baldwin, A. W., *My Father* (London, 1955)
Barnes, J., and Middlemas, K., *Baldwin: A Biography* (London, 1969)
The 2nd Earl of Birkenhead, *F. E., The Life of F. E. Smith, First Earl of Birkenhead* (London, 1965, first published 1933)
Blake, R., *The Unknown Prime Minister; The Life and Times of Andrew Bonar Law, 1858–1923* (London, 1955)
Bondfield, M., *A Life's Work* (London, 1949)
Brockway, A. F., *Socialism over Sixty Years* (London, 1946)
Brockway, A. F., *Inside the Left* (London, 1942)
Viscount Cecil of Chelwood, *All The Way* (London, 1949)
Chamberlain, Sir A., *Down The Years* (London, 1935)
Churchill, R., *Lord Derby, 'King of Lancashire'; the Official Life of Edward, Seventeenth Earl of Derby, 1865–1948* (London, 1959)
Clynes, J. R., *Memoirs, 1869–1924* (London, 1937)
Cole, M. I. (ed.)., *Beatrice Webb's Diaries, 1912–1924* (London, 1925)

Dalton, H., *Call Back Yesterday* (London, 1953)

Elton, Lord, *Life of James Ramsay MacDonald* (London, 1939)

Feiling, K., *The Life of Neville Chamberlain* (London, 1946)

Fisher, H. A. L., *An Unfinished Biography* (London, 1940)

Gallacher, W., *Revolt on the Clyde; An Autobiography* (London, 1936)

George, W., *My Brother and I* (London, 1958)

Gilbert, M., *Plough My Own Furrow; The Story of Lord Allen of Hurtwood as told through his writings and correspondence* (London, 1965)

Graham, T. N., *Willie Graham; The Life of the Rt. Hon. W. Graham* (London, n.d., c. 1948)

Gray, F., *Confessions of a Candidate* (London, 1925)

Haldane, R. B., *An Autobiography* (London, 1929)

Hamilton, M. A., *Arthur Henderson* (London, 1938)

Harris, P., *Forty Years in and out of Parliament* (London, 1947)

Hastings, P., *Autobiography* (London, 1948)

Hewins, W. A. S., *The Apologia of an Imperialist* (London, 1929, 2 vols)

Hyde, H. M., *Lord Birkett of Ulverston* (London, 1964)

Hyde, H. M., *Baldwin: The Unexpected Prime Minister* (London, 1973)

James, R. R., *Davidson: Memoirs of a Conservative* (London, 1969)

James, W., *The Eyes of the Navy; A Biographical Study of Admiral Sir Reginald Hall* (London, 1956)

Jenkins, R., *Asquith* (London, 1964)

Johnston, T., *Memoirs* (London, 1952)

Jones, T., *Lloyd George* (London, 1951)

Kenworthy, J. M., *Sailors, Statesmen and Others* (London, 1933)

Kirkwood, D., *My Life of Revolt* (London, 1935)

Lansbury, G., *My Life* (London, 1928)

Lloyd George, F. *The Years That Are Past* (London, 1967)

McKenna, S., *Reginald McKenna, 1863–1943: A Memoir* (London, 1948)

Macleod, I., *Neville Chamberlain* (London, 1961)

Mallet, C., *Herbert Gladstone: A Memoir* (London, 1932)

Marwick, A., *Clifford Allen, The Open Conspirator* (Edinburgh, 1964)

Masterman, L., *C. F. G. Masterman: A Biography* (London, 1939)

Maurice, F., *Haldane* (2 vols, London, 1937–1938)

Middlemas, R. K. (ed.), *Tom Jones: Whitehall Diary, 1916–1928* (3 vols, London, 1969)

Morgan, Kenneth, O. (ed.), *Lloyd George Family Letters, 1885–1936* (Cardiff, 1973)

Morrison, H., *An Autobiography* (London, 1960)

Mosley, L., *Curzon: The End of an Epoch* (London, 1960)

Nicolson, H., *King George the Fifth: His Life and Reign* (London, 1952)

Norwich, Viscount, *Old Men Forget: The Autobiography of Duff Cooper* (London, 1953)

Owen, F., *Tempestuous Journey: Lloyd George, His Life and Times* (London, 1954)

Earl of Oxford and Asquith, *Memories and Reflections, 1857–1927* (2 vols, London, 1928)

Paton, J., *Left Turn* (London, 1926)

Pease, A. E., *Elections and Recollections* (London, 1932)

Pethick-Lawrence, Lord, *Fate Has Been Kind* (London, 1943)

Petrie, C., *The Life and Letters of the Rt. Hon. Sir Austen Chamberlain, K.G., P.C., M.P.* (2 vols, London, 1940)

Phillipps, V., *My Days and Ways* (unpublished autobiography, n.d., seen by courtesy of Dr Roy Douglas)

Postgate, R., *The Life of George Lansbury* (London, 1951)

Salvidge, S., *Salvidge of Liverpool* (London, 1934)

Samuel, Viscount, *Memoirs* (London, 1945)

Shinwell, E., *Conflict without Malice* (London, 1955)

Simon, Viscount, *Retrospect* (London, 1952)

Smithie, R., *My Life for Labour* (London, 1924)

Snowden, P., *An Autobiography* (2 vols, London, 1934)

Spender, J. A., and Asquith, C., *The Life of Herbert Henry Asquith, Lord Oxford and Asquith* (2 vols London, 1932)

Spender, J. A., *Sir Robert Hudson, A Memoir* (London, 1930)

Steed, W., *The Real Stanley Baldwin* (London, 1930)

Earl of Swinton, *Sixty years of Power* (London, 1966)

Sylvester, A. J., *The Real Lloyd George* (London, 1947)

Taylor, A. J. P., *Beaverbrook* (London, 1973)

Thomson, M., *David Lloyd George, The Official Biography* (London, 1948)

Wedgwood, C. V., *The Last of the Radicals, Josiah Wedgwood, MP* (London, 1951)

Wilson, T. (ed.), *The Political Diaries of C. P. Scott* (London, 1970)

Wrench, E., *Geoffrey Dawson and Our Times* (London, 1955)

Young, G. M., *Stanley Baldwin* (London, 1952)

4. *Electoral, regional and constituency studies*

Bealey, F., Blondel, J., and McCann, W. P., *Constituency Politics: A Study of Newcastle-under-Lyme* (London, 1965)

Benney, M., Gray, A. P., and Pear, R. H., *How People Vote: A Study of Electoral Behaviour in Greenwich* (London, 1956)

Benyon, V. H., and Harrison, J. E., *The Political Significance of the British Agricultural Vote* (Exeter, 1962)

Birch, A. H., *et al.*, *Small Town Politics: A Study of Political Life in Glossop* (Oxford, 1959)

Brockway, F., *Bermondsey Story* (London, 1949)

Bulpitt, J., *Party Politics in English Local Government* (London, 1967)

Butler, D. E., *The Electoral System in Britain, 1918–51* (Oxford, 1953)

Butler, D. E., and Stokes, D., *Political Change in Britain* (London, 1969)

Chaloner, W., *The Social and Economic Development of Crewe* (Manchester, 1950)

Cook, C., and Ramsden, J. (eds.), *By-Elections in British Politics* (London, 1973)

Gibbon, L. O., and Bell, R. W., *A History of the London County Council* (London, 1939)

Hawson, H., *Sheffield: The Growth of a City* (Sheffield, 1968)

James, C., *MP for Dewsbury* (Dewsbury, 1970)

Jones, G. W., *Borough Politics: A History of Wolverhampton Borough Council* (London, 1969)

Keith-Lucas, B., *The English Local Government Franchise* (Oxford, 1952)

Kinnear, M., *The British Voter* (London, 1968)

Lee, J. M., *Social Leaders and Public Persons: A Study of County Government in Cheshire since 1888* (Oxford, 1963)

McCallum, R. B., and Readman, A., *The British General Election of 1945* (Oxford, 1947)

Morgan, K., *Wales in British Politics, 1886–1922* (Cardiff, 1963)

Pelling, H., *Social Geography of British Elections, 1885–1910* (London, 1967)

Pollard, S., *A History of Labour in Sheffield* (Liverpool, 1959)

Thompson, P., *Socialists, Liberals and Labour: The Struggle for London, 1885–1914* (London, 1967)

Williams, J. E., *The Derbyshire Miners* (London, 1962)

5. *General Political Works*

Abel, D., *A History of British Tariffs 1923–42* (London, 1945)

Bassett, R., *1931: Political Crisis* (London, 1958)

Beaverbrook, Lord, *Politicians and the Press* (London, 1925)

Beaverbrook, Lord, *The Decline and Fall of Lloyd George* (London, 1963)

Beer, S., *Modern British Politics* (London, 1965)

Blake, R., *The Conservative Party from Peel to Churchill* (London, 1970)

Chester, L., Fay, S., and Young, H., *The Zinoviev Letter* (London, 1967)

Cline, C. A., *Recruits to Labour, The British Labour Party, 1914–1931* (Syracuse, 1963)

Cole, G. D. H., *A History of the Labour Party from 1914* (London, 1948)

Cowling, M., *The Impact of Labour* (Cambridge, 1971)

Dangerfield, G., *The Strange Death of Liberal England* (New York, 1961; first published 1936)

Dowse, R., *Left in the Centre* (London, 1956)

Fawcett, A., *Conservative Agent* (Driffield, Yorks., 1967)

Fischer, L., *The Soviets in World Affairs* (2 vols., London, 1930)

Fyfe, Hamilton, *The British Liberal Party* (London, 1928)

Graubard, S. R., *British Labour and the Russian Revolution* (Cambridge, Mass., 1956)

Kinnear, M., *The Fall of Lloyd George: The Political Crisis of 1922* (London, 1973)

Klugman, J., *History of the Communist Party of Great Britain* (London, 1968)

Lyman, R., *The First Labour Government 1924* (London, 1957)

Marwick, A., *The Deluge: British Society and the First World War* (London, 1965)

McCallum, R. B., *The Liberal Party from Earl Grey to Asquith* (London, 1963)

McElwee, W., *Britain's Locust Years, 1918–1940* (London, 1962)

McHenry, D. E., *The Labour Party in Transition, 1931–38* (London, 1938)

McKenzie, R. T., *British Political Parties* (2nd edition, London, 1963)

McKenzie, R. T., and Silver, A., *Angels in Marble* (London, 1968)

Middlemas, R. K., *The Clydesiders, A Left-Wing Struggle for Parliamentary Power* (London, 1965)

Mowat, C. L., *Britain Between the Wars, 1918–1940* (London, 1955)

Nordlinger, E. A., *The Working Class Tories* (London, 1967)

Pelling, H., *Popular Politics and Society in Late Victorian England* (London, 1968)

Rasmussen, J., *Retrenchment and Revival: A Study of the Contemporary Liberal Party* (London, 1964)

Rowland, P., *The Last Liberal Governments: The Promised Land, 1905–10* (London, 1968)

Taylor, A. J. P., *Politics in Wartime, and Other Essays* (London, 1964)

Taylor, A. J. P., *English History, 1914–45* (Oxford, 1965)

Tracy, H. (ed.), *The Book of the Labour Party* (3 vols, London, 1925)

Wertheimer, E., *Portrait of the Labour Party* (London, 1930)

Williams, F., *Fifty Years March: The Rise of the Labour Party* (London, 1949)

Wilson, T., *The Downfall of the Liberal Party 1914–35* (London, 1966)

6. *Articles*

Booth, W., 'The Liberals and the 1923 General Election', *Contemporary Review*, 1965

Cook, C., 'Wales and the General Election of 1923', *Welsh History Review*, LV no. 4. (1969)

Dowse, R., 'The Entry of the Liberals into the Labour Party, 1910–1930', *Yorkshire Bulletin of Economic and Social Research*, XIII no. 2. (1961)

Dowse, R., 'The Left-Wing Opposition during the first two Labour Governments. *Parliamentary Affairs,*

Gollin, A., 'Asquith: A New View', in Martin Gilbert (ed.), *A Century of Conflict, 1850–1950.* Essays for A. J. P. Taylor (London, 1966)

Hazlehurst, C., 'Masterman – Lloyd George Split', *New Outlook,* no. 72 (July/August 1968)

Hazlehurst, C., 'The Conspiracy Myth', in Martin Gilbert (ed.), *Lloyd George,* (Englewood Cliffs, 1968)

Koss, S., 'The Destruction of Britain's Last Liberal Government', *Journal of Modern History,* XL no. 2. (June 1968)

Krehbiel, E., 'Geographic Influences in British Elections', *Geographic review,* 1916

McEwen, J., 'The Coupon Election of 1918 and Unionist Members of Parliament', *Journal of Modern History,* XXXIV no. 3 (1962)

McGill, B., 'Asquith's Predicament, 1914–1918', *Journal of Modern History,* XXXIX no. 3 (September, 1967)

Masterman, L., 'Reminiscences of Lib-Lab days', *New Outlook, no. 50 (January 1966)*

Morgan, K., 'The Twilight of Welsh Liberalism: Lloyd George and the Wee Frees, 1918–35', *Bulletin of the Board of Celtic Studies,* XXII pt. 4 (May, 1968)

Morgan, K., 'Cardiganshire Politics: The Liberal Ascendancy, 1885–1913', in *Ceredigion,,* V no. 4 (1967)

Noonan, L., 'The Decline of the Liberal Party in British Politics', *Journal of Politics,* XVI no. 1 (1954)

Pollock, J., 'British Party Organisation', *Political Science Quarterly,* XIV (June, 1930)

Sanderson, G., 'Swing of the Pendulum in British General Elections, 1832–1966', *Political Studies,* 1966

Warth, R. D., 'The Mystery of the Zinoviev Letter', *South Atlantic Quarterly,* October 1950

Wilson, T., 'The Coupon and the British General Election of 1918', *Journal of Modern History,* 1964.

7. *Theses*

Cox, D., 'The Rise of the Labour Party in Leicester', unpublished Leicester M.A. thesis, 1959

Earl, A., 'The Political Life of Viscount Swinton, 1918–38', unpublished Manchester M.A. thesis, 1960

McEwen, J., 'The Decline of the Liberal Party in Great Britain, 1914–1926', unpublished Manchester M.A. thesis, 1952

McKibbin, R., 'The Evolution of a National Party: Labour's Political Organisation, 1910–1924', unpublished Oxford D. Phil. thesis, 1970

Powell, B., 'A Study in the change of Social Origins, Political Affiliation and Length of Service of Members of the Leeds City Council', unpublished Leeds M.A. thesis, 1958

Roberts, D., 'Religion and Politics in Liverpool since 1900', unpublished London M.Sc. thesis, 1965

Rowe, E., 'The British General Election of 1929', unpublished Oxford B.Litt. thesis, 1959

Sommer, R., 'The Organisation of the Liberal Party, 1936–60', unpublished London Ph.D. thesis, 1962

Index